BLACK DOLLS

1820-1991

AN IDENTIFICATION
AND VALUE GUIDE

BY
MYLA PERKINS

COLLECTOR BOOKS
A Division of Schroeder Publishing Co., Inc.

The current values in this book should be used only as a guide. They are not intended to set prices, which vary from one section of the country to another. Auction prices as well as dealer prices vary greatly and are affected by condition as well as demand. Neither the Author nor the Publisher assumes responsibility for any losses that might be incurred as a result of consulting this guide.

On the cover: Konig & Wernicke. Germany. Adorable flirty-eyed toddler boy and girl with Negroid features. 18" tall. Bisque heads, dark brown flirty eyes, open mouth with two glass upper teeth, curly synthetic wig. Composition five-piece toddler bodies. Made during the first quarter of the twentieth century. Marks: K W/g/734/72/(crossed nails), on head.

Searching For A Publisher?

We are always looking for knowledgeable people considered to be experts within their fields. If you feel that there is a real need for a book on your collectible subject and have a large comprehensive collection, contact us.

COLLECTOR BOOKS
P.O. Box 3009
Paducah, Kentucky 42002-3009

TABLE OF CONTENTS

DEDICATION

This book is dedicated lovingly to my parents who made me a doll lover, to my sister who loved dolls with me in our childhood, and to my husband and children who gave me "space" for 25 years of doll collecting as an adult. Without them, none of this would have become a reality.

To Betty Formaz who opened up the world of doll collecting for me through membership in a special doll club. I will never forget her encouragement and love.

To Susan Manos, nationally known doll writer and appraiser, for her encouragement with this project, starting in 1976 to its completion.

PHOTOGRAPHS BY

Edgar Perkins and the following, as noted under the captions with their photographs: I. Roberta Bell, Evelyn Ackerman, Phyllis Houston, Barbara Buysse, Carol L. Jacobsen, Marion Reed Getty, Shindana Toys, and Vogue Dolls.

INTRODUCTION

The importance of black dolls as playthings for children cannot be stressed enough. However, the idea of black dolls representing the black population of our society is not new. Black dolls have been available commercially to some extent, often very limited, since the second quarter of the nineteenth century. Handmade black dolls have been used as far back as one can practically go in our African history.

From the early 1800's to the present, black dolls, like most other things in our society, have gone through many, many changes. They also experienced great surges in popularity at different times, possibly reflecting attitudes prevalent in our society at a particular given time. In doing research on black dolls, many questions arise. Some of the most significant ones are as follows:

1. Who were the commercial manufacturers of dolls from the early 1800's to the present?
2. Where were the dolls made?
3. What market were they made for (black or white children)?
4. What materials were used to make the dolls?
5. When were their peaks in popularity?
6. Most importantly, what do they look like?

These are some of the questions this book will deal with while examining black dolls of the past and present. This book will take you back through the past 170 years through the eyes of children. You will look back, view, and study dolls made for or to represent black children.

This history of black dolls by no means includes *every* black doll made. There are many, many more black dolls yet to be located, documented, and placed in history. The task of finding these dolls will be the work of tomorrow. Searching, more searching, and much more searching, this is the procedure.

Along with researching the marks, manufacturers, descriptions, names of the more than fourteen hundred dolls included in the book, much work went into the price guide. Lists of dolls for sale on the secondary market were studied, results of auctions were analyzed, numerous doll shows were attended to verify selling prices, similar types of dolls were compared, and so forth in order to obtain as accurate a price guide as possible. Prices for dolls made prior to 1965 are based on dolls in good condition but not necessarily in the original clothing or boxes. Prices for dolls made after that period are based on dolls in original clothing and in excellent condition. Values for dolls after 1980 are based on MIB (mint in box), never played with dolls. If a doll during this period is in good condition, but has been played with, the value is approximately one-third of the listed price. Prices also vary according to regions of the country. Dolls are generally higher on the East and West Coasts of the United States. Of course it should be noted that the true value of dolls, like any collectible, depends on how much the collector is willing to pay. Every doll should be purchased with the knowledge that if it cannot be sold for a profit, you love it well enough to keep it forever.

Some of the information in this book was gathered from sources assumed to be reliable but there is no guarantee on total accuracy of information. Whenever possible, however, every attempt was made to verify manufacturer, doll's name, approximate date, and any other information on the dolls.

CHAPTER 1
PAPIER-MACHÉ DOLLS, CIRCA 1820–1860+

The earliest black dolls commercially made as playthings for children are the papier-maché dolls, made between 1820 and 1840. For collectors of today, they are very intriguing and unusual because of their rarity. They are small dolls, approximately 11" tall with heads made of papier-maché, a mixture of paper, paste, and water. The heads were mass-produced with the papier-maché pressed into molds and allowed to harden. After hardening, it was a very durable medium for doll heads and easily withstood minor accidents. The one disadvantage, however, was its inability to withstand moisture.

The dolls made during this period did not generally have wigs. The hair was part of the original molding of the head. The black dolls have hair in a style that resembles what is commonly known as the "afro" today. This indicates that separate molds were made for the black and white dolls of this period because the white dolls have very elaborate and fancy molded hairstyles.

The facial features on these dolls of 1820–1840 were painted. The handmade bodies were either dark cloth or leather, stuffed with sawdust, straw, or cloth scraps while the black painted arms and legs were made of turned wood. Occasionally one will find an originally dressed papier-maché doll from this period. In such cases, the doll is dressed in kitchen-type clothing, indicating that these were used to represent household slaves as they were made during the period of slavery in the United States.

The dolls, 1850 and later, that followed these early papier-maché dolls were generally also made of papier-maché. They were very similar to the earlier dolls with the exception that, at times, pupiless black glass eyes were inserted and wigs sometimes replaced the molded hair. The wigs were primarily made of mohair and usually were short and plainly styled. The bodies were usually made of cloth with papier-maché limbs. Often, the legs were made with molded shoes and stockings. Children, men, or baby dolls were seldom seen during this period as dolls representing ladies were most popular.

From examining original clothes and features, it appears that all of the dolls made between 1820 and 1860 were made to be used as supplementary dolls, used in play situations as maids, servants, slaves, etc., for the white dolls. They were painted the darkest of black possible with no hint of any shading or variety of coloring offered. It should be noted, however, that the materials used in commercial production of black dolls from the early 1800's to the present were generally the same materials used in making the white dolls of the same periods.

The great majority of the dolls commercially produced during this period were made in Europe, probably Germany as Germany was the center of the toy making industry.

Plate 1: Papier-maché from Germany, 1820–1840. Doll is 12" tall; head made of papier-maché with molded hair, painted features; cloth stuffed body; turned wood arms and legs. Doll appears to be wearing original clothes, hand sewn, extremely fine stitching, very well made. Dress is pink print with white apron. Cloth body is stuffed with straw as was commonly used during this period.

Plate 2: Another papier-maché doll similar to doll on previous page. Made in Germany 1820–1840, 12" tall. Doll has been redressed.

Plate 3: Papier-maché doll made in Germany circa 1860. 11" tall. Head, arms, and legs are made of papier-maché, boots and stockings are made onto the legs. Body is made of brown cloth and stuffed with sawdust. Dress is very old print, could be original. Eyes are brown inserted glass eyes. Unmarked.

Plate 4: 11" tall, circa 1860. Papier-maché shoulder head with pupiless black glass stationary eyes, glued-on mohair wig, closed mouth with painted lips, papier-maché arms and legs, brown cloth body, black cloth upper legs. Doll is unmarked.

Plate 5: Germany. Papier-maché, circa 1850. 14½" tall. Papier-maché shoulder head, stationary black glass pupiless eyes, closed painted mouth, molded kinky hair, papier-maché arms and legs with molded-on boots. Brown cloth body stuffed with sawdust. Redressed in old clothing. Unmarked.

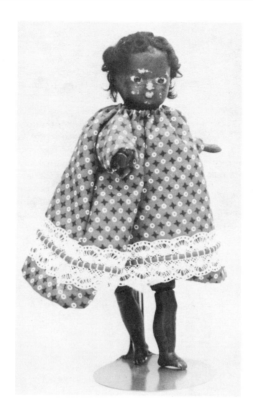

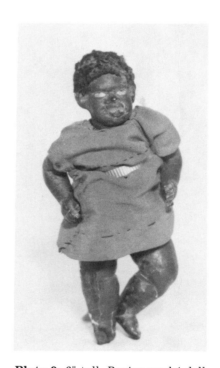

Plate 8: Jack-in-the-Box. An interesting variation of the flip-flop dolls. Papier-maché mask heads covered with cloth at the back. Painted faces. Paper covered wood box 4¾" long x 2¼" high x 2½" deep. Courtesy of Evelyn Ackerman.

Plate 6: Papier-maché. Germany, 6¾" tall. Shoulder head with molded kinky hair, painted features, papier-maché lower arms and legs, very dark brown cloth body stuffed with sawdust. Unmarked.

Plate 7: Papier-maché, 8" tall. Black wax over papier-maché (or composition), shoulder plate. Stationary black pupiless glass eyes, closed mouth, original black mohair curly wig. Cloth body with wood lower arms and lower bare feet. Clothing probably is replaced. Courtesy of Evelyn Ackerman.

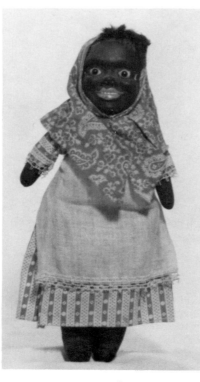

Plate 9: 6" tall. Papier-maché doll jointed at head, shoulders, and hips, glued-on wig that looks like old fur, definite Negroid features, molded and painted. Clothing is old but does not look original. Doll is painted very dark brown, almost black in coloring.

Plate 10: 6" similar doll to plate 9 except this one is painted brown. This doll also has pierced ears with old wooden bead earrings.

Plate 11: Papier-maché. Germany. 8½" tall. All original. Papier-maché head, inset stationary glass eyes, painted open mouth, black fur wig, cloth body stuffed with straw.

CHAPTER 2
BLACK CHINA DOLLS

Black china dolls, dolls with ceramic or porcelain heads that were painted and glazed, were popular during the last half of the nineteenth century. China dolls can be divided into two categories:

    1. Those with china heads with bodies and limbs of various materials, sometimes even china, commonly referred to as "china dolls."

    2. Those made entirely of china, commonly referred to as "Frozen Charlottes."

Most of these dolls were mass-produced in Germany, manufacturers unknown, as dolls were not usually marked by manufacturers during this period. They gradually began to replace the earlier papier-maché heads in popularity. They were more realistic in appearance and able to withstand moisture. They were, however, much more fragile.

The black dolls of this period, like the earlier papier-maché dolls, were usually made in special molds with Negroid features, broader noses, and more exaggerated lips than the white china dolls. For the first time, men or boy dolls were available along with the lady and girl dolls. They all had molded china hair in a very short style that made it difficult to distinguish, ignoring clothing, a black china man doll from a woman doll.

The bodies on most of the black china dolls were made of black cloth with a black kid leather body occasionally seen. The lower limbs are generally made of china although leather or cloth are sometimes found. *Harpers Bazaar*, January (2 or 9), 1869 (page 3 or 17) in an article on dolls, made reference to: "...Negroes with characteristic features..." when discussing the great variety of dolls on the market. The dolls referred to were probably the china dolls as they were the most popular black doll during this period.

The black china dolls, like the earlier papier-maché dolls, were always colored the deepest black possible. Shades of brown were never offered. It is felt that china dolls, in the larger sizes, were also used like the earlier dolls, to represent household help or slaves for white dolls.

The only marks found on the china dolls are single numerals, either 1, 2, 3, or 4. They are found on the back of the shoulder head beneath the neck. This same numeral is also usually found on the china legs and arms. It is apparently a size notation, used to match the proper size limbs to the proper head.

Plate 12: Large china lady doll with Negroid features. Made 1860–1870. 20" tall. Head is made of china with painted features and molded kinky hair. Body is the original cloth body with leather hands and shoes as was typical for china dolls of this period. Body is soft, stuffed with either rags or cotton. Marks: 4, incised on back of head.

Left – Plate 13: China doll, 9½" tall. This doll was probably made during the third quarter of the nineteenth century. Head, hands, and feet are made of china with features painted. For its size, the doll has extremely small feet as was generally the case with china dolls made during this period. The body is stuffed with cotton. Black dolls of this type were made to represent the slaves and used in play by white children along with white dolls. Manufacturer is unknown, but doll was probably made in Germany as Germany was the center of the toy making industry.

Right – Plate 14: China shoulder head. 7" tall. Head has painted eyes looking to one side. Painted features, molded short hair, paint has rubbed off mouth. Body has been replaced. Doll was made during the third quarter of the nineteenth century. Doll is unmarked.

Plate 15: China man doll, circa 1865. 10" tall. China head with molded hair and painted features. Replaced bisque arms and cloth body. Unmarked.

Plate 16: Frozen Charlottes, solid china dolls, 1¼" tall with painted features. They were advertised in Butler Brothers Wholesale catalog of 1895 as follows: "Glazed Nigger baby – open arms and legs, size 1½". One gross in box. 78¢ for gross." The dolls retailed in 1895 for one penny each. The dressed doll at the top of the circle has jointed arms and legs, the remainder are one piece.

Plate 19: China dolls 3½" and 4". Doll on the left is solid china, commonly known as a Frozen Charlotte. Doll on the right is made of solid china with movable arms. Both dolls have molded hair and painted features. Both are unmarked.

Plate 17: China. Germany, 1860–1870, 16½". China shoulder head with molded short kinky hair, painted eyes, painted closed mouth, china arms and legs, brown cloth body stuffed with straw. Feet are unproportionally small for legs and body. Marks: 3, incised on shoulder back.

Plate 18: China dolls 4" to 5" tall. Solid china dolls with painted features, molded hair, hands outstretched. Dolls like these were advertised in Butler Bros. Wholesale 1895 catalog as "Glazed Nigger Dolls." Wholesale price was 22¢ for 6 dozen or more in the smaller size, 38¢ for 6 dozen or more in the larger size. Dolls are unmarked.

CHAPTER 3
LEO MOSS DOLLS

Leo Moss dolls are dolls that were made by a black man, Leo Moss, in Macon, Georgia in the late 1800's and early 1900's. Mr. Moss was not a doll maker by trade, but worked as a handyman for white families in Macon, Georgia. In addition to his regular work as a handyman, Mr. Moss made dolls, both black and white. He would use his amazing talent, when commissioned by a child's parents, to create a doll that had a striking likeness to the child. He made dolls that resembled his own family members. These are the most well known and easiest to locate of the Moss dolls as many of them remained in the possession of the Moss family until the early 1970's.

The Moss doll heads are individually molded of papier-maché. The bodies were, at times, purchased from a white toy supplier and dealer from New York who came to Georgia several times a year to sell parts to Mr. Moss. The dealer, on occasion, would take some of the Moss dolls for payment for the parts, glass eyes, and composition limbs. The toy dealer, while apparently appreciating the beauty and artistry of the dolls, didn't believe there was a market in the United States for black dolls so he sent them to Europe to be sold on the European market. In the 1970's, one of the Moss dolls was purchased at auction from a museum in London. Upon examination, the doll was obviously a Moss doll. The records at the museum, however, did not include the name of the maker, just a mention that he was a black man in the southern part of the United States. The doll had been in the museum's collection since the early 1900's. This leads one to think that there could be other Moss dolls in England even now.

Leo Moss had great talent and feeling for black images. The proof is shown by his dolls. Most of them were made in the image of his family members or other black people close to him. However, his life was tragic at times. He had a wife and five children. During the early 1900's his wife ran away with the toy dealer from New York, taking the Moss baby with her. They were never heard from again. Mr. Moss continued making dolls for some time. His last known doll was made in 1932, of one of his granddaughters. During his lifetime, he did not get the financial rewards that this talent merited. He died in 1936 and was buried a pauper without a headstone.

One question asked frequently about the Moss dolls is why so many of the dolls are crying. According to his daughter, Ruby, when he was making the doll face of one of the toddlers in the family, the child became impatient while sitting and began to cry. Mr Moss tried to get the child to stop crying without success. Finally he said if that's how you want to look, that's how I'll make your doll. The family was amused with the resulting crying doll. Afterwards, whenever a child cried when Mr. Moss was making a portrait doll, the doll then also had tears.

Until 1971, the majority of the known Moss dolls were in the possession of his one known living daughter, Ruby Moss. At that time, she, still living in Macon, Georgia at the age of 83, sold some of the dolls. Other dolls remaining in the Moss home were later sold by a granddaughter named Helen.

Many of the Moss dolls have names. They were given to the dolls by the Moss family. In some cases, the names were incised on the dolls by Mr. Moss, as is the case of "Mina," a Moss baby doll. In most of the named Moss dolls, the names were passed down orally from Ruby Moss, daughter of Leo Moss. A few of the dolls have names written on cloth and sewn to the chest part of cloth bodies.

As mentioned earlier, Leo Moss was often commissioned to make dolls in exchange for services. While he and his wife were working for a white family in Macon, he made three dolls in 1909 for the daughters in the family. One of these dolls, Elaine, is shown with the following collection of photographs of Moss dolls. Elaine was sold in 1972 by the sister of the girl the doll was made for. The following letter accompanied the doll in 1972:

I mailed the doll today. I hope you will love her as she was once loved, long ago. I will introduce you to Elaine. She was my older sister, she passed away near 17 years ago. We were three very happy little girls on Christmas of 1909 when we received our dolls. Each of our dolls were of our own likeness, they were always very dear to us. The wigs were made from our own hair. Mrs. Moss made the wigs and dressed them in clothes of exact copy she had made us girls for Christmas. She did all of our sewing and worked very hard to please my mother. Mother was very fond of her. Mrs. Moss never knew how we missed her.

Mr. Moss used to work for my father. He was such a gentle man with so much love and patience. He made the heads for our dolls. He would just stand and stare at us with his big wistful eyes. This did frighten us – not knowing what he was going to do. We were always afraid to be alone with him, as he made one feel like he was looking right through you. When we would run from him, he would look so hurt. Mrs. Moss would tell us – don't be frightened, Leo only wants to remember your beauty. We didn't know he was working on our dolls. I have my own doll and my sister Lilly. Lilly passed away in '69. I took all 3 dolls to the doll hospital here and had them cleaned and the wigs cleaned. They were very soiled. I don't know what they were cleaned with. But they seem to have faded out some – they are lighter it seems. ...I hadn't looked at the dolls in so many years, I had forgotten how beautiful they were and the many memories that were locked away with them. One of the relatives had a doll also made by Mr. Moss. But I don't know whatever became of it... I hope you will love Elaine and enjoy her for many more years to come – she is 63 years old. Sister Elaine would now be 72. She was 9 years when we got our dolls...

After reading the letter with such vivid description of Leo Moss, it is difficult for doll lovers, or anyone who appreciates art, not to be fascinated, intrigued, and in love with Leo Moss dolls.

Although the Moss dolls were treasured for years by the family of Leo Moss, they were brought to the doll collecting world by doll collector and restorer, Betty Formaz. She personally visited the Moss house in Macon, meeting Ruby Moss, the oldest daughter of Leo Moss, and her daughter Helen. Betty was successful in purchasing thirty-nine of the Moss dolls and getting most of the information on Leo Moss and his doll making that is known today. If it weren't for Mrs. Formaz's willingness to share her "secret" treasure, the doll community would not know the depth of Leo Moss' greatness today.

The Leo Moss dolls were brought to the attention of doll collectors on a national level in 1973 when I entered the then unknown doll "Mina" in national competition in the United Federation of Doll Clubs 24th Annual Exhibit at Louisville, Kentucky. The doll won the blue ribbon in its category, baby dolls. In further judging of approximately 1,800 dolls in competition, "Mina" won a fourth place ribbon. The doll drew much attention and from then on, there was a great deal of enthusiasm and interest in Leo Moss. After that introduction, for the next several years whenever a Moss doll was entered into competition, it won a blue ribbon.

At present, almost fifty Moss dolls can be accounted for. Following are photographs of seventeen Leo Moss dolls.

Plate 20: Leo Moss. "Elaine," Caucasian doll by Moss. 18" tall. Papier-maché shoulder head, glass eyes, fur eyelashes, closed mouth, human hair wig made of the hair cut from the little girl that the doll was made for. Body is made of kid leather with bisque lower arms and hands. All original. Dress was made by Lee Ann, wife of Leo Moss, and is identical to the dress she made for the little girl Elaine for Christmas in 1909. The doll was given to Elaine on the same Christmas. Marks: LM, on back of head.

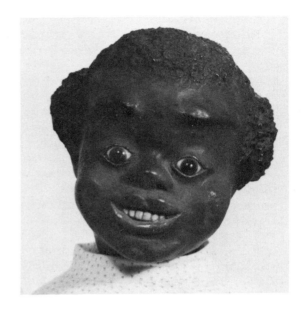

Plate 21: Leo Moss. "Thelma," 20" tall. Circa 1900. Head is papier-maché with brown stationary glass eyes; molded corn-row hairstyle in two braids. Body is cloth stuffed with rags. Arms and legs are composition. Head and body are all original. Doll possibly redressed.

Plate 22: Leo Moss. Smiling girl, 19½" tall. Socket head is papier-maché with inset brown glass eyes, molded hair in two puffs, molded teeth. This is one of the early heads by Leo Moss, probably made in the early 1880's. Only the head was purchased from the Moss family and was put on old composition body. The doll was dressed in 1972 in clothing thought appropriate.

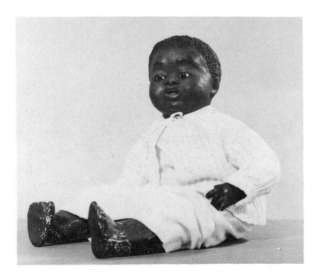

Plate 23: Leo Moss. "Georgie," 18½" toddler boy. Papier-maché shoulder head with inset brown glass eyes, two glass teeth, molded painted hair; rag stuffed cloth body. The clothing on the doll, white nightgown with white hand knitted baby sweater, is very old and could be original. Doll is marked 1888 on back. Doll won a red ribbon at UFDC convention in Miami, Florida, 1974. Another Moss doll, from the collection of the late Ralph Griffin, won the blue ribbon.

Plate 24: Leo Moss. "Lady Doll." Doll is large, 30" tall. Only the head was purchased from the Moss family. It is a shoulder head with molded bustline, papier-maché, with inset brown glass eyes, finely detailed molded hair in braided coils. The head was put on a cloth body matching proportionally in 1972 and dressed in appropriate clothing.

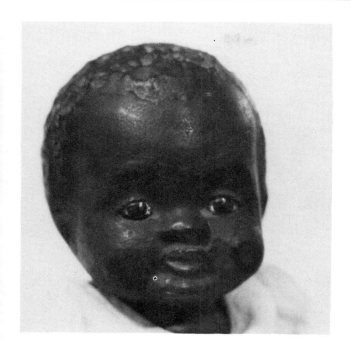

Plate 25: Leo Moss. Tiny baby, 10" tall. This is the smallest of the Leo Moss dolls to have been purchased from the Moss family. It has a papier-maché head and bent leg jointed baby body. Head has inset tiny glass eyes, molded hair. Doll was made in the late 1800's and is unmarked.

Plate 26: Leo Moss. "Bobo," name that was given to this doll by the Moss family, is one of the most comical and interesting of the Moss dolls. After seeing the Moss collection, it is one that all children and adults remember fondly as it is definitely a character doll. He has a teasing, infectious smile and is sticking out his tongue. The doll is all original and 27½" tall. Head is papier-maché with inset brown glass eyes, molded hair and tongue. Limbs are painted composition with cloth body stuffed with what feels like fine straw or sawdust. Doll is unmarked. Doll won the blue ribbon and popular choice ribbon at UFDC regional convention in October, 1973, Rockford, Illinois.

Plate 27: Leo Moss. "Pansy," 23" tall. Papier-maché shoulder head, inset glass eyes, hair has molded pigtails to accommodate ribbons; painted composition limbs, cloth rag stuffed body. Marks: 1888 incised on back of head.

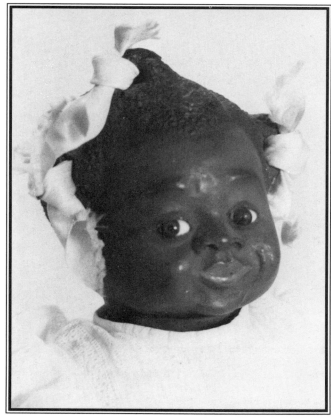

Head shot of Plate 27

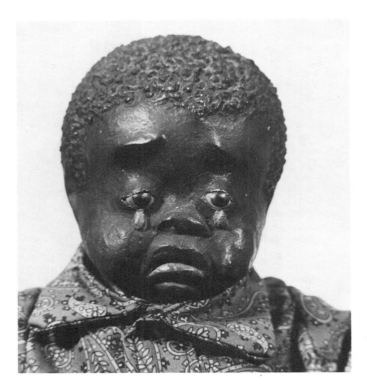

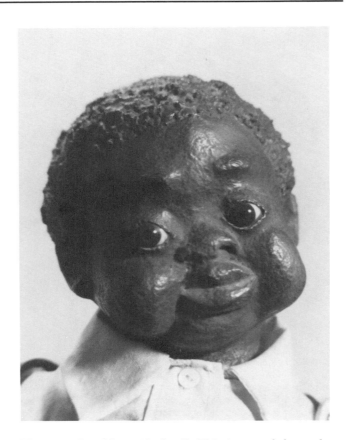

Plate 28: Leo Moss. "Crying Georgie," 16" tall. Papier-maché socket head, three molded tears, painted features, five-piece jointed toddler body. Both body and head are very well proportioned. Clothing is old but does not look old enough to be original. Marks: 1824, incised on back of head.

Plate 29: Leo Moss. 19½" tall. This is one of the early unnamed heads made by Leo Moss. This head, along with several others, was stored in his daughter's attic. He never made a body for any of these heads. An appropriate ball-jointed composition body was added in the early 1970's. His head is a papier-maché socket head with very dark brown eyes, much darker than his later dolls; closed mouth, molded hair. Head is unmarked.

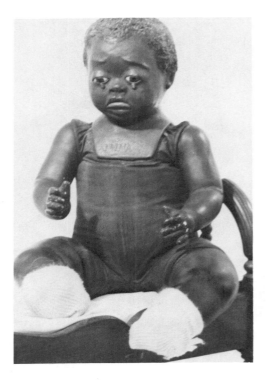

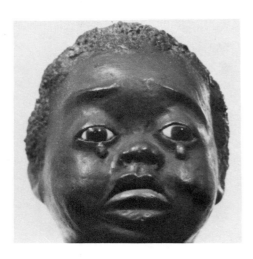

Plate 30: Leo Moss. "Mina." Doll is 22" long with a head circumference of 15½". Papier-maché shoulder head doll. Original clothing was a white silk christening dress and crocheted cap. Doll has medium brown stationary glass eyes, molded hair, closed mouth with corners turned down, molded-on tear under each eye, composition arms and legs, brown cloth body. This was the first Leo Moss doll to win a ribbon in national competition. It won a 1st place ribbon in the baby doll category at the national convention of the United Federation of Doll Clubs in Louisville, Kentucky in August, 1973. At the same convention, it went on to win another ribbon for 4th best doll of the show. There were over 1,800 dolls in competition. Marks: MINA, incised on front of shoulder head; LEO MOSS/1903, incised on back of head.

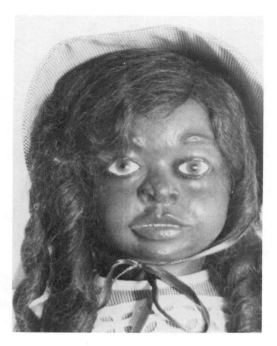

Plate 31: Leo Moss. Serene girl doll, 26" tall. This doll was purchased in the early 1970's from a museum at auction in London, England. The museum's records indicated that they had the doll in their inventory in 1920 and that it was made by a black man in one of the southern states in the Unites States. The doll is one of the rarest of Moss dolls because of the original human hair wig done up in long curls. The doll

has a papier-maché socket head, brown glass stationary eyes, slightly parted mouth with painted teeth faintly showing, ball-jointed body. Redressed. Mr. Moss was known to have used blank bisque heads as a base for molding of the early heads. The blank was apparently made in France as the blank is incised "PARIS." Papier-maché is covering the remainder of the marks, if any. A paper sticker on the head raises several questions. It reads: No BG 3x75 (written by hand)/2158 (stamped on)/MADE IN FRANCE (printed). As the sticker is very old looking, it was probably added when the doll was imported. The reason is unclear as it definitely is a Moss doll.

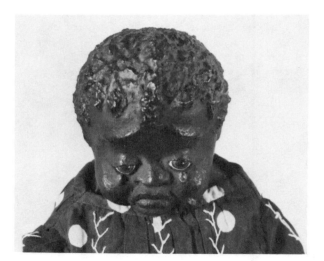

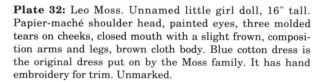

Plate 32: Leo Moss. Unnamed little girl doll, 16" tall. Papier-maché shoulder head, painted eyes, three molded tears on cheeks, closed mouth with a slight frown, composition arms and legs, brown cloth body. Blue cotton dress is the original dress put on by the Moss family. It has hand embroidery for trim. Unmarked.

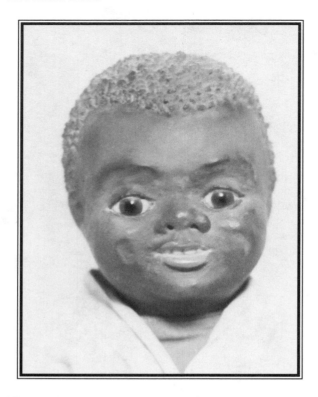

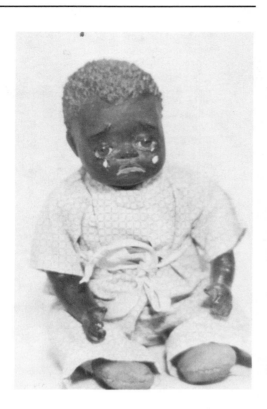

Plate 34: Leo Moss. "Polly," 11" tall. Papier-maché flanged neck head, molded hair, stationary brown glass eyes, closed mouth, papier-maché arms, cloth body and legs. Dressed in very old red and white two-piece print outfit, could be original. Marks: LM, on head; POLLY/1914, on chest. As Leo Moss made dolls representing members of his family, the year 1914 could be the year the girl "Polly" was born rather than the year Mr. Moss made the doll.

Plate 33: Leo Moss. "Leroy, Jr.", 20" tall. Papier-maché flanged neck head with stationary glass eyes, open painted mouth with teeth, pierced nostrils, composition arms and legs, cloth body. Marks: L M, on head; 2-2-33, on cloth sewn to chest.

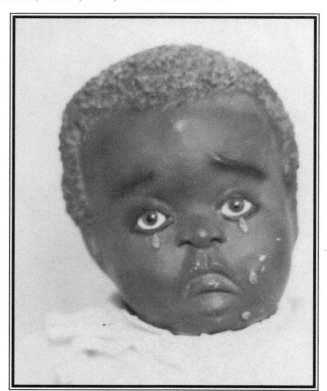

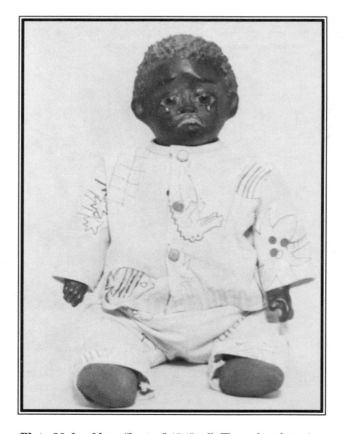

Plate 35: Leo Moss. "Rose," 26½" tall. Papier-maché head, stationary brown glass eyes, closed mouth, four molded tears on face, composition limbs, cloth body. Dressed in beautiful old white embroidered cotton dress. Marks: Rose/1930, sewn to chest dolls square of white muslin.

Plate 36: Leo Moss. "Lester." 13½" tall. Flanged neck papier-maché head, molded hair, stationary brown glass eyes, closed mouth with corners turned down, papier-maché arms, cloth body and legs. Clothing old and could be original. Marks: LM, on head; LESTER/1922, on cloth sewn to chest.

CHAPTER 4
BISQUE DOLLS,
LAST QUARTER OF 19TH CENTURY
TO FIRST QUARTER OF 20TH CENTURY

During the third quarter of the nineteenth century, black china and papier-maché dolls, although still made, were replaced in popularity by the bisque doll. This change in preference from china to bisque is shown in the following articles on toys from *Harpers Bazar* (now spelled Bazaar), January 4, 1879, page 3: "The dolls are more lifelike and in greater variety than in any previous winter...the old-fashioned china dolls are scarcely seen nowadays. To satisfy the child of the period, her doll must move in all the joints, turn her head from side to side, open and close her eyes, and have real hair, or something that passes for it, and is probably lambs wool." Article states that information was supplied to *Harpers Bazar* by Messrs. Ehrich & Co., F.A.O. Schwartz, and E.I. Horsman.

Bisque, the new popular material described in Harpers, is porcelain or ceramic, similar to china except that a glaze was not added to the finished product. This omission of the glaze tended to make the doll's resemblance to human skin more realistic in coloring and texture.

Black dolls, for the first time in history, began to lose their individualism when they were introduced in bisque. The great majority thus offered were made from the same mold as was used for the white dolls. Occasionally, a mold was made with Negroid features and used only for black dolls. These, however, are extremely rare and are quite desirable today. Most of the dark bisque dolls during this period have the color fired in during the second firing of the porcelain heads in the large ovens or kilns. This color will not wash off or peel. There are some, however, not as desirable, that have the brown color painted on after all of the firing has been completed. They are usually the later dolls, after 1915, and were less expensive when originally sold. Most bisque dolls of this type appear to have been made to market as souvenirs for the tourist industry.

The bisque dolls were mass-produced in Germany in great quantities with a lesser number made in France and England, as Germany during this period was the center of the toy making industry. The great extent of German involvement in doll production is illustrated in the following article titled "Dolls" in *Harpers Bazar*, November 22, 1884, page 743.

> ...nine-tenths of all dolls produced are manufactured in the province of Thuringia, in Germany. This comprises but thirty-five square miles, and belongs to the Duke of Saxe-Coburg. The central market of receipt is Sonneberg, a city of some 12,000 inhabitants. The population of Thuringia is about 50,000 or 1,500 people to the square mile. Everyone here is a doll laborer, engaged in making a wig, an eye, a leg, an arm, a dress, some part of doll furniture, or at work in the ovens and clay, or elsewhere.

These very dolls were exported all around the world during this period. They were sold in almost all the large American department and toy stores, advertised as "imported dolls."

Black dolls in bisque, although suffering from their loss of Negroid features for the great majority, displayed advances in materials and detailing parallel to that of white dolls. Most of the black dolls on the market during this period have glass eyes, glass teeth, pierced ears, and wore wigs made of human hair, mohair, or lambs wool. The wigs were sometimes styled in long curls while others wore shorter styles. Much of the coloring on black dolls also changed during this period. For the first time, black dolls varied widely in coloring from black to very light brown. Possibly to account for this variation, they were advertised at times as Negro dolls, mulatto dolls, colored dolls, or pickaninny dolls. Most of the bodies on the dolls during this period were made of composition, a wood pulp mixture. Occasionally, the earlier ones (1880's) were made with leather bodies. The coloring in the leather usually matched the coloring in the bisque heads. Occasionally, the coloring on the composition bodies did not match the bisque heads. This possibly occurred when doll manufacturers had the heads made in one factory, usually a porcelain factory, and bodies made and assembled in another. Because there was such a variety in the coloring of black dolls, they apparently were not always able to have closer matches in coloring on hand.

Why did Germany, a country without a significant black minority as the United States, make black dolls? As was stated earlier, Germany was the center of the doll and toy manufacturing industry. Because they exported dolls worldwide, they considered and produced for all markets. Dark dolls were sent to the United States, the Philippines, Hawaii, India, South America, and various other places where dark races lived. Some were even dressed in original costumes as gypsies.

To a large extent, many of the black dolls thus sent to the United States were still used as supplementary play for the white dolls as were the earlier black dolls. This is illustrated vividly in the following quote from *Harpers Bazar*, January 6, 1877, page 3, when describing Negro dolls in an article reviewing current popular toys:

> ...negresses in gaudy head kerchief and sleeves rolled up as if for washing day...

Later *Harpers Bazar*, December 31, 1881, page 835, in an article on current popular dolls added the following sentence:

> A colored nurse or French bonne with a cap can also be supplied.

The article was entitled "New York Fashions," which was a regular weekly article in *Harpers Bazar*. In the same magazine, December 22, 1888, page 871, the following quote gives one an indication of the still continuing use of black dolls in a subservient manner:

> In the toy shops are seen "all sorts and conditions" of dolls, from the gorgeously attired ladies in Directoire or Empire gowns down to the humble mulatto nurse with her bisque face most naturally colored, a gay bandana on her head, and in her arms her infant charge.

In the January 3, 1885 *Harpers Bazar*, the following description of toys was seen:

> ...Bisque dolls are most liked because they are less easily defaced than those of wax, and these are now shown of any complexion from the fairest blonde to the darkest brunette, and there are also bisque negresses, with woolly hair, to be dressed as maids to fairer dolls.

> ...Whole families of china dolls only two or three inches high to people doll houses are among the favorites of little girls; there are also boy dolls dressed as sailors or soldiers, and the colored dolls are arrayed as cooks with gay turbans or in coachman's attire.

This type of reference to black dolls as maids, etc., was the type frequently found until the 1890's. After this period, an awareness of the possible relationship between black dolls and black children began to develop. The following quote from *Chatterbox*, 1893, pages 214-6, in an article entitled "The Making of Common Things: Dolls," illustrates this relationship:

> Little girls of all nations take the keenest delight in dolls. Some like fair, some like dark beauties, according to whether they are dark or fair. A curious proof that this is so – that a little girl is most fond of that "baby" in which she can see some distinct likeness to herself – is that in America the children of Negroes insist on having black dolls.

This shift in the status of black dolls is also seen in *Youth's Companion*, October, 1895, in an advertisement for "Dolls of Four Races" as follows:

> Our great offer for 1896. Consists of four dolls having bisque heads and jointed arms and legs. The dolls average 9" high and are typical beauties of their race, and are dressed as shown in the illustration. Our stock is limited. Those who wish a set must send up their order early.

This set of "Dolls of Four Races" was given to Companion subscribers for one new subscriber and forty cents for postage and handling. (Although it was advertised as the great offer for 1896, it was actually offered in 1895.) The four races included were Negro doll, white doll, American Indian doll, and Oriental doll. The last two were wearing ethnic-type clothing with the Negro doll in a cotton stripe and the white doll in laces. The Indian and the Oriental had ethnic features while the Negro and white dolls appeared to have been made from the same mold with only color and hair differences. *Youth's Companion* made a similar offer the following year, 1896, called "The Happy Family." It consisted of the same four dolls as in the preceding year with the addition of an Eskimo doll. They were described as: "...typical beauties of their race." This same offer was made in the October 21, 1897 issue of *Youth's Companion*. In this offer, the dolls were not photographed but were described as follows:

> "The Happy Family" consists of five dolls, one each of the following races: American, Indian, Eskimo, African, and Chinese...are typical beauties of their race.

Plate 37: Advertisement from *Youth's Companion*, October, 1895, page 556.

Black dolls and dolls of all races were extremely popular during this period of the 1890's, not only in America, but also in Europe. European children delighted in having a black doll in their collection to play with. This interest in black dolls apparently spread to Canada as in 1908–09, an unusual black doll was advertised along with other dolls in a catalog from the T. Eaton Co., Limited, Toronto, Canada. (Eaton in Canada was the counterpart of Sears, Roebuck in the U.S.) The advertisement which pictured only the white doll was as follows:

Plate 38: Advertisement from *Youth's Companion*, October, 1896, page 568.

This face is photographed and taken from life...Child will take to it at once. This doll comes in two sizes, nicely dressed, with bonnet to match, is unbreakable, and will stand all kinds of wear...

The black rag doll with photographed face was called "The Sunbeam Coon." It was obviously not meant to be marketed for or to black children.

In general, the doll makers in the late 1890's and early 1900's began to dress the black dolls in clothing similar to that of the white dolls. As mentioned earlier, black dolls were not seen as frequently as "servants or domestic dolls." It became obvious that there was a need for a black doll to be used as something other than a supplementary toy for the white doll. Black people were feeling the need to have black dolls available for their children. There was much emphasis on the black dolls for black children being "properly" dressed and presented in a positive manner to black children. This desire of black people to reverse the accepted attitude for black dolls and turn the dolls into toys of pride is shown in the following catalog from the National Negro Doll Company, established in the early 1900's by a black man, Mr. R. H. Boyd. The illustrations and descriptions in this catalog put a great deal of emphasis on the proper dressing of the dolls. Reprint of three pages from the eight-page catalog is shown on the following pages.

23

R.H. Boyd was listed as the president of the firm with H.A. Boyd listed as the manager. Mr. R. H. Boyd was very active in improving conditions for the black segment of the population. In addition to founding the National Negro Doll Company, he also founded the first black bank in Nashville in 1904, the Citizens Savings Bank and Trust Co.

The catalog is a rare find for one interested in research on black dolls. It belongs to NIADA member and doll collector, Roberta Bell of Chicago, Illinois, along with one of the dolls ordered out of the catalog in 1912. The catalog originally belonged to Roberta Bell's great-aunt in Topeka, Kansas. The great-aunt ordered a 36" brown bisque as a prize in a church contest. Roberta, as a young child, won the contest in 1912 and was awarded the doll. It was made by the German firm Schoenau Hoffmeister as were probably all of the dolls in the catalog. The beautiful doll is still in Roberta's doll collection, along with black historical dolls that she creates, and remains her pride and joy.

The National Negro Doll Company remained in business in Nashville until the 1950's, encouraging blacks to purchase black dolls for their children. Lovell Landers, son-in-law of one of the Boyds, was the last president of the company. Although the company reported much success in the early 1900's with their efforts to develop pride in black dolls, because the company was relatively small, the national impact was minimal.

Boyd was not alone in his efforts to encourage blacks to purchase dolls of color for children during the first quarter of the twentieth century. There were many others in history. One of these men was none other than Marcus Garvey, founder of the Universal Negro Improvement Association and organizer of the "Back of Africa Movement." The doll manufacturing firm Garvey established was Berry. It was located in New York City in the area of West 135th Street between Fifth and Lenox Avenues. They were said to have had beautiful dolls. It would be wonderful if one of these dolls could be located now. It is reported that Garvey worked very hard promoting black dolls for black children. According to E. David Cronon in his historical book, *Black Moses: The Story of Marcus Garvey,* Garvey is quoted as stating:

> Mothers! Give your children dolls that look like them to play with and cuddle. They will learn as they grow older to love and care for their own children and not neglect them.

Garvey also ran advertisements for black dolls in *Negro World*, the official publication of the Universal Negro Improvement Association.

In assembling a collection of black dolls, it is fairly easy to find a bisque head doll made during this period. Black dolls didn't again reach a popularity that compared favorably until the 1950's. German and French doll manufacturers who made these black dolls were numerous as shown in the following list. Percentage of black dolls by each manufacturer was small in regards to total production.

Carl Bergner of Germany – made three-faced doll with one face a crying black child, the other two, happier white faces
Bru Jne. & Cie of Paris
Jules Nicholas Steiner of Paris
Mascotte – Paris
Jumeau of Paris – advertised black and mulatto dolls with bisque heads in 1892
Armand Marseille of Germany
Heubach Koppelsdorf of Germany
Kammer and Reinhardt of Germany
Gebruder Heubach of Germany – made character faces in bisque
Heinrich Handwerck of Germany – bisque heads were often marked jointly by Simon & Halbig
Society Francaise de Fabrication de Bebes & Jouets (S.F.B.J.)
Schoenau Hoffmeister of Germany
Kestner of Germany
Recknagel of Germany
Konig & Wernicke of Germany

Dressel, Cuno & Otto of Germany
Kuhnlenz
Simon & Halbig of Germany
F. Gesland of Paris

Dolls marked without the country of origin were probably made before 1891 as this was the year congress passed a law requiring all imported items to be marked with the country of origin.

Although the list of manufacturers that made dolls in a black version is quite lengthy and covers most known manufacturers, there could be other doll manufacturers not included who produced black dolls which the author has not seen as of yet. Many of the black dolls, like the white ones of the same period, are unmarked. These are usually found in the smaller dolls and makes it very difficult, if not impossible, to trace the manufacturer. However, from the black dolls surveyed, it appears that the firm Simon & Halbig made more black dolls than any of the other manufacturers. In the 1880's, Simon & Halbig made black shoulder head dolls with kid leather bodies that are marked 1009 and 1010. Later mold numbers found on black Simon & Halbig socket heads are as follows: #530, very rare; #739, very commonly found in medium brown; #949, usually a lighter shade of brown; #1009, closely resembles the shoulder head with the same mold number; #1039, made before 1891 with open/shut eyes and after 1892 in various shades of brown with flirty eyes; #1078, a beautiful shade of medium brown; #1079, one of the most commonly seen black Simon & Halbigs; #1109, very rare, usually on a jointed well-formed lady body; #1301, closed mouth character pouty with Negroid features, detailed modeling of cheek bones, mouth, and nostrils, dressed as boy or girl; #1348, marked jointly SH-Dressel; #1349 marked S&H – Dressel; #1358, the most desired of the Simon & Halbigs because of its Negroid features, came in various shades from deep black to light brown in a size range from 15" tall to 34" tall; and #1368, also with Negroid features, said to have originally been a brother to mold #1358. Many other Simon & Halbig dolls were made later, early 1900's, and are marked Simon & Halbig – Heinrich Handwerck. Sizes in these range from 10" to 29" tall. It is interesting to note that all of the numbered Simon & Halbig dolls and the majority of those marked jointly with Heinrich Handwerck have pierced ears.

Armand Marseille in Germany appears to have been the second largest manufacturer of different black dolls with bisque heads. The following numbers, indicating various molds that were made, have been found on black Armand Marseille dolls: #351, My Dream Baby or Rock-A-Bye, the most commonly seen black Armand Marseille; #341, Dream Baby, also very commonly seen; #390, frequently seen in varying dark shades of brown or black dressed as girls, ladies, boys or men; #1894, available in many different shades and sizes; baby doll marked "Baby Phyllis," usually on a cloth body; #971, a toddler, open mouth with two upper teeth on a papier-maché body with jointless arms and legs, open crown with wig; mold #990, a baby on a bent leg composition body; and #362, also a baby on a bent leg composition body. Only mold #362 has Negroid features with faintly molded kinky hair. It is also the only mold with pierced ears. All of the molds with the exception of "Dream Baby" and "Baby Phyllis" have open mouths.

The most frequently seen of all the black bisque dolls is the Heubach Koppelsdorf closed mouth mold #399 with Negroid features on a socket head. It was evidently an extremely popular doll during this period as it was made in so many different sizes on both straight leg and bent leg composition bodies. Many of these dolls are found in the original clothes which range from simple grass skirts to extremely "regal looking garments," the latter usually seen on the smaller dolls. The sizes of this doll, commonly referred to as "African," range from 4" tall to life-size babies. Some, usually the later ones, have stickers marked "Bermuda," indicating that they were sold as souvenirs in the islands.

In contrast to most bisque dolls where the closed mouth is rarer, the closed mouth Heubach Koppelsdorf is the most common with the open mouth being much rarer. Mold #414 is the open mouth Heubach African. There is still another open mouth, mold #463, with a wide, wide grin and pierced nose. All of these have solid dome heads, pierced ears, glass eyes, and the same Negroid features. The most desirable of all the Heubach's is, however, the "African" toddler mold #369, on a straight leg stockinette body. Differing from the others, it has a flanged neck with opening in the top of the head and wears an original mohair wig pulled up into a knot on the top of the head. Unlike most other Africans, it has pierced nostrils with a brass ring inserted. This same doll comes in a tiny size, only 4" tall. Unlike the larger version, it has a solid dome head with painted eyes. Another seldom seen Heubach Koppelsdorf is mold #444 with the same Negroid features on a socket head as the other Heubachs. Unlike the more commonly seen African, it has a cut-out crown, wig, and does not have the typical pierced ears. All of the Heubach Koppelsdorfs thus described appear to be variations of the same design with small differences; however, mold #458, found on black Heubachs, is totally different. It is seen in brown fired bisque and original brown painted bisque with Caucasian features only in both the open mouth and closed mouth versions.

Kestner, while not making a large number of black dolls, did make the desirable "Baby Hilda" in black in several different sizes. Other Kestners are a shoulder head bisque on a black leather body, a socket head with Negroid features, and other common doll faced dolls with Caucasian features with the brown color fired into the bisque.

The numbers and descriptions of the dolls made by European Manufacturers for the American market are large and varied. The photographs that follow will give insight on what the dolls are like.

Plate 39: Steropticon photograph from the late 1800's showing a black doll being used as a plaything for white children. In this photograph the doll is used as the "maid" or "servant" for the white girls and their white dolls at a tea party. The steropticon is titled "The Tea Party" by Popular Series.

Plate 40: Another steropticon showing a black doll used as a plaything for a white child. In this photograph, the black doll is sitting in the lap of the larger white doll on the left while the children are having a tea party. The steropticon is titled "Merry Christmas," c 1896 by B. L. Singley, Meadville, Pa., St. Louis, Missouri; Manufactured and Published by Keystone View Company.

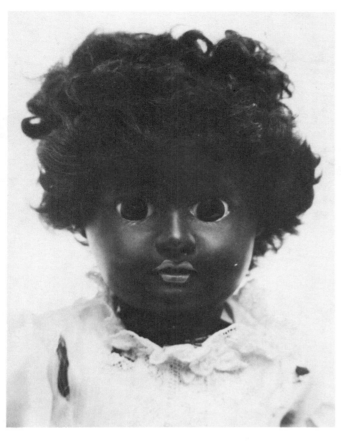

Plate 42: Armand Marseille. "1894," Germany. 9½" tall. Fired medium brown bisque socket head, open mouth, black stationary eyes, dimpled chin, long black human hair wig. Five-piece papier-maché body with molded yellow shoes. Marks: 1894/AM 7/0 DEP.

Plate 41: Armand Marseille. "1894," Germany. 15" tall. Fired black bisque socket head, black stationary glass eyes, open mouth with four glass teeth, curly lambs wool wig. Ball-jointed composition body. Marks: 1894/AM 3 DEP.

Plate 44: Armand Marseille. Germany, first quarter of twentieth century. 13" tall. All original in bandleader costume. Black fired bisque socket head, open mouth with four glass teeth, light brown stationary eyes, mohair wig. Jointed composition body. Black pants with white braid trim, white flannel shirt, pink vest with detailed white trim, pink and white hat with paper trim still intact, spats with four black buttons. Marks: Made in Germany/Armand Marseille/390/A2-0M.

Plate 43: Armand Marseille, "1894." Germany. 19½" tall. Fired brown bisque socket head, stationary eyes, open mouth with teeth; old mohair wig. Ball-jointed composition body. Very old handmade clothing. Marks: 1894/AM 6 DEP, on head.

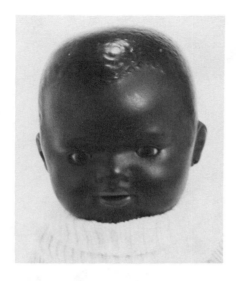

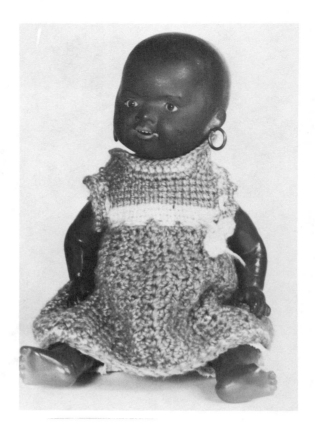

Plate 46: Armand Marseille, Germany. 12½" tall. Bisque socket character face with brown glass sleep eyes, open red mouth with four upper teeth, pierced ears with original brass earrings, molded and painted black hair. Brown composition baby body jointed at neck, shoulders, hips. Old crocheted clothes. Marks: AM/GERMANY/362-12 1-1/2K. Courtesy of Evelyn Ackerman.

Plate 45: Armand Marseille, Germany, first quarter of twentieth century. 12½" tall. Solid dome brown fired bisque head with Negroid features. Open mouth with four upper glass teeth, molded kinky hair, sleeping glass eyes, pierced ears. Bent leg brown composition body matches head closely in coloring. Very unusual and rarely seen baby doll. Marks: A.M./Germany/362/3K.

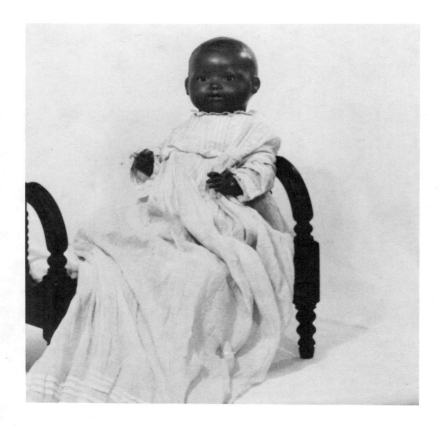

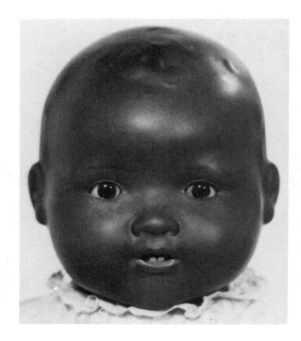

Plate 47: Armand Marseille, Germany, 1924–25. "My Dream Baby" or "Rock-a-Bye." 19" tall, 14½" head circumference. Solid dome fired brown bisque socket head. Open mouth with two lower teeth, sleep eyes, slightly molded painted hair. Bent leg brown composition body. Marks: A.M./Germany/351./6K.

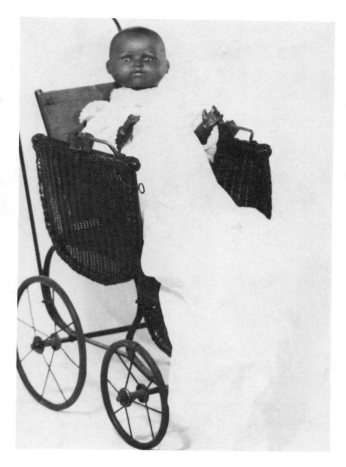

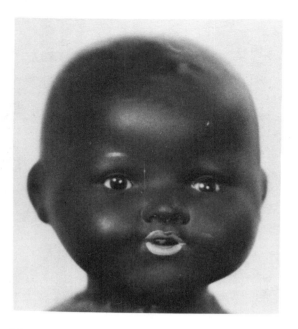

Plate 49: Armand Marseille. Germany, 1924–25, "My Dream Baby." 14½" tall, 11" head circumference. Solid dome black bisque head with flanged neck. Slightly molded hair, sleep eyes, open mouth with "wobble" tongue. Brown cloth body with voice box, jointed cloth arms and legs, composition hands. Marks: A.M./Germany/351./3.

Plate 48: Armand Marseille, Germany. Similar to previous doll except for slightly darker coloring and different head size. Doll is dressed in old long white baby gown. Doll is 19½" long, 13½" head circumference. Marks: A.M./Germany/351/5K.

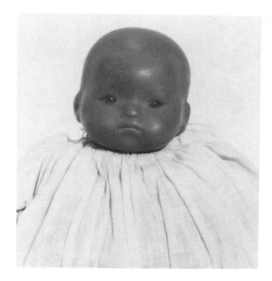

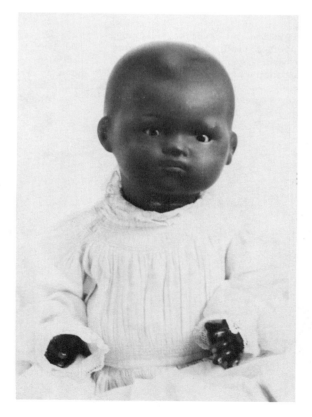

Plate 51: Armand Marseille, Germany, "Baby Phyllis," first quarter of the twentieth century. 10½" long, 7¾" head circumference. Solid dome fired brown bisque head with flanged neck, closed mouth with corners turned down slightly, brown stationary glass eyes, original light brown cloth body, composition hands. Marks: AM/Germany/Baby Phyllis, back of head; 210X, front of neck.

Plate 50: Armand Marseille, Germany, "Dream Baby," 1920's. 17½" tall, 13¾" head circumference. Solid dome fired brown bisque socket head, closed mouth, brown sleep eyes, painted black hair, bent leg brown composition body. Dressed in long white antique baby dress. Marks: A.M./Germany/341/5K.

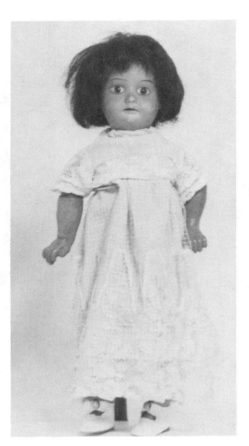

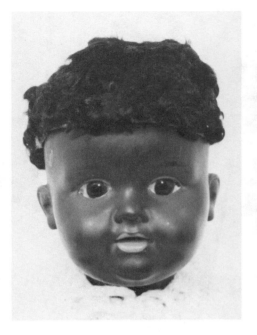

Plate 54: Armand Marseille, Germany, first quarter of the twentieth century. 15" long with 12" head circumference. Open crown dark brown bisque head, open mouth with two upper teeth, dark stationary eyes, black lambs wool wig. Bent leg brown composition baby body. Marks: ARMAND MARSEILLE/Germany/990/ A4M, on head.

Plate 52: Armand Marseille, Germany, circa 1900. 17" tall. Fired brown bisque socket head, sleeping glass eyes with real lashes, dimpled chin, open mouth with four glass teeth, replaced wig. Fully jointed composition body. Redressed. Marks: Armand Marseille/Germany/390/A 0 (1 slash 2) M, on head.

Plate 53: Armand Marseille. Germany, circa 1900. 12½" tall. Fired brown bisque socket head, open mouth with four glass teeth, brown stationary eyes, human hair wig; jointed composition and wood body. Marks: Made in Germany/Armand Marseille/390/A 4-0 M.

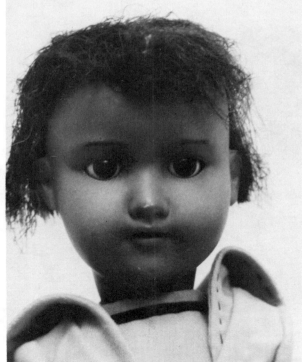

Plate 55: Armand Marseille, Germany. Twin girl and boy dolls, first quarter of the twentieth century. Girl is 19" tall, boy is 18". Open crown fired brown bisque socket heads, dark stationary glass eyes, open mouth with four teeth. Girl has human hair wig, boy has wig made of black string. Bodies are ball-jointed composition and wood. Both have been redressed. Marks: Armand Marseille/Germany/390/A3 M (identical marks on both).

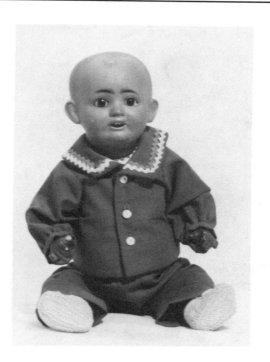

Plate 56: Solid dome bisque head doll made in London, England. 18". Brown glass sleeping eyes, open mouth with two glass teeth, bent leg jointed composition baby body. Redressed. Marks: BND/LONDON/5, on head.

Plate 57: Franz Schmidt & Co., Germany. Approximately 14" tall. Solid dome fired-in brown bisque head, glass sleep eyes, open/closed mouth, pierced nostrils, painted hair. Toddler-type brown composition body. Marks: Germany/F.S. & Co/1255-32/Deponiert.

Plate 58: Light brown bisque head, stationary black glass eyes, closed mouth, wool wig on cardboard pate. Papier-maché body, jointed at neck, shoulders, hips. Clothes may be original. Bisque neck loop for stringing has sometimes been designated as French. Marks: "O" (incised on head). Courtesy of Evelyn Ackerman.

Left – Plate 59: French-type 5" fired brown all bisque, stationary brown glass eyes, black wig, closed mouth, bare feet. Jointed neck, shoulders, hips. Original clothes. Unmarked. Courtesy of Evelyn Ackerman.

Right – Plate 60: 8" tall. Black painted bisque head, black pupiless eyes, closed mouth with full lips; pierced ears, caracul wig. French-type ball-jointed composition body. Redressed. Marks: 6. Courtesy of Susan Manos.

Plate 62: Jumeau. France. 15" tall. Fired medium brown bisque head with closed mouth, dreamy brown sleep eyes, pierced ears. Replaced lambs wool wig. Jointed composition French body with straight wrists. Made in the late 1800's. The only mark is a red check mark below the crown.

Plate 61: French. 13" toddler. Medium brown bisque socket head; stationary brown glass eyes, closed mouth, pierced ears cork pate with black human hair wig (may be replaced). Fully jointed brown composition body, unmarked. Replaced clothes. Marks: PARIS 7/3 BEBE//TETE DEP//3..and with painted red IX, on head. Courtesy of Evelyn Ackerman.

Left – Plate 63: Jumeau. France, circa 1890. 13½" tall. Fired medium brown bisque socket head. Typical Caucasian features, open mouth with four glass teeth, beautiful brown paperweight eyes with large black pupils, pierced ears, jointed composition body. Replaced mohair wig. Redressed. Doll is unmarked.

Right – Plate 64: Jumeau. Paris, France. 12" tall. Dark brown fired bisque socket head, open mouth with six glass teeth, beautiful brown paperweight eyes, pierced ears. Jointed composition body. Made during the third quarter of the nineteenth century and redressed in a style typical of the period. Marks: 3, on back of head.

Left – Plate 65: 13" unmarked French toddler (undoubtedly Jumeau). Light brown bisque socket head incised 3. Stationary brown glass eyes, open mouth with four molded-in porcelain teeth, pierced ears. Cork pate with dark brown human hair wig (probably replaced). Fully jointed brown composition body, unmarked. Replaced clothes. Courtesy of Evelyn Ackerman.

Right – Plate 66: Jumeau. Paris, France. 15" tall with fired light brown bisque head. Open mouth with four glass teeth, pierced ears, beautiful dark paperweight eyes. Jointed composition body closely matches head in coloring. This doll could have been advertised as a mulatto. Only mark on the doll is number 5 on back of neck. Replaced human hair wig.

Plate 67: Jumeau. Paris, France, late 1800's. 16" tall. Fired reddish brown bisque head with heavy black eyebrows, open mouth with six tiny glass teeth. Very realistic looking brown stationary glass eyes, mohair wig, pierced ears. Jointed composition body matches head perfectly in coloring. Clothing could be original. Only mark is number 6 incised on back of head.

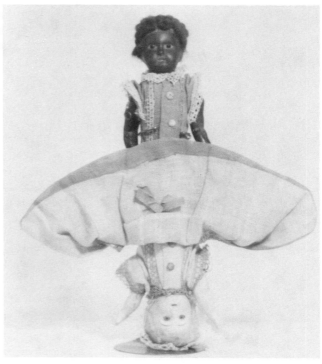

Plate 68: Germany, 1890's. All original black and white double head doll. 11" tall. Both heads are made of bisque with open mouth, five glass teeth, glass stationary eyes, mohair wigs. Shared body is made of wood painted black on one end, faint pink on the other. Painted arms are fastened on with wire through holes drilled into the body. Dolls are dressed identically except for color of outfits. Black doll has light brown dress trimmed with white and blue ribbon and buttons; white doll has cream colored dress with red trim. Similar double head dolls were advertised in Butler Brothers 1895 wholesale catalog for $2.05 per dozen. Dolls are unmarked.

Plate 70: Heubach Koppelsdorf, Germany, early 1900's. 8" tall. Solid dome painted bisque socket head with Negroid features. Closed mouth, open/shut eyes, pierced ears with original brass hoop earrings. Five-piece composition body. Regal looking all original clothing, dressed probably as a tribal chieftan, wearing multicolored grass skirt underneath clothing. Feet are wrapped in braided trim identical to that used to trim outer garment. Multicolored beads are on wrist. Doll is unmarked.

Plate 69: Heubach Koppelsdorf. Germany. 23" long, head circumference 15¼". Solid dome bisque socket head, open mouth with two upper glass teeth, sleeping brown eyes, pierced ears, earrings are missing, jointed composition baby body. Marks: Heubach Koppelsdorf/·414·7·D·R·G·M·/Germany, on head.

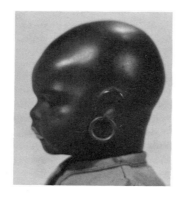

Plate 71: Heubach Koppelsdorf, Germany, early 1900's. 15" tall. Solid dome bisque socket head with Negroid features, closed mouth, painted red lips, pierced ears with original brass earrings, small glass open/shut black eyes, fully jointed straight leg composition body. Head is unmarked. Paper sticker glued to back of body reads: ALA MIGNON-NETTE/POUPEES ET BEBES/Costumes et Trousseaux/Mon GUIGUE/4, rue Notre-Dame de Lorette. Doll is redressed.

Plate 72: Heubach Koppelsdorf, Germany. Solid dome bisque head with inserted tuff of black mohair on top of head. Mohair is attached to and wrapped around wire spring coming out of the head. Stationary black glass eyes looking to the right, pierced ears with earrings, pierced nostrils with inserted earring, open smiling mouth with painted teeth, jointed bent leg composition body. All original in red grass skirt. Marks: 463. 17 (slash) 0, incised on head.

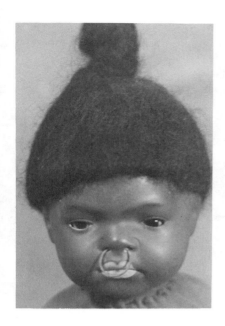

Plate 73: Heubach Koppelsdorf. Germany, early 1900's. 12" tall. Very rare and unusual Heubach "African" with original mohair wig in twisted top knot. Flanged neck painted bisque head with pierced nose instead of ears. Brass ring inserted into nose. Sleeping black eyes, closed mouth. Original brown stockinette body, movable legs connected with metal fasteners. Stitching outlines fingers and toes, dimpled knees. Doll originally came wearing multicolored grass skirt. Marks: Heubach Koppelsdorf/396/10-0 D.R.G.M./Germany.

Plate 74: Heubach Koppelsdorf. Germany, early 1900's. 22" tall. Bisque solid dome socket head with Negroid features. Closed mouth with red painted lips, open/shut glass eyes, pierced ears, original brass hoop earrings are missing, jointed bent leg composition body, same shade of brown as bisque head. Original beads on wrists and in original grass skirt. Doll usually referred to as "Heubach African," is one of the most commonly found black dolls with bisque head. Marks: Heubach Koppelsdorf/399/Germany.

Plate 75: Heubach Koppelsdorf, Germany. 5" tall. Unusual solid dome painted bisque head with flanged neck. Painted eyes, extremely rare on the Heubach "African" dolls. Closed mouth with red painted lips. Ears are not pierced as is usually found on similar dolls. One-piece brown cloth straw stuffed body and legs with papier-maché lower arms and hands. Marks: 396.19/0 (remaining lines, if any, are covered by tightly sewn and glued cloth body).

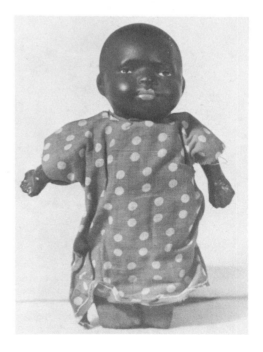

Plate 76: Heubach Koppelsdorf. Germany. 10½" tall. Solid dome dark brown bisque socket head with typical Negroid features. Closed mouth, open/shut glass eyes, pierced ears, original brass earrings, bent leg composition body matches head in coloring. Clothing appears to be original with metal ornament in shape of a quarter moon sewn to headdress. Marks: Heubach Koppelsdorf/399.12-0 D.R.G.M./Germany.

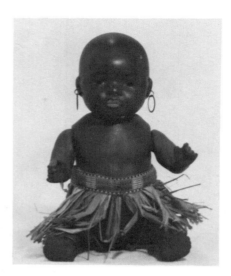

Plate 77: Heubach Koppelsdorf. Germany. 7¼" tall. Solid dome painted bisque socket head. Painted black hair, closed mouth, stationary glass eyes, pierced ears, small brass earrings. Bent leg composition body, brass ring around right leg. Original multicolored grass skirt with colorful woven cloth waistband. Marks: Heubach Koppelsdorf/399.16-0-Germany.

Plate 78: Heubach Koppelsdorf. Germany. 9½" tall. Commonly seen solid dome painted "Heubach African" bisque socket head. Closed mouth, open/shut eyes, pierced ears (earring missing). Five-piece bent leg brown composition body matches head perfectly in coloring. Original natural-colored grass skirt. Marks: Heubach Koppelsdorf/399.13-0/Germany/D.R.G.M.

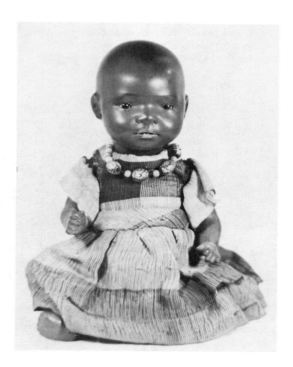

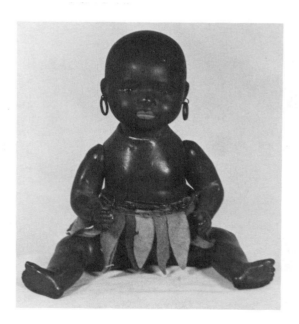

Plate 79: Heubach Koppelsdorf, Germany, early 1900's. 9½" tall. Solid dome painted bisque socket head. Rarely seen open mouth "African" with two lower glass teeth, sleeping eyes, pierced ears with one earring missing, bent leg five-piece composition body. Doll is wearing traditional African trading beads. Clothing is old but does not appear to be original. Marks: Heubach Koppelsdorf/414.13 (slash) 0 D.R.G.M./Germany.

Plate 80: Heubach Koppelsdorf, Germany. 9" tall. Solid dome painted bisque socket head. Doll is all original. Pierced ears with brass earrings, open/closed eyes, closed painted mouth, five-piece composition body. Doll is dressed in multicolored felt skirt with gold and braid waistband. Marks: Heubach Koppelsdorf/399.14/0/D.R.G.M./Germany.

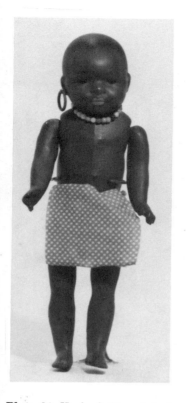

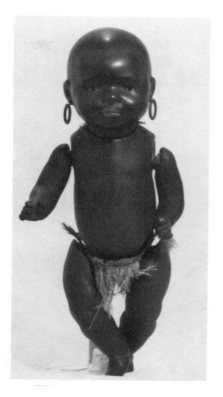

Plate 83: Heubach Koppelsdorf. Germany, early 1900's. 10" tall. Open dome painted bisque head. Stationary eyes, closed mouth, ears not pierced. Wearing original long mohair wig and multicolored beads. Five-piece composition toddler body. Marks: Heubach Koppelsdorf/444.13/Germany.

Plate 81: Heubach Koppelsdorf. Germany. 9½" tall. Unusual Heubach "African" on straight leg composition body. Solid dome painted bisque head. Small glass eyes, pierced ears, one brass earring missing. Doll is wearing original necklace of glass beads. Marks: Heubach Koppelsdorf/ 399.10-0/Germany.

Plate 82: Heubach Koppelsdorf, Germany. 11" tall. Solid dome painted bisque socket head. Tiny, open/shut glass eyes, pierced ears with brass hoop earrings, five-piece bent leg composition body with original natural-colored grass skirt. Skirt is in poor condition. Marks: Heubach Koppelsdorf/399.11-0/Germany/D.R.G.M.

Plate 84: Heubach Koppelsdorf. Germany. 10½" tall. Solid dome bisque head, stationary black glass eyes, closed mouth, five-piece toddler composition body. Original brass earrings in pierced ears, original arm beads, replaced grass skirt. Doll is unmarked.

Plate 85: Heubach Koppelsdorf, Germany, first quarter of the twentieth century. 14" tall. Open dome painted bisque head. Open/closed mouth, stationary eyes, long mohair wig. Five-piece papier-maché body. Very inexpensive doll when originally sold. Dressed in old homemade dress, old shoes and stockings. Marks: Heubach Koppelsdorf/458.12(slash)0/Germany.

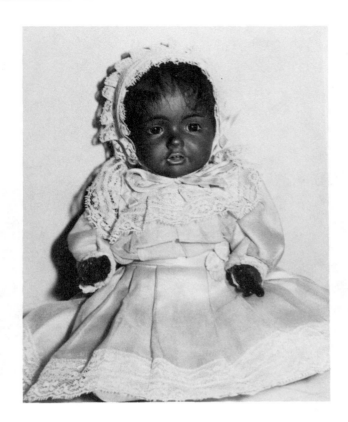

Plate 86: Heubach Koppelsdorf, Germany, early 1900's. 11" tall. Painted bisque originally dressed boy and girl dolls. Open mouth with two upper teeth, sleeping eyes. Girl has pierced ears, intricate gold earrings, human hair wig. Boy does not have pierced ears and has short wig made of mohair. Five-piece inexpensively made papiermaché body. Marks: Heubach Koppelsdorf/458.15 (slash) 0/Germany.

Plate 87: Kestner, Germany. 13". "Baby Hilda," first quarter of twentieth century. Fired brown bisque socket head, human hair wig, brown sleep eyes. Pink satin dress and bonnet. Marks: J.D.K. 245, Hilda, 1914. Courtesy of Carol L. Jacobsen from the *Portrait of Dolls, Volume I,* by Carol L. Jacobsen.

Left – Plate 88: Kestner. 13" tall. "Hilda" toddler. Fired brown bisque socket head, stationary brown eyes, open mouth with two upper glass teeth, red dots painted in nostrils and at corners of eyes, dark brown human hair wig, composition body jointed at the wrists, elbows, shoulders, knees and hips. Clothing is old, could be original. Marks: C made in 7/Germany./245/J.D.K. Jr./1914./C (in circle)/Hilda.

Right – Plate 89: Kestner. Germany, circa 1900. 23" tall. Fired brown bisque socket head, large brown stationary glass eyes, open mouth with four glass teeth, mohair wig, ball-jointed composition body slightly darker than the head. Original shoes and stockings. Dress and underclothing factory made and old, could be original. Marks: 13 1(slash)2 Germany J 1(slash)2.

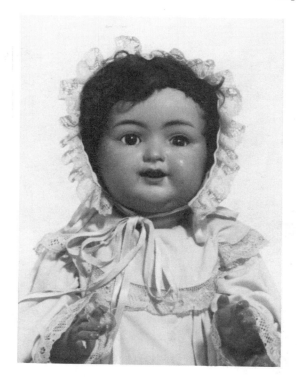

Plate 92: Kammer & Reinhardt – Simon & Halbig. Germany, 1920's. 16" long with 14" head circumference. Fired light brown bisque socket head, open mouth, sleep eyes, bent leg composition body. Dressed in baby blue dress and hat. Marks: K*R/ Simon Halbig/126, on head.

Plate 90: Unmarked, 18" tall. Kestner from Germany during the last quarter of the nineteenth century. Deep black bisque shoulder head with brown stationary glass eyes, open mouth. Body is black leather with lower legs of cloth, lower arms are black bisque.

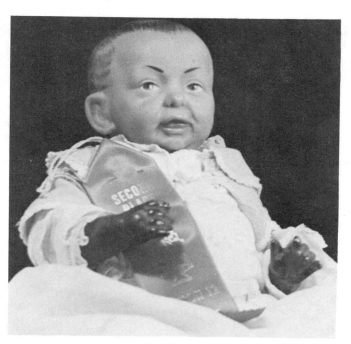

Plate 91: Kammer & Reinhardt, Simon & Halbig, Germany. 11½" tall. Fired light brown bisque head with open mouth, molded tongue, two teeth, sleeping eyes. Bent leg composition baby body. Dressed in old pink knitted two-piece baby suit. Marks: K*R/Simon & Halbig/126/28.

Plate 93: Kammer & Reinhardt, Germany, circa 1910. 16" tall, 10½" head circumference. Solid dome fired light brown bisque socket head, black brush stroked hair, painted eyes, open/closed mouth, bent leg composition body much darker in coloring than head. Doll is the first in a line of realistic character dolls by K*R and is referred to as the "Kaiser Baby" by many collectors. Distributed in U.S. by Strobel and Wilken. Marks: 16/K*R/100.

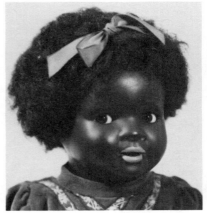

Plate 96: Konig & Wernicke. Germany. Adorable flirty-eyed toddler boy and girl with Negroid features. 18" tall. Bisque heads, dark brown flirty eyes, open mouth with two glass upper teeth, curly synthetic wig. Composition five-piece toddler bodies. Made during the first quarter of the twentieth century. Marks: KW/g/734/72/(crossed nails), on head.

Plate 94: Kammer & Reinhardt – Simon & Halbig. Germany, 1920's. 11" tall. "Originally dressed Twins." Fired light brown bisque heads, open mouth with molded tongue, two upper glass teeth, dark brown sleep eyes, long black mohair wig on girl, short mohair wig on boy. Composition bodies in mint condition, jointed at wrists, elbows, shoulders, knees, and hips. Dolls could have been advertised as mulattoes. Head is identical to K*R mold 126. Marks: K*R/Simon & Halbig/24.

Plate 97: Kresges. 2½" tall. All bisque quintuplets from the 1930's in pink nylon-like wrapper. Movable arms and legs, painted features, slightly molded, painted hair. Stamped on back of wrapper: KRESGES/SPECIAL (in oval)/MADE/IN/JAPAN. Marks: Japan (stamped on the bottom of left foot of each doll). All original.

Plate 98: Kuhnlenz. Germany. 7" tall. Fired brown bisque head, very uneven coloring, brown sleep eyes with black pupils, open mouth with four porcelain teeth, replaced wig. Fully jointed composition body with wooden upper legs, jointed at shoulders, elbows, wrists, hips, and knees. Marks: 34/16, on head.

Plate 95: Konig & Wernicke. Germany. 14" tall. Brown bisque socket head, stationary brown glass eyes with lashes, open mouth with two upper glass teeth, brown synthetic wig, jointed composition toddler body. Redressed. Marks: RW/S/133/16-0, on head.

Plate 101: Recknagel. Germany. Approximately 10" tall. All original brown painted bisque head, painted eyes, open/closed mouth with two painted teeth, pierced ears with brass earrings, short thick mohair wig. Five-piece brown composition body. Original clothing consists of long grass skirt, necklace, paper lei around left ankle, flower in hair. Probably sold to represent islanders or as a souvenir. Marks: R (crossed nails) A/(remainder is impossible to read.)

Plate 99: Mascotte. French "Bebe Mascotte" made between 1891 and 1901. 21" tall. Head is medium brown fired bisque with closed mouth, beautiful dark brown glass stationary eyes, pierced ears, very heavy eyebrows. Lips are soft pink. Body is jointed composition with swayback typical of the Mascotte bodies. Doll is wearing original shoes and stockings. Shoes are incised 75/MODEC DE PARIS A P (in an oval), on the bottom. France is also stamped on the bottom of the shoe. Doll is marked: M/7 on the head.

Plate 100: "Poupee a Transformations." 12½" tall. Interchangeable doll in its original box, circa 1900. The set is complete with three bisque heads, two white and one black; a set of white bisque arms and legs; a set of black arms and legs and a cloth body with cork filled torso. Heads are secured to the body by using long pins that go through holes in the front and back of the shoulder heads. Legs and arms are secured to the body by using elastic bands. The heads are closed mouth with molded, painted hair; painted eyes. One of the white heads has a molded green ribbon in her hair. Both of the white heads have blond hair and blue eyes while the black head has black hair and brown eyes. The original dress is aqua silk with white dots. The dolls were made in England; however, French writing is probably used on the box because French dolls were of higher status than those from England or Germany during this period. Marks: ENGLISH/MAKE/D.P.C. O 58-6, black head; ENGLISH/MAKE/D/P.Co 59-6, white somber face head; ENGLISH/MAKE/D.P.C 0 28-6, white smiling face head.

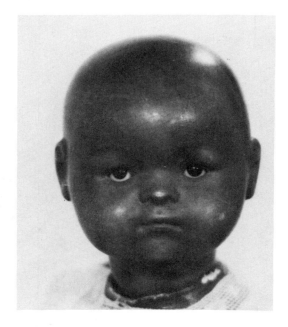

Plate 103: Germany. 23" tall. All original jester or clown doll. Fired-in brown bisque head, open mouth with teeth, stationary black eyes, red mohair wig, jointed brown composition body. Clothing is said to be original. Face has heart, diamond, club and spade painted on cheeks, forehead and chin. Doll has incised mark on back of head that is only found on black dolls. Marks: SP/S (inside a shield), back of head.

Plate 102: Recknagel. Germany. 15" long, 11" head circumference. Solid dome brown fired bisque head with very motley coloring. Closed mouth, sleep eyes, bent leg composition baby body. Marks: Germany/31/2/R127A, on head.

Plate 104: Schoenau Hoffmeister, Germany. 7½" tall. "Hanna," light brown painted bisque with open mouth, sleep eyes, original mohair wig, five-piece jointed composition body. Originally dressed in grass skirt, it was sold to represent Polynesians. Marks: S PB (in a star) H/Hanna/11(slash)0.

Plate 105: Schoenau Hoffmeister, Germany, early 1900's. 19" tall. Fired light brown bisque socket head, open mouth with glass teeth, sleeping eyes, human hair wig, ball-jointed composition body. Redressed. Marks: S PB (in a star) H/1909/3/Germany.

Plate 106: Schoenau Hoffmeister, Germany. 6" tall. Fired brown bisque socket head, black stationary glass eyes, open mouth with glass teeth, composition and wood body jointed at shoulders, hips and knees. Replaced wig. Marks: 4000 17/O/S PB (in star) H.

Plate 109: Simon & Halbig. Germany, last quarter of the nineteenth century. 18" tall. A body made of kid leather is the outstanding feature of this doll. Leather bodies, although commonly seen in white dolls of this period, are rarely seen in black dolls. The tint of the leather closely matches coloring in the bisque shoulder head. Fired brown bisque head has open mouth with four glass teeth, brown stationary glass eyes, pierced ears, dimpled chin. Lower arms and hands are bisque. Marks, if any, are impossible to see as kid leather is tightly secured to shoulder head where marks could be found.

Plate 108: Simon & Halbig. Germany #949. 18" tall. Fired light brown bisque socket head, open mouth, beautiful dark brown glass eyes with black pupils, pierced ears. Ball-jointed composition body. Doll was probably advertised as a mulatto. Marks: S 10 H/949, on head.

Plate 107: Simon & Halbig. Germany. #739. 17" tall with fired medium brown bisque socket head. Dark brown stationary glass eyes, pierced ears, open mouth with glass teeth, original human hair wig. Jointed composition French body has been repainted. Marks: S 10 H/739/DEP, on head.

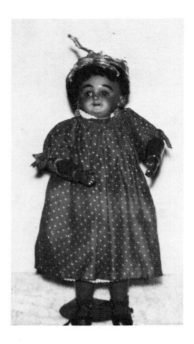

Plate 110: Simon & Halbig. Germany. Mold #1009. 12" tall. Fired medium brown bisque socket head, open mouth, glass eyes, pierced ears. Ball-jointed composition body, slightly darker than head. Original mohair wig. Marks: S & H 1009/ DEP/SC, on head.

Plate 111: Simon & Halbig. Mold #1010. 16" tall. Fired brown bisque shoulder head, brown paperweight glass eyes, pierced ears, open mouth with four tiny porcelain teeth, lambs wool wig, brown bisque lower arms, hands, brown kid leather body, legs and feet. Body matches bisque very closely in coloring. Redressed. Marks: SS 1/2 H 1010 DEP. on shoulder.

Plate 112: Simon & Halbig. Germany. Mold #1039, late 1800's. 20" tall. Medium brown fired bisque socket head. Glass sleeping eyes, open mouth with four glass teeth, pierced ears, old human hair wig, replaced eye lashes. Ball-jointed composition and wood body. Marks: SH 1039/9DEP, on head.

Plate 113: Simon & Halbig. Germany. Mold #1039. 21" tall. Fired medium brown bisque socket head with flirty eyes. Open mouth with four glass teeth, pierced ears, dimpled chin. Original mohair wig. Ball-jointed composition body. Very similar to previous doll except that eyes are flirty and doll is marked with country of origin, which indicates that this doll was made after 1891. Marks: S H 1039/Germany/DEP/8, on head.

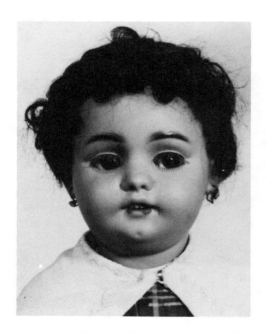

Plate 114: Simon & Halbig. Germany. Mold #1039. 23" tall. Mulatto version of previous doll with same flirty eyes, open mouth, pierced ears. This one has original brown silk eyelashes. Ball-jointed composition body, darker in coloring than head. Marks: 1039/Germany/Halbig/S & H, on head.

Plate 115: Simon & Halbig. Germany. Mold #1078. 21" tall. Fired medium brown bisque socket head. Glass eyes, open mouth, pierced ears, black caracul wig, ball-jointed composition body. Marks: 1078/HALBIG/S & H/GERMANY/10 1-2, on head. Courtesy of Susan Manos.

Plate 116: Simon & Halbig. Germany, late 1800's. Mold #1079. 16" tall. Fired medium brown bisque socket head. Open mouth, glass sleep eyes, pierced ears with glass earrings, human hair wig. Jointed composition body attached to head with coil spring. One of the more commonly seen Simon & Halbig black dolls. Marks: SH 1079/DEP, on head.

Plate 117: Simon & Halbig. Germany. Mold #1079. 17" tall. Fired brown bisque socket head similar to previous doll except that head is slightly larger, doll taller. Open mouth porcelain socket head, glass teeth, stationary brown glass eyes, pierced ears with glass earrings, human hair wig, composition body jointed at wrists, elbows, shoulders, knees, and hips. Dressed in very old handmade clothing. Marks: SH 1079 DEP/7/GERMANY, on head.

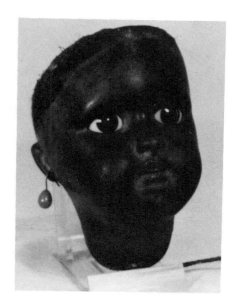

Plate 118: Simon & Halbig. Germany. Mold #1109. Fired black open crown bisque socket head; open mouth, glass sleep eyes, pierced ears. Old black wax remains on glass eyes, shown when sleeping. This head used to be on a well-formed jointed composition lady body. Marks: SH 1109/DEP 6 1/2, on head.

Plate 119: Simon & Halbig – Dressel. Germany. Mold #1348. 17" tall. Medium brown fired bisque socket head. Open mouth with four glass teeth, pierced ears, dark brown stationary eyes, dimpled chin, original mohair wig. Ball-jointed composition body. Marks: 1348/Dressel/SIMON & HALBIG, on head. Head was probably made by Simon & Halbig.

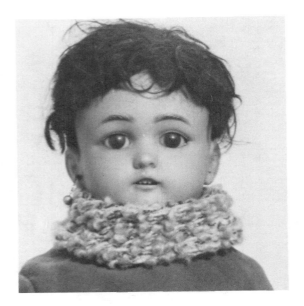

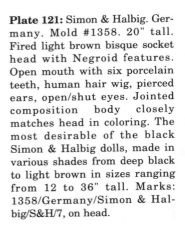

Plate 121: Simon & Halbig. Germany. Mold #1358. 20" tall. Fired light brown bisque socket head with Negroid features. Open mouth with six porcelain teeth, human hair wig, pierced ears, open/shut eyes. Jointed composition body closely matches head in coloring. The most desirable of the black Simon & Halbig dolls, made in various shades from deep black to light brown in sizes ranging from 12 to 36" tall. Marks: 1358/Germany/Simon & Halbig/S&H/7, on head.

Plate 120: Simon & Halbig. Germany. Mold #1349 marked jointly with Dressel. 20" tall. Made in early 1900's. Light brown fired bisque socket head, open mouth, pierced ears, open/shut brown glass eyes, mohair wig. Jointed composition and wood body. Marks: 1349/DRESSEL/S & H/8, on head.

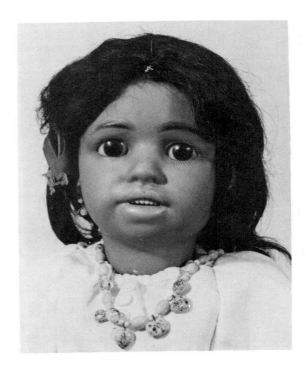

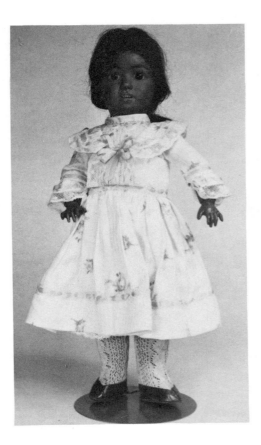

Plate 122: Simon & Halbig. Germany. Mold #1358. 22" tall. Bisque socket head, brown sleep eyes, open mouth, six porcelain teeth, pierced ears, ball-jointed body, black silk mohair wig. Marks: 1358/Germany/Simon & Halbig/S&H/8, on head. Courtesy of Susan Manos.

Plate 123: Simon & Halbig. Germany. Mold #1368. Early twentieth century. 15" tall. Chocolate fired bisque socket head, stationary brown glass eyes, black mohair wig, pierced ears, open mouth with four upper teeth (grown-up type face). Fully jointed brown composition body. Replaced clothes. Marks: 1368/Germany/S&H 4. Courtesy of Evelyn Ackerman.

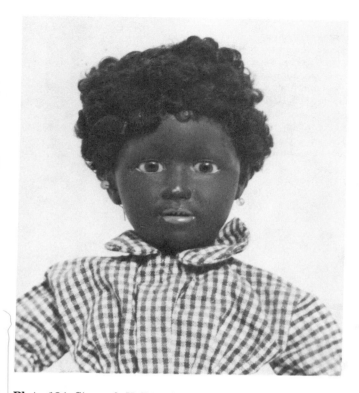

Plate 125: Simon & Halbig – Heinrich Handwerck. Germany, first quarter of the twentieth century. 26" tall. Light brown fired bisque socket head. Open mouth with four glass teeth, large glass sleep eyes, pierced ears. Probably advertised as a mulatto. Body is ball-jointed composition, matches head closely in coloring. Marks: Germany/Heinrich Handwerck/Simon & Halbig/4 1/2.

Plate 124: Simon & Halbig. Germany. Mold #1368. 14½" tall. Fired black bisque socket head, Negroid features, open mouth with four glass teeth, pierced ears, stationary brown eyes, mohair wig. Ball-jointed wood and composition French body. Marks: 1368/Germany/Simon & Halbig/S&H/ 4.

Plate 126: Simon & Halbig – Heinrich Handwerck. Germany, first quarter of the twentieth century. 29" tall, very difficult to find black bisque dolls in this size. Fired light brown bisque socket head, open mouth with four glass teeth, pierced ears, dark brown glass sleeping eyes, dimpled chin, original long curly human hair wig. Ball-jointed composition body. Marks: Germany/Heinrich Handwerck/SIMON HALBIG/5 1/2.

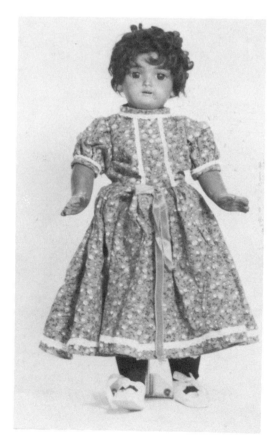

Plate 127: Simon & Halbig – Heinrich Handwerck. Germany. 17" tall. Medium brown fired bisque socket head, open mouth with four teeth, brown glass sleep eyes with black pupils, short black mohair wig, pierced ears. Brown composition jointed body. Redressed. Marks: Germany/Heinrich/Handwerck/SIMON HALBIG/0 1 (slash) 2.

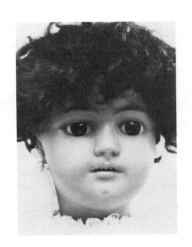

Right – Plate 128: Simon & Halbig –Heinrich Handwerck. Germany, early 1900's. 18" tall. Fired brown bisque socket head. Open mouth, pierced ears, glass eyes, old human hair wig in two long braids. Ball-jointed brown composition body closely matches head in coloring. Marks: Germany/Heinrich Handwerck/SIMON HALBIG/1, on head.

Plate 129: Simon & Halbig – Heinrich Handwerck. Germany. 22". Medium brown fired bisque socket head, open mouth with four glass teeth, pierced ears, glass open/shut eyes, dimpled chin. Ball-jointed composition body closely matches head in coloring. Made from the same mold as the white dolls. Marks: Germany/HEINRICH HANDWERCK/SIMON & HALBIG/3.

Plate 130: Simon & Halbig. 4" tall. Fired medium brown bisque socket head, brown stationary eyes, closed mouth, brown composition body, jointed arms and legs. Courtesy of Paul Johnson.

Plate 131: Simon & Halbig – Heinrich Handwerck. Germany. 19½" tall. Light brown fired bisque socket head. Open mouth with four glass teeth, open/shut eyes, pierced ears, long mohair wig. Ball-jointed composition body, slightly darker in coloring. Marks: Germany/HEINRICH/HANDWERCK/SIMON & HALBIG/2.

Plate 132: Simon & Halbig – Heinrich Handwerck. Germany. "Bride," circa 1900. 14" tall. Head is light brown fired bisque, open mouth with glass teeth, original earrings of wire and green glass beads in pierced ears, stationary brown glass eyes, black caracul wig. Jointed composition body. Outstanding feature on this doll is the original silk wedding dress with long train, ribbons, and laces. Replaced veil. Marks: Germany/Heinrich/Handwerck/SIMON HALBIG, on head.

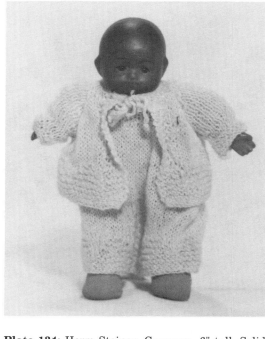

Plate 134: Herm Steiner. Germany. 6" tall. Solid dome fired brown bisque head with flanged neck, closed mouth, black stationary eyes. One-piece brown cloth body, papier-maché hands. Marks: 79/H/S, on head.

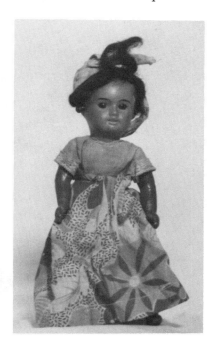

Plate 135: SFBJ. "Unis France." 8½" tall. Fired brown bisque socket head, stationary black eyes, black mohair wig, open mouth with four porcelain teeth, jointed composition body. All original in cotton print island dress with headpiece. Marks: UNIS/FRANCE (in oval)/60, on head.

Plate 133: Jules Steiner. France. 8" tall. Fired brown bisque head, dark brown stationary eyes with black pupils, open mouth with painted teeth. Composition body jointed at wrists, elbows, shoulders, hips, and knees. Marks: A1 (incised); LE PARISIEN, stamped on (unable to read remainder). Courtesy of Paul Johnson.

Plate 136: Societe Francaise de Fabrication de Bebes et Jouets. (SFBJ). "Unis France." Paris, France, first quarter of twentieth century. Doll is 13½" tall and came in sizes from 6" to at least 16" tall. Head is light brown fired bisque with dark brown glass stationary eyes, open mouth, original mohair wig. Five-piece composition body matches head closely in coloring. Many of the black dolls produced by this manufacturer do not have fired-in coloring, they were painted brown in the factory after the final firing. Marks: UNIS/71 FRANCE 149/60.

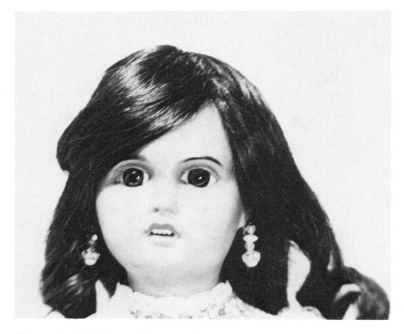

Plate 137: SFBJ. Paris, France, early 1900's. 18½" tall. Very smooth fired brown bisque head. Dark lifelike paperweight eyes, open mouth with four glass teeth, pierced ears. Ball-jointed composition body, slightly darker than head. Replaced human hair wig. Marks: 1/R/S.F.B.J./Paris/7, on head.

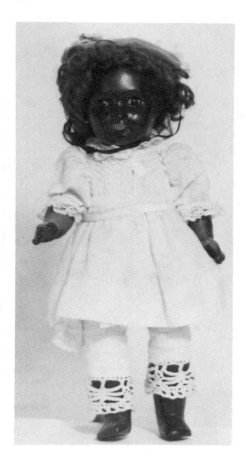

Plate 139: SFBJ. 10½" tall. Painted bisqueloid socket head, stationary amber eyes, black synthetic wig, closed mouth, five-piece jointed composition body. All original in flowered "island" dress. Doll was probably made for the tourist trade. Marks: SFBJ/PARIS, on head.

Plate 138: SFBJ. France, first quarter of twentieth century. 12" tall. Painted black bisqueloid head, closed mouth, pupiless black stationary eyes; five-piece black composition body. Marks: SFBJ/PARIS, on head.

Plate 141: 4" tall. C. 1890. Black bisque socket head, stationary brown glass eyes, closed mouth. Composition body, jointed arms and legs, molded, painted shoes and stockings. Marks: 4/0, on head. Courtesy of Paul Johnson.

Plate 140: SFBJ. "Unis France." 12" tall. Fired bisque socket head, stationary black glass eyes, open mouth with four teeth, jointed five-piece composition body, long human hair wig. All original in light blue chemise trimmed with ecru lace with bead necklace. Marks: UNIS/FRANCE (in oval)/71 60 140, on head.

Plate 142: Musical Mechanical Male Smoker, 24" overall height. Brown bisque head and hands to above wrists. Stationary black glass eyes. Open mouth (for smoking). Pierced ears. Cork pate with original black coarse woolly wig. Broad features beautifully modeled. Original clothes, box and mechanism. Courtesy of Evelyn Ackerman.

Plate 143: England, circa 1925. 18" tall. Bisqueloid head, pierced ears, brown sleep eyes, open mouth with two upper teeth, glued-on short lambs wool wig. Jointed bisqueloid toddler body, painted black. Cry box is inserted in back of body, bisqueloid molded around box. Marks: MADE IN ENGLAND/PAT. NO 535811/&/FOREIGN PATENTS, on head.

Plate 144: Germany. 5¾" tall. Tiny fired black bisque head doll, wig missing; stationary glass eyes; open mouth with four porcelain teeth. Five-piece black papier-maché body; molded orange stockings and black shoes. Very old handmade clothes. Only mark is number 34 on back of head.

Plate 145: Germany. 14" tall. Light brown fired bisque socket head, open mouth with five porcelain teeth, stationary glass eyes, mohair wig. Fully jointed wood and composition body, closely matches head in coloring. Body has a pull string attached to voice box inside body. Original brown painted gauze joins portion of body cut for insertion of voice box. Clothing is old but does not appear to be original. Only identification marks are 62 2, on head. Dolls very similar to this one were advertised in a 1901 wholesale catalog as "Assorted Darky Dolls." They were offered boxed as a group containing six different moving jointed dolls with voice, including two Negro cooks, a Negro nurse, Uncle Tom and two mulatto girls. Price per dozen wholesale was $2.10. This little doll, before it was redressed, could have been one of the mulatto girls.

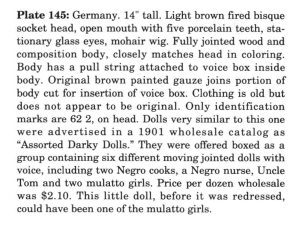

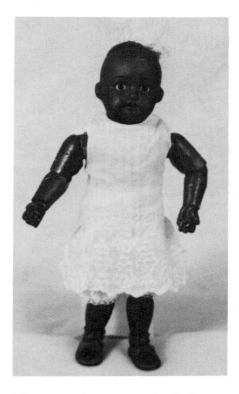

Plate 146: Germany. 5½" tall. Bisque socket head, black stationary glass eyes, open mouth with five porcelain teeth, dimpled chin. Wig is missing. Composition and wooden body, fully jointed at wrists, elbows, shoulders, knees, and hips. Marks: 50/R.DEP./ 79/0, on head.

Plate 147: Germany. 12" tall. Fired brown bisque socket head, open mouth with four porcelain teeth, black stationary eyes, long black mohair wig; five-piece papier-maché body with molded, unpainted shoes. Redressed. Marks: 11/0, on head.

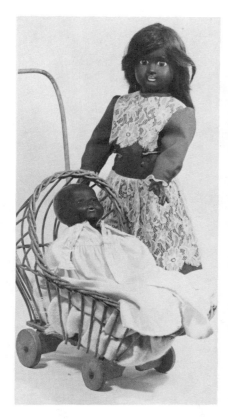

Plate 148: Germany, circa 1900. 24" tall. Black bisque socket head, open mouth, stationary eyes, pierced ears, human hair wig. Ball-jointed composition body. Doll is incised with a mark usually found on black dolls only. Marks: 13 (looks like an iron), on head. Baby in buggy is an Armand Marseille doll.

Plate 150: Germany. "Alice". 11" tall. Brown fired bisque shoulder head, stationary glass eyes, open mouth with four porcelain teeth, mohair wig. Brown cloth body, feet and upper arms, papier-maché lower arms and hands. Marks: Alice/No. 191/14/ 0A, on head.

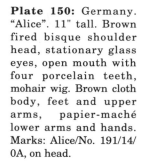

Plate 149: Germany. 13" tall. Bisque head with open mouth, porcelain teeth, dark stationary eyes, short lambs wool wig, jointed composition and wood body. Dressed in old white cotton dress, could be original. Marks: 50 9/0/Made in Germany.

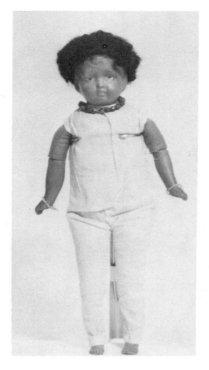

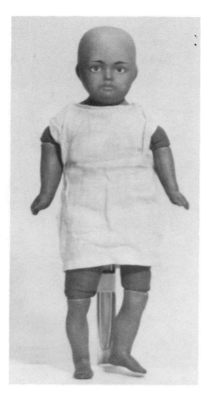

Plate 151: England, circa 1900. Dolls are 11 and 12" tall. Solid dome bisque shoulder heads, slightly open/closed mouth, two upper painted teeth, painted eyes, cloth bodies, bisque lower arms and legs. Boy has a bald head without wig; girl has mohair wig over molded hair. Boy is marked DPC 149-5, on head; 170-4, on legs and arms. Girl is marked: DPC 154-5, on head; 170-4, on legs and arms.

Plate 152: England. 16" tall. Earthenware head, molded kinky hair, brown sleeping glassine eyes, open mouth with two upper teeth, five-piece bent leg baby body. All original in two-piece white cotton undies. Marks: Made in England, on paper sticker on back of head. Underpants are tagged "PETIT NEGRO."

Plate 153: Germany. 6½" tall. Brown fired bisque socket head, black sleep eyes, open mouth with inset porcelain teeth, lambs wool wig, composition body, upper legs wood, jointed at shoulders, elbows, hips, and knees. Marks: Made in Germany/17-0, on head.

Plate 154: Germany. 15" tall. Fired bisque head, stationary black glass eyes, open mouth with six porcelain teeth, mohair wig, jointed composition body. Redressed. Marks: (incised horseshoe)/1900-7, on head.

Plate 155: Germany. 12" tall. Fired brown bisque socket head, stationary black eyes, open mouth with four porcelain teeth, black mohair wig, five-piece strung brown composition body. Clothing is old and appears to be handmade. Marks: 3/0/F, on head.

Plate 156: Japan. 4¾" tall. All bisque doll. Molded kinky hair, exaggerated Negroid features, jointed arms and legs, molded and painted shoes and stockings. Marks: MADE IN JAPAN. Courtesy of Paul Johnson.

Plate 157: 5" tall. Another all bisque doll jointed at shoulders and hips. Molded hair with loop for bow, painted features, molded, painted shoes and socks. All original in pleated yellow nylon skirt. Marks: MADE IN/JAPAN, on head; JAPAN, stamped on skirt in the back. Purchased in the 1940's. Courtesy of Sammye Sheard.

Left – Plate 158: 4" tall. Bisque doll with movable arms, molded hair, painted features. Marks: MADE IN/ JAPAN, on back.

Right – Plate 159: Japan. Pre-World War I. 5" tall. All bisque, movable arms, molded kinky hair; painted features; molded, painted clothes. Marks: Nippon.

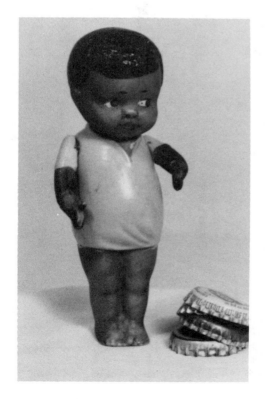

Plate 161: Similar 5½" all bisque story-book doll in red print dress. All original.

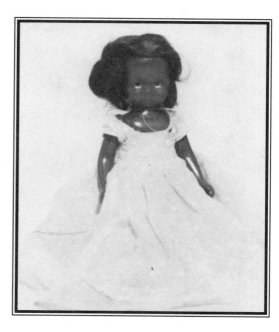

Plate 162: Storybook. "Nancy Ann Storybook Doll." 5½". Later Storybook doll made of hard plastic. Jointed head, arms, and legs, mohair wig, sleep eyes. All original in pink and white dotted dress. Hard plastic dolls were made from 1949–late 1950's. Marks: StoryBook/U.S.A./Trade Mark/Reg., on head. Courtesy of Marge Betts.

Plate 160: Storybook. "Nancy Ann Story-book Doll Topsy," 5½". All bisque doll with painted features, glued-on mohair wig, jointed arms at shoulders. All original. Marks: Storybook Doll U.S.A., on body. Dolls were made 1939–1948. They are included in this section because they are made of bisque. The following Nancy Ann dolls made of plastic are included also.

Plate 164: German. Dollhouse doll (Butler). 7⅜" tall. Black bisque shoulder head. Painted brown eyes; molded black hair, slightly glazed; closed red lips. Lower limbs of black bisque. Feet have molded boots with heels and are painted black. Original clothes. Unmarked, if marked it would probably only have mold numbers. Courtesy of Evelyn Ack-erman.

Plate 163: Storybook. Hard plastic Nancy Ann with painted eyes. All original. 5½" tall, jointed head, arms, and legs, black mohair wig. Marks: STORYBOOK/DOLLS/U.S.A./TRADE MARK/ REG., on body.

Plate 165: Another "Nancy Ann Storybook," plastic with sleep eyes in different all original dress. Hairstyle is also different. Dress is orange print with orange ribbon in hair. Marks: STORYBOOK/DOLLS/TRADE MARK/REG., on body.

Plate 166: 2½" tall. All bisque with swivel necks, painted features. Girl has black glued-on wig; boy has molded, painted hair. All original clothing on both dolls. Courtesy of Paul Johnson.

Plate 167: Germany. 14" tall. Bisque head, stationary black glass eyes with red dots in corners, black mohair wig, open mouth with four porcelain teeth, jointed five-piece toddler body. Redressed. Marks: 4 (slash) 0, on head.

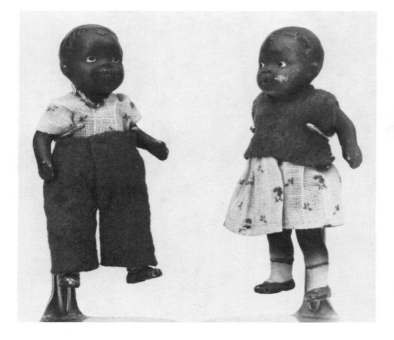

Plate 168: Germany, 1920's. 2¾" tall. Rare dollhouse dolls. All original. All bisque, dark brown, molded black curly hair, painted faces, closed mouths. Jointed at shoulders and arms. Molded shoes painted orange, painted white socks with orange top stripe. Original felt and printed gauze clothes. Marks: 11/Germany, incised on body. Courtesy of Evelyn Ackerman.

Plate 169: Approximately 5" tall all bisque baby. Painted eyes, closed mouth, tuffs of hair inserted into three holes in head, jointed body.

CHAPTER 5
CLOTH DOLLS,
MID-1800's TO THE PRESENT

Dolls can and have been made by hand with cloth by many generations of mothers, fathers, grandmothers, aunts, and even children themselves. The desire to make dolls can be created by need or it can be stimulated by a creative experimenting mind. Whatever the case may be, the final product is a doll, made to love.

Manufacturers of cotton fabrics were well aware of this desire or need to create and as early as 1886 often offered dolls printed on cloth. The cloth was purchased by the yard or piece in the yard goods department to be cut, sewn, and stuffed at home. In other cases, cloth with dolls printed on were given as premiums for boxtops, magazine subscriptions, etc. One of the most popular of the commercially printed black rag dolls was the set made in 1910 by the Davis Milling Co., later called Aunt Jemima Mills, Inc. The set, advertised as "Funny Rag Dolls," consisted of Aunt Jemima, Uncle Mose, and children Wade Davis and Diana Jemima. The complete set was available in exchange for four flour coupons and sixteen cents. This was not the first set of Aunt Jemima dolls made however, an earlier set was made in 1905. They are extremely rare. The original design for the set of Aunt Jemima dolls changed several times. Sets are known to have been made for the following years: 1905, 1910, 1924, 1929, and 1949. It is possible that other sets may also exist.

With each issue of the Aunt Jemima sets, the dolls were available with coupons and/or a small amount of money. It is doubtful that these dolls were marketed for black children. Most black parents probably would not have found the dolls appropriate playthings for their children. However, it is possible that some black children did play with these dolls.

Rag dolls, as well as being totally made at home or partially made at home, were also sold completely finished at various times in the late 1800's and throughout the 1900's. They fulfilled a need – they could be dropped, stepped on, misused, washed, and loved again. They were also less expensive than other dolls on the market. Commercially made rag dolls popular during the turn of the century were those made by Arnold Print Works, Massachusetts; Albert Bruckner, New York; Averill Manufacturing Co., New York; Elms and Sellon Company, New York; The Saalfield Publishing Company, Akron, Ohio; and the Spring Mills Co. From these companies and many more unknown manufacturers, rag or cloth dolls were available in a size range of 5½" to 22½" tall. They were given a variety of names such as: "Darky Doll," patented August 15, 1893; "Mammy Doll," copyright 1910 by the Saalfield Publishing Co., "Topsy" dolls; and "Pickaninny," patented July 5, 1892 and October 4, 1892 in the U.S. and England by the Arnold Print Works.

Plate 170: Handmade cloth doll with embroidered features and hand sewn black yarn hair knotted. All original, 1940's–50's. Doll resembles the Terri Lee doll made in composition and hard plastic during the same period. As this cloth doll is frequently seen, there possibly was a pattern for a Terri Lee like doll.

The advertisement for these dolls, at times, was very descriptive, as shown in the following quotes from Montgomery Ward and Co. 1903 catalog:

"Darky" Nurse Rag doll, a well-made and appropriately dressed doll in bright colored clothing; length, 14". Sure to please little folks; also suitable for use as a booby prize for card parties, etc. Ought to be in every collection of dolls. Price fifty cents...

"Mammy" Rag Doll, 16" long, appropriately dressed in a facsimile costume such as was worn by the real old Southern mammy, with bandana kerchief on head, white kerchief over shoulders, long colored dress and white apron. Each seventy-five cents...

"Dusky Dude" Rag Doll...length, 14". A novel and desirable doll for boy's use, and will make an appropriate addition to any doll collection...price fifty cents.

Butler Brothers wholesale 1914 catalog offered an uncut cloth doll as follows:

To be cut out and stuffed. Lithographed in bright oil colors on strong cloth. Simple to make up, parts fit accurately, practically indestructible. Each doll on separate sheet with instructions.

Included in the above offer was a 23" "Mammy" doll and a 17" "Topsy." Sheets were about 23" by 24" at $1.25 per dozen, wholesale.

The following pages contain photographs and detailed descriptions of many black cloth and rag dolls available from the mid-1800's to the present. Cloth dolls made by Shindana Toys, Division of Operation Bootstrap, are shown in this book with the vinyl Shindana dolls. Included are personality dolls Rodney Allen Ripey, Redd Foxx, J.J. Walker, Flip Wilson, and fun dolls Li'l Souls and Li'l Friends.

Plate 171: Arnold Print Works, North Hampton, Massachusetts. "Pickaninny," uncut printed cloth doll patented July 5, 1892 and October 4, 1892 in the U.S., also registered in England. Completed doll would be 14" tall. Doll came in either red dress with blue hat or blue dress with red hat. Directions printed on cloth read: "Sew up the sides and head and stuff with cotton. Cut paste board oval to fit bottom piece then sew together."

Plate 172: Arnold Print Works. "Pickaninny," 14" tall. Identical to previous doll, already cut, sewn, and stuffed. Doll is printed with red dress holding blue hat.

Plate 173: Arnold Print Works. "Blossom." Completed doll is 14" tall. Reproduction of previous two dolls with the only difference being the name change from "Pickaninny" to "Blossom." Reproductions were made by The Toy Works Inc., Middle Falls, New York, c1977. Cloth is stamped with their logo and the logo of the Museum of the City of New York. Colors are the same as those in the provious dolls.

Plate 174: Arnold Print Works. "Blossom" cut out and sewn up.

Plate 176: Uncut version of front and back of previous Aunt Jemima doll.

Plate 175: Quaker Oats Company. "Aunt Jemima," 1929. Printed cloth, 16" tall. Doll has been cut and sewn but not stuffed. Marks: Aunt Jemima, back of doll. Advertisement for "free Aunt Jemima and her rag doll family" in exchange for the coupons on each package of Aunt Jemima Pancake flour by Davis Milling Co., St. Joseph, Missouri, was shown in *Playthings*, a toy directory, February, 1912, page 26.

Plate 177: Aunt Jemima Mills Co. "Diana Jemima," circa 1910. 12" doll from the earlier Jemima dolls offered as premiums. Diana is the daughter of Aunt Jemima. Doll is unsewn. Marks: Diana Jemima, on back. It is interesting to note that Diana is holding a black rag doll. She is not doing this in later issues.

Plate 178: Quaker Oats Co. "Uncle Mose," printed on cloth uncut doll. Cloth is 16½" by 14", circa 1929. Doll is wearing blue jacket, yellow and red checked pants, holding white top hat. UNCLE MOSE is written on back of doll's collar. Issued along with previous Aunt Jemima doll.

Plate 179: Aunt Jemima Mills Co. 1924, "Aunt Jemima." Front and back of cloth ready to cut out and stuff to make Aunt Jemima doll. Printed on front of cloth: Our full set of rag dolls, Aunt Jemima, Uncle Mose, and the Pickaninnies, Diana and Wade, ready to cut out and stuff, will be sent to any address postpaid upon receipt of four tops taken from packages or backs cut from bags of – AUNT JEMIMA PANCAKE FLOUR/AUNT JEMIMA BRAN FLUFFS/AUNT JEMIMA BUCK-WHEAT FLOUR/AUNT JEMIMA BRAN/AUNT JEMIMA GRITS/AUNT JEMIMA SELF-RISING FLOUR/AUNT JEMIMA CREAM MEAL and twent-five cents in stamps or coin or any one of these dolls of one package top on back of bag and ten cents in stamps or coin. Be careful to give full name, street number, town and state. Address all mail to AUNT JEMIMA MILLS COMPANY, DEPT. A. ST. JOSEPH, MISSOURI. ALSO MAN-UFACTURERS OF AUNT JEMIMA WHEAT FLOUR/RED TOP WHEAT FLOUR/FIDDLE AND BOW SELF-RISING FLOUR/AUNT JEMIMA SALAD AND COOKING OIL. Printed in U.S.A. Directions for completing the doll were printed as follows: Cut around body on dotted line, and lay printed sides together. Sew all around body on BODY LINES, except a 2" space at side. Now turn right side out and stuff with sawdust, bran, cotton batting or soft rags through the opening left in the side. Fill until doll is plump, sew up and it is ready to play with. (No feet with mother doll.)

Plate 180: Aunt Jemima Mills Co., "Aunt Jemima." 16½" tall. Completed doll like uncut previous one.

Plate 181: Aunt Jemima Mills Co. "Uncle Mose," 15½" tall, offered the same time as the previous doll. Marks: Uncle Mose/Aunt Jemima's/Husband, printed on back.

Plate 182: Aunt Jemima Mills Co. "Diana Jemima," 12" tall. She is holding a cat in this later 1924 version. Marks: Diana/Aunt Jemima's/Little Girl, printed on back.

Plate 183: Aunt Jemima Mills Co., 1924, "Wade." 11½" tall. Doll is unmarked.

Plate 186: Norah Wellings, England. 18" tall. Cloth doll with hard pressed velvet face. Glass inset googlie eyes, mohair wig. All original. Collection of Susan Manos.

Plate 184: Aunt Jemima Mills Co. "Aunt Jemima Family," 1949. Printed, stuffed plastic dolls were heat sealed around edges except for bottom at the feet. They were probably issued unstuffed, as the bottoms are hand sewn. Cost of the set of four dolls was seventy-five cents and three Aunt Jemima box or sack tops. Aunt Jemima or Uncle Mose could be purchased separately for twenty-five cents each.

Plate 185: Cloth doll said to be a Voodoo doll from Haiti. 16" tall with embroidered features, chicken quill fingernails. All original. Similar dolls were also sold in Brazil.

Plate 188: Norah Wellings, England. 14" tall. Cloth stuffed doll with movable arms, legs, and head, painted eyes, brown caracul wig. Tag with "Bermuda" sewn on chest. Tag sewn on bottom of left foot: MADE IN ENGLAND/BY/NORAH WELLINGS. This doll was probably sold as a souvenir.

Plate 187: All original boy and girl cloth dolls with hard cloth pressed faces, circa 1920. 15" tall. Features are painted, glued-on wigs look like mohair. Attached to back of each doll is a tag with following information: Childhood Classics/An Original Creation/By A.P.I. Ltd. New York.

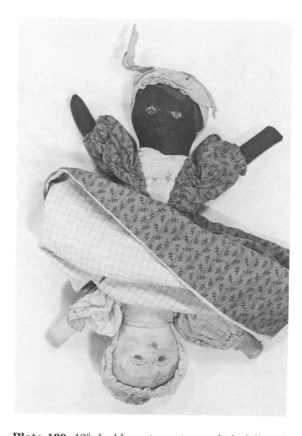

Plate 189: 9" tall cloth topsy-turvy or double doll with painted features. Body and arms are made of the same material as used for skirt. One head is brown cloth with tuff of dark brown mohair for hair, other head is white cloth with light brown tuff of mohair for hair. Unmarked doll appears to have been commercially made.

Plate 190: 12" double or topsy-turvy cloth doll with painted features, first quarter of twentieth century. Black face has orange kerchief tied around head, wears red and black printed dress with white yoke, arms are black cloth. White face has white lace cap, wears blue and white dress with white yoke, arms are white. Clothing is old, looks handmade and was sewn on doll. Doll is unmarked.

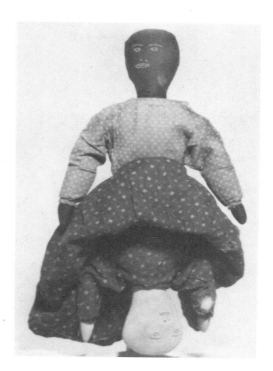

Plate 191: "Topsy-turvy," 12" tall. 1920–1930. All cloth with pressed face and painted features. Black face has tuff of black hair sticking out of bandana. All original in sewn-on clothing except for removable skirt, red print for black doll, blue print for white doll. Unmarked.

Plate 192: Cloth topsy-turvy, 13½" tall. Early 1900's. Both dolls have embroidered features, no hair. Clothing is old and handmade, could be original.

Plate 193: 16" tall cloth doll with printed facial features, glued-on black yarn hair, blue gingham cloth body, removable red felt dress. 1960's. Doll is unmarked.

Plate 194: 16" tall cloth doll with painted facial features, three loops of black yarn for hair, sewn-on bandana and stockings with matching removable dotted pink dress. Unmarked. 1920's–1930's.

Plate 195: 15½" tall all original handmade cloth doll from the 1870's. Well-dressed doll has eyes made of black beads, embroidered features, finely detailed black string hair styled in coil at the back, very old black leather shoes.

Plate 196: 11" tall cloth topsy-turvy doll with printed features, yarn hair, printed bodices, off-white skirt. Early 1900's. Dolls are unmarked.

Plate 197: 14" long. Handmade cloth doll with embroidered features, including eyelashes made of embroidery thread, black yarn hair. Doll appears to have been made during second quarter of twentieth century.

Plate 198: Collection of cloth dolls purchased in the 1940's and 1950's in the Caribbean. Dolls are unmarked.

Plate 199: Golliwogg from England, 1970's. Character doll taken from an English children's story *The Adventures of Two Dutch Dolls and a Golliwogg*. Original doll was first made following the publication of the book in 1895. It was advertised in a 1901 wholesale catalog as: "Golliwogg Dolls. Grotesque, bushy-headed Negro dolls, in old-fashioned red flannel swallowtail coat; yellow vest, with brass buttons; striped flannel pants and white collar; made of cloth and unbreakable: 13" long. Per dozen…$2.25." Early Golliwogg dolls are very rare. Golliwogg is sometimes spelled Golliwog.

Plate 200: 16" tall novelty looking cloth doll with painted and slightly molded features. Material used for face has shiny appearance, similar to early oil cloth. Body is blue cotton. Appears to have been made during first quarter of twentieth century. Unmarked.

Plate 201: 14" & 15" handmade cloth dolls from first quarter of twentieth century. Features are painted on by hand. Clothing is removable.

Plate 202: Averill Manufacturing Co. "Chocolate Drop" 1923–24. Brown rag doll made in the U.S. Doll was designed by Grace Drayton and is 11" tall. Head has three tuffs of yarn inserted for braids, facial features and the rest of hair appear to be lithographed except for portion of eyes which are painted white. Voice box is inserted into chest. Doll is wearing original undies.

Plate 203: "Rastus," advertising cloth Cream of Wheat doll, uncut. 1924. Doll was a premium from Cream of Wheat Company, Minneapolis, Minnesota. Finished doll is 18" tall. Doll has white shirt, brown pants with black stripes, red bow under chin and on shoes, white cap and apron. Some of the cut Rastus dolls on the market have been sewn up incorrectly. All of them should have separate legs, stuffed individually. On the incorrectly sewn dolls, one leg, fully open, was used for the front of the body, the other for the back.

Below – Plate 204: Letter that was sent along with the Cream of Wheat doll Rastus. The letter and folded uncut doll were sent in a #10 business envelope.

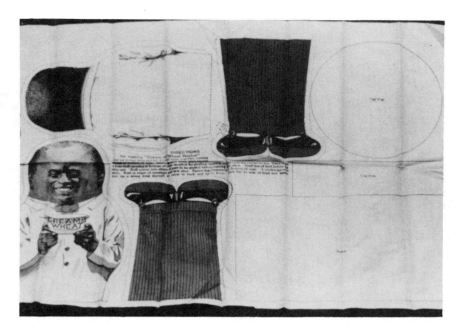

GEO. B. CLIFFORD, PRESIDENT
J. WALKER SMITH, VICE PRESIDENT

D. F. BULL, TREAS. AND GEN. MANAGER
G. V. THOMSON, SEC. AND ASST. MGR.

CREAM OF WHEAT COMPANY

MINNEAPOLIS, MINN.

Dear Friend:

We are very glad to send you along with this letter your Rastus Doll, for which you recently asked. He is a jovial, good-natured individual, and is always ready to serve you with a delicious, nourishing breakfast. On the well-known Cream of Wheat package he stands for wholesomeness and purity in a product which has been building healthy children for many years.

Enclosed you will find booklet, "The Important Business of Feeding Children," which has been prepared with the approval of well-known children specialists and dietitians.

For years Cream of Wheat has been recommended by doctors and health authorities as a wholesome and nutritious food for infants and growing children. Authorities stress particularly the importance of a hot cooked cereal breakfast for children. This is essential, not only during their younger years, but during the grade and high school periods.

Cream of Wheat is made from the best hard wheat. It is extremely rich in energy-producing elements, and is also easily digested. These two qualities--high energy, quickly available--make it an unusually well-fitted food to meet the child's daily demand for energy, and to supply this energy with little tax on digestion.

Buy a package of Cream of Wheat today and try the healthful and delicious energy dishes illustrated in this book. They are not only good for the children, but are sure to become great favorites with the whole family. And bear this in mind--you get forty generous dishes from one big package.

Yours very truly,

CREAM OF WHEAT COMPANY.

Plate 205: Albert Bruckner, New York. Black cloth doll with stiffened mask face, patented July 9, 1901. 13" tall. Features are printed on the face which has been fastened to a stuffed dummy head of brown cloth. Four tuffs of hair are attached to the edges of the face mask. An extension below the chin forms the neck. The date, "Pat'd July 9, 1901" is printed on the right front side of the neck. Body and limbs are brown, tightly stuffed cloth. Face is identical to one used by Bruckner for their "topsy-turvy" dolls. Red print dress could be original.

Plate 206: "Rastus," Cream of Wheat advertising doll, cut, sewn, and stuffed, 1949 version. 18" tall. Doll is very similar to earlier Rastus except pants are red and white striped, bowl is blue.

Plate 207: Topsy-turvy doll is 15" tall. 1920's. Both heads have embroidered features. Black doll has button eyes. White doll has Betty Boop type face. All original.

Plate 208: Commercially made double lithographed doll, circa 1900. 15" tall. Black doll is printed on one side, white doll on the other. Doll is stuffed with cotton. Black doll has a wide smile, printed kinky hair, wears green and yellow checkered dress; white doll has printed blond curls, red dress.

Plate 209: Reverse side of previous doll.

Plate 210: Albert Bruckner. Patented July 9, 1901. 12½" tall. Doublehead or topsy-turvy cloth doll. Both faces are lithographed. Black head has black mohair wig, laughing mouth with teeth, red dress and kerchief. White head has lithographed blond hair, blue eyes, red checked dress, and bonnet. All original.

No. 2 "TU-IN-ONE"
TRADE MARK

"Turn Me Up
Turn Me Back
First I'm White
Then I'm Black"

SPECIALTIES

"Dollypop"
Trade Mark Reg. U. S. Pat. Off.
The Popular Fashion Dolls
"TUBBY-TOT"
Trade Mark Reg. U. S. Pat. Off.
Design Patent May, 1926
The Durable Rubber Dolls

Albert Bruckner's Sons
"One of America's Oldest Doll Manufacturers." Established 1901.
Specialists in Soft, Novelty and Character Mama Dolls
31 UNION SQUARE W., NEW YORK CITY

Plate 211: Advertisement for previous doll by Albert Bruckner & Sons.

Plate 212: Handmade "Sewing Basket" doll, 10" tall. Doll is made of items normally found in sewing baskets around 1950. Head is made of ball of black crochet or tatting thread, body is made of skein of heavy knitting or crochet yarn, arms and legs are made of wooden spools of thread. Clothes are a zipper top with felt pants. Shoes, hands, and facial features are old buttons. Doll can stand alone.

Plate 213: Spring Mills Company. "Black Mammy" from "Black Mammy and Child." 15" tall. Caricature-type doll was sold printed on cloth to be cut, sewn, and stuffed along with the following boy doll.

Plate 214: Spring Mills Co. "Child" from "Black Mammy and Child." 9" tall. Both dolls are printed in red, white, and blue clothing.

Plate 215: Approximately 14" tall. Handmade one-piece cloth boy doll marketed to preschools from catalogs in the mid-1960's when black dolls were relatively hard to find. Boy's clothing has been lost. Doll is unmarked. Black yarn hair, embroidered features.

Plate 216: Sold along with previous boy doll through preschool toy catalog. All original in cotton print dress. Yarn hair, embroidered features.

Plate 217: Handmade 19" cloth doll made from a popular commercial pattern in the mid-1970's. The pattern was sold in fabric stores and department stores. Black yarn hair, embroidered features. The pattern for the clothing was included with the doll pattern. The doll was made by Julie Perkins Scott for her mother's doll collection.

Plate 218: Another handmade cloth doll the same size as the previous one, probably made from the same pattern as dolls are identical except that this one does not have the red cheek circles sewn on. The patterns used for the clothing are also identical except that different fabrics and trims were chosen. Courtesy of Cheryl Larry Perkins.

Plate 219: Toy Works. "Egyptian Mummy Doll," printed cloth, 9" tall. Purchased new in 1988.

Plate 220: McCall Pattern Company. "Raggedy Ann" doll made from McCall's pattern 4268. 36" tall. Made by Julie Perkins Scott in 1981. Doll has iron-on decal features. Yarn hair was planned but never added. Included with the pattern for Raggedy Ann was a pattern for Raggedy Andy and patterns for clothing for both dolls.

Plate 221: Concord Fabrics. "Samantha and Polly," printed-on cloth dolls that you cut out and stitch at home. Samantha is 18" and Polly is 7½". Designed by Joan Kessler for Concord Fabrics.

Plate 222: Uncut cloth version of previous dolls, "Samatha and Polly." Fabric for making the dolls was sold by the piece from bolts at fabric stores.

Plate 223: Melco Textile Corp. Heartline, Cabbage Patch Kids Collection, cloth cut-out, stuff, and sew at home doll. Finished doll is 18" by 13½". One piece, with printed brown yarn hair, lavender print dress. In the background there are three brown cabbages in the patch. Marks: 1983 Original Appalachian Artworks, Inc., bottom left-hand corner.

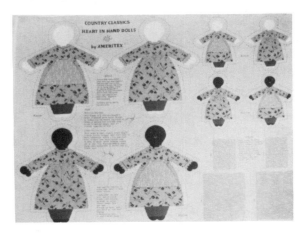

Plate 224: Ameritex. "Hattie" from Country Classics Heart in Hand series. 1980's. Cut out and sew dolls sold by the piece from bolts at fabric stores. Large completed Hattie is 15½" tall. Smaller Hattie is 8". White doll is Katie. Except for coloring, black and white dolls are identical.

Plate 225: Springs Industries, Inc. "Topsy-Turvy, Rose & Marie," Pattern 4908. Printed-on cloth cut out, stuff and sew at home doll. Completed doll is approximately 20" tall. Marks: Springs Industries, Inc. Pattern 4908, printed on selvage of cloth.

Plate 226: Commercially made "Topsy-Turvy," 1930–1940. 9¾" tall. Painted faces with a hard finish, paint is chipping off, particularly noticeable on the black face; yarn hair, black on black doll, yellow on white doll. Red dotted sewn-on dress and cap for black doll, print dress for white doll.

Plate 227: Cranston Print Works Co. "Rachel and Cotton-Tail" from Oh, You Beautiful Doll series. A screen print cut out and sew at home doll. Completed doll is 18½" tall. Printed on the cloth, along with the doll, is the following story: "Rachel lives on a big, old farm with her parents and her brother Amos. Rachel likes to help her mother in the kitchen and she knows how to make wonderful blueberry muffins. Rachel goes to Sunday School and can recite the names of all the books in the Bible. There are lots of animals on the farm and she has her very own rabbits to raise. Here she is shown with Cotton-Tail (her favorite) and one of the new baby rabbits." Doll was available in fabric stores in the mid-1980's.

Right – Plate 228: Cranston Print Works Co. "Amos and Spot" from the Oh, You Beautiful Doll series. Companion cut out and sew screen print to the previous doll. Completed doll is 18½". Printed-on story about Amos is as follows: "Amos lives on a big, old farm with his parents and his sister Rachel and his dog, Spot. There are lots of animals on the farm and Amos likes them all. His favorites are the horses and sometimes his father lets him hitch up the team and drive to town with him. In the winter, Amos goes to school and is a good student. However, he likes summer best because there are so many interesting things to do around the farm...picking (and eating) strawberries...caring for the newborn animals and going fishing with Spot." Doll was available in fabric stores in the mid-1980's.

Plate 229: Cranston Print Works Co. "Plantation Pals" from the Once Upon A Time series, 1980's. Cut out, sew up, stuff dolls with clothing printed along with the dolls. Completed mother and father are 9½" and baby is 3½". Dolls were sold from the bolt at fabric stores.

Plate 230: Completed "Plantation Pals" from previous piece of fabric.

Plate 231: Annette Shelly. "Sala," 17" cloth doll with soft, sculptured face, black button eyes, embroidered lashes and mouth, sewn-on black yarn hair. All original in removable pink blouse and shorts. Tag sewn to body: Little Love/Rag Doll Industries, Inc./Made in Taiwan..." Cloth book attached to arm of doll says the doll is named Sala and was copyright 1984 by Annette Shelly.

Plate 232: Handmade cloth doll, 21" tall. Soft, sculptured nose, dimpled cheeks and mouth, painted eyes, black looped yarn sewn-on hair, soft, sculptured hands and feet. Dressed in purple and lavender jogging suit. Made by Cheryl Larry Perkins in the mid-1980's. Doll is similar to Cabbage Patch Kids. Courtesy of Cheryl Larry Perkins.

Plate 234: H. Lee Toy Co. "Little Sis," 14" doll from Little Sis and International Friends series. The following is printed on the box: "Little Sis came about in Columbus, Ohio, in 1975, from a father's love for his daughters, and his desire to give them a soft, cuddly doll that would reinforce their positive self-image." Doll has black button eyes, sewn-on red felt nose and mouth, black yarn hair.

Plate 233: Gambina. "Nankie and Jody," 17" rag dolls. All cloth with matching embroidered facial features. Dozens of black yarn braids tied with colored ribbons are on the girl. All original. Purchased new in 1990.

Plate 235: Black double doll, one end happy, the other end sad with eyes closed and tears. All original, 13" tall. Purchased new in 1990.

Plate 236: Hallmark. "George Washington Carver," 7½" tall, all cloth with removable laboratory coat. Tag sewn to body: Hallmark Cds., Inc./K.D. Mo./Made in Taiwan/400 DT 113-7/George Washington/Carver/Doll Toy. Reverse side: February, 1979. This was probably made for Black History Month.

Plate 237: Fanny's Playhouse. "International Friends," 14" tall. All cloth boy and girl learn-to-dress dolls that button, zip, snap, buckle and lace. Sewn-on clothing, black yarn hair, painted features. Tag sewn to body: International Friends…, one side; Fanny's Playhouse…, other side. Dolls are primarily marketed to preschool.

Plate 238: McCall Pattern Company. "Kenya." Iron-on color transfer from book *International Dolls*. Pictures were transferred to fabric by ironing, cut-out, sewn, and then stuffed to make a doll. Book included four boys and four girls representing eight different countries (Poland, Japan, Spain, India, Greece, Scotland, Holland, and the above doll from Kenya). Completed doll is 10" tall. Copyright c1977 by The McCall Pattern Company.

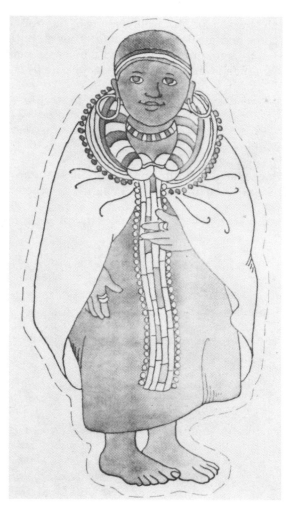

CHAPTER 6
COMPOSITION, RUBBER AND
WOODEN DOLLS, 1900–1950+

In the early 1900's when most of the dolls sold in the U.S. were still the imported bisque dolls from Germany, American toy companies began competing noticeably with imports by making large numbers of dolls in composition, a wood pulp mixture similar to that used for most of the imported doll bodies. Horsman, one of the leading American Manufacturers, advertised these dolls as "Can't Bread-Em Heads." These composition dolls made in America eventually gained popularity and after World War I, when there was much devastation in Europe and anti-German feelings in the U.S., the American-made doll replaced the European dolls in the American market. Although the great majority of dolls made by the American companies were made of composition, a few companies used rubber in making dolls.

Perhaps because of social changes during this period, the black dolls were not as popular or favorably received as they were in the late 1800's and early 1900's. Dolls of all races were not featured. Good quality, large black dolls were relatively scarce. Like the majority of the European manufacturers around the turn of the century, most of the American manufacturers made black dolls using the same molds as were used for the white doll. American manufacturers, however, usually made the black dolls in the less expensive models, using simpler, less stylish clothing.

In the 1920's, black dolls began to take on a different form. The black dolls, although still made from the same mold as the white dolls, were "doctored" up. Often, three holes were drilled in the head and tuffs of yarn or string was inserted for "Topsy" type hair. Character dolls like "Aunt Jemima" were introduced occasionally and judging by advertisements, Aunt Jemima was by far the most popular black doll made in composition, on the market in the mid-1920's. Ironically, many of the Aunt Jemima dolls were made with Caucasian features and molded straight hair. They were then dressed and advertised as "Aunt Jemima." In a manufacturing and wholesale monthly periodical, *Playthings*, December, 1924, the following advertisement was run by the Toy Shop:

Aunt Jemima – known to all Jobbers as an unfailing seller will be an important part of our 1925 line of white and colored dolls.
Never before have we offered such a comprehensive assortment of white and colored dolls.

The popularity of the Aunt Jemima doll continued to grow. In *Playthings*, January, 1925, the Toy Shop altered its ad slightly to read:

Aunt Jemima – known to all Jobbers as an outstanding profit maker is an important part of our line.

The February, 1925 *Playthings* ad from the Toy Shop was:

Aunt Jemima is more popular than ever! The only genuine Aunt Jemima doll is made by the Toy Shop...

Also sharing the other half of the advertisement from the Toy Shop was a description of their newest hit doll on the market:

"Pickaninny Baby"
The only Colored Infant Doll!
There are White Infant Dolls galore, but
nothing so cute as "Pickaninny Baby," the
Toy Shop's new colored infant doll. Its
ingenious likeness of a little Darky Baby who
has just entered the world means instant
sales for your Doll Department...

Sears, Roebuck and Co., calling itself the "World's Largest Doll Store" and claiming in 1923 to serve more than one-quarter of all families in the U.S. with its 8 million customers, first advertised the Aunt Jemima doll in their Fall 1924 catalog. It came in two sizes, 20" and 14" for $2.35 and $1.19 respectively. Also advertised in the same catalog were 10" character baby dolls in your choice of white or colored with the following description:

Strong all composition character dolls. Chemise included with each. Painted hair, eyes and features. Jointed at hips and shoulders.

The dolls were pictured undressed and sold for forty-three cents each. To illustrate the comparative availability of black dolls, a total of sixty-three dolls were offered for sale in this particular Sears catalog with only the two mentioned above being black. However, large quantities of the cheaper black dolls were evidently sold during this period as shown by the frequency of ads appearing during this period, the 1920's and 1930's, and the great number available on the market for doll collectors today. Presently, if desired, it is relatively easy to add this type of doll to a collection.

The Spring 1925 Sears catalog didn't show any black dolls; however, the Fall catalog of 1925 again repeated the ads for Aunt Jemima and the "Colored" character baby as it appeared in the Fall 1924 catalog. The following description was given by Sears:

Aunt Jemima doll with "Ma-Ma" voice, strong composition finished in dark chocolate color. Painted hair, eyes and features. Regular "Jemima" costume of colored cotton material with large white apron and collar and red "bandana." Cotton stuffed body and legs. 14" tall—98¢.

On a national level, black dolls continued to be mentioned occasionally, as in the article "Stauffer's Doll Show a Big Hit in Cleveland" in *Playthings*, November 24, 1924. The article described a doll show arranged by a famous toy buyer for the May Company in Cleveland, Ohio. Each girl entering a doll was encouraged to select a favorite from her collection. Included in the exhibit were Negro dolls; however, not mentioned was the type or number of Negro dolls or awards, if any, they received.

Not merely "another" doll, but a brand new kind of doll was the introduction given to the new doll, "The Famlee Doll" in December, 1924 by the Berwick Doll Company, New York. The Famlee doll consisted of one doll with a large variety of additional heads that could be attached one at a time, changing the doll from one character into a totally different character whenever desired. The various combinations offered from two to twelve heads and costumes that could be used with the desired head. One of the heads included in the set was a smiling Negro boy. *Playthings*, in an editorial commentary, February, 1925, reported that the Famlee dolls were well and favorably known to trade. In 1926, in the

Plate 239: Toy Shop. "Aunt Jemima." 14" tall. All original. Head and hands are medium brown composition. Body legs and arms are brown cloth; hair is molded in Caucasian style and painted black. This doll was highly advertised in Sears 1924–25 catalogs. Made in U.S.A.

Sears, Roebuck, & Co. Fall catalog, the Famlee doll was advertised for the first time; however, the black head was not included in the set offered.

The American Character Doll Co., a manufacturer, exhibited a comprehensive line of 150 dolls in February, 1925. The chief attraction in the line was a white infant doll, "Teensie-Eencie," with mention given to others in the line, including pickaninny infants. The prices ranged from one to twenty-five dollars with no mention given to specific prices.

Schoen and Yondorf, Co., New York, makers of composition character dolls advertised two black dolls in their line of ten dolls and soft toys in the Spring of 1925. The black dolls' faces had comical expressions as did all of the dolls in the Schoen & Yondorf (Sayco) line. Sayco advertised their line frequently during this period and reported good sales. The name "Mistah Sunshine" was given to one of their black dolls while a black and white double doll was called "Helen and Maria."

In the Sears Fall, 1926 catalog, a series of three dolls from "Our Gang" called "Our Gang Comedy Dancers" were introduced. You would wind the dolls and they would spin around. Included were white dolls, May and Fatt, and Farina, a black doll. They were all composition and 12" tall. Also repeated in this catalog were the 10" composition dolls in both black and white.

The fact that black dolls in the 1920's were used largely as novelty or just for sport is illustrated in the following quote from *Playthings*, February, 1925 in an article entitled: "Mardi Gras and Costume Fetes, New Orleans Does a Big Business in Favors and Novelties During the Mardi Gras." The article is quoted as follows:

...Another window that interested all visitors, especially those from the north, was that installed by the toy department of the big Holmes Store, which featured plantation dolls made of cloth, as well as log cabins and cotton bales filled with candy. In the centre was a log cabin, surrounded by a picket fence. In the front yard stood a Sambo doll, in red and blue. The interior of the house was brightly lighted and in the window was Mandy, a black doll, with red bandana, black dress, and big white apron. In both the front and back yard were bales of cotton, inside of which reposed a dozen of the delicious Creole pralines...

Black dolls were not advertised in the Sears 1927 Spring or Fall or 1928 Spring catalogs although white dolls were available. In the Sears Fall, 1928 catalog, "Beloved Belindy," black character from *The Raggedy Series Story Books* was advertised along with Raggedy Ann and Raggedy Andy. Fourteen-inch "Beloved Belindy" was described as follows:

Belindy has bandana cap, two-piece dress and bloomers, price $1.95.

Although black dolls of some sort were advertised during the 1920's, probably less than one percent of dolls advertised were black. Monthly, only two or three companies out of over 200 in the category "The Market Place" in *Playthings*, made any reference to carrying black dolls in their line. One company, however, did specialize in Negro dolls, N.V. Sales Co., 2540 Seventh Ave., New York. Their advertisement in *Playthings*, 1924–25 reads as follows:

Negro Dolls
Ask for catalog showing biggest variety,
snappiest designs and best prices.

A second ad appearing in "The Market Place" was as follows:

Colored Infant Dolls
Write for samples of our new infant and
other original colored dolls.

This ad was from the Blum-Lustig Toy Co., Inc., 495 Broome Street, New York. It should be noted, however, that the Blum-Lustig Toy Co., ran, in addition, a separate advertisement for their white dolls. Another advertisement for black dolls was placed by the American Style Doll Mfg. Co., 164 Eldridge St., New York. It featured both black and white dolls as follows:

Jointed
Composition Dolls
White and Colored
9½ x 12"
Attractively Dressed...

This particular advertisement ran for several years.

Sears, Roebuck Spring 1932 catalog again advertised the 10½" composition white and colored dolls. They were priced at thirty-four cents each or set of two for seventy-nine cents. The set of dolls differed noticeably in accessories from the same set advertised in the previous years. Earlier, the black and white dolls offered together were dressed identically; however, now the white doll had a frilly cap with a fancier dress while the colored doll had three tuffs of yarn sticking out of the molded head with a plainer print dress. This same set of dolls was again advertised in the Fall, 1932 Sears catalog for thirty-nine cents each or set of two for sixty-nine cents under the names of "Eva" and "Topsy." Topsy, the black doll, now came in a one-piece romper suit with the three yarn braids while Eva, the white doll, came in a white dress and bonnet. Also advertised for the first time in this catalog were "Metal Head Babies" in white or black. The 15½" tall dolls were identical except for coloring and were described as follows:

Metal Head Babies
15½" tall. Short dress baby dolls that are regular tin boys for play. Have soft kapok bodies, sleeping eyes, organdy dresses, rubber panties, metal heads, and composition legs and arms.

There were eight pages of dolls advertised in the 1932 Fall catalog with Topsy and above mentioned dolls being the only black dolls.

The Spring and Fall 1933 Sears catalogs did not advertise any black dolls. The companion white dolls to both of the black dolls advertised a year earlier were still available; however, only three pages of dolls were advertised as compared to eight pages in the Fall, 1932 catalog. Evidently, the depression was affecting availability and sales of toys.

"Dusky," a colored all-rubber doll, was first introduced in the Sears, Fall, 1934 catalog. She was probably made by Ideal Doll Co. as the caption at the top of the page read: "Famous Ideal Rubber Babies." She was dressed in a diaper with movable arms and legs, painted eyes, molded Caucasian looking hair. Topsy was again offered by Sears in the 1934 Fall catalog with the following description:

9½" colored pickaninny with three yarn braids and diaper. All composition – jointed arms and legs.

After this catalog, 1934, black dolls did not appear in Sears Roebuck catalogs until Fall, 1955.

Plate 240: Sun Rubber Co., Canada. "Viceroy," 11" tall, circa 1930. Rubber head, molded painted hair, painted eyes looking to the left, nursing mouth, jointed rubber baby body. Marks: A VICEROY/SUN RU CO DOLL/Made in Canada/Patent Pending, on body.

Although black dolls were seldom seen on the toy shelves in the late 1930's and 1940's and were not carried in most mail-order catalogs, some black parents through diligent searching or by chance were able to find sources for acceptable black dolls. This was usually through small black mail-order companies. One of these sources in 1936–37 was the Humania Hair Products Co. in New York. The company included several pages of black dolls in their hair products catalog. The catalog was advertised in a nationally distributed black weekly newspaper, the *Pittsburgh Courier*.

The periodical, *Toys & Novelties*, Buyers Guide for 1935–1936, "A Complete Directory of the American Toy Industry," copyright, 1935 by Porter-Spofford-Langtry Corporation, Chicago, Illinois, made reference to black dolls. In their classified section under "Dolls, Colored," the following company was listed:

Lujon Colored Doll Co.
56W. 22nd St., New York, N.Y.
Manufacturers of Colored Dolls Only

In the 1937 Buyers Guide for *Toys & Novelties*, the same company was listed at 34 W. 32nd St. NYC with the notation, Mfg. of colored dolls only. In the 1939 thru 1941 Buyers Guides, Lujon was listed at 1107 Broadway, N.Y., New York. By 1949, the same Buyers Guide had several more listings under colored dolls. They were the following:

Francesse Doll Co., 1758 Third Ave. NY 29, NY.
Halpern Company J., 810 Pennsylvania Ave., Pittsburgh PA.
Leslie-Henry Co., Inc., 1107 Broadway, NY (former address of Lujon).
Lujon Colored Doll Co., 36 W. 32nd St., NY, NY.
Rex Novelty Co., Inc., 152 Wooster St., NY 12, NY.
Terri Lee Co., 132 S. 13th St., Lincoln, NE.
Wolfset & Co. I.B. 27 E. 22nd St., NY, NY.

Some of the above companies described their dolls while others simply listed their company names. Descriptions, when given, are as follows:

Francesse Doll Co. "Suntan-colored and white baby doll brides, bridesmaids and Nuns, soft body, composition, and plastic dolls, character dolls."

Halpern Company. "Mfs. of masquerade costumes, character colored, composition, plastic, and rubber dolls..." Halpern used the trade name "Dolls by Halco."

Leslie-Henry. "Mfs. of composition dolls, dressed and undressed; colored dolls..."

Lujon. "Mfs. of only colored dolls."

Rex Novelty Co., "Mfrs. of colored dolls."

In 1950, the Buyers Guide listed 12 companies under their classified section on colored dolls. The most significant of these was the Allied Grand Doll Manufacturing Co. Their promotional hit was the composition Jackie Robinson doll. It was well received by the black community in 1950. Other significant black dolls introduced in the early 1950's were the Saralee doll by Ideal Doll Co., designed by sculptress Sheila Burlingame and Patti-Jo and Benji dolls by Terri Lee Incorporated. Probably the most well received doll of this postwar period was Amosandra. She appeared in stores on Valentine's Day, 1949, a week after the birth of a radio child bearing the same name to Amos and Ruby Jones, fixtures on the Amos 'n Andy show. Amosandra was made by the Sun Rubber Company. All of these black dolls of the late 1940's and early 1950's were well received by both the black and white community. *Ebony Magazine*, the leading black monthly periodical said the following about the new dolls on the market, January, 1952, page 46, in an article titled: "Modern Designs for Negro Dolls":

This Christmas a half million little girls of many races found under their Christmas trees some of the most beautiful Negro dolls America has ever produced. A transformation has taken place in toyland and new colored dolls with delicate features, lighter skin, and modish clothes are being introduced into the world of childhood fantasy where always before the Negro doll was presented as a ridiculous, calico-garmented, handkerchief-headed servant.

Following are advertisements and photographs of dolls made during the period from approximately 1900–1950.

COMPOSITION
Character Dolls

To Retail For

25c to 50c

White, Colored and Clown Characters in a Variety of Costumes

Specially Made and Priced for Chain Stores

An entire building devoted to making popular priced Dolls — over 12 years' experience in supplying leading Chain Stores — an unbroken record of 100% Deliveries and Satisfaction — NOW — a Bigger and Better Line than ever.

ALLIED-GRAND
DOLL MFG. CO.
66-68 Greenpoint Avenue
Brooklyn, N. Y.

One of Our Big Value Numbers

Plate 241: Advertisement for colored composition character dolls by the Allied Grand Doll Manufacturing Co., Inc. in *The Playthings Directory*, 1927–28, page 185. Republished with permission from *Playthings* and *The Playthings Directory* copyright 1927–28 by Geyer-McAllister Publications, Inc., New York.

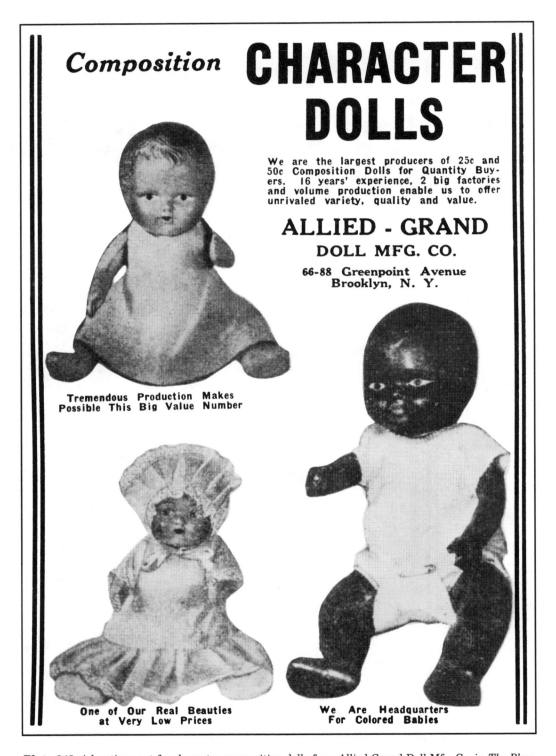

Plate 242: Advertisement for character composition dolls from Allied-Grand Doll Mfg. Co. in *The Playthings Directory*, 1931, page 172. The company advertised that they were the headquarters for colored babies. Republished with permission from *Playthings* and *The Playthings Directory* copyright 1931 by Geyer-McAllister Publications, Inc., New York.

The Famlee Doll
REG. U. S. PAT. OFF.

The Doll with Extra Heads

A Brand New and Patented Idea

Plate 243: Advertisement for "The Famlee Doll," the doll with extra heads, made by the Berwick Doll Company, New York. This advertisement appeared in *Playthings*, January, 1925, page 32. Republished with permission from *Playthings* and *The Playthings Directory* copyright 1925 by Geyer-McAllister Publications, Inc., New York.

Why Not Get More Birthday Business?

IN every community, every day in the year brings a bunch of birthdays—and the buying of birthday gifts.

For a little girl's birthday, one of the first things people think of is a doll.

But—

If the little girl already has a perfectly good doll, then no one is likely to give her **another—**

Unless—

You can show a doll **so totally and entirely different** that it doesn't in any way **duplicate.**

That's the big sales advantage of the Famlee Doll—for birthdays, Easter and all the time.

Not merely "another" doll but a **brand new kind** of doll.

The only doll which **changes faces**—changes from one character into a **wholly different character** whenever desired. Many dolls in one.

That's why it catches the eye and **captures** the fancy where other dolls are passed by.

Because it gets away from the commonplace duplication that limits the sale of ordinary dolls, the Famlee Doll with its extra heads and many characters stimulates a lot of **extra** birthday business for every store that displays it.

Even if a little girl already has a Famlee Family she is still a good prospect —she will want **additional** heads and costumes to **enlarge** her family.

And don't forget that every Famlee Family you sell starts a little chain of sales—each little girl who gets one has many little playmates; and they will all soon be begging for a Famlee Family.

You can't expect to sell any Famlee Families unless you've got them in your store—and unless you put them out where people can see them.

Berwick Doll Company

Makers of the Famlee Doll

478 Broadway, New York City

The Famlee Doll

REG. U. S. PAT. OFF.

A Whole Family of Dolls in One

A Brand New and Patented Idea

Plate 244: Advertisement for "The Famlee Doll" in *Playthings*, December, 1924, page 133. Republished with permission from *Playthings and The Playthings Directory* copyright 1924 by Geyer-McAllister Publications, Inc., New York.

A Sensational New Doll Will Be Shortly Introduced!

WATCH FOR THE

"U-MAN DOLL"

PATENT APPLIED FOR

Made By a Special Process of a Material Heretofore Totally Unknown In Doll Manufacture

After extensive experimentation, we have succeeded in producing a Doll which more closely resembles Natural Human Appearance than any Doll yet shown.

You have a big surprise in store when you see the "U-Man Doll" on display for the first time at the

NATIONAL TOY FAIR

Bush Terminal Sales Building
ROOM 564

AUNT JEMIMA—

known to all Jobbers as an unfailing seller will be an important part of our 1925 line of white and colored dolls.

Write For Sample Assortment

The TOY SHOP

Mama Doll Specialists
149 WOOSTER ST.   **NEW YORK**

Kindly mention PLAYTHINGS when writing to advertisers.

Plate 245: Advertisement for the Aunt Jemima doll from The Toy Shop. This ad appeared in *Playthings*, December, 1924, page 138. The doll was made of composition and cloth. Republished with permission from *Playthings and The Playthings Directory* copyright 1924 by Geyer-McAllister Publications, Inc., New York.

Mid-Summer Sales That Mean Profits!

SAYCO SOFT TOYS AND DOLLS **SHOW THE WAY**

NOVELTY Is the Life of Summer Sales. Here We Show a Dozen Specialties That Will Mean Holiday Activity to Your Mid-Season Months. Write For a Sample Dozen Today.

SCHOEN & YONDORF CO.

Makers of High Class Composition Character Dolls

207-209 Wooster Street   New York, N. Y.

"SEE SAYCO FIRST"

Kindly mention PLAYTHINGS when writing to advertisers.

Plate 246: Advertisement for a line of dolls and toys that included black dolls from Schoen and Yondorf Co. that appeared in *Playthings*, March, 1925, page 87. Republished with permission from *Playthings and The Playthings Directory* copyright 1925 by Geyer-McAllister Publications, Inc., New York.

Plate 247: Advertisement for the Jackie Robinson doll by the Allied Grand Doll Manufacturing Co., Inc. in the *Playthings Directory*, 1950, page 255. Republished with permission from *Playthings and The Playthings Directory* copyright 1950 by Geyer-McAllister Publications, Inc., New York.

My! what fun changing one dollie into another—
Change from French dollie into Tim, the clown,
then Simple Sue and all the others.

The Right Costume

When you are changing the characters I suppose you will give each doll her own costume. For example: Little Miss Sweet Face owns the ni(
white party dress. The Dutch Girl owns the Du .n
Dress, and so on. Each doll has her own costume,
as you can easily see.

Of course, they can borrow from each other if
you will allow that. And maybe borrowing would
be good fun too. Can you imagine Black Face Sam
wearing the white party dress instead of his colored
trousers? Wouldn't that look funny? Or Susie
Bumps dressed up in pants? Oh, my! Yes, when
you just feel in the mood to mix things up it would
be lots of fun having the dollies loan their costumes
to each other.

BERWICK DOLL COMPANY
Makers of
Famlee Doll Sets
A whole family of dolls in one
478-482 Broadway,
New York, N. Y.

Plate 248: Advertisement for "Famlee Doll Sets." A black doll was often included in the set of dolls. Notice the third doll from the right. Republished with permission from *Playthings and The Playthings Directory* copyright 1925 by Geyer-McAllister Publications, Inc., New York.

Changing Doll Parties

You probably will enjoy your Famlee Doll Set more if you invite your little friends to play too. While you are unscrewing the head, Mary can be choosing another head, and Alice can be looking over the Famlee wardrobe and selecting the right costume.

Here is a little story about a magic Doll Party—

Once upon a time there was a little girl who had a magic doll. She called to her little playmates, "Come on everybody and see what my wonderful dolly can do."

"Now," she said, "This doll is named Ruth. See her pretty blond hair? And her nice rosy cheeks? And her lovely white dress?"

"Well all of you just turn your backs—only for one minute . . . R-e-a-d-y! everybody look!"

And there her little blondie with the white dress had changed just like magic into a little French girl with coal black curls and a different dress that wasn't white at all but blue.

And then as the children sat around, Presto Chang-O— the little French girl was changed into a regular laughing happy circus clown—and then the clown was changed into a grinning li'l black boy—and the black boy into a Ching Ching Chinaman— and on and on it went from one to another.

My but those children all had heaps and heaps of fun at that magic Famlee doll party. And as they were very good children all afternoon, the little girl said she would invite them again soon to play at changing round and dressing up her magical Famlee Doll.

There is such fun in Magic Famlee Doll Parties. Why don't you have one too? You and your little playmates would enjoy it very much.

BERWICK DOLL COMPANY
Makers of
Famlee Doll Sets
A whole family of dolls in one
478-480-482 Broadway,
New York.

Plate 249: Advertisement for "Famlee Doll Sets." A black doll was often included in the set of dolls. Notice the third doll from the right. Republished with permission from *Playthings and The Playthings Directory* copyright 1925 by Geyer-McAllister Publications, Inc., New York.

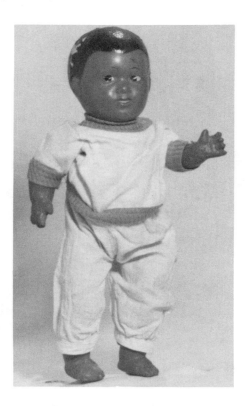

Plate 251: "Topsy-Turvy" or double doll, 8" tall. All composition with black head on one end, white head on the other. Both faces are from the identical molds with painted features. Black head has three tuffs of black string inserted into holes in the head for hair even though black head has the same molded hair as the white head. Both dolls have movable arms. This doll probably dates to the mid-1930's. Doll on the left is all original, other one has been redressed.

Plate 250: Allied-Grand Doll Mfg. Co. "Jackie Robinson," 13". All composition, jointed at the neck, arms and legs, painted features and hair, eyes looking to the right. Redressed. Original clothes were a Brooklyn Dodgers baseball uniform, including cap and baseball bat. Jackie Robinson was the first black to play professional baseball. He was signed by the Brooklyn Dodgers in 1947. Doll is unmarked and was made in 1950.

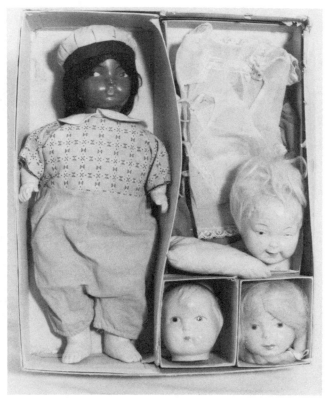

Plate 252: Berwick. "The Famlee Doll," 16" tall. Composition heads, arms and legs, cloth body. Painted features, mohair wigs. Doll heads screw on similar to a light bulb. Dolls are unmarked.

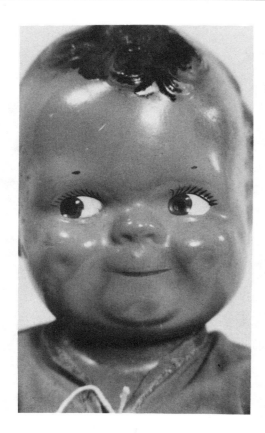

Plate 254: Cameo. "Kewpie Hottentot," 11½" tall composition doll, painted features, eyes looking to the left, jointed shoulders, stationary head. All original with painted red Kewpie heart label. Doll was designed and copyright by Rose O'Neill.

Plate 253: Cameo. "Scootles," 13" unmarked composition doll. Molded, painted hair, painted features, jointed arms and legs. 1925. Redressed. Designed by Rose O'Neill.

Plate 255: Effanbee. "Lucifer," marionette, 14" tall. Designed and patented by puppeteer Virginia Austin. Head, arms, and feet are molded papier-maché; body, wooden blocks. All orignial in over-alls and white checked shirt, bare feet. Made in 1937 by Effanbee, a trade-mark registered in U.S. by Fleischaker & Baum, doll manufacturers. Marks: Lucifer/V. Austin/Effanbee. 1937. There is a matching female marionette. Photo unavailable.

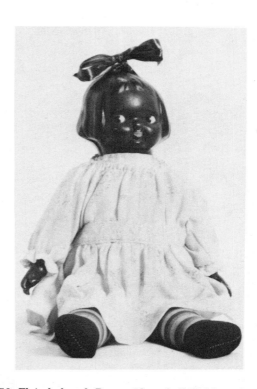

Plate 256: Fleischaker & Baum, "Campbell Kid," 10½" character doll designed by Grace Drayton. Made in U.S. circa 1915 under the trademark "Effanbee." Head is dark brown composition with painted features. Hair is molded black in "bob" style with molded loop on top for ribbon. Lower arms and hands are composition. White cloth, jointed body with striped cloth in red, green, and gold used for legs. Feet are black cloth. Marks: F & B, on head.

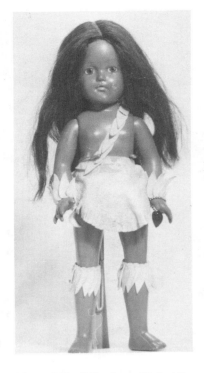

Plate 257: Effanbee, "Toonga from the Congo," marionette (Talen-Toy Puppet). Head, body, and limbs are made of hardwoods with joints solidly pinned, stapled, or joined with eyelets; skirt made of pink, blue, and yellow strings sewn together at waistband; hair made of fur-like material; painted facial features; metal hands. Puppet came with a Talen Toon photograph record, with two sides of original Talen Toon stories and tunes written especially for Talen Toon Puppets and booklet of instructions for handling and working Talen Toy Puppets, with stories and lyrics of the shows on the record made for each puppet. Other puppets sold separately were "Pim-Bo the Clown," "Mac Awful the Scot," "Kilroy the Cop," and "Jambo the Jiver." Toonga was the only black puppet from the group. Box is Marked: COPYRIGHT 1948/EFFANBEE DOLL Co., 45 Green Street, NY 13, NY.

Plate 258: Effanbee. "Primitive Indian," from Historical Doll series, 1939. 15" tall. Composition head, painted eyes, closed mouth, dark brown glued-on wig, jointed composition body. All original in white leather clothing. Marks: EFFANBEE/ANNE.SHIRLEY, on body.

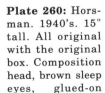

Plate 259: Madame Hendren. 12" tall. Composition shoulder head and arms, painted eyes and mouth, molded, painted hair with three tuffs of yarn-like hair inserted into drilled holes. White cloth body with cry box, brown cloth sewn-on legs. Marks: GENUINE/MADAME HENDREN/DOLL/112/MADE IN U.S.A., stamped on back of cloth body.

Plate 260: Horsman. 1940's. 15" tall. All original with the original box. Composition head, brown sleep eyes, glued-on mohair wig, painted closed mouth, arms and legs are stuffed vinyl, white cloth body with "crybox." Blue organdy dress and bonnet, white slip, pink rubber panties. Tag pinned to doll reads: Lifelike/Horsman/Softee/Plastic/Skin-like arms and legs/Flexible fingers/sleeps and cries. Doll is unmarked.

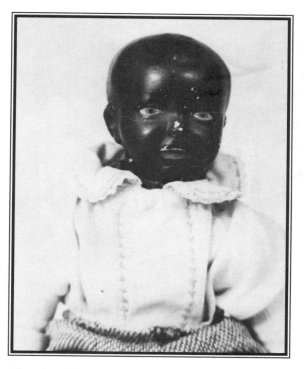

Plate 262: Horsman. "Twins," 16" tall. Sleeping brown eyes, black mohair glued-on wig, composition arms and legs, cloth body. Circa 1918. Marks: HORSMAN/Doll, on head.

Plate 261: Horsman. "Baby Bumps," 12" character doll made by E.I. Horsman Company of New York, circa 1910. Head is composition with painted features and hair. Body is jointed, tightly stuffed white cloth. Arms and legs are brown cloth. Doll came in black or white versions, identical except for coloring. Unmarked.

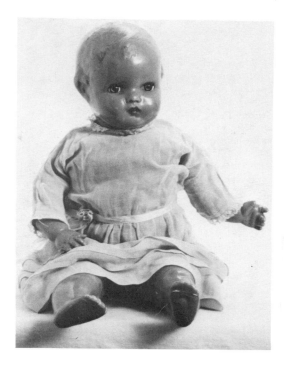

Plate 263: Horsman. "Mama" doll. 22" tall. Brown composition flanged head, lower arms and lower legs, hair slightly molded around hairline, wig missing, open/shut brown glassine eyes, closed mouth, white cloth stuffed body with cry box. Marks: HORSMAN/DOLLS. Collection of Mary Ann Floyd.

Plate 264: 14" tall character doll with gutta percha head and hands, molded hair, painted eyes, closed mouth, cloth arms, body, and legs. Redressed. Marks: N.D. Co., on head.

Plate 265: Reliable Toy Co., "Topsy," 13" all composition bent leg baby. Painted features, eyes looking to the right, molded painted hair, swivel head. All original, including tag pinned to clothing. Marks: RELIABLE/DOLL/MADE IN CANADA, on head. Tag reads: MADE IN CANADA/TOPSY/A Reliable Doll/A British Empire Product/Mfg. By RELIABLE TOY CO.–Limited. 1930's.

Plate 266: Reliable Toy Co. Rubber doll, 12" tall. Head and body are stuffed rubber; hair molded in two braids; painted features, molded-on shoes and socks. Marks: 1132/Reliable/Made in Canada. Doll was made in the 1950's.

Plate 267: Sun Rubber Co. "So-Wee," 9", drinks and wets, rubber head, molded and painted curly hair, inserted glassine eyes, nursing mouth, jointed rubber baby body. Marks: SUNBABE/"SO-WEE"/RUTH E. NEWTON/NEW YORK. N.Y. on head; THE SUN RUBBER CO., on body. Patent #597920 filled 5/1950 by Sun Rubber Co. of Barberton, Ohio for So-Wee doll.

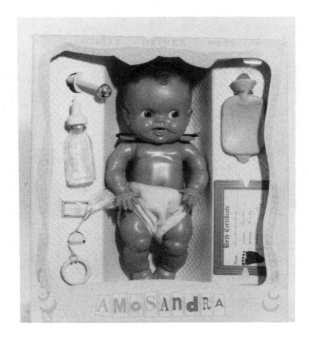

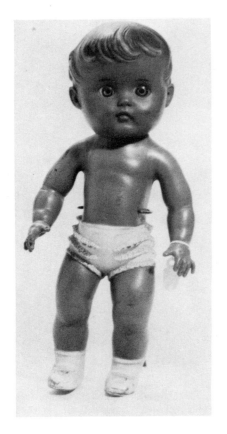

Plate 269: Sun Rubber Co. 10½" tall. Soft rubber head, molded painted hair, inserted glassine eyes, closed mouth, one-piece rubber toddler body with molded-on white panties and shoes. Marks: THE SUN RUBBER CO./1956, head; same marks on body.

Plate 268: Sun Rubber Co., Barberton, Ohio. "Amosandra," from Amos and Andy radio and TV series. 10" tall. Rubber head, molded painted curly hair, painted eyes, looking to the left, nursing mouth, jointed rubber baby body. Marks: AMOSANDRA/COLUMBIA BROADCASTING/SYSTEM, INC./DESIGNED BY/RUTH E. NEWTON/MFD. BY/THE SUN RUBBER CO./BARBERTON, O. U.S.A./PAT. 2118682/ PAT. 2160739, on body. Doll was sold from 1949 into the 1950's.

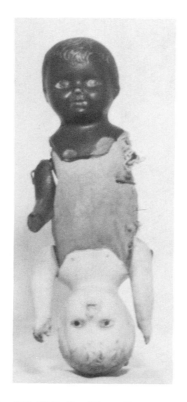

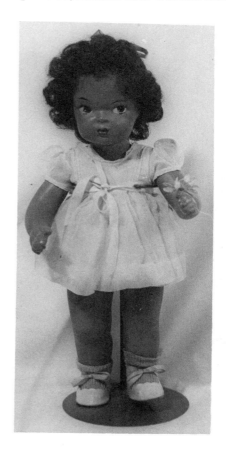

Plate 270: Sun Rubber Co. "Tot-L-Tot," 10½" rubber doll. Head moves, body is one piece, circa 1950. Brown inset glassine eyes, nursing mouth, molded painted hair, molded-on brown diapers, shoes and socks. Marks: 21A/TOT-L-TOT/The Sun Rubber Co./Barbertown O.U.S.A., on back.

Plate 271: W.D. Co. "Topsy-Turvy." 11½" tall. composition heads and arms, painted eyes, molded hair, closed mouths, cloth body stuffed with sawdust. Both heads are identical except for coloring. One arm is missing from the black doll. Marks: W.D.Co., on both heads.

Plate 272: Composition Terri Lee, 16". Circa 1950. All original. Painted features; stiff, glued-on synthetic brown wig. Jointed composition body. Yellow organdy dress marked "Terri Lee" on back of neckline. Yellow ribbon in hair, on wasitband and on shoe ties. Holding daisy in her right hand through hole drilled between thumb and index finger. Marks: TERRI LEE/PAT PENDING, on shoulders.

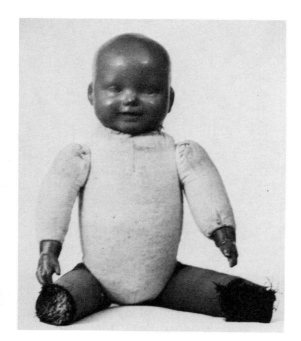

Plate 274: 10½" tall. All original Topsy-type composition baby doll. One-piece head and body, movable arms and legs, spring strung; painted features; molded, painted hair with three braids made of black string inserted into head. Body underneath clothing is painted white, only limbs and head are brown. Clothing and booties are original. Unmarked.

Plate 273: Unmarked composition circa 1910. 11½" tall. Interestingly molded composition head, no hint of hair; once painted eyes and mouth have almost totally faded. White cloth sawdust stuffed body with movable white cloth arms and brown cloth legs. Hands are composition. Cloth feet are missing.

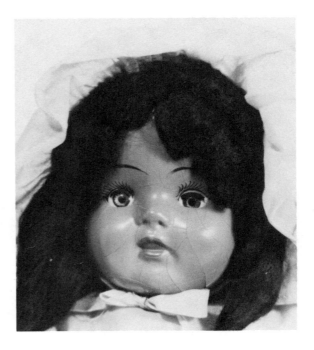

Plate 275: 9½" tall. Originally dressed Topsy-type composition. Painted eyes and mouth; molded, painted hair with two tuffs of string hair inserted into holes in head, third tuff of hair missing. One-piece body and head, movable arms and bent legs, rubber strung. Unmarked, 1920–1940.

Plate 276: Unmarked 25" tall "Mama" doll. Composition head with open/shut eyes, painted mouth; stuffed rag body with composition limbs. All original clothes, long mohair wig.

Plate 279: 10" composition Topsy-type doll from the 1930's. Painted features, holes drilled in head for three tuffs of black string hair. Head and body are one piece with movable arms and legs. Redressed.

Plate 277: Unmarked 17" doll from the 1920's. Composition head, painted features, open/closed mouth, glued-on wig made of brown string braided into two long braids, composition arms and legs, white cloth body.

Plate 278: Smiling composition head doll, 12" tall, circa 1900. Stationary glass eyes, open painted mouth with painted teeth, glued-on mohair wig. Papier-maché hands and legs, cloth stuffed body. Clothing is old and could be original. Doll is unmarked.

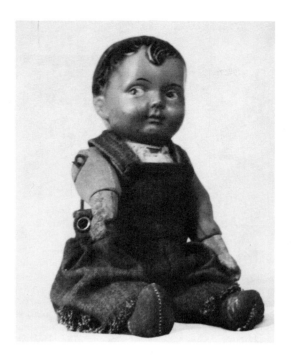

Plate 280: Composition shoulder head, circa 1910. 10" tall. Painted eyes looking to the right, molded painted black hair, painted closed mouth, slightly dimpled chin. Off-white cloth body is stuffed with straw. Brown cloth arms and legs are fastened to the body by means of steel pins over tin washers. Finely modeled papier-maché hands. Doll is unmarked.

Plate 281: All composition girl, 7" tall with movable arms, molded painted hair with molded bow and molded booties. Painted eyes looking to the right. Doll is unmarked.

Plate 282: "Whistling doll," 14" tall. Composition shoulder head, paint is flaking badly. Composition arms, one-piece cloth body and legs. Small whistling hole in mouth, legs have spring mechanism, when feet are pushed up, air is forced out of mouth to make the whistle sound. Marks: PATENT PENDING, stamped on chest.

Plate 284: 9½" tall composition doll made in Germany. Spring jointed composition body, painted features, red dots at corner of eyes and in nostrils. Slightly molded, painted hair. Redressed. Marks: "Germany," stamped on back of body.

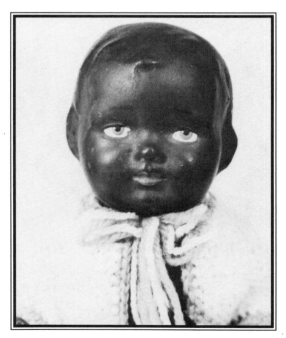

Plate 283: Unmarked composition baby, circa 1930. 12" tall. Painted eyes and mouth, black mohair wig stapled over molded, painted hair. Movable arms and legs.

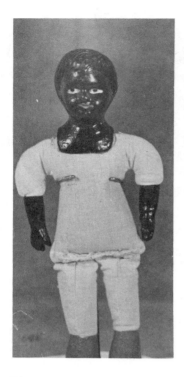

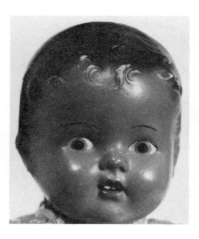

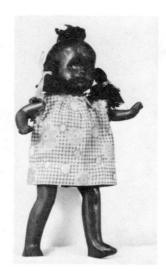

Plate 285: 9" tall unmarked shoulder head composition doll. Circa 1900. Cloth body and feet, composition arms and hands. Molded hair, painted features.

Plate 286: 16" tall unmarked composition "Mama"-type doll from the 1930's. Composition head with painted features, molded painted hair; composition arms and legs, cloth body.

Plate 287: Composition girl, 9" tall. 1930's–1940's. Molded hair with three string pigtails hanging out of holes. Five-piece composition body, rarely seen with straight legs. Doll is unmarked.

Plate 288: Unmarked composition, 1930's. 12" tall. Very crudely made – note seams. Only shoulders and hips are jointed; painted eyes to the side; open/closed mouth; molded painted hair; two holes in head – one on each side – for hair which is missing. Doll is dressed in old but not original dress as these dolls usually came nude or with diapers only. Courtesy of Phyllis Houston.

Plate 289: Unmarked composition baby, 1930's. 7" tall. Painted eyes looking to the left, slightly parted lips, molded painted hair with three tuffs of yarn hair inserted into holes in head. Jointed at neck, arms, and hips. Courtesy of Phyllis Houston.

Plate 290: Shoulder head composition doll. 16" tall. Molded, painted hair; painted eyes; painted open, smiling mouth; composition lower arms; brown cloth body with voice box, brown cloth legs and feet. Clothing is old and could be original, red cotton dress, bloomers and hat. Shoes look replaced. Marks: C, on head.

Plate 291: Composition "Marotte," musical toddler toy. Also used by photographers to make children smile. Composition head, wooden lower arms and legs, wire upper arms and legs, cardboard body. Painted exaggerated features, closed mouth. All original. Unmarked.

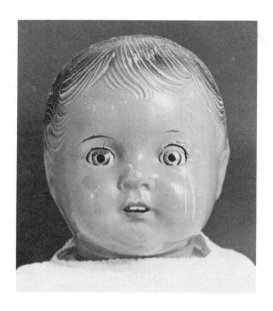

Plate 292: Composition shoulder head "Topsy-Turvy." 13" tall. Painted eyes, molded hair, closed mouth. Except for coloring, both heads are identical. Brown cloth hard stuffed body. Doll is unmarked. Clothing is very old, could be original.

Plate 293: Composition shoulder head doll, light brown sleeping eyes, open mouth with two upper teeth, composition arms and legs, cloth body. This type of doll was commonly known as a "Mama" doll because of the cry box inside cloth body. Doll is unmarked.

Plate 294: 15" tall composition head doll with flanged neck, sleeping hazel eyes, closed mouth, glued-on synthetic wig, stuffed rubber arms and legs, white cloth body. Doll is unmarked. Redressed.

Plate 295: Two glove puppets from a late 19th–early 20th century Punch & Judy puppet set. Approximately 15" tall. Wood heads, hands, legs, and feet (one foot missing from black man); painted heads. Clothes are original. Courtesy of Evelyn Ackerman.

Plate 296: Schoenhut Negro dude. Original clothes. Black paint worn off his hands. Unusual Schoenhut dude because African Native head was used. Courtesy of Evelyn Ackerman.

Plate 297: Similar Schoenhut dude with African Native head. 8" tall. Mouth is slightly different. Hat and coat are missing. All original.

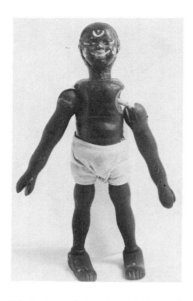

Left – Plate 299: "Dancing Dan," 10½" tall jointed all wooden man that was part of a "dancing" toy. Shoulders, hips, and knees are jointed. Molded painted facial features, painted clothing.

Right – Plate 300: Avis Lee. "Digitalis." 10" tall. Carved wooden head; painted features; glued-on black yarn hair; cloth stuffed posed body. Doll is holding small white doll made entirely of wood. All original. Tag attached to arm: An Original/Avis Lee/Doll; other side of tag: "DIGITALIS" This youngster's name is taken from that of an actual case on record in a social workers files/AVIS LEE/Chicago. (handwritten) Courtesy of Paul Johnson.

Plate 298: Schoenhut. "African" from the "Teddy Roosevelt Safari" set. 8" tall. All wood, jointed and strung, painted features. Clothing is missing. Courtesy of Susan Manos.

Plate 301: Celluloid. "The Dolly Sisters." Japan, 1930's, celluloid quintuplets sold in their own little cardboard suitcase. 2" tall. Sticker on suitcase is imprinted: "The Dolly Sisters," Japan. Dolls are all celluloid with movable arms, molded hair, painted features, painted shoes and socks, glued-on cloth skirts, each a different color: blue, orange, pink, yellow, and green with glued-on pink ribbons on hair. Marks: JAPAN, on back.

Plate 303: Celluloid girl. Wind-up crawling doll. 6" long. Celluloid movable head with molded wavy hair with four molded, painted ribbons, molded painted Negroid features, movable arms and legs that crawl. Clothes are sewn on.

Plate 302: Celluloid boy, 6" tall. Body and head, one piece; movable arms and legs. Molded, kinky hair, painted features, painted-on clothing. Marks: JAPAN/PATENT, on back.

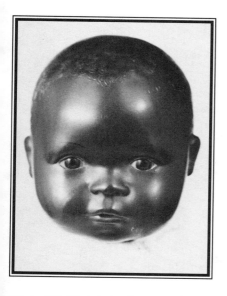

Plate 304: Rheinische Gummi and Celluloid Fabric Co., Germany, late 1920's to early 1930's. 13" tall. Dark brown celluloid doll with Negroid features, stationary brown glassine eyes, molded and painted curly hair, slightly open mouth, jointed body. Doll has been redressed. Marks: Turtle mark (turtle inside of diamond)/32/34, on head; Turtle mark/34, on body.

Plate 305: Celluloid Carnival girl — made between 1946 and 1948. Approximately 7" tall. Wears silver cardboard hat, glass beads, and earrings; carries cane. Sox, shoes, bra, hair are molded and painted. Made in Occupied Japan is marked on back. Only shoulders are jointed. Courtesy of Phyllis Houston.

Plate 306: Celluloid "Cooking Chef." 3" tall, including base. All original in one piece with molded and painted clothes. When bulb in back is touched, body head makes liquid bubble up and appear to be cooking under the frying pan. Made in Japan.

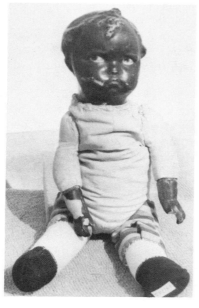

Plate 307: Black mask face from Germany, extremely rare in a black doll and in a doll this size, 16" tall. Blown glass eyes, composition mask face, four-part jointed cloth body. Doll is unmarked. Courtesy of Susan Manos.

Plate 308: Effanbee. "Baby Grumpy." 12" tall. Composition head and hands, cloth body filled with a very fine cork-like material, painted eyes, molded hair, closed pouty mouth. The original legs were of striped material with black cloth feet. The legs had to be repaired but you can see the remaining original stripe material on the left leg. Courtesy of Marion Reed Getty.

Plate 309: Celluloid dollhouse dolls, 3½" to 5¾" tall. Celluloid heads, molded, painted hair and features; celluloid hands and feet; poseable cloth bodies. All original in sewn-on clothing. Dolls are unmarked.

CHAPTER 7
COLLECTIBLE DOLLS,
1950–1991

By 1951, many people were becoming concerned about the lack of black dolls on the market and disturbed about the apparently unfulfilled needs of a relationship between black children and black dolls. An example of this concern is the doll "Saralee Negro Doll," introduced in 1951 with Negroid features as the "Doll for Negro children." This doll, manufactured by the Ideal Toy Corporation, made such an impact that she, as well as several other black dolls designed by her creator, were featured in the December 17, 1951 issue of *Life Magazine* as follows:

Dolls for Negro Children
New Toy Which is Anthropologically Correct Fills an Old Need

At an early age U.S. Negro children have had their many disadvantages illustrated for them by one fact: there has never been a doll they could call their own. They have always had to play with unsatisfactory "pickaninny" dolls or white dolls painted brown. But recently Sara Lee Creech of Belle Glade, Florida, reflecting on that fact, decided to have a doll made that would be anthropologically correct and something a Negro child could be proud of. The result is the first truly Negro doll ever made.

To make sure that the doll would be just right, Miss Creech photographed and carefully measured scores of Negro children in her home town and got sculptress Sheila Burlingame interested in the project. Mrs. Burlingame, who has done many statues of Negroes, used Miss Creech's material for reference in creating four head models which are a fair sample of anthropological characteristics of U.S. Negroes. The Ideal Toy Corporation agreed to manufacture them. Then a jury, including Dr. Ralph Bunche, Walter White, and Eleanor Roosevelt, met to determine the exact shade of the doll's skin.

The baby doll model, introduced last month as the "Saralee Negro Doll," is made of Vinylite plastic, has eyes which move, and sells for $6.95. Stores reported it was selling unusually well and noted that the doll is so cute that it is enjoying a brisk trade not only among Negro children but among white children as well.

Photos of seven black children of all ages up to eight, used as models for the doll, were shown in the *Life Magazine* article. Miss Creech sent a composite of detailed head measurements of the children along with the individual photographs of them to the sculptress, Miss Burlingame. A full black family was scheduled for the future to include "Little Miss," "Little Brother," "Little Sister," along with the newly introduced baby. It is not known whether the dolls were ever produced however.

Around this same period, another revolution occurred in doll making. Hard plastic had become the most common material used. This was gradually replaced by vinyl in the late 1950's. Also, as the 1960's emerged, more and more black dolls began appearing on store shelves. Black people again, as in the early 1900's, began to show an awareness of the importance of black images for their children. A rejection of black dolls with Caucasian features began to grow. Demands were made by civil rights groups to have nationally advertised dolls made in a black version.

During this period of growing awareness, Remco Industries, a national doll manufacturer, introduced four "ethnically correct" Negro dolls in 1968. All of their dolls, although they had negroid features, carried the same names as their Caucasian counterparts in the line: Winking Winnie, Growing Sally, Tippy Tumbles, and Baby Grows-A-Tooth.

In order to make the black dolls as ethnically correct as possible, Remco Industries hired a young black freelance artist, Annuel McBurrows, to design the dolls. According to *Playthings*, a national publication for wholesalers and manufacturers, July, 1968, the Remco management, under board chairman, Saul Robbins, outlined

102

for Mr. McBurrows standards that the doll would have to meet. The most important of these were 1) it had to be cute and appealing and 2) it had to have realistic elements that would find favor with as many members of the Negro community as possible. In the same issue of *Playthings*, Mr. Robbins, in discussing the addition of black dolls with Negroid features, is quoted as saying:

> *The key to the success of just about any item in the toy industry is the degree of its realism. A girl playing with a doll is engaged in a mother-child fantasy. And if she's a Negro girl, we're certain she'll want a doll that most closely resembles Negro babies and toddlers.*
>
> *What we want the trade and public to realize is that we didn't come out with these dolls as some kind of gesture. There's no tokenism in our decision...We're not looking for thanks, but for business. We're trying to fill what we believe is an unfilled market demand. If we're right in our assumptions, these four Negro dolls will turn a profit, which is why we're in business.*

The dolls were scheduled to be advertised in store newspaper ads, on Negro radio shows, and in the black publications, *Ebony* and *Jet*, October, 1968. The white counterparts of the Negro dolls were advertised on TV with the hope that the black market would become familiar with the white product and then choose the Negro version when they confronted them in the store. It was felt by Remco that the final acceptance to the dolls was left to the black public because buyers from all parts of the U.S. responded favorably to the idea of ethnically correct dolls and the dolls themselves.

Black dolls designed for Remco by Annuel McBurrows are shown on pages 239-243 in this book with the Remco dolls.

Also during the 1960's, a period of social unrest, Shindana, the first large scale national black owned and operated doll manufacturing company, was founded. Unfortunately, it ceased operation in 1983. More information on Shindana is included in the section on Shindana dolls, pages 247-278.

Another black owned doll company of the mid-1960's was Beatrice Wright Dolls. They were ethnically correct with beautifully sculptured features. More information on this doll company can be found with the Beatrice Wright Dolls later on in this chapter.

Following are hundreds of dolls made as playthings for children from approximately 1950 to the present. The great majority of them are made of vinyl, the most commonly used material for dolls in this period. The dolls for the most part are very unique. Many of them feel, look, and can move like real children. Horsman Dolls, Inc., in a booklet on the history of dolls entitled "Dolls, From the Beginning of Time," c1974, described the dolls of this period as follows:

> *At last we have dolls whose bodies look and feel natural; whose hair is held to the scalp by its roots, to be washed, combed, curled, and set repeatedly; whose hearts can beat; who can drink and wet; who can blow bubbles, laugh, or cry tears; who can lie down, sit up, stand, crawl, or walk; who can talk, write, or draw; who can sing and dance, hug and kiss...also wear regular childsize clothes, assume almost any position and perform almost any function.*

This is a significant change from the dolls of the early and mid-1800's.

Plate 310: Alexander. "Africa," 1989–90, from International series. 8" tall. All original in dark print African dress. Hard vinyl head, five-piece jointed hard vinyl body. Sleeping black eyes, black caracul type glued-on wig. Marks: Alexander, on back.

Plate 313: Alexander. "Cynthia," 18". 1952–1953. Hard plastic head, black saran wig, brown sleep eyes with lashes, closed mouth, jointed hard plastic body. Hair is in its original set. Doll is redressed. Marks: ALEXANDER, on head.

Plate 311: A & H Doll. "1890's Bell System Operator Doll," 15". Designed exclusively for "Telephone Pioneers of America." Vinyl head, dark brown sleeping eyes, rooted black hair; jointed hard vinyl body. All original in long black taffeta skirt, white silk-like blouse with telephone appropriate with the period. Marks: 4444/10/A&H Doll/N.Y.1981, on head.

Plate 312: Alexander. "Cynthia," 14" tall. All original. Hard plastic head with sleep eyes, painted closed mouth, glued-on black saran wig, jointed hard plastic body, yellow organdy dress with ruffles and lace trim. 1952. Doll is unmarked. Tag on dress: "Cynthia"/Madame Alexander/New York, U.S.A. Doll was also made 18" and 23" tall.

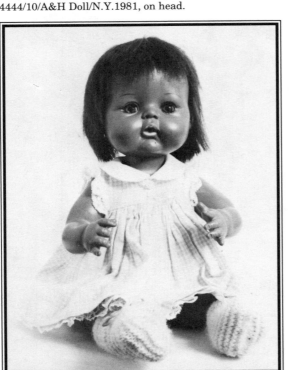

Plate 314: Alexander. "Baby Ellen," 13" all original baby doll made for only a short period. All vinyl, jointed baby body; dark brown sleep eyes; nursing mouth. Some of the Baby Ellen dolls have pink lips with faint pink toned coloring on the cheeks while others have bright orange-red lips with red tinted cheeks. Marks: ALEXANDER/19c65, on head; 14f, on body.

Plate 315: Alexander. "Katie," fully jointed little girl. 12" tall. Soft light brown vinyl, sleeping eyes with lashes, rooted dark brown hair and expressive hands. She has a mischievous smile on her face. Doll is all original in yellow organdy dress marked Alexander. Marks: Alexander/19c62, on head. "Katie" is a black version of white doll "Smarty."

Plate 316: Alexander. "Pussy Cat," 14" long baby doll. Soft vinyl head, lower arms and legs; brown rooted hair; brown sleep eyes; closed mouth; brown cloth body with cry box. Original blue checked dress and bloomers. Marks: Alexander/1965, on head. Courtesy of Susan Perkins.

Plate 317: Alexander. "Pussy Cat," 18". Vinyl head, arms and legs; brown cloth body; brown sleeping eyes with lashes, rooted brown hair, closed mouth. All original in pink rosebud print dress with matching rompers. Cry box inside cloth body. Marks: 3/ALEXANDER/19c77, on head.

Plate 318: Alexander. "Leslie" with Polly face. 17" tall. Vinyl head, arms and legs; hard vinyl body. Rooted brown synthetic wig was originally longer, has been cut. Head has dark brown sleep eyes; closed painted mouth; pierced ears, earrings missing. Doll is wearing original green dress with half-slip, replaced shoes. Marks: Alexander Doll Co Inc/1965. Courtesy of Michele Hill Grier.

Plate 319: Alexander. "Leslie" with Polly face. 17" tall. All original in a bridal gown and hairpiece. This gown has lace going down the bodice with tiny sequins sewn down the center. Headpiece has hundreds of tiny sequins sewn on. Brown rooted hair with bangs, pierced ears with diamond-like earrings. Marks: cALEXANDER DOLL CO. INC./1965, on head.

Plate 320: Alexander. "Leslie" with Polly face. Different all original bride doll, 17" tall. Vinyl head, closed mouth with corners turned up, sleeping brown eyes, rooted brown hair with center part, jointed vinyl body with high-heeled feet, pierced ears with pearl earrings. Marks: cALEXANDER DOLL CO. INC./ 1965, on head.

Plate 321: Alexander. "Leslie," blue formal with Polly face, corners of the mouth are turned up and chin is slightly different than Leslie with Elise face. All original. Vinyl head and jointed body, brown hair with cut bangs, sleeping brown eyes.

Plate 323: Alexander. "Leslie," Elise face, in pink formal gown. 16½" tall. All original. Rooted brown hair with bangs, sleeping brown eyes, closed mouth with corners turned down, pierced ears, earrings are missing. Marks: ALEXANDER/19c66, on head (marks are very faint).

Plate 322: Alexander. "Leslie," Polly face. All original in pink cotton dress with ecru lace shawl and trim, pink high-heel shoes and nylons. Long brown rooted hair with bangs, sleeping amber eyes, closed mouth. Marks: cALEXANDER DOLL CO. INC./1965, on head. Identical doll was also available in a blue dress of the same style. Courtesy of Michelle Bady.

Plate 324: Alexander. "Leslie." Elise face. All original in blue ballerina costume. 16½" tall. Vinyl head, closed mouth with corners turned down, brown sleeping eyes, rooted brown hair with bangs, pierced ears, hard plastic body. Marks: Alexander/19c66, on head. Clothing is marked Madame Alexander.

Plate 325: Alexander. "African," 7½" doll from the International series. All original. Hard vinyl, brown sleep eyes, black caracul glued-on wig. Pierced ears with gold earrings. Jointed knees. Marks: Alex, on back. "African"/By Madam Alexander/New York, U.S.A., on clothing tag. Doll was made from 1966 to 1971. Collection of Julie Perkins Scott.

Plate 326: Alexander. "Africa," 1991 from the International series. Doll is identical to Africa on page 103 except for clothing. Dress is now a two-piece print with matching gele (headpiece). Doll is wearing African-type beads around the neck and gold sandals.

Plate 327: Alexander. "Morocco," 8". 1968–1970. Hard vinyl head and body. Sleeping dark eyes, glued-on wig, fully jointed, including knees.

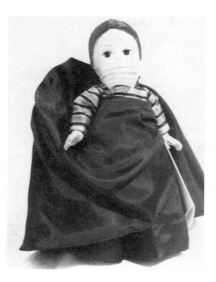

Plate 328: Alexander. "Jamaica," 8" doll from the International series. All original. Hard vinyl, dark brown wig, black sleep eyes, five-piece jointed body. This is the first doll from the Carribean that Alexander has issued in the series. Marks: Alex, on head. Alexander on back of doll. Clothing tag on doll: "Jamaica"/By Madame Alexander/Made in U.S.A. Jamaica was on the market from 1986–1989.

Plate 329: Alexander. "Egypt," 8" doll from International series. All original. Hard vinyl head and body, dark brown glued-on wig, black sleep eyes, five-piece jointed body. Marks: Alex, on head. Alexander, on back. Egypt/By Madame Alexander/Made in U.S.A., on clothing tag. 1986. Doll was discontinued in 1989.

Plate 330: Alexander. "Mammy." 8", from the Scarlett Jubilee II collection from *Gone With the Wind*. All original. Hard plastic head and body, caracul-type glued-on wig, black sleeping eyes. Actress Hattie McDaniel played the part of "Mammy" in the 1939 Academy Award Winner. Marks: Alex, on head. Alexander, on back. Mammy/Madame Alexander/Made in U.S.A., on clothing tag. Production limited to 1989.

Plate 331: Alexander. "Mammy," 1991. 8" tall. All original in blue checked dress, beige apron, white lace shawl, red plaid turban, red taffeta petticoat.

Plate 332: Alexander. "Prissy," 8" doll from the Scarlett series. All original. Hard vinyl head and five-piece jointed body, dark brown glued-on wig, black sleeping eyes. Actress Butterfly McQueen played the role of Prissy in the movie *Gone With the Wind*. Marks: Alexander, on back. Prissy/Madame Alexander/Made in U.S.A. on clothing tag. 1989.

Plate 333: Alexander. "Ballerina," 1991 from the Miniature Showcase series. 8" tall. Vinyl head, sleeping black eyes, black wig. Jointed five-piece body. All original in white with gold accents. Marks: ALEXANDER, on body.

Plate 334: Alexander. "Cheerleader," 1991 from the Miniature Showcase series. 8" tall. All original in red and white cheer outfit. Doll is the same as previous Alexander.

Plate 335: Alexander. "Bride," c1991, from the Americana collection. 8" tall. Hard vinyl head, body, and limbs. Black sleeping eyes, glued-on short black synthetic wig, closed mouth. All original in white bridal gown, headpiece, shoes, and stockings. Marks: ALEXANDER, on body. Clothing is tagged: "Bride"/By MADAME ALEXANDER/MADE IN U.S.A.

Plate 336: Alexander. "Graduation," c1991, from the Miniature Showcase collection. 8" tall. Except for clothing, identical to previous Alexander bride. All original in baby blue taffeta short dress with matching slippers and black taffeta gown with black felt cap.

Plate 337: Am Toy, Inc. "Holiday Holly Hobbie," 18" all cloth doll, special collector's edition designed exclusively for Zayre. Doll is Hollyberry scented and comes with collector's edition Christmas ornament dated 1988. Brown and black yarn hair in two long braids with two loops of yarn for bangs and painted features. All original in green print dress with matching hat and pantaloons. Hat is sewn on. Tag sewn to body: HOLLY HOBBIE/1988 THOSE CHARACTERS/ FROM CLEVELAND, INC.

Plate 338: American Character. 12" tall. "Tressy," high-fashion cosmetic doll with growing hair and magic makeup face. All vinyl; painted features; rooted black hair; fully jointed poseable body, growing mechanism on stomach. All original. High-fashion clothes and cosmetics for face sold separately. Marks: AMER. CHAR. TOY CORP./1963.

Plate 339: American Character. "Honey." 18" tall. Hard plastic head, sleeping brown eyes, open mouth with four upper teeth, red felt tongue; glued-on black wavy wig in two pigtails; hard plastic body. When doll "walks," her head turns. Clothing is appropriate with period of doll, 1950's, and could be original. Doll is unmarked.

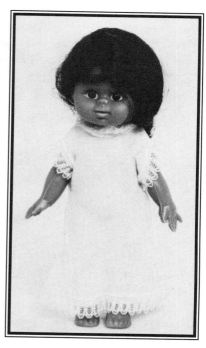

Plate 340: Amsco. "Polly Pretend." 14" tall. Vinyl head, painted features, rooted dark brown hair; jointed hard plastic toddler body. She came with a trunk and oversized clothing to play dress-up in mommy's clothes. All original. Marks: AMSCO/1974, on head.

Plate 341: Arkin A-OK Products. "Sweetheart," 1975. 7" tall. Vinyl head, painted eyes, nursing mouth, black rooted hair, jointed baby body. All original. Marks: MADE IN HONG KONG/ P.KROKOW & CO./BKLYN, N.Y. 11222, head; MADE IN/HONG KONG, body.

Plate 342: Arkin. "Little Angel," 6½" tall. Mid-1970's. Vinyl head with rooted black hair, painted features, five-piece jointed body. All original in long yellow gown trimmed in white lace. Marks: MADE IN HONG KONG/ P.KROKOW & Co./BKLYN, NY 11222, on head.

Left – Plate 343: Arkin A-OK Products. "Melanie," 1975. 11" tall. Vinyl head, painted eyes looking to left, rooted black hair, forehead has unusual molded ridge extending to both ears (hairdo covers), jointed vinyl body. All original. Marks: Made in/Hong Kong, body.

Right – Plate 344: Georgene Averill. 12½" tall character doll with rubber head, inset brown glassine eyes, molded hair with three tuffs of black yarn inserted, cloth body and limbs. All original in blue and white checkered dress with red sash. Marks: GEORGENE, on head.

Plate 345: Avon. "Kenzie," 11½" fashion doll. Soft vinyl head, painted features, long brown rooted hair; hard vinyl poseable body. All original. Created in China exclusively for Avon Products, Inc. Marks: could be 23 or 25, not clear, on head. 1991.

Plate 346: Avon. "Courtney," from the Colorsnaps collection. 14" tall. Vinyl head and hands, painted eyes, long dark brown rooted hair; cloth body and legs. All original in removable blue print sweatshirt. Marks: AVON PRODUCTS Inc. DISTR./cAVON 1987 – ALL RIGHTS RESERVED/REG. NO. PA940 H17, tag sewn to body.

Plate 347: Barval. "La Baby," 11" natural-looking baby whose skin looks and feels like a real baby. Head, arms, and legs are vinyl with a very soft light brown cloth body. The eyes are beautiful brown stationary eyes that almost look like the glass eyes of antique French dolls. Short curly hair is rooted. LaBaby came with a pacifier in his open mouth. Doll was made in Spain by Berjusa for Barval Toys, Miami, Florida. Marks: Berjusa, on head.

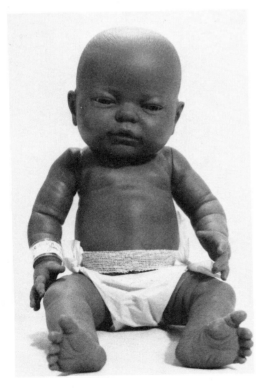

Plate 348: Barval. "La Newborn," 17" realistic looking newborn baby, available in two different sizes in boy, girl, and non-sexed versions. All vinyl with inset plastic eyes, open/closed mouth; jointed body. All original. Marks: BERJUSA, on head. Made in Spain.

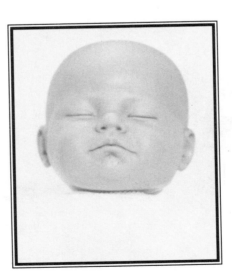

Plate 349: Barval. "La Baby," 21" sleeping baby doll. Vinyl head, molded lightly painted hair, molded closed eyes and mouth, vinyl arms and legs, cloth body. All original in two-piece white nightie trimmed in pink. Also available trimmed in blue. Marks: Berjusa/Made in Spain, on head.

Plate 350: Belle Doll & Toy Corp. 17" hard plastic Hawaiian walker. Brown sleep eyes, open mouth with four teeth, black glued-on mohair wig, walking hard plastic body. All original in two-piece blue and white print bathing suit with grass skirt, lei, and grass anklet. Unmarked. Marked on original pink and white striped box: A doll of QUALITY/A BELLE DOLL (inside bell logo)/BELLE DOLL & TOY CORP. Brooklyn, N.Y.

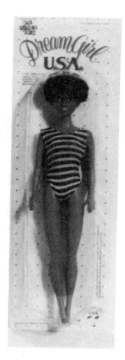

Plate 351: Ben Cooper Toys. "Dream Girl USA," 11½" fashion doll. Vinyl head, painted eyes, rooted black hair, vinyl jointed body. Doll came dressed in swimsuit in either red, green, or blue stripes. Marks: cBen Cooper Toys/MADE IN CHINA, on head. Copyright 1986 TWENTIETH CENTURY FOX FILM CORP. All RIGHTS RESERVED, on package.

Plate 352: Cameo. "Miss Peep," 15" tall. Vinyl head with stationary brown inset eyes, molded, painted hair; vinyl squeaker body with hinged legs and arms. All original in white robe trimmed in pink. Marks: USE 53 CAMEO, on head; CAMEO, on body. Early 1970's. Collection of Julie Perkins Scott.

Plate 353: Flirty-eyed doll from Canada, early 1970's. 13" tall. Hard vinyl head, glued-on caracul wig, closed mouth, jointed hard vinyl body. Dressed in red hat and loincloth that could be original. Doll is unmarked.

Plate 354: Children at Play. "Blooming Dolls." Approximately 12" tall. 1987. Soft sculptured face, pink yarn hair, glued-on plastic eyes, painted mouth, cloth body and limbs. Doll comes in a purple cloth flower pot, her hat becomes a flower when she is pushed inside the pot.

Plate 355: Cititoy. "Beauty Salon," for makeup and styling fun. Stand with doll, 8" tall. All original. Box is marked: No. 600010 (copyright sign) 1985 CITITOY. Made in China.

Plate 356: Cititoy. "My Little Angel," 13" tall. She can kneel down to say her prayers and hold her hands together; fingers are lined with velcro. Vinyl head, painted features, curly brown rooted hair; cloth body and limbs. All original. Marks: 8515, on head. Made in China. Box marked: No. 68530 (cw)1987.

Plate 357: Cititoy. "Holiday Kelly," 11½". Vinyl head, painted features, rooted brown hair; fully poseable. All original. Made in China, copyright 1988. Marks: MADE IN CHINA/(cw) 1985 CITITOY, on head.

Plate 358: Cititoy. 9" all vinyl little girl, long black rooted hair, painted features, jointed body. All original in long yellow print and white dress. Marks: 1989 CITITOY, on head. Courtesy of LaKenya Mixon.

Plate 359: Coleco. "CPK," 1983. 16" tall. Vinyl head, cut brown yarn hair, dimple in left cheek, painted eyes. All original in short white sailor suit with blue trim. Marks: COPY R. 1978, 1982/ORIGINAL APPALACHIAN ART WORKS INC/MANUFACTURED BY COLECO IND. INC./108 3, on head. Brown signature, 1983, face #3.

Plate 360: Coleco. "CPK" boy, 1983. 16" tall. Vinyl head, looped brown yarn hair, painted features. All original in blue jean rompers with checked shirt and orange windbreaker. Marks: COPY R. 1978, 1982/ORIGINAL APPALACHIAN ART WORKS INC./MANUFACTURED BY COLECO IND. INC./118 3, on head. Brown signature. Dimple in left cheek, 1983, face #3.

Plate 361: Coleco. "Cabbage Patch Kids" girl, 1983. 16" tall. Vinyl head with two looped brown yarn ponytails, dimple in left cheek. All original in pink two-piece sunsuit and white bib. Marks: COPY R. 1978, 1982/ORIGINAL APPALACHIAN ART WORKS, INC./MANUFACTURED BY COLECO IND. INC./15 3, on head. Brown signature.

Plate 362: Coleco. "Cabbage Patch Kids" bald boy. 1983. 16". Bald vinyl head with dimple in left cheek. All original in red rompers and white t-shirt. Marks: COPY R. 1978, 1982/ORIGINAL APPALACHIAN ART WORK INC./MANUFACTURED BY COLECO IND. INC./3, on head. Tag sewn to body: Cabbage Patch Kids/1978, 1982. Brown signature, face #3.

Plate 363: Coleco. "Cabbage Patch Kids" boy. 1984. 16" Vinyl head with one dimple, rooted brown yarn hair, cloth body. All original in blue jeans and white and orange striped shirt. Marks: COPY R. 1978, 1982/ORIGINAL APPALACHIAN ART WORKS INC/MANU-FACTURED BY COLECO IND. INC./105 3, on head. Brown signature, face #3.

Plate 364: Coleco. "Cabbage Patch Kids Preemie." 1984. 14". Bald vinyl head, no dimples. All original in yellow print gown. Marks: COPY R. 1978, 1982/ORIGINAL APPALACHIAN ART WORKS, INC/ MANUFACTURED BY COLECO IND. INC./73 1, on head. Brown signature.

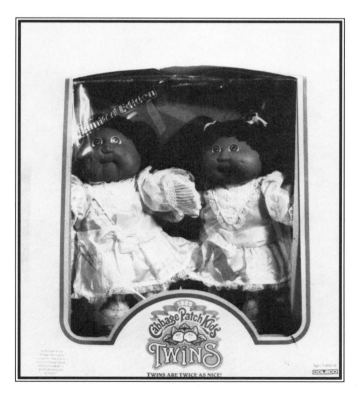

Plate 365: Coleco. "Cabbage Patch Kids Twins," limited edition. 1985. Marks: COPY R. 1978, 1982/ORIGINAL APPALACHIAN ART WORKS INC./MANUFACTURED BY COLECO IND. INC/ 107 3, on head. Face #3.

Plate 366: Coleco. "Cabbage Patch Kids Preemie," 1985. 14". Vinyl head, rooted tuff of looped yarn hair, cloth body and limbs, dimple in left cheek. All original in long yellow gown and matching bonnet. Marks: COPY R. 1978, 1982/ORIGI-NAL APPALACHIAN ART WORKS INC./MANUFAC-TURED BY COLECO IND. INC./3/29, on head.

Plate 367: Coleco. "CPK Circus Kids," 1985. 16". Vinyl head, brown cut loop yarn hair, dimple in left cheek. All original in clown suit in orange, yellow, and green with orange clown shoes and hat. Doll came with a colorful mask, collectible "Circus Kids" trading card and Big-Top poster. Marks: cCOPY R. 1978, 1982/ORIGINAL APPALACHIAN ART WORKS INC/MANUFACTURED BY COLECO IND. INC./MADE IN HONG KONG/3, on head. Face #3, Red Signature.

Plate 368: Coleco. "Cabbage Patch Kids Young Astronaut," 1986. 16". Boy, all original, dimple in left cheek, cut yarn hair. Face #3.

Plate 369: Coleco. "Cabbage Patch Kids All-Stars," 1986. 17". Vinyl head, rooted cut yarn hair. Dressed in Detroit Tigers uniform. Marks: 1978, 1983 O.A.A., INC./11, on head; Cabbage Patch Kids/1978, 1982/Original Appalachian Art Works, Inc., on tag sewn to body. Clothing is also labeled. Red signature, face #11.

Plate 370: Coleco. "CPK Cornsilk Kids," 1986. 16". Vinyl head, decal eyes, rooted curly dark brown hair in the full Afro fluffy hairstyle, two dimples. Marks: c1978 1983 O.A.A., Inc./35 (raised) 12 (not clear), on head.

Plate 371: Coleco. "CPK Circus Kids Ringmaster." 1986. 17" tall. Vinyl head, brown cut loop yarn hair, dimple in each cheek. All original in white cotton shirt, white satin pants, gold vest, red velveteen jacket lined in black, black vinyl boots, black plastic top hat, and plastic megaphone. Marks: 9/c1978, 1983 O.A.A., INC./12, on head. Red Signature.

Plate 372: Coleco. "CPK Talking Kids," 1987. Vinyl head, open mouth, rooted brown curly synthetic hair. All original in purple velveteen dress with white eyelet pinafore.

Plate 373: Coleco. "CPK Talking Kids," 1987. All original in white cotton dress under sky blue velveteen cotton pinafore. Dark brown synthetic hair pulled up in one ponytail, curly bangs in front; open talking mouth. Marks: c1979, 1983 O.A.A. INC./T9, on head. Green signature.

Plate 374: Coleco. "CPK Splashin' Kids" boy, 1987. 14" tall. Rooted synthetic brown curly hair. All original in red swim trunks and red windbreaker trimmed in yellow and white. Marks: 1978, 1982 O.A.A/Made in China/13 20, on head. Aqua signature, face #20.

Plate 375: Coleco. "CPK Splashin' Kids" girl. 1987. 14". Open mouth, rooted dark brown "cornsilk" hair, vinyl jointed body. All original in white swimsuit with multi-colored dots and white cotton knit cover-up. Marks: c1978, 1983 O.A.A. INC./Made in China/20 (embossed) 21, on head. Aqua signature, 1987, face #21.

Plate 376: Coleco. "CPK Designer Line" girl. 1988. 16" tall. Vinyl head, rooted black synthetic or "cornsilk" hair, painted eyes, dimpled chin, cloth body. All original in dress decorated with buttons in style made popular by dress designer, the late Patrick Kelly, who coincidently had a collection of over 6,000 black dolls. Dress is aqua, lavender, and yellow. Marks: 1978, 1982 1988/O.A.A. 44/MFG. BY COLECO IND. INC., on head. Pink signature. Face #44.

Plate 377: Coleco. "CPK Designer Line" boy, 1989. 16". Rooted synthetic hair, dimple in left cheek. All original in gray, yellow, and blue jogging suit and athletic shoes. Marks: 3, everything above this is hidden in rooted hair. Tag sewn to body: CABBAGE PATCH KIDS/Copyright 1989. Face #3.

Plate 378: Coleco. "CPK with Growing Hair," 1988. Vinyl head, decal eyes, long rooted brown synthetic "growing" hair, tongue sticking out. All original in pastel print dress. Marks: cCOPY R. 1978, 1982–1987/ORIGINAL APPALACHIAN ART WORKS, INC/MANUFACTURED BY COLECO IND. INC./MADE IN CHINA/H23. Purple signature.

Plate 379: Coleco. "Brenton Rudy and His Barnyard" from "Cabbage Patch Kids Pin-Ups," 5" tall. Vinyl head, painted features, rooted brown yarn hair. All original in removable overalls, shirt is sewn on. Marks: 1978, 1983 O.A.A. Inc., on head.

Plate 380: Spindex Corp. "CPK Poseable Figure, Carly Pam," July 16, 1984. Baby with orange rompers, removable yellow bib, holding a baby spoon. Marks are the same as Plate 382.

Plate 381: Spindex Corp. "Cabbage Patch Kid Poseable Figure, Marjorie Pat." Created in the Cabbage Patch August 1, 1984. Dressed in molded-on blue and white romper set with removable pink bib. Doll is holding a tiny black doll. Marks are the same as previous figure.

Plate 382: Spindex Corp. "Cabbage Patch Kids, Poseable Figure," Madella Jill. First edition figure 3½" tall. All vinyl with molded, painted hair and features. Clothing is molded, painted-on white dress with pink trim and lavender socks. Doll is holding a teddy bear. Pink ribbons tied through molded loops in hair are removable. Certificate on back of box states that doll was created in the Cabbage Patch on August 12, 1984. Marks: 1984 O.A.A., on head; 5/China, left leg; 4/1984/O.A.A. Inc., right leg.

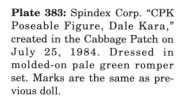

Plate 383: Spindex Corp. "CPK Poseable Figure, Dale Kara," created in the Cabbage Patch on July 25, 1984. Dressed in molded-on pale green romper set. Marks are the same as previous doll.

Plate 384: Coleco. "Princess Magic Touch," 5½" tall. Poseable vinyl with painted features and long dark brown rooted hair. All original. Marks: c1987 COLECO/Made in China, on back.

Plate 385: Collette. "Collette Doll," 24" walking doll. 1970's. All original. Soft vinyl head, rooted black hair, sleeping eyes, hard vinyl body and limbs. Doll is unmarked. Box is marked: Another Beautiful Collette Doll/24" Walking Doll/Hold my left hand and/I will walk with you.

Plate 386: Colombo Doll Co. "Jilly and her Playthings," 1975. Soft vinyl head; sleep eyes with real lashes and painted lashes on sides; open/shut painted mouth; short black rooted hair; jointed vinyl body. All original in tights, blouse, and hat; comes with two extra wigs. Marks: MADE IN HONG KONG, head; MADE IN/HONG KONG, body.

Left – Plate 387: Colombo Doll Co. "The Talking Walking Doll," talks, sings, and recites. 23" tall. Four records that play on both sides are included with doll. Record player is inside back of doll. When records are in place, button on stomach of doll is pressed to start record. Battery operated. Soft vinyl head, rooted black hair, sleep eyes, jointed hard plastic body. Marks: COLOMBO, body; MADE IN JAPAN/DTD/6/PAT. P., on record player.

Right – Plate 388: Corolle, Inc. "Jessie," designed by Catherine Refabert, the master doll artist for Corolle. All original, 14½" tall vinyl doll. Beautiful black eyes with lashes, rooted black hair, five-piece jointed body. Doll is very well made. Coloring is realistic. Marks: Corolle/87-4/2014, on head. This type of doll is only carried in finer toy stores. Made in France. Corolle dolls are distributed in the U.S. by Timeless Creations, the collectible/specialty division of Mattel, Inc.

Plate 389: Corolle. "Pamela," 21" doll designed by Catherine Refabert. All original. Vinyl head with sleeping black eyes, black rooted hair. Very soft brown cloth body with vinyl limbs. Beautifully dressed with white and pink dress and pantaloons, white stockings and black shoes. Made in France. Marks: Corolle/87-4/2014, on head. Dress is marked Corolle.

Plate 390: Corolle. "Canelle," 22" tall. The first in a series of Catherine Refabert designed Corolle dolls influenced by the works of great artists. Canelle brings to life the great paintings of Gauguin and the beauty of the Caribbean and Tahitian islands. The colors in the dress are pink, fuchsia, lavender, gold, typical colors used by Gauguin. Vinyl head, beautiful dark sleeping eyes, rooted dark hair; vinyl lower arms and legs, cloth body and upper limbs. All original. Marks: COROLLE /87/4/2014, on head. Tag on body: Corolle Inc. 1989 Timeless Creations/a division of Mattel Inc./Made in France. Doll came to market in 1990.

Plate 391: Corolle. "Sabrina," designed by Catherine Refabert. 22" tall. Vinyl head in medium brown, sleeping black eyes, long black rooted hair, closed mouth; vinyl lower arms and legs; cloth body, upper arms and legs. All original in pink and aqua print dress marked Corolle on the collar and hemline and matching print pantaloons. Marks: Corolle; 87/4/2014, on head; Corolle Inc. 1989., tag sewn to body.

Plate 392: Corolle. Baby doll, 16" tall. Vinyl bald head, slightly molded hair; sleeping black eyes, closed mouth; jointed vinyl body. All original in blue and white striped rompers. Marks: CAROL 80/MADE IN FRANCE, on head. Courtesy of Marge Betts.

Plate 393: Corolle. "Timmy," #5032. 13" tall. Vinyl head, rooted black hair, sleeping black eyes, vinyl arms and legs, brown cloth body. All original in white cotton knit sleepers. Marks: MADE IN FRANCE/88/4 M10/COROLLE, on head. Courtesy of Marge Betts.

Plate 394: Corolle. "Kim," a Catherine Refabert design. 21" tall. Vinyl head and hands, cloth body and legs; brown sleeping eyes, closed mouth, black curly rooted hair. All original in red striped sweater dress with matching leg warmers and yellow tights. Marks: COROLLE/1981, on head.

Plate 395: Creata. "Heather's Secret," 11½" doll with glamour secrets. One of three dolls in the collection. Each doll wears a lacy romantic undergarment hidden beneath her fancy outfit. Also, beauty and grooming tips are printed on the box. The dolls are all vinyl with painted features and long rooted hair. They are completely poseable with movable arms, twist waist and poseable, bendable legs. Other dolls in the series are Tiffany and Vanessa. Marks: CREATA/1988, in head. Made in China.

Plate 396: Creata. "Vanessa's Secret," one of the three dolls in the Glamour Secrets collection. Marks: CREATA/1988, on head.

Plate 397: Creata. "Tiffany's Secret," one of the three dolls in Glamour Secrets collection. Marks: Creata/1988, on head.

Plate 398: Creata International Inc. "Lace," 11½" celebrity rock star with fashion and fame. Vinyl head, painted features, rooted long brown/blond hair; hard vinyl jointed body. All original. Marks: CREATA, on head. 1986.

Plate 399: Creata. "Kelly," 6" doll from Today's Girls series. Other 6" dolls in the series were Katie, Marina, and Pepper. Vinyl head, painted features, long black rooted hair, hard vinyl jointed girls body. All original, dolls were sold in a variety of outfits as shown in the photograph, style No. 1034. Marks: Creata/1985, on head; Creata/1985/China, on body.

Plate 400: Creata. "Marina," 6" doll from Today's Girls Beach Kids series of dolls. Except for clothing, doll is like previous 6" Today's Girls. Style No. 1034. The dolls were individually sold in a variety of beach wear as shown.

Plate 401: Creata. "Today's Girls," 11½" fashion doll. Vinyl head, rooted long dark hair, painted features, poseable vinyl body. Doll came in a variety of different clothes with different hairstyles. Each of the boxes was also a different color; however, they were all style No. 1360. Dolls names were Cookie, Candy, and Trish. It was not clear who was named what as all three names were on each box. Marks: CREATA, on head; CHINA/CREATA 1988, on body.

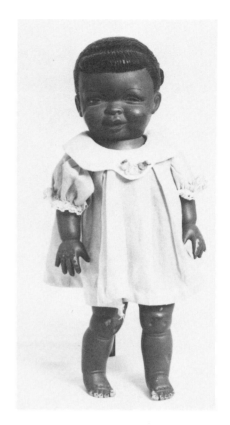

Plate 402: Dakin. "Twinkie" from the "Dream Dolls" collection. 7" tall. Vinyl head, painted eyes, closed mouth, rooted brown hair, jointed soft vinyl body. All original in blue and white dress, white shoes. Marks: R. Dakin & Co./COPYRIGHT 1969/PROD. OF JAPAN, on head. Clothing is marked: DREAM DOLLS.

Plate 403: Dee&Cee. "Calypso Jill," 15½" doll from a Canadian Doll Company. Soft vinyl head; painted features; open smiling mouth; molded, painted hair with bangs and two pigtails; hard plastic jointed body. Marks: DeeCee, on head (very faint). This doll is included, along with other dolls, in the Dolls in Canada series of stamps issued by the Post Office, Canada Post, to celebrate the memories of past childhood. Doll was made in 1960.

Plate 404: It is either a Horsman "Polly" or Dee&Cee "Calypso Jill." 12" earlier version of the previous doll. This one is made of soft, stuffed rubberlike material. It also has molded, painted features. Doll is unmarked, circa 1950.

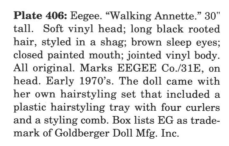

Plate 406: Eegee. "Walking Annette." 30" tall. Soft vinyl head; long black rooted hair, styled in a shag; brown sleep eyes; closed painted mouth; jointed vinyl body. All original. Marks EEGEE Co./31E, on head. Early 1970's. The doll came with her own hairstyling set that included a plastic hairstyling tray with four curlers and a styling comb. Box lists EG as trademark of Goldberger Doll Mfg. Inc.

Plate 405: Ebony Jr. "Sunny and Honey," cloth dolls ordered through Johnson Publication's *Ebony Jr*. magazine. 17" tall. Mid 1970's. Dolls were reissued in 1991.

Note: Eegee dolls are made by Goldberger Doll Mfg. Inc.

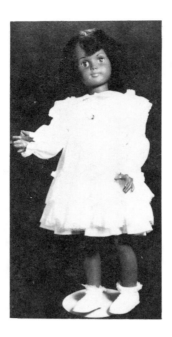

Plate 408: Eegee. Walking doll, 31" tall. All vinyl with sleeping brown eyes, solid one-piece lashes; rooted short black hair. Marks: 30N/Eegee Co./Made in Taiwan. Redressed.

Plate 407: Eegee. "Army Girl," 32" walking doll. Mid-1970's. Vinyl head, sleeping brown eyes, long black rooted hair; hard plastic walking body. All original in army uniform. Marks: EEGEE Co. 74, on head.

Plate 409: Eegee. 1960's. Vinyl doll, 14", painted black eyes, rooted black hair, nursing mouth, one-piece body. Redressed. Marks: EEGEE CO./14P, on head; DULLON/PAT. NOS. 3.432.581/3.456.046/OTHER PAT'S PEND'G/EEGEE CO., on back.

Plate 410: Eegee. Vinyl wet and drink baby, 13" tall, painted black eyes, rooted black hair, nursing mouth, one-piece soft vinyl stuffed body with tube where baby wets. Childhood toy of Cheryl Larry, mid-1970's. Marks: EEGEE CO./14P, on head; Dublon/PAT. NO. 132.58/3.456.046/OTHER PAT'S PEND'G./EEGEE CO., on back. Courtesy of Cheryl Larry Perkins.

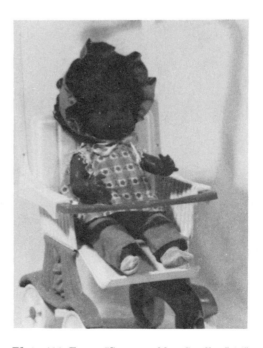

Plate 411: Eegee. "Susan and her Stroller." 14" tall. Soft vinyl head, rooted curly black hair, sleep eyes, nursing mouth, jointed baby body. Stroller is hard plastic, blue and white. Marks: cEEGEE CO. 14BA/N.F. HONG KONG. 1970's.

Plate 412: Eegee. 16" vinyl head doll, molded fancy hairdo, brown stationary glassine eyes, jointed vinyl body. Redressed. Marks: Eegee, on head.

Plate 413: Eegee. Similar doll in smaller version, 10½" tall. Soft vinyl head with painted eyes; the same molded hairdo; molded-on panties, shoes, and stockings; one-piece vinyl body. Marks: KS9, on head; A, on body.

Plate 414: Eegee. "Sojourner Truth," of the Liberty Belle series, 1975. 11½" tall. Doll came with historical information of the life of Sojourner Truth (Isabella Baumfree). Doll has soft vinyl head; painted features; black rooted hair; jointed body. Doll is all original in long red dress with yellow trim and yellow print bandana on head. Marks: HONG KONG, on head; made in HONG KONG, on body.

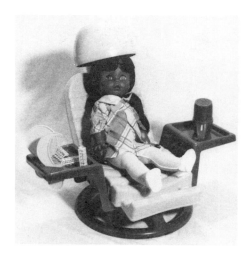

Plate 415: Eegee (Goldberger). "Li'l Carol," 1975. 9" tall. Soft vinyl head, painted features, long black rooted hair, jointed vinyl body. All original. Marks: HONG KONG, on head; PLAY-MATES (in logo)/HONG KONG/5092, on body.

Plate 416: Eegee. "Sugar Kandi," 13½" drinking and wetting doll. Vinyl head, sleeping brown eyes with lashes, rooted black hair; jointed baby body. All original. Marks: Made in Hong Kong/EEGEE CO./14BA/N.F., on head. 1967–1970.

Plate 417: Eegee. "Sue and Her Beauty Salon Too," includes plastic beauty chair. 19" tall. Vinyl head, painted eyes, rooted long black hair, closed mouth, jointed hard plastic body, vinyl arms. All original. Marks: 16 BP/cEEGEE CO., on head.

Plate 418: Eegee. "Lester." 27" tall. Ventriloquist doll, pull string in back opens mouth. Hard vinyl head, painted eyes, molded painted teeth, vinyl hands, cloth stuffed body and legs, rooted black hair. Glasses are missing. Marks: c1973/LESTER/cEEGEE CO./24, on head. This same doll remained on the market from the 1970's to the 1990's. This one was purchased in the early 1970's.

Plate 419: Eegee. "Baby Little One," 20" baby. Vinyl head, sleeping brown eyes, curly rooted short black hair; vinyl limbs, brown cloth body. All original. Marks: 19RG/EEGEE Co., 3, on head. Doll wears hospital wrist tag, not filled in. Doll was made in U.S.A.

Plate 421: Eegee. "Baby Little One," 14" musical moving baby, wind-up key in back. Vinyl head, arms and legs; cloth body; molded, closed eyes; open/closed mouth; molded hair. All original in flannel sleepers with bunny ears. Marks: EEGEE/19c87, on head.

Plate 420: Eegee. (Goldberger Doll Mfg. Co.) "Willie Tyler's Lester," 20" tall talking doll. Pull string in back of doll and it says 16 different sayings and sounds. Doll looks like a ventriloquist dummy. Vinyl head, painted features, rooted black hair; vinyl hands; cloth body, legs, and feet. All original. Marks: 1973/LESTER/EEGEE CO./24, on head. Made in Taiwan. 1990.

Plate 422: Eegee. "Sugar Pudd'n," 19". Vinyl head, painted eyes, rooted black curly hair, closed mouth, vinyl arms and legs, cloth body. All original in pink knit pant outfit and matching cap. Box says doll was created by James W. Royland and brought to life by Marcella Welch. Marks: SP/18/EEGEE HP/86, on head.

Plate 423: Effanbee. "Gumdrops," character faced doll. 15" tall. Vinyl head and arms, brown sleep eyes, rooted brown hair, hard plastic jointed body. Marks: c1962/EFFANBEE. Doll was purchased new in the early 1970's. Courtesy of Susan Perkins.

Plate 424: Effanbee. "Half-Pint." 11" tall. All original character doll with soft vinyl head, jointed body. Head has brown sleep eyes; rooted brown hair; closed mouth. Marks: 10ME/Effanbee/ 19c66, head; EFFANBEE/2400, body.

Plate 425: Effanbee. "Half-Pint" with black googlie sleeping eyes, brown straight rooted hair; closed mouth. All original in white cotton eyelet dress, old-fashioned shoes and natural straw bonnet. Marks are the same as on previous Half-Pint.

Plate 426: Effanbee. "Suzie (Susie) Sunshine," from the Pajama Kids collection, #1856, 1975. 18" tall. All original. Soft vinyl head with freckles; dark brown rooted hair; brown sleep eyes, real eyelashes; painted mouth. Soft vinyl arms; hard plastic body and legs. Doll came with small brown teddy bear with glassine eyes, felt nose and mouth. Marks: EFFANBEE/c1961. Teddy bear is 6½" tall. Marks: TRUDY TOYS CO. INC. NORWALK, CONN., tag sewn to body. Collection of Susan E. Perkins.

Plate 427: Effanbee. "Girl Scout." 8½" tall. Official Junior Girl Scout doll, sold originally in Girl Scout department where scout clothing was purchased. Original price was $4.50 and the doll came in a green girl scout box. All original. Soft vinyl head; brown glassine sleep eyes; brown rooted hair; closed, painted mouth. Jointed vinyl body. Marks: EFFANBEE 19c65, on head.

Plate 428: Effanbee. "Brownie Scout." Identical to Girl Scout doll except for clothing. Dressed in brown brownie scout uniform. Hat, shoes, socks are missing. Collection of Julie Perkins Scott.

Plate 429: Effanbee. "Miss Chips" in original bridal gown. 18" tall. Vinyl head; brown rooted hair; brown sleep eyes; hard plastic jointed body. Purchased new in mid-1970's. Marks: EFFANBEE/19c65/1700, on head.

Plate 430: Effanbee. "Chipper" from the Bridal Suite collection, 1973. 15" tall. Vinyl head, sleep eyes, closed mouth, long rooted brown hair, hard plastic body and arms. Marks: EFFANBEE/19c66, on head.

Plate 431: Effanbee. "Chipper" in another all original bridal outfit. This dress has much more lace and hairstyle has changed from a bun in the back to hanging loose. Doll was issued in the mid-1970's. Marks: EFFANBEE/19c66, on head.

Plate 432: Effanbee. "Chipper" from the Bridal Suite collection, 1973. 15" tall. All original in pink and white bridesmaid gown. Marks: EFFANBEE/19c66, on head.

Plate 433: Effanbee. "Chipper" from Yesterday's collection, 1977. 15" tall. Vinyl head, sleeping brown eyes, long rooted brown hair with center part, closed mouth, jointed vinyl body. All original in long gown with a multicolored skirt and white bodice. Doll is wearing a straw hat trimmed with the same fabric. Marks: EFFANBEE/19c66, on head.

Plate 434: Effanbee. "Chipper" from A Touch of Velvet collection, 1977. Except for clothing, doll is identical to previous Chipper. All original in white eyelet dress trimmed in burgundy velvet. Marks: EFFAN-BEE/19c66, on head.

Plate 435: Effanbee. "Chipper," 1981 from Over The Rainbow collection. 15" tall. All original in pastel gingham and white dress. Marks: EFFANBEE/19c78/1578, on head.

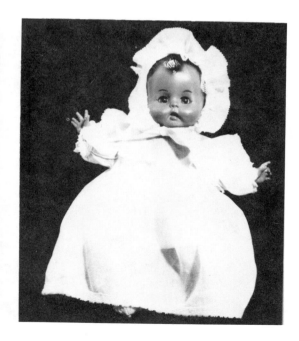

Plate 436: Effanbee. "Baby Button Nose." 12" tall. Vinyl head, molded painted hair, brown sleeping eyes with lashes, open/closed mouth, vinyl arms and legs, brown cloth body. Redressed. Marks: EFFAN-BEE/1971/8171, on head. Baby Button Nose was made until 1983.

Plate 437: Effanbee. "Baby Button Nose." 12". Vinyl head, hazel sleeping eyes, molded black hair, vinyl arms and legs; open/closed mouth with molded, painted tongue; brown cloth body. All original in white rosebud print sleepers. Marks: EFFANBEE/19c80/8180, on head.

Plate 440: Effanbee. "Pun'kin." 11" tall. Jointed vinyl head and body; rooted brown hair; brown glassine sleep eyes. Purchased new in the early 1970's. All original. Marks: EFFANBEE/19c66, on head.

Plate 438: Effanbee. "Tiny Tubber." 10½" tall. Soft vinyl head and jointed toddler body; drinks and wets; brown sleep eyes; brown rooted hair. All original. Marks: EFFANBEE (remainder of marks are indistinguishable).

Plate 439: Effanbee. "Tiny Tubber," 1975, from the Crochet Classics collection. #2373. All original in pale pink hand-crocheted dress and booties. Vinyl head, sleeping brown eyes, rooted dark hair, nursing mouth, jointed vinyl baby body. Marks: EFFANBEE/19c66, on head.

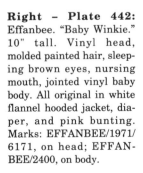

Left – Plate 441: Effanbee. "Baby Face," toddler girl. 16" tall. Vinyl head, sleeping brown eyes, closed mouth, rooted brown hair, jointed hard plastic body and legs, vinyl arms. Marks: EFFANBEE/19c67/2600, on head.

Right – Plate 442: Effanbee. "Baby Winkie." 10" tall. Vinyl head, molded painted hair, sleeping brown eyes, nursing mouth, jointed vinyl baby body. All original in white flannel hooded jacket, diaper, and pink bunting. Marks: EFFANBEE/1971/6171, on head; EFFANBEE/2400, on body.

Plate 443: Effanbee. "Sugar Plum." 19" mama baby doll. Vinyl head, sleeping brown eyes, rooted brown hair, vinyl arms and legs, cloth body. All original in white organdy dress trimmed with tucks and white lace. Marks: 17/EFFANBEE/1969/9669, on head.

Plate 444: Effanbee. "Little Luv," 1975, from the Pajama Kids collection #9356B. 15" tall. Vinyl head, arms, and legs; brown cloth body with cry box; molded, black painted hair; brown sleep eyes; painted mouth. Heart-shaped tag reads: I AM YOUR LITTLE LUV/THE PERFECT IMAGE OF AN ADORABLE BABY/AN EFFANBEE DURABLE DOLL. Marks: 10/ EFFANBEE/19c70.

Plate 445: Effanbee. "Sissy," black doll from Effanbee's One World collection. Other dolls were Kim, oriental and Jane, white. Sissy is 11⅓" tall, all vinyl with black sleeping eyes and short dark brown rooted hair. Her toddler body has movable arms and legs. All original. Made in U.S.A., 1983. Marks: Effanbee/19c80/1480, on head; F-B, on body.

Plate 446: Effanbee. "Frontier," one of four 12" dolls from the Through the Years limited edition collection. "Frontier" is #1401, all original in red print dress, blue hat with matching red trim, carrying basket. Doll is identical to "Sissy" doll by Effanbee. Vinyl head, sleeping black eyes, one-piece lashes; rooted brown hair; vinyl jointed body. Marks: EFFANBEE/1980/1480, on head; F-B, on body. Copyright 1985.

Plate 447: Effanbee. "Civil War," 12" doll from the Through the Years collection. All original in white dress trimmed in lavender ribbon and white lace. Style #1402.

Plate 448: Effanbee Doll Corp. "Today," 12" doll from Through the Years collection. All original in red velveteen dress trimmed in white lace. Style #1404.

Plate 450: Effanbee. "Caroline," 11" bride doll. All original. Vinyl head, sleeping brown eyes, long brown rooted hair and jointed vinyl body. Marks: Effanbee/1975/1176, on head; Effanbee, on body.

Plate 449: Effanbee. "Turn of the Century," from Through the Years limited edition collection. All original in white dress and pantaloons trimmed in white lace and blue ribbon. Doll is wearing a cameo. Style #1403.

Left – Plate 451: Effanbee. "Red Shoes" from the Dance Ballerina Dance collection. 11" tall. Hard vinyl head and jointed body, brown rooted straight hair, sleeping brown eyes. All original. Marks: EFFANBEE/1975/1176, on head; EFF & BEE on back. Hang tag: ...#1141 Red shoes... EFFANBEE/1984/EFFANBEE DOLL CORP./NEW YORK/MADE IN USA.

Right - Plate 452: Effanbee. "Miss Black U.S.A.," limited edition of 300 made for Treasure Trove. This is doll #4. 11". Vinyl head, brown sleeping eyes with one-piece black vinyl eyelashes and painted eyelashes, long black rooted hair, closed mouth, jointed hard vinyl body. All original in denim and red gingham outfit with red felt hat. Marks: EFFANBEE/c1975/1176, on head; EFFANBEE, on body.

Plate 453: Effanbee. "Miss Black America," 11". Vinyl head, brown sleeping eyes, rooted brown hair, jointed hard plastic body. All original in traditional African styled gown and head wrap. Marks: EFFANBEE/1975/1176, on head; EFFANBEE, on body.

Plate 454: Effanbee. "Dover" from the Victorian Miniatures collection. Doll is 11". She is wearing her original ecru dress made of lace and organdy fabric, ecru straw hat and carrying lace parisol. Vinyl head, sleeping brown eyes with solid lashes, rooted brown hair, hard vinyl jointed body. Style No. 1148. Certificate of authenticity that comes with the doll says, "Effanbee's 1986 Victorian Miniatures collection consists of Cornwall, Coventry, Dover, and Salisbury. The production of each of these prestigious collectibles is limited to 4,000 pieces, to be made during 1986 only." Marks: Effanbee/1975/1176. Made in U.S.A.

Plate 455: Effanbee. "Annabelle" 13" limited edition bride, #6 out of 500 dolls. Vinyl head, sleeping brown eyes, rooted dark brown hair. All original in beautiful white gown and head-piece, carrying a bouquet of roses. Doll was made as a limited edition for Treasure Trove. Marks: EFFANBEE/3381/1981, on head; Effanbee, on body.

Plate 456: Effanbee. "Louise," 13" limited edition Maid of Honor, #6 of 250 dolls made for Treasure Trove. All original in pink satin dress with dotted white net overskirt and white straw hat trimmed with pink ribbon. Marks are the same as those of "Annabelle" bride, previous doll.

Plate 457: Effanbee. "Lorraine," from the Grandes Dames. Numbered limited edition of 700 made exclusively for Treasure Trove. #142/750. 11" tall. Vinyl head, closed mouth, sleeping brown eyes, long rooted brown hair, jointed vinyl body. All original in long red dress with thin black stripes, velvet-like black jacket, black velvet hat. Marks: EFFANBEE/c1975/1176, on head.

Plate 458: Effanbee. "Amanda," from the Grandes Dames collection. 11" tall. All original in long mauve gown trimmed with lace and burgundy ribbon, natural straw hat with flowers and ribbons. Vinyl head, sleeping eyes, rooted brown hair, closed mouth, jointed hard vinyl body. Marks: EFFANBEE/c1975/1176, on head; EFF BEE, on body.

Plate 459: Effanbee. "Grandes Dames, Summer" from the Four Seasons collection. 11½" tall. Vinyl head, sleeping brown eyes, rooted dark brown hair, closed mouth; jointed vinyl body. All original in long white organdy dress over pale pink; white mesh hat trimmed with lace and ribbon, white mesh flower basket. Marks: EFFANBEE/c1975/1176, on head.

Plate 460: Effanbee. "Grandes Dames, Autumn" from the Four Seasons collection. All original in long brown velveteen dress with capelet collar and matching bonnet.

Plate 461: Effanbee. "Grandes Dames, Winter" from the Four Seasons collection. All original in long dress with red velveteen bodice and white cotton skirt, red velveteen cape with matching bonnet, white felt scarf.

Plate 462: Effanbee. "Grandes Dames, Spring" from the Four Seasons collection. All original in long green faille skirt with white cotton blouse and petticoat, natural straw hat.

Plate 463: Effanbee. "Louis Armstrong, 15" doll from the Great Moments in Music collection. Vinyl head and body, molded painted facial features and hair. Marks: 1984/EST. Louis Armstrong/Effanbee, on head. Effanbee, on back. Hang-tag on doll reads, "...Our 'Satchmo' is so realistic you can almost see the beads of perspiration on his brow. (His ever present white handkerchief is tucked in his hand) as he belts out a tune with his raspy voice and his beloved horn." Satchmo died in 1971. The doll was produced for 1984 and 1985 only. One of his most popular songs was "Hello Dolly."

Plate 464: Effanbee. "Muhammad Ali," 18". "I am the Greatest" doll, from Effanbee's Great Moments in Sports series. This doll was available for 1986 only. All vinyl with painted features, molded-on boxing shoes and gloves. All original. Marks: Effanbee/1986/M.ALI, on head. Crafted with Pride in U.S.A., wrist tag. Booklet attached gives a brief biography of Muhammad Ali.

Plate 465: Effanbee. "Buckwheat," 11" character from the Little Rascals series. Hard vinyl head, five-piece jointed vinyl body, painted features, rooted black synthetic hair. All original. Marks: Effanbee F81131/King World, 1989, on head. Hang tag: "The Little Rascals and their timeless humor have spanned generations, filling us with laughter. These wonderful characters will bring back to your heart many fond memories of yesterday. The Little Rascals, with their intricate detail, will delight fans of all ages." Buckwheat was played by child actor William Thomas. Thomas died in 1980.

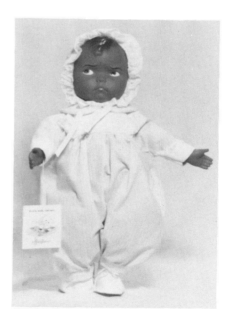

Plate 466: Effanbee. "Patsy," 13" vinyl limited edition. Molded hair with red ribbon, red gingham dress, panties, shoes, socks. Patsy is a reproduction of an original Patsy doll made in the 1920's in composition. Production of this doll was limited to 900 pieces. Marks: Effanbee/Patsy 1986, on head; Effanbee, on back.

Plate 467: Effanbee, "Patsy Boy," 16" vinyl doll limited to production in 1986. Boy is dressed in red and white checked shorts with suspenders, white shirt, and matching cap. Marks: Effanbee/Patsy 1986, on head; Effanbee, on body.

Plate 468: Effanbee. "Baby Grumpy." Made exclusively for Shirley's Dollhouse 1988–1989, limited to 1,500 pieces. 16" tall. Vinyl head, painted eyes, molded painted hair, closed mouth, vinyl arms, cloth body and legs. All original in yellow and white striped rompers with matching hat. Marks: 176 BABY GRUMPY LE/c1915, 1988 Effanbee Doll Co./New York, N.Y. 10010, on head.

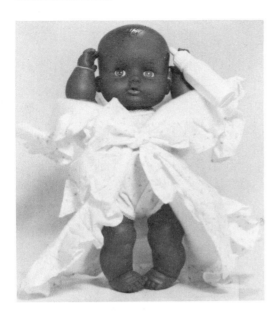

Plate 469: Effanbee. "Butterball." 12" tall. Vinyl head, molded hair, brown sleeping eyes, nursing mouth, jointed vinyl baby body. All original in white rosebud romper suit with white blanket trimmed in rosebud print. Marks: cEFFANBEE/ 1969/6569, on head.

Plate 470: Effanbee. "Dydee." 18" tall. Vinyl head, nursing mouth, dark brown rooted hair, brown sleeping eyes, jointed vinyl baby body. Marks: cEFFANBEE/56/71, on head. All original in white rosebud print sleepers. Doll is carrying a bear by Russ named "Bashful."

Plate 471: Effanbee. "Baby to Love." 14" tall. Vinyl head, sleeping brown eyes, molded hair, closed mouth, vinyl arms and legs, brown cloth body. All original in white cotton rosebud print dress, bonnet, and booties. Marks: 41460/c1988 EFFANBEE DOLL CO./NEW YORK, N.Y., on head. Courtesy of Marge Betts.

Plate 472: Ertl. "Tanya" and her Teeter Rockin' Totter from the Playground Kids. 7" tall. Vinyl head with closed mouth, rooted long dark brown hair, pulled up on top of her head. All original sewn-on purple shirt and gray print shorts, pink tights, and removable yellow print smock. Marks: 3/c1990 TCFC, on head.

Plate 473: Ertl. "Carrie" and her On-the-Go Cart from Playground Kids. 7", c1990. Vinyl head, painted features, rooted dark brown hair, vinyl hands, poseable cloth body. All original in sewn-on red and blue dress with removable blue vest. Those Characters From Cleveland, Inc. Marks: 2/c1990 TCFC, on head.

Plate 474: Ertl. "Amanda" and her Silly Spring Thing from the Playground Kids. 7" tall. All original in bright pink sewn-on shirt, green sewn-on tights, removable green skirt. Vinyl head and hands, open/closed mouth with painted teeth, rooted dark brown hair. Comes with her Silly Spring Thing. Marks: 4/c1990 TCFC, on head.

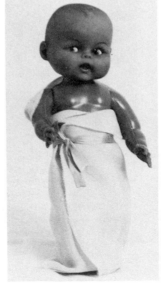

Plate 475: Eugene. Drink and wet baby, 10" tall. 1970's. Vinyl head, painted eyes; molded, painted hair; nursing mouth; jointed vinyl body. All original. Marks: LORRIE DOLL/1971 17/MADE IN TAIWAN, head. MADE IN TAIWAN, body.

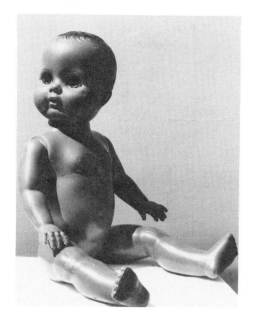

Plate 476: Eugene. "Baby Sister," 8" doll in her carrier. Soft vinyl head, painted features, rooted black hair; hard vinyl body and movable jointed limbs. Marks: Made in Taiwan, on back. 1976.

Plate 477: Eugene Doll Co. "Sweet Lorrie." 20" tall. Molded, painted black hair; brown sleep eyes; open mouth, nurser; dimples at the corners of her eyes. Vinyl head; hard plastic body and limbs. Doll was originally dressed in a pink sleeper, socks, and was wrapped in a pink blanket. Unmarked. Courtesy of Phyllis Houston.

Plate 478: Eugene. "Pastel Miss." 23" tall. Vinyl head, rooted bobbed black synthetic hair, brown sleeping eyes, closed mouth, dimples in both cheeks, hard plastic body and limbs. Redressed. Marks: LORRIE DOLL/19c64, on head.

Plate 479: Eugene. All vinyl fully jointed 24" doll. Sleeping brown eyes, rooted long black hair. Marks: E7020/Made in Taiwan/Eugene Doll/1977/53. Redressed.

Plate 480: Eugene. "Growing Hair Girl," 11½" hairstyling doll. Hair grows with a simple tug and retracts easily. All original with vinyl head, painted features, rooted long black hair; soft vinyl arms and body, hard vinyl legs. Marks: cEugene Dolls/China, on head. Style No. 43125. Copyright 1988.

Plate 481: Eugene. "Twinkle Toes," 13" prima ballerina. Vinyl head, brown sleeping eyes, rooted black hair, hard plastic jointed body. All original in white trimmed in lavender. Doll was available in white costumes with various colored trims. Marks: China, on back. 1990.

Plate 482: Eugene. Walking doll, 24". Vinyl head, brown sleeping eyes with solid lashes, black rooted hair; hard plastic jointed body. Redressed. Marks: E7020/MADE IN TAIWAN/EUGENE DOLL/1977/67, on head.

Plate 483: Eugene. "My Christmas Baby," 17". Vinyl head, sleeping brown eyes, rooted black hair, cloth body, vinyl arms and legs. All original in white satiny dress trimmed in red. Marks: 1987 Eugene Doll Co., on head. Made in China for the Eugene Doll Co., tag sewn to body.

Plate 484: Eugene. "My Christmas Baby," 13" smaller version of previous Christmas baby by Eugene. Vinyl head with dark sleeping eyes and rooted, curly black hair. All original in green corduroy dress with My Christmas Baby written in front. Doll is also available in red dress. The marks are the same as those on previous Christmas Baby.

Plate 485: Eugene. "Campbell Kids," 17". c1984 Campbell Soup Co. Vinyl head, arms, legs, painted eyes, molded painted black hair, cloth bodies. Girl is all original in yellow cotton print dress, white bloomers; boy is all original in rompers with blue bottoms, white top and red ribbon suspenders. Marks on boy: #96-61782/Campbell Soup Co./c1984. Marks on girl: Campbell Soup Co./c1984 #96-61781.

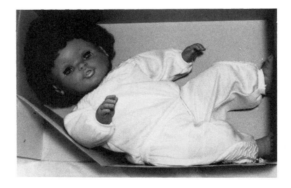

Plate 486: Famosa. "Nitey-Nite Baby," 21" baby. Vinyl head, sleeping brown eyes, rooted brown hair, open/closed mouth; vinyl arms and legs, cloth body. All original in yellow sleeper trimmed in white. Marks: FAMOSA/MADE IN SPAIN, on head. Dolls are distributed in the U.S. by International Bon Ton Toys Inc. 1989.

Plate 487: Eugene. "Neat Teen," life-size walking doll, 32" tall. All original. Vinyl head with sleeping dark brown eyes, rooted black curly hair. Five-piece jointed vinyl body. Marks: 10/Eugene Doll Co./1974/Made in China, on head. Purchased new in 1990.

Plate 488: Famosa. "Nitey-Nite Baby Bubbles," 16" anatomically correct baby boy. After you feed him from bottle, he gurgles little bubbles when you squeeze his left hand. Vinyl head, molded painted hair, stationary glassine eyes, nursing mouth, jointed vinyl baby body. All original in white flannel bib and diapers trimmed in blue. Marks: FAMOSA/MADE IN SPAIN, on head. On the market in 1990.

Plate 489: Famosa. 19" baby girl made in Spain. Vinyl head, arms, and legs; cloth body. Sleeping dark brown eyes, rooted dark brown hair, open/closed mouth. All original in red and white striped dress with white printed bodice. Created and designed exclusively for Formosa by A.d'Angulo. Marks: FAMOSA/MADE IN SPAIN. Courtesy of Xzena Moore of the Cubby Hole.

Plate 490: Fisher Price. "Baby Soft Sounds," 17" baby doll with a motion sensitive electronic "voice box," removable from her zippered body. The battery operated voice box makes a whole range of happy baby sounds as you play with the baby. Doll has vinyl head, arms, and legs with painted features, curly black rooted hair and pink and white cloth body. Pink part of body is unremovable underpants. Marks: 27351/Fisher Price Toys/1979.

Plate 491: Fisher Price. "Nicky," cheerleader from the My Friend series. 16½" tall. Vinyl head, arms and legs, printed cloth body, painted eyes, rooted black hair, closed mouth. All original in blue and white cheerleading outfit. Marks: 14/23088/FISHER-PRICE TOYS/C1978, on head.

Plate 492: Fisher Price. "Sara," 5", from the Smooshers collection. All cloth, painted-on clothing and features, comes with sweatshirt and shopping bag. Marks: 1987 FISHER PRICE/DIVISION OF THE QUAKER OATS CO., tag sewn to body.

Dolls marked 14R are a collection of glamour dolls made between 1957 and 1965. It is not a company mark. Dolls marked 14R were sold undressed to a variety of companies who then dressed and marketed them. Companies known to have used the 14R doll were Belle, Deluxe Reading, Eegee, Natural, Rita Lee, Royal and Sayco. In some cases, other marks were added to the 14R. An example of this is the doll marked 14R-1. Some dolls with this mark are known to have been made by Eegee.

Right – Plate 494: "14R" Lady doll 19½" tall. 1950's. Vinyl head, rooted synthetic dark brown hair, sleeping brown eyes, closed mouth; hard vinyl well-made jointed body, high heels. Redressed. Marks: 14R, on head.

Plate 493: Fisher Price. "Billie." 10" tall. Vinyl head, painted features, rooted black hair, cloth body and limbs. All original in white print dress, only the skirt portion is removable. Legs and body are bright orange. Marks: 225871/FISHER-PRICE-TOYS/ 19c78, on head.

Plate 495: "14R.". Similar to the previous doll except doll is 18½" tall, hair is black synthetic and doll is a slightly lighter shade of brown. Details like molded fingers and toes and slightly dimpled knees are identical to previous doll. Redressed. Marks: 14R-1, on head; V20, on body.

Plate 496: 24" high-heeled lady doll. Vinyl head, rooted long black synthetic hair, sleeping brown eyes, closed mouth, jointed vinyl lady's body. All original in blue nylon dress trimmed in black with white lining/slip. Shoes are missing. Although slightly taller, doll looks similar to those marked 14R. Doll is unmarked. Courtesy of Cheryl Larry Perkins.

Plate 497: 14R 19½" high heel fashion doll. Vinyl head and body, hard vinyl arms and legs, long brown frosted silky hair with bangs, brown sleep eyes, closed mouth, pierced ears with earrings. Doll is very well made. 1950–1960. Redressed in hand crocheted dress. Marks: 14R, on head.

Plate 498: 14R. "Bride," 19½" tall. Vinyl head, rooted reddish brown short hair, sleeping brown eyes, pierced ears, closed mouth, hard vinyl jointed body with high heel feet. All original in white lace bridal gown. Marks: 14R, on head. Late 1950's, early 1960's.

Plate 499: Fun World. "Lullaby Luv," 7½" baby in a cradle. Soft vinyl head, painted features, rooted black hair; hard vinyl jointed bent leg baby body. Wet and drink doll. All original. Marks: Hong Kong, on head; Made in Hong Kong, on body. Stock No. 9620. 1976.

Plate 500: Fun World, Inc. "Soul Sister." 8" tall. Fully jointed vinyl doll, rooted hair, painted features. All original. 1960's. Courtesy of Donna Cochran.

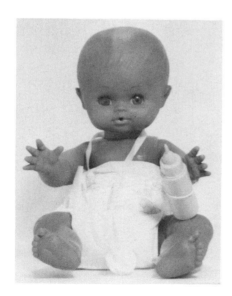

Plate 501: Furga. "Baby Bimbo," 16½" anatomically correct drinking and wetting baby boy. Vinyl head, sleeping brown eyes, nursing mouth with pacifier, jointed vinyl baby body. Doll came wearing only a diaper. Made in Italy. Marks: (logo) Furga/Italy/20340, on head; 10256/(logo)Furga/Italy, on body.

Plate 502: Furga. "Florence," 30" tall, from the Furga Boutique collection. Vinyl head, stationary brown glassine eyes, rooted long full curly black hair, closed mouth, vinyl arms and legs, cloth body. All original in yellow sweatshirt, yellow corduroy pants and red print overblouse. Marks: FURGA/ITALY, on head. Available 1990–91.

Plate 503: Furga. Florence in another all original outfit. Fuchsia print long overblouse, fuchsia synthetic pants, yellow knit shirt, yellow tennis shoes.

Plate 504: Furga. "Maggie," 24", from the Furga Vogue collection. Vinyl head, stationary brown plastic eyes, open mouth with two painted teeth, rooted long black curly hair, pierced ears with earrings, vinyl arms and legs, cloth body. All original in red velvet and white cotton print dress. Marks: FURGA/ITALY/603, on head. Available 1990–91.

Plate 505: Furga. "Just Born Boy and Girl," anatomically correct, vinyl heads, jointed vinyl bodies, rooted black hair, open/closed mouth, stationary black eyes. Girl has pierced ears with stud earrings. Marks on girl: FURGA ITALY/474/c1988, on head; FURGA/ITALY/459, on body. Marks on boy: FURGA ITALY/474/c1988, on head; FURGA/ITALY/458, on body.

Plate 506: Galoob. "Mr. T" action figure as B.A. Baracus, Bad Attitude, from the "A-Team" TV series. 6½" tall. Fully jointed, molded-on clothing. Marks: 1983 Cannell Prod./All Rights Reserved.

Plate 508: Galoob. "Talking Mr. T." c1983. Doll looks like previous Mr. T doll except for different clothing and jewelry. Four messages are given in Mr. T's voice: "Always listen to your parents," "Study hard in school," "I pity the poor fool," "Ralph, you're crazy." All original in blue jeans vest and black cotton pants.

Plate 507: Galoob. "Mr. T," 12" action figure of the "A-Team" star, dressed as B.A. Baracus (Bad Attitude). All vinyl, fully jointed and poseable, dressed in jeans, red shirt, and jewelry with molded, painted hair and features. Marks: c1983 CANNELL PROD./ALL RIGHTS RESERVED/MADE IN HONG KONG, on back.

Plate 509: Galoob. "Lieutenant Geordi La Forge," 3½" action figure from "Star Trek, The Next Generation." Role was played by actor LaVar Burton. Poseable hard plastic, painted features. Marks: c1988 P.P.C/MADE IN CHINA, on back.

Plate 510: Galoob. "Lieutenant Worf," 4" figure from "Star Trek, The Next Generation." Poseable hard plastic. Role of Worf was played by actor Michael Dorn. Marks: c1988 P.P.C./MADE IN CHINA, on body.

Plate 511: Galoob. "Princess Ruby," 8" doll from the Bouncin' Princess series. Vinyl head, painted eyes with pink around the pupil, long rooted dark brown hair, painted open mouth with smiling teeth, vinyl jointed body. All original in pink gown with white lace overlay, pink tiara that lights up. Batteries required. Marks: 1989 L.G.T.I. on head.

Plate 512: Galoob. "Princess Amethyst." 8" tall. Jointed vinyl doll, painted eyes with lavender around the pupils, closed mouth, rooted black hair. All original in lavender gown and pale lavender tiara. Marks: c1989 L.G.T.I., on head.

Plate 513: Galoob. "Princess Pearl." Jointed vinyl doll, painted eyes with aqua around the pupils, rooted black hair, closed mouth. All original in white gown with white tiara. Marks: 1989 L.G.T.I., on head.

Plate 514: Galoob. "Princess Sapphire" in blue dress and tiara. Painted eyes with blue around the pupils, painted open mouth with smiling teeth, rooted black hair. Marks: 1989 L.G.T.I., on head.

Plate 515: Galoob Toys, Inc. "Cyclin Kid," 7½" doll from the Bouncin' Kids series, the dolls that really move. Battery required, comes with her tricycle. Vinyl head, painted features, including freckles; rooted black hair; hard vinyl jointed body. Marks: 1988 L.G.T.I., on head. 1988 L.G.T.I./CHINA, on body.

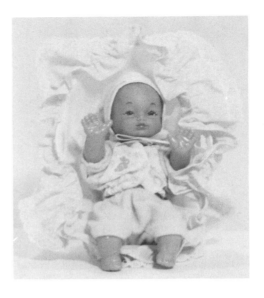

Plate 518: Galoob. "Bouncin' Babies Crawlin' Baby," 6½". Tilt her head and she crawls and wriggles like a baby. Includes carry basket. All vinyl, painted features, molded painted hair. Battery operated. Marks: 1988/LGTI, on body.

Plate 516: Galoob. "Tumblin' Kid" and her parallel bars, from the Bouncin' Kids series. 7" tall. Vinyl head, painted brown eyes, open mouth with painted teeth, rooted black hair, hard plastic body and limbs. All original in aqua and purple jumpsuit. Battery operated. Marks: c1988 L.G.T.I. CHINA, on body.

Plate 517: Galoob. "Skatin' Kid" and her beach chair from the Bouncin' Kids series. 7½" tall. Vinyl head, painted brown eyes, rooted brown hair, closed mouth, jointed hard plastic body and limbs. All original in white sweatshirt, fuchsia pants and aqua roller-skates. Battery operates. Marks: c1988 L.G.T.I./ CHINA, on body.

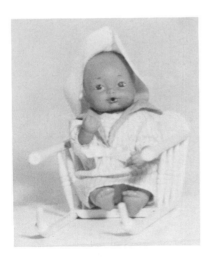

Plate 519: Galoob. "Bouncin' Babies Roll Over Baby." 6½". Turn her on her side and she rolls over like a real baby. All original in white with aqua stripes nightie and cap. Doll comes with a portable chair. Vinyl head, nursing mouth, molded hair, painted eyes; hard plastic body. Marks: c1988 LEWIS GALOOB TOYS, INC./ MADE IN CHINA, on tag sewn to unremovable undies.

Plate 520: Galoob. "Bouncin' Babies Bouncin' Twins." All original with pink stroller for two. One doll is the playful baby and wiggles and kicks, the other is the cuddly baby and cuddles and snuggles. Batteries required. One doll is dressed in pink print trimmed with aqua print, the other in aqua print trimmed with pink print. Marks: c1989 LEWIS GALOOB TOYS, INC./MADE IN CHINA, on tag sewn to unremovable undies.

Plate 521: Galoob. "Bouncin' Kids Ballerina," 7½". No batteries required, mechanism at the top of her head works like an old-fashioned spinning top. When one ballet toe is pointed downward, the doll spins on her toes. Hard vinyl head and body, painted features and dark brown rooted hair. All original in lavender and pink, comes with mirror/ballet bar. Marks: 1988 LGTI, on head; 1988 LGTI/China, on back.

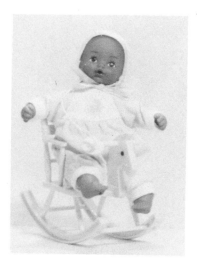

Plate 522: Galoob. "Bouncin' Babies Cuddly Baby." 6½". She cuddles and snuggles and comes with a pink rocking horse. All original in pink and white rompers with matching hat. Vinyl head, arms, and legs; white cloth body with battery case inside. Doll is battery operated. Open nursing mouth with pacifier attached to body, painted brown eyes, painted hair. Marks: c1988 LEWIS GALOOB TOYS, INC./MADE IN CHINA, on tag sewn to body.

Plate 523: Galoob. "So Playful Penny," #3209. c1990. From the Baby Face collection, each with a special expression. 13" tall. Vinyl head, open mouth, painted upper teeth and molded, painted tongue showing; stationary brown eyes with lashes; rooted dark brown hair; fully jointed, even knees and elbows, body. All original in lavender, pink, and orange two-piece outfit with matching cap. Her "magic heart" message is "I love playing with you." Marks: c1990 L.G.T.I./#10 CHINA, on head; c1990 L.G.T.I./CHINA, on body.

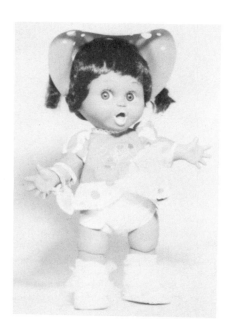

Plate 524: Galoob. "So Surprised Suzie" from the Baby Face collection. Vinyl head, open mouth with two lower teeth, eyes looking to the right. All original in red top trimmed with dots and stripes, matching vinyl visor and white vinyl diapers. Marks: c1990 L.G.T.I./#2 CHINA, on head. Her secret message is "Surprise—I Love You."

Plate 525: Galoob. "So Funny Natalie" from the Baby Face collection. Vinyl head with open mouth, four upper teeth, six lower teeth, stationary brown eyes looking straight. All original in two-piece green outfit with fuchsia dots and trim, fuchsia shoes and white socks, matching visor. Secret message is "We Always Have Fun Together." Marks: c1990 L.G.T.I./#5 CHINA, on head.

Plate 526: Galoob. "So Delightful Dee Dee" from the Baby Face collection. Vinyl face with tongue sticking out. All original in pink and yellow two-piece short outfit with white diapers, yellow cowboy boots, white socks and pink hat. Top of dress has "cool" printed on front. Marks: c1990 L.G.T.I./#8 CHINA, on head.

Plate 527: Galoob. "So Shy Sherri" from the Baby Face collection. Vinyl head, body and jointed limbs; stationary brown eyes; closed mouth; rooted dark brown hair. All original in pink and lavender print dress with lavender boots. Marks: c1990 L.G.T.I./#9 CHINA, on head; c1990 L.G.T.I./China, on body.

Plate 528: Galoob. "So Small Babies," 2½". C.1989. Cloth doll with vinyl face and sewn-on clothing. Doll comes with bed and playhouse.

Plate 529: Gambina. "Marie Laveau,' 14" historical doll. Vinyl head with painted features, brown rooted hair. Authentically dressed. doll is unmarked. Hang-tag gives an 8-page biographical sketch of the life of Marie Laveau, a New Orleans Voodoo Queen who lived from 1794–1881. Doll also comes with a wooden name plaque.

Plate 530: Gambina. "Natalie," 11", pioneer. Vinyl head, brown sleeping eyes, rooted black hair, jointed vinyl body. All original in outfit typical of the early pioneers who settled the West and Midwest, red print dress with matching cap and yellow apron, both trimmed in ecru lace. Marks: Gambina Doll, on head. Purchased new in 1990.

Plate 531: Gambina. "April," 14". Vinyl head, painted features, rooted dark brown hair, vinyl jointed lady body. Doll has definite ethnic facial features. All original in black velvet and pink chiffon dress with jewelry. Doll #641. Doll is also available in several different outfits, each doll still named April. Marks: Tanline Products, on head. Although doll is marked tanline, it was purchased from Gambina, has a Gambina tag hanging from clothing and is shown in Gambina catalog No. 4.

Plate 532: Gambina. "Jo Anne" 16" southern belle. Vinyl head, sleeping brown eyes, rooted black hair, jointed vinyl body. All original in blue organdy dress trimmed in white lace with matching hat and pantaloons. This type of doll usually adorns a bed. Doll is unmarked.

Plate 533: Gatabox. "Toys 'R' Us Kids," 16" vinyl head doll with rooted brown yarn hair, painted features, cloth body. All original. Marks: 1983 GATA BOX LTD, on head.

Plate 534: Gatabox. "Frosty Spice," 5", from the Cooky Box series. Fully bendable, all vinyl flat doll that smells like real ginger. Painted features, sewn-on black yarn hair, removable clothes, sewn-on bakers hat. All original. Marks: c1981/ INTRA ENTERPRISES/MADE IN HONG KONG, on body.

Plate 535: "Gerber Baby," 12" baby with flirty dark brown eyes. All original. Vinyl with molded hair, one-piece body. Gerber baby came with his own bathtub, towel, and accessories. Doll came dressed in white and pink or white and blue with matching bathtub. Marks: GERBER PRODUCTS CO./1985, on head.

Plate 536: "Gerber Baby," all original 15" baby with brown sleeping eyes. Head, arms and legs are vinyl with brown cloth body. Doll is dressed in white nightgown. Marks: 1989 Gerber Products Co./"All Rights Reserved," on head. Body and clothes have sewn-on tag from manufacturer, Lucky Industrial Company. Doll was made in China.

Plate 537: Atlanta Novelty, Sub. of Gerber Products Company. "Gerber Baby Doll," 12" tall. Vinyl head with brown flirty eyes, open/closed mouth, one-piece vinyl body. Doll came with plastic feeding dish, bottle warmer and stuffed teddy bear. All original in white knit baby suit trimmed in pink. Marks: GERBER PRODUCTS CO./1985, on head.

145

Left – Plate 538: Atlanta Novelty. "Gerber Baby," 12". Vinyl head, brown gravity controlled rolling eyes, open nursing mouth, painted hair, vinyl arms and legs, cloth body. All original in white printed flannel sleepers in its own natural straw basket with cardboard suitcase, boxes of cereal, feeding dish, Oneida spoon, pink rubber mouse toy, baby bottle, pink bottle warmer, baby lotion, shampoo, eyelet trimmed baby pillow and complete set of clothing, including a white print dress and booties. Marks: GERBER PRODUCTS CO./c1981, on head.

Right – Plate 539: Golden Doll Co. "Cindy." 19" tall. Vinyl head, rooted black hair, closed mouth, sleep eyes with heavy eye makeup, jointed vinyl body. All original. 1970's. Marks: 27 EYE/NEW/SM/AE 2/P.M. SALES INC./c1966, on head.

History of Huggy Bean Dolls

Huggy Bean was introduced in 1985 and is the trademark of Golden Ribbon Playthings, Inc. The company is 100% black owned with Yvonne C. Rubie as president. The company prides itself on being the leader in establishing and promoting correct images of and for the black child. According to their quarterly magazine *Huggy Bean Up-Date*, January/February 1991, Volume 1, Number 1, the following is a complete list of their outstanding achievements and history from their beginning in 1985 to 1991:

First black character doll to be mass-produced, and having her own story line.

Gained distribution through major accounts across the nation.

Scored 85% sell-through during her first Christmas season, and has maintained that record.

Passed all product safety standard tests.

Coverage by over 500 magazines and newspapers across the country in the first year.

Successful introduction of Oni Bean and Hispanic Friends, Pepita and Carlos.

Scored among the top ten safest, most played with toys in the CBS-TV Annual Toy Test (3,500 toys from leading toymakers were entered).

Licensed Huggy Bean sleepwear and active wear.

Successfully introduced the play *Huggy Bean & the Origins of Her Magic Kente Cloth.* These live performances were seen and enjoyed by children of all ages in schools and community centers in the New York Tri-State area.

Regular participant in the Macy's Thanksgiving Day Parade in New York.

Recognized by leading educators, child psychologists, kids, parents, and media, as "A positive image product line of and for the black child."

Signed and successfully executed a 20 city multimedia promotional tie-in with Kraft.

Regular participant in effective cooperative print media advertisements with retailers.

Successful introduction of the Huggy Bean Family collectibles.

Successful introduction of the Huggy Bean Radio Show – half hour family program – hosted by Huggy Bean.

Huggy Bean Family of dolls selected as the symbolic Kwanzaa Family by the New York Urban Coalition.

Successful introduction of the educational entertainment audio and video cassette series.

Successful introduction of the new 17" Super Style Huggy Doll, with fully combable hair.

Following are photographs and descriptions of the dolls in the Huggy Bean Family marketed from 1985 to 1991.

Plate 540: Golden Ribbon Playthings. Current product line shot of "Huggy Bean" collection. New for 1991, among many items, are the "Kulture Kids," a collection of 12" dolls designed to reflect the positive impact of cultural awareness in kids. Also new is a "Super Style Huggy" with combable, synthetic hair; and three videos for children of all ages starring Huggy Bean. Photograph courtesy of Golden Ribbon Playthings Inc.

Plate 541: Golden Ribbon Playthings. "Super Style Huggy," 17" doll from the Huggy Bean collection. All original with clothes from the Kente collection. Vinyl head, painted features, rooted brown hair; vinyl limbs, brown cloth body. Marks: Golden Ribbon Playthings/1984 HG-1084, on head; Huggy Bean/1984 Golden Ribbon Playthings Inc., tag sewn to body. Box marked No. 47110, 1990.

Plate 542: Golden Ribbon Playthings. "Huggy Bean," 17" doll from the Huggy Bean Doll Family collectibles. Vinyl head, painted features, rooted brown yarn hair; vinyl arms and legs, brown cloth body. All original. Marks: Golden Ribbon Playthings/1984 HB 1084, on head; Huggy Bean/1984 Golden Ribbon Playthings, tag on body. Box marked 1985. Made in Taiwan. Other members of the Huggy Bean Family are Oni Bean, Huggy's best friend; Femi Bean, a second cousin; Mama Bean; Papa Bean; Baby Bean; Kofi Bean, big brother; Damali; Mama Maria; Pepita and Carlos.

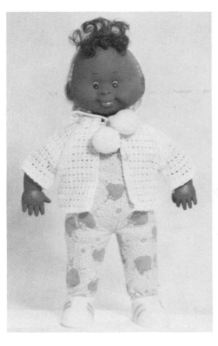

Plate 543: Golden Ribbon. "Oni Bean," 17" doll from the Huggy Bean Doll Family collectibles. Vinyl head, painted features, short rooted yarn loops for hair; vinyl arms and legs, brown cloth body. All original. Marks: same as for Huggy Bean.

Plate 544: Golden Ribbon. "Papa Bean," 12" doll from the Huggy Bean Doll Family collectibles. Vinyl head, painted features, rooted yarn loop hair; vinyl arms and legs, cloth body. All original. Marks: 1985 Golden Ribbon Playthings Inc./Made in China, tag sewn to body. Tag is also printed in Spanish.

Plate 545: Golden Ribbon. "Baby Bean," 12" baby from the Huggy Bean Doll Family collectibles. Vinyl head with painted features, tuff of rooted synthetic hair, vinyl arms and legs, brown cloth body. All original. Marks: same as Papa Bean.

Plate 546: Golden Ribbon. "Kofi," 12" Huggy Bean Doll Family collectible. Vinyl head, painted features, short yarn hair without loops, vinyl arms and legs, white cloth body. All original. Marks: same as Papa Bean.

Plate 547: Golden Ribbon. "Carlos," 12" doll from Huggy Bean Doll Family collectibles. Vinyl head, painted features, rooted looped yarn hair; vinyl arms and legs, white cloth body. All original. Marks: 1985 Golden Ribbon Playthings, Inc./Made in China, tag sewn to body.

Plate 548: Golden Ribbon. 12" member of the Huggy Bean Family collectibles. Vinyl head, painted features, rooted brown yarn hair in two ponytails, vinyl arms and legs, cloth body. All original in blue overalls and yellow shirt trimmed in orange. Marks: Golden Ribbon Playthings/Made in China, on tag sewn to body. Copyright 1985, on box.

Plate 550: Gotz. "Joy," 18" "Black Fanouche" from the collection Fanouche and Her Friends designed by Sylvia Natterer. All original. Soft vinyl with painted features, natural-looking and feeling black rooted hair. Body is poseable vinyl. Doll is not only a beautiful collectors doll, but is well made to withstand lots of play in children's hands. The design of this doll and all of Natterer's dolls shows doll designer Sasha Morgenthaler's influence on Natterer's dolls. Morgenthaler's dolls are listed under Sasha. Joy was made in West Germany. Marks: Gotz/737/SN (superimposed together), signet of the artist.

Plate 549: Golden Ribbon. "Mama Bean," 10" according to the Huggy Bean Legend, keeper of the secret of the Magical Kente Cloth and ticket manager for the Chocolate Forest Airport. Vinyl head, rooted brown yarn hair pulled up in a bun, painted features, vinyl arms and legs, cloth body. All original. Marks: Made in China, tag sewn to body.

Plate 551: Gotz. "Sophie," 25½" from Fanouche and Her Friends, 1990, No. 79863. Vinyl head, handpainted eyes, rooted hair in combination of curls and braids, cloth lower body, vinyl upper body, arms, and legs. All original in white cotton dress. Doll designed by Sylvia Natterer. Marks: Gotz/144/N N, on head; GOTZ, on body.

Plate 552: Gotz. "Cherry" baby doll from the series Fanouche and Her Friends by Sylvia Natterer. Doll is 14" tall. Head, body, arms, and legs are from high-quality vinyl and are fully poseable. The eyes are painted. Cherry has short, curly, rooted black hair that can be combed and washed. All original. Marks: SN (signet of the artist)/Gotz '89, on neck. Doll made in West Germany.

Plate 553: Gotz. 1970's. Vinyl head, sleeping dark brown eyes, long black rooted hair, open/closed mouth, jointed vinyl cry body. All original in white cotton-knit short jumpsuit, long red and white cotton knit print vest, white vinyl boots, belt with gold links. Marks: 16/42/71/Gotz-Puppe, on head.

Plate 554: Gotz. "Soft Baby," 17". Vinyl head, arms and legs, cloth body, sleeping brown eyes, rooted black hair, open/closed mouth. All original in mauve cotton dress with smocking, white lace collar. Marks: GOTZ.PUPPE, on head.

Plate 555: Gotz. 18" toddler doll. Vinyl head, dark brown sleeping eyes, black rooted hair, closed mouth, vinyl arms and legs, brown cloth body. All original in pastel print dress with white cotton bib. Marks: GOTZ PUPPE, on head. Courtesy of Marge Betts.

Plate 556: Gotz. "Cherry," 1990. All original in white cotton dotted two-piece sundress with matching bloomers and white knitted sweater. Marks: SN/Gotz 1989, on neck. Made in West Germany.

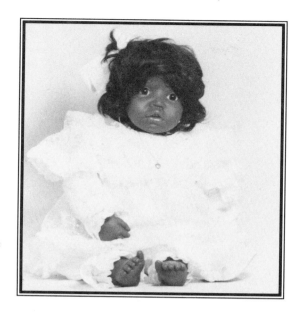

Plate 557: Gotz. "Larene," baby doll designed by Carin Lossnitzer for the Dribble Babies collection. No. 86864. Vinyl head, arms and legs, cloth body, glass crystal eyes, rooted dark brown hair, open mouth. Dressed in white baby outfit with lots of white lace. Doll is marked "Carlos" on the back of the neck which stands for CARin LOSsnitzer and comes with a certificate. Doll is 26" tall. Pictured in Gotz 1990 catalog. Marks: Gotz/CARLOS/90/133, on head.

Plate 558: Gotz. "Aretta," 18", No. 44061. Dressed in red polka dot jumpsuit. 18" tall. Brown sleeping eyes, black rooted hair. Vinyl head, arms, legs, brown cloth body. Marks: Gotz/139-17/(Gotz initials), on head.

Plate 559: H.M.S. Corporation. "Joann," one of the Sunny Valley Kids, 14" tall. Vinyl head, painted features, rooted synthetic dark brown hair; cloth body, including arms, hands, legs, and feet. All original. Marks: cHENRY ORENSTEIN/ HMS, on neck.

Plate 560: Hasbro. "G.I. Joe Adventurer," 11½" tall. All vinyl action figure, flocked hair, painted features, fully articulated body. Marks: G.I. Joe Reg. T.M./RD 1964/Hassenfeld Bros. Inc./Patented 1966.

Plate 561: Hasbro. "GI Joe, Adventurer," 1974. 11½" tall. Soft vinyl head, painted features, flocked black hair, fully jointed vinyl body, hands have Kung-fu grip. Marks: G.I. JOE/Copyright 1964/BY HASBRO/PAT NO. 3277,602/MADE IN U.S.A. Collection of Steven Perkins.

Plate 562: Hasbro. "G.I. Joe Talking Commander." Vinyl action figure with flocked hair, beard, and mustache; painted eyes. Pull string in chest makes the figure talk. Marks: Patent Pending/ G.I. JOE R/COPYRIGHT 1964/BY HAS-BRO R/PAT.NO.3,277,602/MADE IN U.S.A., on back.

Plate 563: Hasbro, "Hanna," one of the four Hugabees, 1976. 9" tall. All cloth; glued-on felt features; black yarn hair; wire in arms allows them to hold three positions. Red cloth sewn-on shoes; removable clothing. Extra accessories and yellow trunk sold separately. Tag sewn on doll: HUGABEE 4514/ 1976 HASBRO INDUSTRIES INC/PAW-TUCKET, RHODE ISLAND/MADE IN HONG KONG...

Plate 564: Hasbro. "Soul" from "The World of Love." Vinyl head; real lashes; rooted black curly hair; painted features; hard vinyl body that turns, twists, and bends. All original. Marks: 5/Hong Kong/HASBRO/U.S. Pat. Pend., on body. Clothing marked: The World of Love. 1970's.

Plate 565: Hasbro. "Leggy Sue" c1973. 10½" high-fashion doll. Vinyl head, rooted short black hair, painted eyes, closed mouth. All original in long yellow knit dress with split up the front and imprinted rose. Doll has extremely long legs. Marks: c1972/HASBRO/ HONG KONG, on body.

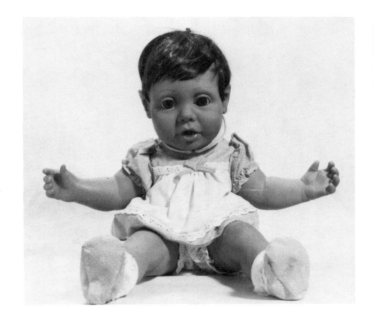

Plate 566: Hasbro. "Real Baby," 20". Vinyl head, stationary brown eyes with eyelashes, open/closed mouth, glued-on brown wig, vinyl arms and legs, cloth body. All original. Marks: 1984 J. Turner/HASBRO IND., on head. Some of the Hasbro "Real Babies" have rooted hair.

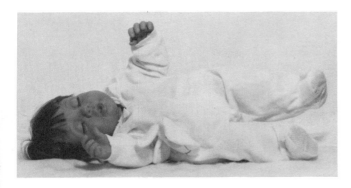

Plate 567: Hasbro. "Sleeping Real Baby," 20". Vinyl head, glued-on brown synthetic wig, sleeping eyes with real lashes, open/closed mouth, vinyl arms and legs, weighted cloth body. All original in white flannel hooded rompers with bunny ears. Marks: c1984 Turner/HASBRO IND MA (MA is very faint), on head. This particular doll is hand signed by the artist, Judith Turner, on the neck.

Plate 568: Hasbro. "Real Baby Newborn," 17". Vinyl head, glued-on brown wig, stationary large brown eyes, real eyelashes, closed mouth, vinyl arms and legs, cloth body. All original in two-piece white print flannel undies and white flannel bonnet. Doll comes with a white and yellow rattle. Marks: c1985 JTurner/HASBRO INC/MADE IN CHINA, on head; c1986 Hasbro, Inc., tag sewn to body.

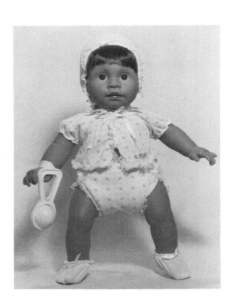

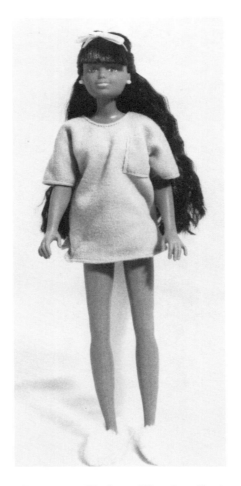

Plate 569: Hasbro. "Kristen," 11½" tall, from the Maxie series. Vinyl head, painted features, rooted long hair, poseable vinyl body. All original in white blouse, denim skirt, white socks, and yellow shoes. Marks: c1987/HASBRO, on head; c1987 HASBRO/ CHINA H-15, on body.

Plate 570: Hasbro. "Slumber Party Simone," 11½" poseable fashion doll. All original. Marks: HASBRO, on head; 1987 HASBRO/CHINA H-15, on body.

Plate 571: Hasbro. "Sun Splash Simone," from the Maxie series, 1989. All original in pink two-piece swimsuit. Marks: c1987/HASBRO, on head; c1987 HASBRO/CHINA H-15, on body.

Plate 572: Hasbro. "Joline," toddler doll from Canneto line #9730. 18" tall. Vinyl head, rooted long black hair, sleeping black eyes with lashes, vinyl arms and legs, soft cloth body. All original. Marks: Hasbro, Inc./Made in Italy, on tag sewn to body. Reverse side of tag: Canneto Dolls/1990 Hasbro, Inc. Pawtucket, RI.

Plate 573: Hasbro. "Dominique," 18" toddler from Canneto line #9730 along with previous doll Joline. Except for hairstyle and dress, identical to Joline.

Plate 574: Hasbro. "Love-A-Bye Baby," 5½" fully jointed vinyl baby doll. Painted features, dark brown rooted hair. All original. Marks: HA, on head; China, on back. 1987.

Plate 575: Hasbro. "CPK Designer Line," girl 17" tall. Vinyl head with rooted fancy yarn hair, open mouth with molded painted teeth, cloth body. All original. Marks: 1978, 1983 O.A.A. INC/19, on head. Copyright 1989.

576: Coleco. "CPK Designer Line" boy, 16". Vinyl head, rooted brown cut yarn hair, dimple in right cheek. All original in multicolored sweatsuit. Marks: MFG. BY COLECO IND. INC., on head. Red signature. 1988.

Plate 577: Hasbro. "CPK Designer Line" girl, vinyl head with dimple in chin, fine crimped brown yarn hair. All original purple print jumpsuit and matching jacket, yellow knit shirt. Marks: 1978, 1982–1988/ OAA INC./MFG. BY COLECO IND. INC., on head. Red signature.

Plate 578: Hasbro. "CPK" boy. 16". Vinyl head, rooted synthetic black straight hair; dimple in right cheek, closed mouth, cloth body. All original in black vinyl jacket trimmed in red, green, and white over green and white striped shirt, gray cotton pants; green and white athletic shoes. Marks: MFG. BY COLECO IND. INC., on head; wrist tag marked Hasbro. Red signature.

Plate 579: Hasbro. "CPK Designer Line," 16". Vinyl head, rooted "cornsilk" hair, eight teeth, painted eyes, cloth body. All original in purple print cotton overalls and matching jacket with yellow knit shirt. Marks: 19, on head (marks above this are under rooted hair). Red signature, Face #19. Copyright 1989, on hang tag.

Plate 580: Hasbro. "CPK Birthday Kids," girl, 16" tall. Vinyl head, rooted fancy yarn hair, open mouth to hold party favor; cloth body. When tummy is pressed, doll makes sounds with the party favor. Marks: First Edition/Copyright 1990/O.A.A. Inc./Manufactured by HASBRO Inc. HB 22 2, on head. Made in China. This doll is named Mahala Cleo. Red signature.

Plate 581: Hasbro. "CPK Birthday Kids," boy with party kazoo. Vinyl head, brown cut yarn hair, short on sides and back, longer on top. All original in mint green cotton pants, green print shirt, and pink striped vest. Marks: First Edition/Copyright 1990/O.A.A. INC./Manufactured by HASBRO Inc. HB20 (1 inside a circle), on head.

Plate 582: Hasbro. "CPK Birthday Kids" girl with dimple in her chin. Vinyl head, brown twisted yarn hair, open mouth for party blower. Marks: First Edition/Copyright 1990/ O.A.A. Inc./Manufactured by HASBRO INC. HB 20, on head.

Plate 583: Hasbro. "CPK Poseable" boy with Weebok CPK shoes and $5.00 certificate for Weebok or Reebok shoes. vinyl head, rooted brown cut yarn hair, smiling mouth. All original. Marks: First Edition/ Copyright 1990/O.A.A./ Manufactured by HASBRO Inc./K 5 2 (has circle around the numeral 2) 19/Made in China, on head.

Plate 584: Hasbro. "CPK Sippin' Babies," 14" long. Vinyl head, tuff of rooted black synthetic hair, painted eyes, cloth body. Baby comes with bottle and bottle holder/bib. Copyright 1989. Marks: Copyright 1978, 1982/ORIGINAL APPALACHIAN ART WORKS INC./9, on head.

Plate 585: Hasbro. "CPK Toddler Kids," 13". Vinyl bald head, cloth body, decal eyes, open mouth with tongue, dimple in right cheek. All original in blue romper suit. Marks: c1978, 1983 O.A.A. INC./12 (embossed) 18, on head. Face #18, deep pink signature. Copyright 1988, 1989, on box and arm tag.

Plate 586: Hasbro. "CPK Toddler Kids," 13". Vinyl head, rooted brown yarn hair, painted features, cloth body. Marks: First Edition/Copyright1990/O.A.A. Inc./Manufactured by HASBRO Inc., on head. Collection of Leanne Johnson.

Plate 587: Hasbro. "CPK Babies," 12". Vinyl head with small tuff of rooted yarn in front, painted eyes, pacifier in mouth; cloth body filled with polypropylene pellets. Marks: 1978, 1982 O.A.A., Inc., on head; HASBRO/Made in China, tag sewn to body. 1990.

Plate 588: Coleco. "Cabbage Patch Babyland Kid," 10". Vinyl face, painted features, sewn-on clothing, including bib. Marks: CABBAGE PATCH BABYLAND KIDS/Copy. 1988, tag sewn to body under bib. Tag sewn to side seam: Xavier Roberts, reverse side, Cabbage Patch Babyland Collection. Collection of Haille Perkins.

Plate 589: Hasbro. "CPK Preemie," 14". Vinyl bald head with dimple in right cheek, open mouth with molded, painted tongue sticking out. All original in lavender bunting with drawstring at bottom. Marks: First Edition/19 Copyright 1990/O.A.A. INC./Manufactured by Hasbro Inc./P13 4 (4 is in a circle).

Plate 590: Hasbro. "CPK Babyland Bunny," 11". All cloth with sewn-on bunny outfit, including ears and tail, with vinyl face. Decal eyes, dimple in right cheek, two upper teeth. Babyland Bunnies came dressed in pink, blue, yellow, and lavender. Marks: Cabbage Patch Kids/cCopyright 1991, ORIGINAL APPALACHIAN/ARTWORKS INC., tag sewn inside mitten on left hand.

Plate 591: Hasbro. "CPK Preschool Kids," girl. 14" tall. Vinyl head, painted eyes, rooted brown fancy yarn hair, cloth body and limbs. All original in animal print rompers and matching pink blouse. Marks: First Edition/Copyright 1990/O.A.A. INC./Manufactured by HASBRO INC./T25 9 (9 is in a circle), on head.

Plate 592: Hasbro. "CPK Preschool Kids," boy. 14" tall. Vinyl head, painted eyes, rooted brown yarn shag hair, cloth body and limbs. All original in animal print pants and matching knit shirt. Marks: First Edition/Copyright 1990/O.A.A. INC./Manufactured by HASBRO INC./T84 (4 is in a circle), on head.

Plate 594: Hasbro. "Cheryl Ann," CPK poseable figurine, 3¾" tall. All vinyl with movable arms, legs, and head; molded, painted hair with two long black yarn ponytails inserted; molded-on clothing. Marks: c1984 O.A.A. on head; 6/c1984/O.A.A. INC., left leg; 2/CHINA, right leg. Copyright 1991, on package.

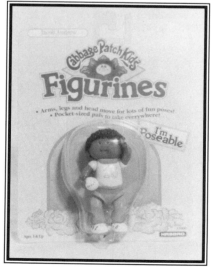

Plate 595: Hasbro. "Jacob Andrew," 3¾". The other black doll in the 1991 collection of CPK figurines. Similar to above doll except that hair is all molded. Marks are the same as those on above doll.

Plate 593: Hasbro. "Tyler," 18", from My Beautiful Doll series. Vinyl doll, long rooted hair, painted eyes, closed mouth. All original ballerina comes with a locket for the child to wear. Marks: 1988 Hasbro Inc/Made in CHINA, on head. Box: 1989 Hasbro Inc., Pawtucket, R.I.

Plate 597: Hasbro. "Steve Urkel" talking doll from TV's "Family Matters." Steve Urkel is played by actor Jaleel White. 17½" tall. Vinyl head, painted eyes, painted smiling mouth, molded black hair, molded-on saddle shoes, vinyl hands, cloth body. Doll is all original in sewn-on shirt and jeans with removable glasses. Tag sewn to body: FAMILY MATTERS/URKEL 9600/FAMILY MATTERS, STEVE URKEL, the FAMILY MATTERS character names, likenesses, slogans, and related indicia are trademarks of Lorimar Television c1991.

Plate 596: Hasbro. "Lindy," 18" tall, from My Beautiful Doll series. All original in an aqua party dress.

Plate 598: Horsman Dolls, Inc. 13" toddler doll. Soft vinyl head, sleeping brown eyes, rooted black hair, open/closed mouth; vinyl arms; hard plastic jointed body and legs. Redressed. Marks: Horsman, on head. 1961.

Plate 600: Horsman Dolls, Inc., "Thirstee Walker," 26" walking doll. Soft vinyl head; sleep eyes; open nursing mouth; rooted black hair; hard plastic jointed body. Redressed. Marks: Horsman Dolls Inc./1964/TB26, on head. body is unmarked. This is an early Thirstee Walker, 1960's. Later Thirstee Walker dolls, on the market in the late 1980's, are marked the same on the head but are marked China on the body. They also are slightly darker in coloring and have dark brown hair instead of black.

Plate 599: Horsman. Vinyl 15" baby doll with brown sleeping eyes, black rooted hair, nursing mouth. Five-piece bent leg vinyl body with movable limbs. Marks: Horsman Dolls Inc./1964/BC161, on head.

Plate 601: Horsman. "Tammy Tears," 1964. 12½" tall. Vinyl doll with open nursing mouth, brown sleep eyes, rooted brown hair. All original in pink flannel dress trimmed in lace. Marks: HORSMAN DOLLS INC./19c64/B144, on head; HORSMAN DOLLS INC., on body.

Plate 602: Horsman. "Thirstee Walker," smaller version of above doll, 21" tall. Vinyl head, sleeping brown eyes, rooted dark brown hair, nursing mouth, jointed walking body. Clothing is said to be original. Marks: HORSMAN DOLLS INC./1969, on head; HORSMAN DOLLS INC., on body.

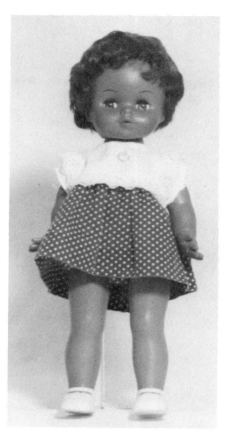

Plate 603: Horsman. 14" tall. Vinyl baby doll, painted eyes looking to the left, nursing mouth, jointed baby body, rooted black hair. Redressed. Marks: 3-5/67152/HORSMAN DOLLS INC./19c67, on head.

Plate 604: Horsman. "Ruthie." 13" tall. Vinyl head, brown sleep eyes, rooted brown hair, closed mouth, five-piece straight leg hard plastic body, vinyl arms with beautifully molded hands. Marks: Horsman Dolls, Inc./1967, on head; Horsman dolls Inc./Pat. Pend., on body. Redressed.

Plate 605: Horsman. "Li'l Softee." All original baby doll. 10½" tall. Vinyl head, arms, and legs; painted features; closed mouth; dark brown rooted synthetic hair; brown cloth body. All original in orange cotton dress with lace. Marks: 29/HORSMAN DOLLS, INC/19c68. An Irene Szor Design.

Plate 607: Horsman. "Softee Baby." 14" tall. Vinyl head, legs, and arms; dark brown rooted hair; painted eyes; open/closed mouth with molded tongue; brown cloth body. All original in yellow polished cotton dress with organdy and lace overlay. Beautifully molded fingers and toes. Marks: 2760 (immediately under rooted hair)/6/HORSMAN DOLL INC./19c68, on head.

Plate 606: Horsman. "Baby," 13". Vinyl head, sleeping brown eyes, rooted dark brown hair, open/closed mouth, vinyl arms and legs, brown cloth body. Marks: 2386/13 EYE/12/HORSMAN DOLLS INC./1968, on head. Courtesy of Cheryl Larry Perkins.

Plate 608: Horsman. "Teachers Pet." 11½" tall. Vinyl head, rooted dark brown hair, painted eyes, closed mouth, vinyl arms, hard plastic body and legs. All original in red dress trimmed in blue, imprinted "Teachers Pet" on front. Doll comes with school play accessories. An Irene Szor design. Marks: 13/HORSMAN DOLLS INC./19c69, on head; HORSMAN DOLLS INC./T11, on body.

Plate 609: Horsman. "Bootsie." 12½" tall. Vinyl head and arms; brown synthetic rooted hair; sleeping brown eyes; closed mouth, hard vinyl legs and body. Marks: 2907/13EYE/T125/10/cHORSMAN DOLLS INC./1969, on head.

Plate 610: Horsman. Baby doll. 18" tall. Vinyl head, arms, and legs; dark brown rooted hair; brown stationary glassine eyes looking to side; painted closed mouth; brown cloth body; redressed. Marks: 16/HORSMAN DOLLS INC./19c70. Collection of Susan Perkins.

Plate 611: Horsman. "Peggy Pen Pal." 18" tall. Vinyl head, painted eyes, dark brown rooted hair; hard plastic body with swivel waist and neck, jointed at shoulders, elbows and hips. Right hand is molded to hold a pencil. Doll came with a table and panograph; both are missing. Marks: HORSMAN DOLLS INC./ 19c70, on head; HORSMAN/ DOLLS/ INC./(c in a circle), on body.

Plate 612: Horsman. "Bye-Lo Baby." 14". Vinyl head and limbs, painted eyes, nursing mouth, molded hair, brown cloth body. Marks: HORS-MAN DOLLS, INC./c1972. An Irene Szor Design. All original in white gown and cap with blue rose-bud print.

Plate 613: Horsman. "Walt Disney's official Mouseketeer." 8½" tall. All vinyl; brown sleep eyes; dark brown rooted hair; painted open/closed mouth, rosy cheeks; jointed body with fat tummy. Marks: HORSMAN DOLLS INC./19c71, head; 12, body.

Plate 614: Horsman. "Bye-Lo Baby," 17" open mouth vinyl head, painted features and hair; vinyl arms and bent legs; brown cloth body. This is a copy of an earlier bisque and composition doll from 1924 by Horsman, also called the Bye-Lo baby. Crying voice mechanism is inside this new version. All original. Bottom of the box doll came in has handles making box a carrying case for doll, resembling a basket. Marks: Si8/HORSMAN DOLLS INC/1980, on head.

Plate 615: Horsman. All vinyl 12" baby with painted eyes; painted, molded hair; hard plastic legs and body; vinyl arms. Redressed. Marks: HORSMAN (the rest is unclear)/19c74, on head.

Plate 616: Horsman. "Happy Baby," a doll that laughs and giggles when tossed or bounced. 16" tall. Battery operated. Vinyl head, painted eyes, rooted dark brown hair, open mouth with two upper teeth, vinyl arms and legs, cloth body with zippered back for batteries. All original in aqua and white flannel pajamas. Marks: 125/HORSMAN DOLLS INC./19c76, on head.

Plate 617: Horsman. "Buttercup," an Irene Szor design. Vinyl head, sleeping amber eyes, rooted brown hair, nursing mouth, jointed vinyl baby body. All original in blue nylon dress trimmed with white lace and matching bonnet. Marks: 3 75/HORSMAN DOLL INC./19c74, on head.

Plate 618: Horsman. "Softee Love." 21" Mama doll. Vinyl head, brown sleeping eyes with lashes, long rooted dark brown hair; vinyl arms and legs, brown cloth body with cry mechanism inside. All original in pink and white. Marks: 3/HORSMAN DOLL/1984/S-22, on head. Box: Made in China 1987/HORSMAN, Division of GATA BOX LTD.

Plate 619: Horsman. "Tynie Sofskin," 12" drinking and wetting baby. Vinyl head, sleeping brown eyes with lashes, rooted brown hair, bent leg baby body. All original in white print gown. Marks: HORSMAN DOLLS INC/1977, on head; 84 2/HORSMAN DOLLS INC/1977, on back. Box marked 1988 HORSMAN–DIVISION OF GATA BOX LTD. Made in China.

Plate 620: Horsman. "Dollhouse Family," 1" equals 1' scale. c1990. Vinyl dolls, painted features. Mother and girl have rooted brown hair; father and boy have painted hair. Removable clothes, fully jointed. 2" to 6" tall. Dad has definite Negroid features.

Plate 621: Ideal. "Tiffany Taylor." All original. Glamorous 19" beauty whose hair color changes from black to red. Vinyl with movable arms, legs, and head; painted features; rooted hair. Extra clothing sold separately, including a "mink" coat. Marks: 1973 Ideal (in logo)/CG-19-h-230/HONG KONG, on head. On body: 1974/IDEAL (in logo)/Hollis, N.Y. 11423/2M-5854-01/1. All original.

Plate 622: Ideal. "Hair Magic Crissy," 18" tall. Vinyl head, painted eyes, rooted black hair, plastic body, vinyl arms. All original in white eyelet camisole and pink satiny skirt. Marks: 1977/IDEAL TOY CORP./M.H.C.-19-H-281/HONG KONG, on head; 1974/IDEAL/HOLLIS N.Y. 11423/2M-5854-01/1, on body.

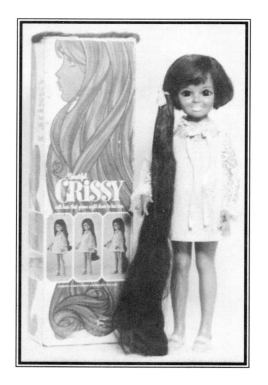

Plate 623: Ideal. "Crissy," with hair that grows right down to her toes, 1969. Vinyl head, jointed vinyl body, black sleep eyes, long black rooted hair, open, smiling mouth. All original in green lace dress, green shoes, and pink ribbon at neck. Marks: c1968/IDEAL TOY CORP./GH-17-129, on head; 1969/IDEAL-TOY-CORP/GH-18/U.S. PAT. #3,162,976, on lower body.

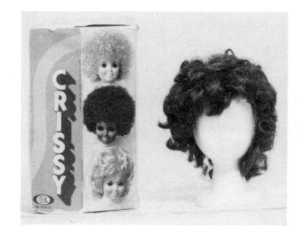

Plate 624: Ideal. "Crissy's Way-out Wig." c1972. Natural styled wig for black Crissy doll, dark brown in color. Included with the wig was a wig stand and styling brush. Natural styled hairdos were very popular in the early 1970's.

Left – Plate 625: Ideal. "Look Around Crissy," 1972. 18" tall. Soft vinyl head and arms, black rooted growing hair, large black sleep eyes, painted open mouth. Hard vinyl body jointed at arms, legs, and waist. When "look around" pull string in back of doll is pulled, upper torso and head of doll gracefully move back and forth. Marks: HONG KONG/1968/IDEAL TOY CORP/GH-17-H129, head; 1972 IDEAL TOY CORP./HONG KONG P./U.S. PAT. NO.3,162,976/OTHER PATENTS PENDING, on body. All original in long green plaid dress and green shoes. Courtesy of Julie P. Scott.

Right – Plate 626: Ideal. "Crissy with Twirly Beads Hairdo Dangle." 18" tall. All original in pink and white checked long dress. Marks: 1968/IDEAL TOY CORP./GH-17-H12/Hong Kong, on head; MADE IN HONG KONG/1969/IDEAL TOY CORP/GH-18, on body.

Plate 627: Ideal. "Swirla Curler Crissy," 1973. All original in red plaid jumper with holly leaf trim on shoulder and red blouse. Curler device came with the doll for curling her hair. Extra outfits were sold separately. Marks: 96/HONG KONG/1968/IDEAL TOY CORP/GH-17-H129, on head; 1969/IDEAL TOY CORP/GH-18/U.S. Pat 3,162,976, on body. Courtesy of Julie P. Scott.

Plate 628: Ideal. "Tara," 1976. 16" tall. This doll from the "Crissy" family was only made in black. Vinyl head and arms, hard plastic body and legs; rooted black grow-hair, black sleeping eyes, closed mouth. All original in yellow and white checkered pant outfit. Marks: IDEAL TOY CORP./H-250/HONG KONG, on head; MADE IN HONG KONG/c1970/IDEAL TOY COR/GH-15/2M 5169-01, on body. Box reads: The AUTHENTIC Black Doll With Hair That Grows.

Plate 629: Ideal. "Country Fashion Growing Hair Crissy," 1982, 15". All original in lavender checked pinafore and white and lavender print long-sleeved blouse with natural straw hat. Although she was sold as a "Crissy" doll, she is made from the earlier Velvet mold. The earlier "Crissy" doll was 18" tall. Marks: 13 EYE/1969/IDEAL TOY CORP./GH-15N-157, on head; 1970/IDEAL TOY COR/GH-15/2M 5169-01, on body. The marks on the head are the same marks as those on the Velvet dolls from the early 1970's. Doll's hair grows by pulling a string in her back. No. 1036-3 Blk.

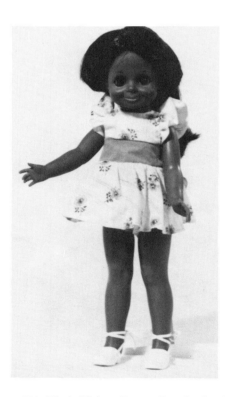

Left – Plate 630: Ideal. "Crissy," 1982 reissue with head and body of Velvet from the early 1970's. Instruction sheet enclosed in original box also gives instructions from growing "Velvet's" hair. 15" tall. All vinyl with long black hair, brown eyes, not black like the earlier Crissy and Velvet dolls, closed mouth. All original in white cotton dress trimmed in pink. Marks: 13 EYE/c1969/IDEAL TOY CORP./GH-15-H-157, on head; 1970/IDEAL TOY CORP./GH-15/2M5169-01, on body.

Right – Plate 631: Ideal. "Velvet." 1981 reissue. Although dressed the same as the previous Crissy made in 1982, there are slight differences. This Velvet has curly hair with bangs, Crissy has straight hair without bangs; this Velvet has amber eyes, Crissy has brown eyes; Velvet has redder coloring in face and body, particularly the arms. Also, Velvet's head and body are marked Hong Kong. This is missing on the Crissy doll. Marks: 13 EYE/c1969/IDEAL TOY CORP./GH-15-H-157/HONG KONG, on head; MADE IN/HONG KONG/c1970/IDEAL TOY COR/GH-15/2M5169-01, on body.

Plate 632: Ideal. "Velvet Beauty Braider." Velvet is a cousin of Crissy. 16" tall. Soft vinyl head and arms, black rooted growing hair, black sleep eyes, painted smile. All original in lavender printed dress, replaced shoes. Marks: 13EYE/c1969/IDEAL TOY CORP/GH-15-H157/Hong Kong, on head; c1970/IDEAL TOY CORP/GH-15/2m5169-01/MADE IN HONG KONG, on body.

Plate 633: Ideal. "Velvet Swirly Daisy," 1974. All original in pink, purple, and green plaid dress with white bodice. Marks: 1969 IDEAL TOY CORP/GH-15-H-157, on head; 1970 IDEAL TOY CORP./GH-15-2M516901, on body.

Plate 634: Ideal. "Movin' Groovin' Velvet," 1970–1971. All original in two-toned drop waisted pink dress with purple bow. Doll has posing waist. Marks: c1969/IDEAL TOY CORP./GH-15-H-157, on head.

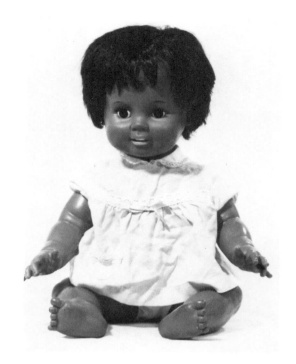

Plate 635: Ideal. "Velvet," 1970–71. All original in lavender brushed corduroy A-line dress with white ribbon at hips and lavender shoes. Marks: 13 EYE/c1969/ IDEAL TOY CORP./GH-15-H-157, on head; c1970/IDEAL TOY CORP/ GH-15/ 2M5169-01, on body.

Plate 636: Ideal. "Cinnamon with Curly Ribbons," 1974. 12". All original in short denim overalls and yellow gingham blouse with navy blue t-strap shoes. Marks: 66/c1971/IDEAL TOY CORP./GH-12-H-188/HONG KONG, on head; c1972/IDEAL TOY CORP./U.S. PAT. PEND/HONG KONG P., on body.

Plate 637: Ideal. Life-size "Baby Crissy." 24" tall. Soft vinyl jointed baby body and head; black stationary glassine eyes with lashes; painted open mouth and teeth; black rooted growing hair. Marks: c1972/IDEAL TOY CORP/GHB-H-225, head; c1973/IDEAL TOY CORP/ GHB/2M5611/6, on body. All original in pink cotton dress with matching panties. Courtesy of Susan E. Perkins.

Plate 638: Ideal. "Baby Crissy," 1980. Identical to previous doll except for clothing and marks on body. All original in white sunsuit trimmed in green gingham. Marks on body: c1973/ IDEAL. TOY. CORP./GHB/2M-5611-01/1. Head has the same marks as previous Baby Crissy.

Plate 639: Ideal. "Tressy," early 1970's. 18" tall. All original. Soft vinyl head and arms; black growing hair; large brown sleep eyes with real painted lashes; painted closed mouth. Hard plastic jointed body. Doll was purchased at Sears. Marks: c1970/IDEAL TOY CORP./SGH-17-H15L/HONG KONG on head; MADE IN/HONG KONG/C1969/IDEAL TOY CORP, on body. Collection of Julie Perkins Scott.

Plate 640: Ideal. "Tressy." 12" fashion doll you can give a permanent to. Vinyl head, black rooted hair, brown sleeping eyes, closed mouth, jointed vinyl body. All original in long dress with blue print skirt and pink gingham bodice. Marks: c1982/IDEAL-TOY-CORP./H373, on head; IDEAL (in oval)/c1982 Gabriel Ind./a division of CBS Inc.

Plate 641: Ideal. "Me So Glad," Belly Button Baby. 9" tall. Soft vinyl head, arms, and legs; rooted black hair; painted features; hard plastic body; pushbutton in stomach makes head, arms and legs move in amusing positions. Marks: 1970/IDEAL TOY CORP. E9-2-H165/HONG KONG, on head; IDEAL TOY CORP./HONG KONG/ 2A-0156, on body.

Plate 642: Ideal. "Jody," Party Formal. 9" tall. Jody is an old-fashioned doll in times-gone-by outfit. Vinyl doll with painted features; poseable legs and arms; long black rooted hair. All original. Marks: 1974/G-H/241, head; c1975 IDEAL (in logo)/HONG KONG, body.

Plate 643: Ideal. "Jody" in Gibson Girl outfit.

Plate 644: Ideal. "Fashion Flatsy." 5" tall. Flat (½") flexible vinyl doll. Long black rooted hair; painted features. Marks: IDEAL (in logo) c1969/PAT. PEND/ HONG KONG. Collection of Julie Perkins Scott.

Plate 645: Ideal. "Jody" in Country Calico outfit.

Plate 646: Ideal. "Trixy Flatsy." The doll is the same as Flatsy doll on page 166, but came with a real bicycle in different packaging.

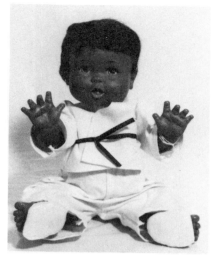

Plate 647: Ideal. "Rub-A-Dub Dolly," 16" chubby vinyl baby. Painted eyes, short rooted black hair, open/closed mouth, jointed vinyl baby body. Redressed. Marks: c1973/IDEAL TOY CORP./RAD-16-H-233, on head; c1973/ IDEAL TOY CORP./HOLLIS N.Y. 11423/R.A.D. 17/2M-5852-01/2, on body. Courtesy of Susan Perkins.

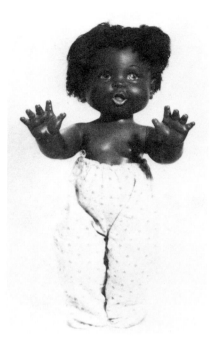

Plate 648: Ideal. "Rub-A-Dub Dolly." 16½". Vinyl head, black rooted hair, painted eyes, open/closed mouth with tongue, jointed bent leg baby body. Marks: 1973/IDEAL TOY CORP./HOL- LIS N.Y. 11423/R.A.D. 17/2M-5852- 01/3, on body. The last line of marks on this body is different from previous Rub-A-Dub Dolly. Courtesy of Cheryl Larry Perkins.

Plate 649: Tyco. "Tropical Rub-A-Dub Dolly." c1990. Except for clothing and accessories, identical to the follow- ing doll. All original in one-piece pink and yellow swimsuit.

Plate 650: Tyco. "Rub-A-Dub Dolly," 16". All vinyl, rooted hair, painted eyes, open/closed mouth, stationary black eyes with lashes. 16" tall. All original in pink and white terry cloth and flannel sunsuit and yellow plastic shoes. Marks: RUB-A- DUB DOLLY/c1989 Ideal Subsidiary Tyco Toys/Made in China, on head.

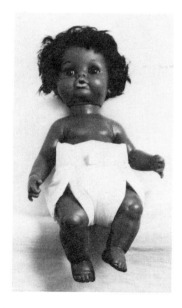

Plate 651: Ideal. "Tiny Tears with Rock-A-Bye Eyes," 1973, 13" tall with vinyl head, rooted black hair, black eyes that close as you rock her to sleep; one-piece vinyl body. Original clothing was a Newborn Pamper diaper. Marks: 1972/IDEAL TOY CORP./TNT-14-N- 219, on head; 1971/IDEAL TOY CORP./ TNT-14-5-34, on back.

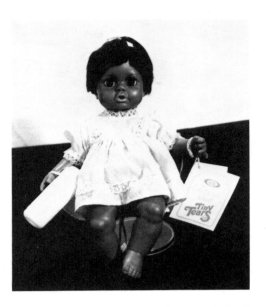

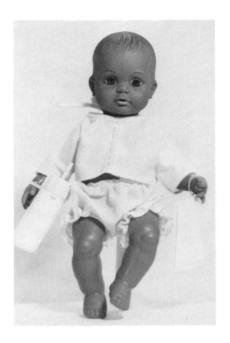

Plate 652: Ideal. "Tiny Tears," 1971, 13" tall. Vinyl head, stationary brown eyes, rooted black hair, nursing mouth; one-piece vinyl body. Marks: 1971/IDEAL TOY CORP/TNT (the remainder is blurred), on head; 1971/IDEAL TOY CORP/TNT-14-5-34, on body.

Plate 653: Ideal. "Tiny Tears," 1982, 13½" tall with vinyl head, stationary brown eyes with lashes, rooted short black hair, nursing mouth; one-piece vinyl body. All original in blue print dress and blue panties. Marks: 1971/IDEAL/ TNT-14-N 370, on head; 1971/IDEAL TOY CORP./TNT-14-5-34, on back. Reissued as Classic Doll.

Plate 654: Ideal. "Tiny Tears," 1982. 14". Similar to previous doll except for molded, painted hair. Doll is all original in pink two-piece flannel outfit. Marks: 1971 0 IDEAL/TNT-14-H195, on head; 1971/IDEAL TOY CORP./TNT-14-5-34, on body.

Plate 655: Tyco (View-Master Ideal Group, Inc.). "Tiny Tears," a crying doll that has been reissued many times, always popular. This latest one is 17" tall with vinyl head, plastic stationary "tearing" eyes, rooted dark brown hair, open nursing mouth; vinyl arms and legs; brown cloth body. All original in pink, lavender, and aqua rompers. She cries real tears when you squeeze her hand. Marks: TINY TEARS/1989 IDEAL INC/MADE IN CHINA, on head.

Plate 656: View-Master Ideal Group, Inc. "Baby Bubbles." 16½" tall. She blows bubbles and girgles like a real baby. Vinyl head, rooted dark brown hair, open nursing mouth, sleeping black eyes, vinyl arms and legs, cloth body. All original in pink and white two-piece flannel outfit with lavender shoes and fancy headband. Marks: BABY BUBBLES TM/ c1989 IDEAL INC./Made in China, on head.

Plate 657: View-Master Ideal Group, Inc. "Betsy Wetsy." 17" tall. Reissue of a popular doll from the 1950's. Vinyl head, rooted dark brown hair, nursing mouth, black sleeping eyes with lashes, jointed vinyl body. All original in pink cotton knit undershirt and pink rubber pants. Doll comes with pink plastic potty chair. Marks: Betsy Wetsy R/c1989 Ideal Inc./ Made in China, on head.

Plate 658: Ideal Toy Corp., Hollis, New York. "Saralee Negro Doll," 1950. 18½" tall. All original. Soft vinyl head, arms, and legs; brown cloth stuffed body with cry box; brown sleep eyes, eyelashes; painted open mouth; slightly curly molded, painted hair; rosy cheeks. Doll is dressed in pale yellow organdy dress and bonnet with white undies, shoes and socks. Head is marked: C-17/IDEAL DOLLS. Original yellow tag on arm reads: Ideal (in oval) Beautiful/Saralee/Dolls/Made in U.S.A. By IDEAL TOY CORP. HOLLIS 7, N.Y. Sticker on original box reads: Ideal's Beautiful "Saralee Negro Doll/More Than Just a Doll...An Ambassador of Good Will."

Plate 659: Ideal. "Kitt and Kaboodle," soft body doll and action pony. Kitt is 15" tall with vinyl head and hands; painted features, including freckles; dimpled chin; rooted black hair; cloth body and legs with sewn-on clothing. All original in blue overalls with red and white checkered shirt. Kaboodle, the pony, is hard plastic. When pony is pulled back, she winds up and can then trot around with a bobbing tail and a clip-clop sound. No batteries are required. Marks on Kitt: 1977/IDEAL TOY CORP., on head.

Plate 660: Ideal Toy Corp. "Whoopsie," 14" toddler doll. Vinyl head, smiling mouth, rooted black hair, painted eyes; jointed toddler body. When stomach is pressed, her hair flies up in the air and she squeaks. Marks: IDEAL TOY CORP./HONG KONG/ 1978/H-298, on head; IDEAL TOY CORP./ 1978/B-66/5 1, on body.

Plate 661: Ideal. "Wake up Thumbelina," 18". Vinyl head with black rooted hair, painted eyes, open/closed mouth, vinyl body and arms, cloth legs. Battery operated. All original in yellow and white romper suit with legs attached to clothing. Marks: 1975/IDEAL TOY CORP./WB-18-H-251, on head; 1976/IDEAL (in logo)/HOLLIS N.Y. 11423/2. Courtesy of Cheryl Larry Perkins.

Plate 662: Ideal. "Chew Suzy Chew," 15" long. Vinyl head with breathing nostrils, open mouth that "chews" when a button on the doll's back is pushed, rooted black hair, painted features. Doll is all original in salmon rompers. Jointed hard plastic bent leg baby body. Marks: 1979/IDEAL TOY CORP./H332/CSC, on head; 1979/IDEAL TOY CORP/B86, on body.

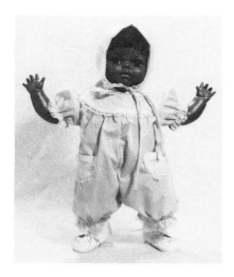

Plate 663: Ideal. "Thumbelina," 20". Vinyl head, rooted black hair, brown sleeping eyes, open/closed mouth, vinyl arms and legs, cloth body with "Ma-Ma" voice. Marks: 1965/IDEAL TOY CORP./ FL 20-E-H-354, on head. Redressed. Courtesy of Xzena Moore.

Plate 664: Ideal. "Thumbelina," 1982. 20" long, vinyl head, molded painted hair and eyes, vinyl arms and legs, cloth body with "Ma-Ma" voice. All original in white romper suit trimmed in pink. Marks: Ideal (in logo)/1982 CBS INC./ H393, on head.

Plate 665: Ideal. "Baby Thumbelina," 7". Vinyl head with rooted black hair, stationary dark brown glassine eyes, open nursing mouth, one-piece vinyl body. All original with pink trimmed diaper in print carry-all lined with pink checked fabric. Marks: 1974/IDEAL (in logo)/B-6-H-36.L, on head.

Plate 666: Ideal. "Taylor Jones," 11½" fashion doll. Vinyl head, painted features, long rooted hair that changes from black to brunette, fully poseable vinyl body. All original in long red gown. Marks: c1975/IDEAL/H-248/HONG KONG, on head.

Plate 667: Ideal. "Tuesday Taylor," 12" super model. Poseable vinyl doll, painted eyes, long black rooted hair. All original in white pantsuit with matching scarf trimmed in hot pink. Marks: 1977/IDEAL/H-293/HONG KONG, on head; 1978 IDEAL/HOLLIS N.Y. 11423/ HONG KONG P, on lower back.

Plate 668: Ideal. "Pretty Curls." 13" tall. Vinyl head, painted eyes with stars, long black rooted hair, closed mouth, one-piece vinyl body. All original in pink sundress. Marks: c1980/IDEAL TOY CORP./H-341, on head; cIDEAL TOY CORP/1980 B-95, on body.

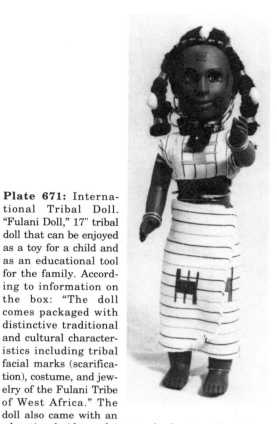

Plate 669: Ideal. "Baby Sees All," 13". Her eyes move, her head turns, she looks this way and that. No batteries required. Vinyl head, movable inset eyes, rooted black hair, cloth body and limbs. All original in pink sewn-on outfit. Marks: c1980/IDEAL TOY CORP./H-234-SEE/HONG KONG, on head.

Plate 670: Ideal. "Patti Play Pal," 35". Reissue of the very first life-size three-year-old to be mass-produced. Vinyl head, rooted black hair, stationary brown eyes, jointed hard vinyl body and limbs. All original in red and white cotton dress, white socks, and black shoes. Marks: c/IDEAL TOY CORP./G-35/H-346, on head; IDEAL (in logo)/35-5, on back. Copyright 1981, 1959, on box.

Plate 671: International Tribal Doll. "Fulani Doll," 17" tribal doll that can be enjoyed as a toy for a child and as an educational tool for the family. According to information on the box: "The doll comes packaged with distinctive traditional and cultural characteristics including tribal facial marks (scarification), costume, and jewelry of the Fulani Tribe of West Africa." The doll also came with an educational video and 14-page book giving the history and background of the Fulani Tribe. All vinyl with sleeping brown eyes and rooted black hair. Marks: Made in China, tag stuck to body. Copyright 1986.

Plate 672: Ja-Ru, Jacksonville, Florida. "Betty," 1975. 11" tall. All vinyl fashion doll, painted features, rooted black hair, movable arms and legs, twisting body. Marks: MADE IN HONG KONG, on body.

Plate 673: Jesco. "Kewpie Party Boy," 8" identical to the following party girl except for clothing. Style #879.

Plate 674: Jesco. "Kewpie Party Girl," from the Kewpie Kouples collection along with previous boy. 8". All original vinyl copy of a popular composition doll from the 1930's. Painted features, molded hair; vinyl jointed body. Doll has squeak mechanism inside body. Style #878. Marks: JESCO c1986/T.M./Made in China, on back.

Plate 675: Jesco. "Kewpie Play Girl and Boy" from the Kewpie Kouples collection. Available 1991. 8" tall. All original in identical navy blue rompers. Girl has blue print blouse trimmed in white lace, boy has blue and white pinstriped shirt. Marks on both dolls are the same: Jesco c1986/T.M./Made in China, on body.

Plate 676: Jesco. "Kewpie Girl," 16" tall. Vinyl head, painted features, molded hair; jointed vinyl body with squeaker inside. All original. Marks: Cameo 11-7-67, on head. Style #6116.

Plate 677: Jesco. "Kewpie Boy." 16" tall. Doll is identical to previous doll. All original in light blue shirt with white stripes and navy blue cotton pants with red felt tie. #6117B.

Plate 679: Jesco. "Kewpie Jack and Jill," 12" tall. Both dolls are all original in light blue and matching blue rosebud print with white plastic pails. Girl is looking to the left, boy is looking to the right. Jack is style #2146B, Jill is #2147B. Marks: 20/CAMEO, on head; Jesco/cCAMEO/12, on body.

Plate 678: Jesco. "Kewpie Goes to School," 12" tall. Vinyl head, painted features, molded hair; jointed vinyl body. Boy is all original in burgundy and pink corduroy, style #2106B. Girl is all original in pink print dress, style #2105B. Both dolls are marked: 6/CAMEO JDK, on head; JESCO/CAMEO/10, on body.

Plate 680: Jesco. "Scootles," girl and boy. 12" tall. Copy of a very popular composition doll from the 1920's. See composition dolls in this book for picture and further information on the original Scootles. Identical dolls have vinyl heads, painted features, molded painted hair; jointed vinyl bodies. All original. Style #2204 and #2205. Marks: J K 1964/CAMEO, on head; JESCO/CAMEO/12, on back.

Plate 681: Jesco. "Scootles" boy, 1991. #2209. 12" tall. All original in blue pants and white print shirt. Marks: JLK 1964/cCameo, on head; Jesco/cCameo/11, on body.

Plate 682: Jesco. "Scootles," girl, 1991. 12" tall. All original in floral print dress with blue ribbon trim. #2208. Marks: JLK 1964/cCameo, on head; Jesco/cCameo/10, on body.

Plate 683: Jesco. "Christening baby," 15", vinyl head, open/closed mouth, molded hair, sleeping brown eyes with lashes; vinyl jointed bent leg body. All original in beautiful long white baby gown and cap. Marks: JESCO TM/(copyright sign) 1987/Made in China, on back. Hang tag: Cameo Babies by JESCO.

Plate 684: Jesco. "Scootles." 14" all porcelain doll is the third doll in Jesco's porcelain series and the first black porcelain doll in the series. The original Scootles doll was designed in the 1920's by Rose O'Neill and was made on composition. See the composition section of this book for a photograph and description of the original Scootles. This porcelain Scootles is limited to production in 1991 and is a numbered edition. This particular doll is number 47. All original in aqua and white dress. Doll has stationary brown glass eyes. Marks: 47, on head; JESCO/Limited Edition, on body.

Plate 685: Jesco. "Kewpie Astronaut" from Kewpie Thru the Ages collection. 12" tall. All original in silver astronaut suit. Available 1991, #1969. Marks: JLK/4/ Cameo, on head; Jesco/cCameo/12, on body.

Plate 686: Jesco. "Kewpie Basketball" from Kewpie Aktivities collection. 12" tall. All original in white basketball uniform trimmed in blue. Available 1991, #2134. Marks: JLK/ 21/CAMEO c, on head; Jesco/ cCameo/ 6, on body.

Plate 687: Jesco. "Kewpie Celebration, 1991 #823. 8". All original in blue dot jumper with white blouse. Marks: Jesco c1986/T.M./Made in China.

Plate 688: Jesco. "Kewpie" girl from the Kewpie Klassics collection, #2111. 1991. 12" tall. All original in pink dot dress. Marks: JLK/21/Cameo c, on head; Jesco/cCameo/4, on body.

Plate 689: Jesco. "Kewpie Kottontail" #2144, 1991. 12" tall. All original baby blue flannel. Marks: JLK/5/ Cameo c, on head; Jesco/cCameo/4, on body.

Plate 690: Jesco. "Deluxe Kewpie," #6110, 1991. 16" tall. All original in yellow print dress with white pinafore and pantaloons. Marks: 11-7-67/cCameo 6, on head; cCameo (very faint), on body.

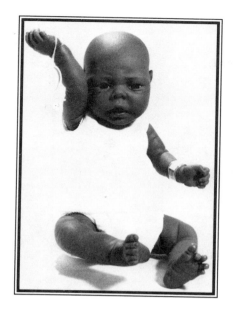

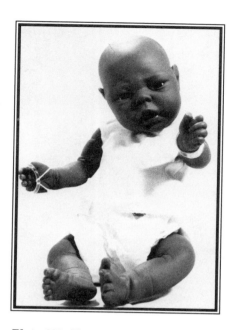

Plate 691: Jesmar. "Natiora," 18" vinyl, fully jointed newborn baby boy. Anatomically correct, dark brown stationary eyes, open mouth, wrinkled skin on folds like a newborn. All original in white blue trimmed diapers with pacifier. Marks: JESMAR/MADE IN SPAIN, on head. Same marks on body. Doll wears hospital wrist tag with words printed in Spanish. Doll was purchased new in the mid-1980's.

Plate 692: Identical to previous doll, but this one is anatomically correct baby girl. Shirt is white trimmed in pink. Marks are the same.

Plate 693: Jolly Toys, Inc. "Linda." 18" tall. Soft vinyl head; nursing mouth; black rooted hair; jointed toddler body. All original. Said to be the first doll made commercially in U.S. to represent the black race with ethnic features. However, Shindana dolls had an earlier copyright date. Marks: JOLLY TOYS INC./19c69/13.

Plate 694: Jilmar. "Sleepy Angel," 20" tall. Kneels down and says her bedtime prayer "Now I Lay Me Down to Sleep." Battery operated with miniature record player in her tummy. The flip side of record plays "Brother John." Vinyl head with painted closed eyes, black rooted hair, vinyl hands, cloth body and feet. Marks: Sleepy Angel by JILMAR CO. INC, on tag sewn to body. Doll was advertised and distributed by Niresk Industries as "Patty Prayer."

Plate 695: Jolly Toys. Smaller version of the above doll. 15" tall. Marks: Jolly Toys Inc./ 19c69/3.

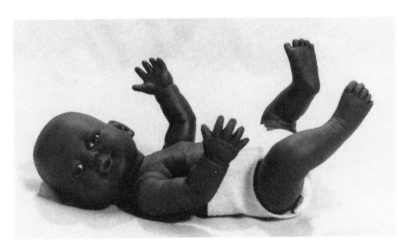

Plate 697: Just For Kids. "My Newborn Baby," 10" soft vinyl doll with diaper. Doll is anatomically correct baby girl. Doll is realistically detailed with lots of newborn wrinkles, fully jointed, inset glassine eyes. Marks: 1986/JUST FOR KIDS/(HK) LTD. on head. The same marks are on the body.

Plate 696: Juro Novelty Co. "Lester," 30" ventriloquist doll. Hard plastic head, molded hair, painted features; cloth body. All original, model 1200 Lester. Purchased new in 1972.

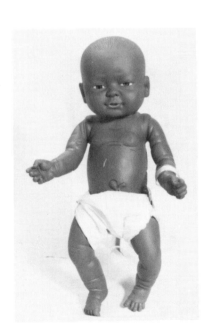

Plate 698: Just For Kids. "My Newborn Baby," 14". Identical to previous doll except this one is larger. Marks are the same as previous doll. Replaced diaper.

Plate 699: Justin. "Darling Denise," 18" tall, numbered D4579 from the Second Generation Dollies, Loving Legacy series. A very collectible doll as each is numbered. Vinyl head, arms, and legs, sleeping eyes; rooted black hair; cloth body. Comes with matching teddy bear. All original in blue plaid dress. Marks: LOVING LEGACY DOLLS/BY JPI 1990/NY NY 10003 U.S.A., on head. Tag sewn to body: Second Generation Baby/D4579 Darling Denise/Loving Legacy Dolls, a Division of/JPI, New York, NY 10003.

Plate 700: Justin. "Darling Debbie," 24", from Second Generation Babies series of limited edition numbered dolls. This one is doll A 000752. Sticker affixed to cloth body reads: Limited Edition/DARLING DEBBIE/A 000752/Second/Generation/BABIES. Vinyl head, arms, and legs; cloth body; large brown sleeping eyes; rooted black hair. All original in peach flowered dress with matching bloomers, booties, socks, and teddy bear. Item No. D4506. Marks: LOVING LEGACY DOLLS R/BY c JPI 1989/NY, NY 10003 USA, on head.

History Of The Keisha Doll Co.

The Keisha Doll Company was established in 1981 by Helen J. Steward. At that time, Helen Steward was a school teacher in New York. Out of her love for children and interest in dolls, grew this wonderful product that would enrich children while at the same time "put starch in children's backs." Ms. Steward retired from teaching in 1984 and devoted full time to the development of her doll company in Harlem. In the beginning, a standard, generic-type doll was used. Later, she designed her own doll by making the lips and nose slightly fuller for a more ethnic effect.

Keisha offers a wide range of dolls while still definitely being considered an ethnic doll company with emphasis on Third World Dolls. Although many of the dolls are made from the same mold, it is the costuming that makes every doll unique. Much research goes into all the clothing and accessory details to insure accuracy of dress. Braids, pigtails, plaits, and cornrows are a part of our culture and are special features of many of the dolls.

According to Ms. Steward, the name KEISHA was selected because of its popularity among black students. When teaching in Harlem, each class seemed to have one or more KEISHA's. After doing business in Harlem, the Keisha Doll Company moved to Florida where it currently is located. Dolls shown in the 1991 catalog are as follows:

"Tiye," The Nubian Queen of Egypt (CA 1415–1340 B.C.). A wise and beautiful woman from Nubia so captured the heart of the Pharaoh, she changed the course of history. Style #100.

"Makeda, Queen of Sheba" (960 B.C.). I Kings, 10:10, a Bible passage which refers to the gifts that Makeda presented to King Solomon. Makeda had a son for King Solomon whose name was "Menelek." A beautifully dressed doll with an extra hairpiece. Style #701.

"Ann Nzinga, Amazon Queen of Matamba," West African (1582–1663). Nzinga was excellent as a military leader. She led her people into war against the Portuguese for many years. The doll is elegantly dressed with costume jewelry. Style #18.

"Cleopatra VII," Queen of Egypt (69–30 B.C.). The Keisha Doll Company offers three different versions of Cleopatra, 200B Cleopatra has braids and beads, 200A & 200C have an extra hairpiece which can be removed and placed back. Each doll comes with jewelry.

"Nefertiti," a very beautiful and gracious Queen (1375–1358 B.C.). The wife of the Pharaoh of Egypt, Akhenaton. Style #10.

"Ndeble Tribe and the Ashanti." Style #102 &12.

"The Mighty Shaka, King of the Zulus." A strong leader and military innovator. Shaka is noted for revolutionizing nineteenth-century Bantu warfare. A beautifully illustrated book accompanies this doll. Style #40A & 40B.

"Stardoll," (head only, on a stand), with a booklet showing how to braid, bead, and cornrow. The stand holds curlers, comb, rubber bands, and beads. Style #1650.

"Carnival J. Bluette," carnival doll. Style #5.

"Brandi," carnival doll with turban and exotic plume carnival affair. Style #41.

"Dominique," Mardi Gras doll. Style #7.

"African American Princess." Style #1555.

"Naziah the Bride." Style #922.

"The Groom." Style #922M.

"Bridesmaid Minon." Style #806.

"Chocolate Chip." Style #220.

"Prince Hammer." (not available) Style #909.

"Khadja." Style #101.

"Jameelah, The Island Girl."

"Miss Cinnamon Brown." Style #801.

"Beautiful Jasmine." Style #23.

"Keisha Easter." Style #24.

"A Little Nostalgia," the Shindana Babies. Style #36.

"Neecie." Style #26.

"Sandy." Style #505.

"Whitney." Style #28.

"Toussaint L'Overture," historical doll, one of our first Freedom Fighters. Style #90.

"Marcus Garvy," historical doll. Style #80.

"Sojourner Truth," historical doll. Style #91.

"Harriet Tubman," historical doll. Style #88.

"Frederick Douglass," historical doll. Style #60.

"Prince and Princess," baby dolls. Style #30 & 31.

"Tiger Lily." Style #33.

"Queen Hapshetsut." Style #1100.

"Massai Girl." Style #14.

"African Princess Atella." Style #32.

"Satla." Style #34.

"Fulani Tribe." Style #35.

All of the above dolls are 23" vinyl dolls with the exception of the babies.

Available in 1992 are 11½" Keisha Fashion dolls, style #1333.

The following dolls are available in porcelain:

"Elise." Style #4205.

"Lola." Style #FH207.

"Lucy." Style #34.

"Keisha." Style #212.

"Lil Brown Baby with Sparkling Eyes." Style #22.

"Baby Girl." Style #23.

"Porcelain Head." Style #45.

The following dolls are available in cloth:

"Brandi." Style #50.

"Dawn." Style #51.

"Chrystal."

"Nyota."

"Nola."

The size of the porcelain, cloth, and baby dolls is not mentioned in the catalog.

Plate 701: Keisha. "Sandy," curly hair, 23". All original in plaid pinafore and white blouse with lace, white tights, and shoes. Black hair is styled in a combination of braids with plastic beads and a ponytail on the top. This doll was also available with dark brown hair.

Plate 702: Keisha. "Shaka Zulu," 23" ethnic vinyl doll, rooted black hair, sleeping dark brown eyes, jointed well-formed body. All original in typical Zulu styled clothing. Included with the doll was a hard-cover children's biography of Shaka Zulu. Marks: KEISHA II/H.J.S./1983/008695, on head; same marks on back. Keisha dolls were created by Helen J. Steward and made in Harlem, U.S.A. Also included on each doll box are paper dolls "Savannah," "Neecie," and "Keisha."

Plate 703: Keisha. "Ashanti," 23" from the collection of Third World Dolls. All of the dolls in this series are from the same mold but differ in hairstyles and authentically created clothing. Only the boy, Shaka Zulu, does not have painted lips, the rest have them painted in a soft natural-looking hue.

Left – Plate 704: Keisha. "Cleopatra B.," 23". All original in one-piece pant outfit in a beautiful African print, gold colored plastic necklace, gold sandals, white beads in braided hair. Doll is holding gold painted grass fan.

Right – Plate 705: Keisha. "Cleopatra A.," 23". All original in yellow taffeta one-piece pant outfit with gold colored accessories. Long loose hairstyle with coins in hair.

Plate 706: Keisha. "Khalilah," 23". One-piece loose pant outfit in strong African-like print, with matching head cover, braided hair, neck beads, and black sandals.

Plate 707: Keisha. "Yoruba," 23". Authentically styled dress in blue striped cloth with a different but similar cloth for headpiece. Hair is in many braids pulled to the back. Doll is wearing beads and black sandals.

Plate 708: Keisha. "Ronnie," 23". All original with dark brown curly hair, dressed in yellow print dress trimmed in black with black tights and shoes.

Left – Plate 709: Keisha. "Miss Cinnamon Brown," 23". All original with long curly black hair dressed in blue jean outfit with matching cap and red t-shirt.

Right – Plate 710: Kenner. "Gabbigale." 1972. 18" tall talking doll with pull string. Vinyl head, painted eyes, open painted mouth with teeth, rooted black hair; hard plastic jointed body and limbs. All original in gold dress with red print sleeves and trim around the neck. Marks: c1972/KENNER PRODUCTS CO./3, on head; Gabbigale T.M./c1972 GENERAL MILLS FUN GROUP INC./KENNER PROD. CINCINATTI, OHIO/PATENTS PENDING, on back.

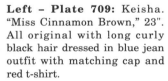

Plate 713: Kenner. "Baby Yawnie," 1974. 14" tall. Vinyl head; tuff of black rooted hair at forehead; brown sleeping eyes. Doll yawns and closes its eyes when left hand is squeezed. Cloth stuffed body with sewn-on clothing. Tag sewn to body: BABY YAWNIE/C1974 G.M.F.G.I.,/Kenner Products/ Cincinnati, Ohio 45202/Made in Taiwan/Republic of China/ALL NEW MATERIALS/consisting of 100% Polyester. Collection of Susan Perkins.

Plate 711: Kenner. "Baby Alive," 16" eating and drinking doll. She eats from a spoon and drinks from a bottle. The food was a specially prepared mix purchased separately. Battery operated. Vinyl head with painted features, rooted black hair, open mouth, one-piece vinyl body. Marks: 3564/BO/KENNER PROD./19c73, on head. Courtesy of Susan Perkins.

Plate 712: Kenner. "Baby Alive," reissue, 15½" tall, all vinyl with painted features and rooted hair. Sucks her thumb and eats specially prepared food. Battery operated. All original in pink striped sunsuit. Marks: 65, on head; U.S. PATENT NO. 3,858,352/ 1990 KENNER MADE IN CHINA/CC, on back. Courtesy of Candace Gates.

Plate 714: Kenner. "Nancy Nonsense," 1974. 18" tall. Soft vinyl head; curly rooted black hair; painted, molded features; painted, freckles above the nose; hard plastic body. All original. Nancy Nonsense says 216 different things when talking string is pulled. Marks: 1974 General Mills Fun Group Inc./by its DIV. KENNER PROD. Co./Cincinnati, Ohio 45202/ NANCY NONSENSE/CAT. NO. 2800-2805.

Plate 715: Kenner. "Baby Bundles," 1975. 14½" tall. A cuddly soft drink and wet doll that won't hold still. Soft vinyl head; black rooted hair; painted eyes; open nursing mouth; jointed soft vinyl body. Marks: GENERAL MILLS/FUN GROUP INC/1975/KENNER PROD/CINN. OHIO/MADE IN HONG KONG/NO.26000. All original clothing.

Plate 717: Kenner. "Bob Scout." 1974. 9½" tall action figure in official uniform. All vinyl, painted features; fully jointed with action arm movement. Doll was approved by Boy Scouts of America and comes with scouting booklet. Additional high adventure accessories sold separately. Marks: c1974 G.M.F.G.I./KENNER PROD./ CIN'TI, OHIO 45202/NO 7005/MADE IN HONG KONG.

Plate 716: Kenner. "Skye," 1975 (left), 1976 trade-in (right) fashion-action doll. All vinyl; black rooted hair; molded, painted features, open/closed mouth with teeth. Poseable 1975 doll has fully articulated spring-loaded arms and torso, including movable wrists and wears a pink swimsuit; 1976 doll is fully jointed and poseable but does not have the jointed wrists or spring-loaded arms and torso. She wears a yellow swimsuit. Both dolls are 11½" tall. Marks: (doll on left) 25/c1975/GMFGI, on head; c1974 G.M.F.G.I. Kenner PROD/Cincinnati, Ohio 45202/MADE IN HONG KONG, on body, Doll on right: 23/c1975/GMFGI, on head; body is marked the same as the other doll.

Plate 718: Kenner. "Orange Blossom," 14" baby doll. Vinyl head, arms, and legs; cloth body; painted features; rooted dark brown hair; nursing mouth. All original in yellow print rompers trimmed in orange and matching booties. Marks: 685011/AMERICAN GREET- INGS/CORP. 1983/HONG KONG, on head.

Left – Plate 719: Kenner. "Dave Cub," 1975, in official Cub Scout uniform. 9" tall. All vinyl, painted features, fully jointed. Approved by the Boy Scouts of America. Marks: 49, on head; cG.M.F.G.I./KENNER PROD CIN'TI. OHIO 45202/MADE IN HONG KONG, on body.

Right – Plate 720: Kenner. "Berry Baby Orange Blossom," from the Strawberry Shortcake series. 5" tall. Fully jointed hard vinyl baby, painted features, rooted hair, wets and drinks. All original. Marks: cA.G.C., 84/H.K., on back.

Plate 722: Kenner. "Orange Blossom," from the Strawberry Shortcake series; 6" tall, vinyl head with painted features, including freckles, long rooted dark brown hair; hard vinyl jointed body. All original in orange and yellow print dress, matching bow and shoes. Marks: AMERICAN GREETINGS/CORP. 1979, on head; AMERICAN/GREETINGS/CORP. 1984/Made in H.K./ on body.

Plate 721: Kenner. "Sweet Sleeper Orange Blossom with Marmalade," 5½" tall. All original in yellow and white dress with orange sleeves, green and white stockings and white slippers. Marks: AMERICAN GREETINGS 1984/MADE IN HONG KONG, on head. Doll has brown sleep eyes. This is the only Orange Blossom with sleep eyes.

Plate 723: Kenner. "Orange Blossom," 15". All cloth doll, black yarn hair, painted features, sewn-on bonnet, brown cloth arms, orange cloth body and feet, green and white striped cloth legs. Clothing is missing. Courtesy of Kelley Jackson.

Plate 724: Kenner. "Orange Blossom," 6". From the Strawberry Shortcake series. All original in yellow print and orange dress with matching hat, green and white legs. Marks: cAMERICAN GREETINGS./CORP. 1981, on head; MADE IN HONG KONG, on body.

Plate 725: Kenner. "Orange Blossom with Marmalade," 1981. No. 43070. 6" tall. All original in orange and yellow print dress and matching hat. Marks: cAMERICAN GREETINGS/CORP. 1981/HONG KONG, on head.

Plate 726: Kenner. "Orange Blossom Party Pleaser," 6" tall. All original with yellow print dress and matching bonnet, green and white striped stockings. Marks: AMERICAN GREETINGS/CORP. 1979, on head.

Plate 727: Kenner. "Orange Blossom with Marmalade," 6". All original in yellow print skirt and orange top with matching bonnet in a different style from previous Orange Blossom dolls. Marks: AMERICAN GREETINGS/CORP 1984, on head.

Plate 728: Kenner. "Dana," cover girl, 12½". Fully poseable vinyl doll with painted features and rooted dark brown hair. All original in long white slim gown with portfolio, magazine covers and posing stand. Copyright 1979. Marks: 56 HONG KONG/G.M.F.G.I. 1978, on head.

Plate 729: Kenner. "Jana," 4½" from the Glamour Gals collection. All original in the "Sweet Romance" costume.

Plate 730: Kenner. "Blair," 4¼" tall, one of the Glamour Gals. All vinyl poseable, painted features, rooted long brown hair. 1982. Made in Hong Kong. All original in the "Wedding Belle" costume.

Plate 731: Kenner. "Bubbles and Chumley," 1986. 7" and 2", from the Hugga Bunch series. Bubbles is all vinyl with movable limbs and head, painted features, rooted dark brown hair. Chumley is one-piece hard vinyl with painted features, hair, and molded-on clothing.

Plate 732: Kenner. "Rose Petal." 6" tall. Vinyl head, painted eyes, closed mouth, rooted dark brown head, jointed hard vinyl body. Painted-on green tights and purple shoes. Marks: A53/cDKP 1984, on head; cDKP 1984, on body.

Plate 733: Kenner. "Cool Cuts Kara," you can cut and style her replaceable hair, 13½" tall. Vinyl head, painted features, rooted dark hair; hard vinyl body. All original in purple dress with pink print overskirt, molded-on pink panties and purple shoes. Marks: cKENNER 1990/MADE IN CHINA/ CE, on body.

Plate 734: Kenner. "Always Sisters Vanessa," 20" tall. All original, oldest sister. Vinyl head, stationary glassine dark brown eyes, rooted dark brown hair, closed mouth, vinyl hands, cloth poseable body. Marks: KENNER PARKER TOYS INC. (KPT) 1988/ALWAYS SISTERS COLLECTION/VANESSA/ 13040/Made in China, tag sewn to body.

Plate 735: Kenner. "Always Sisters Gina," 17" tall, middle sister. Vinyl head, stationary dark eyes, dark brown hair, closed painted mouth, cloth poseable body. All original in pink striped skirt and pink sweater with pink and white shoes. Marks: KENNER PARKER TOYS INC./(KPT) 1988/ ALWAYS SISTERS COLLECTION/GINA/ 13110/Made in China, tag sewn to body.

Plate 736: Kara. "Always Sisters Kara," 14" tall, baby sister. Vinyl head, stationary dark brown eyes, dark brown rooted hair, closed mouth, vinyl hands, cloth body. All original in white eyelet dress and pink tights. Marks: KENNER PRODUCT TOYS INC./(KPT) 1988/ ALWAYS SISTERS COLLECTION/KARA/ 13180/Made in China, tag sewn to body.

Plate 737: Kenner. "Tonya," Miss America. c1991. 11½". Vinyl head, painted features, long brown and black hair, jointed vinyl body. All original in purple and pink gown with Miss America banner. Marks: cKenner 1991/CE, on body.

Plate 738: Kenner. "Sergeant Reed," 4½" action figure from RoboCop and the Ultra Police series.

Plate 739: Kenner. "Winston Zeddmore," 5¼", from The Real Ghostbusters with Fright Features. All vinyl with molded hair and clothing. Head spins 360 degrees and jaw drops. Marks: 1987/COLUMBIA/PICTURES.

Plate 740: Kenner. "Winston Zeddmore," 5¼", from The Real Ghostbusters Screaming Heroes series.

Plate 741: Knickerbocker. "Punjab," 7" from the Orphan Annie series The World of Annie. Vinyl jointed doll with molded painted black hair, painted features. All original in white cotton suit with turban. Marks: c1982 CPI,–c1982 CTNYNS, INC./1982 KNICKERBOCKER TOY CO. INC./H22, on back.

Plate 742: Knickerbocker Toy Company, Inc. "Beloved Belindy," character from the Raggedy Ann books created by Johnny Gruelle. 15" tall. All cloth, black button pupils, remainder of the features are painted. Brown face, body, and arms; back of head is red. Removable clothing. Marks (tag sewn to dress): BELOVED BELINDY/©BOBBS-MERRILL CO., INC 1965/CAL T-5 ALL NEW MATERIALS. (reverse side): JOY OF A TOY TM/Knickerbocker R/Knickerbocker Toy Company, Inc./Made in Hong Kong.

Plate 743: Knickerbocker Toy Co. "Lindy," "Missy," and "Silky" (left to right) from the Sugar 'n Spice series. Vinyl heads, closed mouths, black rooted hair; five-piece vinyl jointed bodies. All original. Marks: K T C 1975/Made in Taiwan, on head. Box is marked 1976.

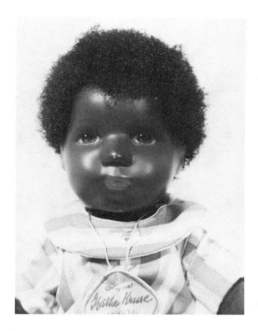

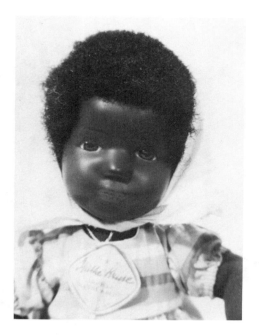

Plate 744: Kruse. "Benji," 10" tall. Cellulite-type head; painted eyes; closed mouth; glued-on synthetic wig; cloth body, legs, and arms with inset wire for posing. All original in aqua, pink; and white striped shirt; aqua corduroy pants; and pink felt shoes. Hang tag reads: Original/Kathe Kruse/MODELL/HANNE KRUSE/Made in Germany. Doll was made in the early 1970's.

Plate 745: Kruse. "Bessie." Identical to previous doll except for clothing. All original in orange, yellow, and purple striped dress, yellow bandana; and pink felt shoes. Hang tag is identical.

Plate 746: L.J.N. (Goldberg Productions). "Terry," 1973. 8" fully jointed action figure from TV show "The Rookies." Vinyl head; painted Negroid features; molded afro hairstyle; fully jointed vinyl body. The role was played on TV by George Sanford Brown. Marks: (in logo) LJN TOYS LTD/HONG KONG/ALL RIGHTS RESERVED.

Plate 747: L.J.N. "Michael Jackson" in Grammy Awards outfit. 11½" tall. All vinyl, painted features, fully jointed. Marks: 1984 MJJ PRODUCTIONS/LJN TOYS LTD., on body.

Plate 748: L.J.N. "Michael Jackson" in Beat It outfit.

Plate 749: L.J.N. "Michael Jackson" in Thriller outfit.

Plate 750: L.J.N. "Michael Jackson" in American Music Awards outfit.

Plate 751: L.J.N. "Flo Jo," 12" Florence Griffith Joyner, the 1988 Olympic Gold Medal Winner in track. All vinyl, painted features, rooted hair. Marks: c1989 L.J.N./MADE IN CHINA, on body.

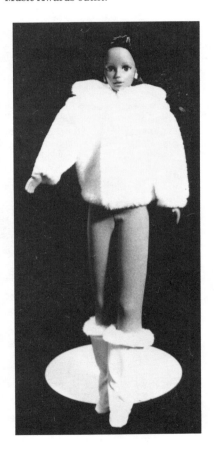

Plate 752: Lanard Toys. "Jet Setter" Nikita. 18" fashion doll. Vinyl head, painted features, long dark brown rooted hair, and aqua earrings. Hard vinyl jointed body. All original in white fake fur jacket aqua stretch pants and white boots. Marks: A13, on head; 1987 LANARD TOYS LTD./ Made in China, on body.

Plate 753: L.J.N. "Police Nurse" from the Police Girl series. c1975. 9" tall. All vinyl jointed doll with painted features, rooted black hair. All original. Marks: L.J.N./1974, on head. Courtesy of Marge Betts.

Plate 754: Lanard. Another "Jet Setter." This one is all original in the Leilani outfit, two-piece yellow swimsuit with green print wrap around.

Left – Plate 756: Lanard. "Jet Setter," Kenya. All original in two-piece safari outfit, hiking boots, helmet, bandana, and socks.

Right – Plate 757: Lanard. "Glitter." 1987. Poseable fashion doll, 18" tall. Vinyl head, painted eyes, painted open mouth, long black rooted hair, earrings. Doll was sold in either a white evening gown or a black evening gown. Marks: c1987 Lanard Toys Ltd./Made in China, sticker on lower back. Dolls wear "real" rhinestones.

Plate 755: Lanard. "Jet Setter," Nina. All original in Mardi Gras outfit, pink and silver party dress, neckpiece, Mardi Gras mask and fancy tights.

Plate 759: The Little Tikes Company. 1990. "Little Tikes Family," 3" to 5½" tall. Mother, father, brother, sister, and baby. Hard plastic, molded hair and clothing, painted features, movable head and arms, swivel waist. Unmarked.

Plate 758: Larami Corporation. "Julie." 11" tall. All original vinyl doll with black rooted synthetic hair, sleeping eyes, movable arms and legs. Purchased new in 1976. Marks: HONG KONG/MADE IN (remainder is missing.)

Plate 760: Lomel Enterprises. "Baby Whitney," 21" doll with vinyl head, arms, and legs; soft cloth body; curly rooted dark brown hair, painted eyes, pierced ears. Baby Whitney is the first Afro-American doll selected by the Smithsonian Institute. Her face was designed by Rosalind Jeffries, a noted art historian and curator of the New York Center for African Art. Lomel Enterprises is a black-owned doll company based in Washington, D.C. Marks: 1985 LOMEL ENT. INC./P.O. BOX 2452/WASH. D.C. 20013/ FIRST EDITION/BABY WHITNEY TM.

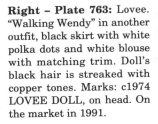

Left – Plate 762: Lovee. "Walking Wendy," 32" doll. vinyl head, dark brown sleeping eyes, long black rooted hair; hard plastic body and limbs. All original in blue and white blouse, blue skirt, and white tights. Marks: 20/1974 LOVEE DOLL/Made in China, on head. Doll was purchased new in 1990.

Right – Plate 763: Lovee. "Walking Wendy" in another outfit, black skirt with white polka dots and white blouse with matching trim. Doll's black hair is streaked with copper tones. Marks: c1974 LOVEE DOLL, on head. On the market in 1991.

Plate 761: Lomel Ent. "Baby Whitney," all original in African Kente styled clothing.

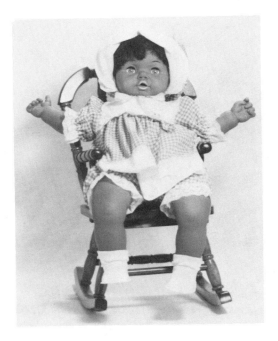

Plate 764: Lovee Doll & Toy Co. "Fashion Flo." 18½" tall, 1970's. Soft vinyl head, long black rooted hair, dark brown sleep eyes, closed mouth, jointed vinyl body. All original. Marks: SM, on head; 6419, on body.

Plate 765: Lovee. "Baby Alexandra," 24" baby doll with soft vinyl arms, legs, and head with sleeping brown eyes and rooted black hair; white cloth body. All original in purple and white checked dress and bonnet. Marks: A9, on head; Lovee Doll & Toy Co. Inc., tag sewn to body. Copyright 1987, on box. Doll made in China.

Plate 766: Lovee. "Fran," 1990. 24" walking doll, style No. 5026. Vinyl head, sleeping dark brown eyes with lashes, long black rooted hair; hard plastic jointed body. All original in red and white print cotton dress. Marks: 1974 LOVEE DOLL, CHINA, on head.

Plate 767: Lucky Ind. "Just Like Me Baby Puddin'," 14" all vinyl doll with five-piece bent leg body. Doll has brown sleeping eyes, rooted black hair and drinks and wets. All original in yellow and white dress. Tag on wrist says doll is a Marcia Neal design. Marks: Lucky logo (rabbit)/1988 Lucky Ind. Co. STD/Made in China, on head; Made in China, on body.

Plate 768: Lucky Ind. "Just Like Me Baby Alisa," 12". All vinyl doll similar to Baby Puddin' except that she is smaller and has brown hair. All original. Marks: Logo (rabbit)/1988 Lucky Ind. Co. LTD/Made in China, on head; Made in China, on body. This doll also wears a Marcia Neal design wrist tag.

Plate 769: Lucky. "Julie," 8" doll from the Dreamland series. Vinyl head, painted features, rooted black hair; vinyl bent leg baby body. All original in blue and white knitted outfit. Marks: Made in/China, on back. Box marked 1989.

Left – Plate 770: Lucky. "Nikki," from the Just Like Me series. 12" vinyl doll, long brown curly rooted hair, smiling mouth with two painted teeth, painted eyes, jointed vinyl body. All original in pink sweatsuit with green and gold trim. Marks: (Rabbit logo)/1987 LUCKY IND. CO. LTD/Made in China, on head.

Right – Plate 771: Lucky. "Fashion Corner," 11½" fashion doll. Vinyl head, painted smiling mouth, with dimples in her cheeks, long black rooted hair, jointed hard vinyl body. All original in two-piece blue dress. Marks: (Rabbit Logo) 1987/LUCKY IND. CO. LTD./Made in China, on body. Doll was available in a variety of outfits.

Plate 772: Lucky. "Fashion Corner," c1991. Same as previous doll in all original wedding gown. Marks: (Rabbit Logo) c1987/ LUCKY IND. CO. LTD./MADE IN CHINA, on body.

Plate 773: Marvel. "Black Girl and Boy," 13". Vinyl heads, painted eyes, closed mouths, jointed vinyl baby bodies. Girl has rooted black curly hair, boy has molded painted hair. All original, yellow print cotton dress on girl; denim pants with red gingham shirt on boy. These dolls were marketed for preschools. Marks: MARVEL EDUCATION/ MADE IN HONG KONG, on head.

Plate 774: Marvel. "Pliable Black Family," 7½" to 4". All rubber bendable dolls that can hold their position when bent. Molded, painted hair, painted features, molded-on clothing. Marks: MARVEL EDUCATION/ MADE IN HONG KONG, on feet.

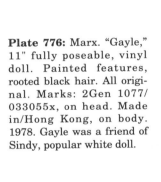

Plate 776: Marx. "Gayle," 11" fully poseable, vinyl doll. Painted features, rooted black hair. All original. Marks: 2Gen 1077/ 033055x, on head. Made in/Hong Kong, on body. 1978. Gayle was a friend of Sindy, popular white doll.

Plate 775: Marx. "Sgt. Kogo," 7½" action figure from an African Safari collection. 1970's. All original with removable coat and molded-on blue safari suit. Vinyl head and arms; painted, molded features; hard plastic fully jointed body. Right hand is movable with control in back. Marks: Marx Toys/Made in U.S.A., on back.

Plate 777: Marx. "First Love," 1979, 17" fully poseable doll with a twist and turn waist. Vinyl head, brown sleeping eyes with lashes, rooted black hair; vinyl jointed body. Marks: MARX/c1978, on head.

Plate 778: Matchbox. "Reba," 6" poseable character from Pee Wee Herman series. All vinyl in postal workers uniform with removable skirt and mail bag, painted features, molded painted hair. Marks: Copyright 1988/Herman Toys Inc./All Rights Reserved/Matchbox Int. Ltd./Made in China, on back.

Plate 779: Matchbox. 10" tall. "Cinnamon," the only black doll in a series of nine "Sweet Treats" dolls. Other treats were Coconut Cupcake, Blueberry Cheesecake, Cotton Candy, Candy Cottage, Treatmaker Trike, Banana Split, Raspberry Sherbet and Sugar Plum Pudding. Vinyl head; painted features; rooted hair; cloth body, legs, and arms. Doll smells like cinnamon. Marks: CHINA, on head. Tag on body: Sweet Treats Doll. 1988 MATCHBOX INTERNATIONAL LTD. Box: 1989.

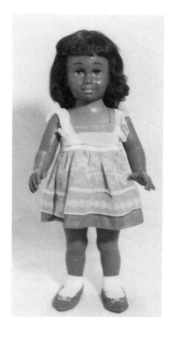

Plate 780: Matchbox. "Beverly Johnson," 11½", from The Real Model collection. Other models were Christie Brinkley and Cheryl Tiegs. All vinyl, painted features, long full rooted dark brown hair, jointed hard plastic body and limbs. Beverly Johnson donated 20% of her proceeds on the sale of the dolls to the Make A Wish Foundation. Marks: Beverly Johnson, on head; Matchbox 1989/Made in China, on body.

Plate 781: Matchbox. "Talking Baby Hush-A-Bye," 18" secret telling doll. Vinyl head, painted features, rooted dark brown hair; vinyl hands, cloth body and legs. Blue print fleece clothing is sewn on. Battery operated. Marks: CHINA, on head. Made in China. Copyright 1988.

Plate 782: Mattel. "Chatty Cathy," 20" talking doll. Vinyl head, sleeping brown eyes, rooted dark brown hair, open mouth with two teeth, hard vinyl arms and legs, hard plastic body. All original in red cotton sunsuit under red cotton pinafore with white organdy overskirt and white organdy shoulder straps. Marks: CHATTY CATHY R/c1960/CHATTY BABY TM/c1961 BY MATTEL, INC./U.S. PAT. 3,017,187./OTHER U.S. &/FOREIGN PATS. PEND., on body.

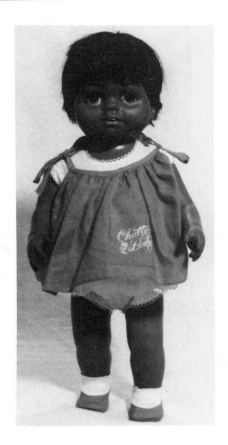

Plate 783: Mattel. "Chatty Cathy" first edition. 20" tall. Dark brown hair is styled differently and is longer than that on previous Chatty Cathy. Marks: CHATTY CATHY T.M./PATENTS PENDING/cMCMLX/BY MATTEL, INC/ HAWTHORNE, CALIF. (on rectangle on back); MATTEL, INC./M/TOYMAKERS (in circle on back).

Plate 784: Mattel. "Chatty Cathy," c1969. 17½" tall. Vinyl head, painted eyes, closed mouth, rooted black hair, jointed vinyl body. Doll talks, sings, and whispers with pull talking ring. All original in red dress with dotted skirt and white lace over red bodice, red shoes. Marks: c1969 MATTEL INC. MEXICO, on head; c1964 MAT- TEL, INC./HAWTHORNE, CALIF., U.S.A./ PATENTED IN U.S.A./PATENTED IN CANADA 1962/OTHER PATENTS PENDING MADE IN MEXICO, on body.

Plate 785: Mattel. "Chatty Baby," 18". Vinyl head, brown sleep eyes, rooted black hair, jointed vinyl body. All original in red top and white undies. Marks: CHATTY CATHY/1960/CHATTY BABY TM/1961/By Mattel Inc./U.S. Pat. 3,017,187/Other U.S. &/Foreign Pats Pend'g.

Left – Plate 786: Mattel. "Tiny Chatty Baby." 15½" tall. Vinyl head, brown sleep eyes, black rooted hair, two upper teeth, hard plastic body, jointed vinyl limbs. Marks: TINY CHATTY BABY/TINY CHATTY BROTHER/1962 MATTEL, INC./HAWTHORNE, CALIF. U.S.A./U.S. PAT. 3,017,187/OTHER U.S. AND FOREIGN/PATENTS PENDING/PATENTED IN CANADA 1962, body.

Right – Plate 787: Mattel. "Chatty Patty," 16½", pull string talking doll. She says different things about the plaything she holds and can even talk without a toy. Vinyl head and legs, painted features, dark brown rooted hair, hard plastic arms and body. All original in dark pink sunsuit with pink print dress. Marks: MATTEL INC. 1983, on head; MATTEL INC 1964/MEXICO, on body.

Plate 788: Mattel. "Lilty," 1974. One of the "Love Notes" dolls. 13" tall. Vinyl head, rooted dark brown curly hair; molded and painted features. Cloth stuffed body that plays different musical notes when squeezed on hand, legs and tummy. Songbook is included. All original, Marks: 1974 MATTEL, INC, on head. Made in U.S.A.

Plate 789: Mattel. "Hi Dottie." Battery operated talking doll talks with telephone. Vinyl head, legs, and right arm; plastic body and left arm. Rooted black hair, painted features. Plug in left hand to connect phone. Marks: 1969 MATTEL INC. Mexico, head; 1971 Mattel Inc./Mexico/U.S. Patent Pending, body. Doll was made for 1972 market.

Plate 790: Mattel. "Curly Q" from the Honey Hill Bunch series. 5" tall. Vinyl head, painted eyes, rooted red hair, smiling mouth with painted teeth, cloth body and limbs, removable printed dress. Doll is holding yellow felt cat. Marks: c1975 MATTEL INC./TAIWAN, on head.

Plate 791: Mattel. Another black doll from the Honey Hill Bunch series. This one has a green and white checkered shirt rather than the striped one in previous doll. Clothes are sewn on. Marks are the same.

Plate 792: Mattel. "Solo," 1975. Member of the Honey Hill Bunch. 6" tall. Soft vinyl head, painted features, rooted black hair, cloth stuffed body. Marks: 1975 MATTEL INC./TAIWAN, tag sewn to body.

Plate 793: Mattel. "Nan," from Pretty Pairs Nan 'n Fran, 1966. 6½" tall all vinyl with poseable arms and legs; painted features; rooted black hair. Missing "Fran" was a small baby doll. Marks: SN/443, head; 1966/MATTEL, INC/JAPAN/25, body. Redressed.

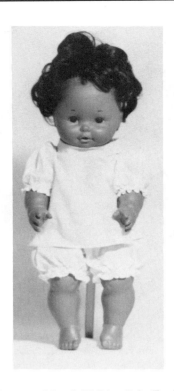

Plate 794: Mattel. "Timey Tell," 1971–72. 17½" tall. Pullstring talking doll with wristwatch. Vinyl head and body, rooted black hair, painted features. When watch is set, she tells the time and suggests an appropriate activity. All original. Marks: 1969 MATTEL INC. MEXICO, on head; c1964 Mattel Inc/Hawthorne, California U.S.A./PATENTED IN U.S.A. PATENTED IN CANADA 1962 OTHER/PATENTS PENDING MADE IN MEXICO, on body.

Plate 795: Mattel. "Talking Baby Tender Love," 16" toddler doll. All vinyl, one-piece doll, head and limbs are stationary. Painted features, rooted black hair in inset scalp, nursing mouth. Redressed. Doll was marketed 1970–73.

Plate 796: Mattel. "Baby Brother Tender Love," 1976. 13" tall anatomically correct drink and wet boy doll. Vinyl head; painted eyes; drinking mouth; brown rooted hair. One-piece vinyl body. After doll is fed, he wets when you squeeze his tummy. Marks: c1972 MATTEL INC., head; c1975 MATTEL INC. U.S.A., body.

Plate 798: Mattel. Another doll with Tender Love-type body from the 1970's. 14" tall. Vinyl head, painted features, rooted brown hair. Closed mouth, brown hair, vinyl body is one piece, only the head is movable. Marks: 1978 Mattel Inc. U.S.A., on head. 1975 MATTEL INC./USA, on body. Redressed.

Plate 797: MATTEL. "Happy Birthday Tender Love," 1975. Toots her party horn, blows out her "magic" candles, blows bubbles. No batteries required. Vinyl head; rooted dark brown hair; painted eyes; open mouth for blowing. One-piece vinyl body. 14" tall. Marks: c1975 MATTEL INC U.S.A., on head; c1975 MATTEL INC/U.S.A., on body. All original in yellow party dress with white dotted overskirt.

Plate 800: Mattel. "Baby-That-a-Way." 15" tall. Battery operated; she crawls, walks, squirms; soft vinyl head, rooted hair; hard vinyl body. All original in pink sunsuit. Marks: cMATTEL INC. 1974 U.S.A., on head; cMattel, Inc. 1974/U.S.A. Patents Pending, body.

Plate 799: Mattel. "Baby Magic Tender Love." Identical to previous Tender Love doll except for eyes and left hand. This doll has white lines painted around the black pupils to make it appear the eyes are glistening and has a hole in the palm of the left hand for holding her wand. All original in pink print vest and shorts with pink cape and shoes. Marks are the same as previous doll.

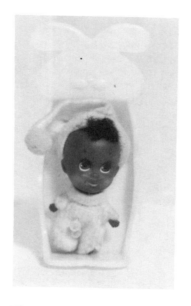

Plate 801: Mattel. "Spangle," 1981. 4½" doll from the series Dazzle and Her Friends. Of eight dolls, she was the only black one. All vinyl painted features, rooted long brown hair; poseable. Made in Taiwan. Doll is unmarked.

Plate 802: Mattel. "Kiddles," 2", 1967. Vinyl head, rooted dark brown hair, painted features, hard jointed vinyl body. Both dolls are all original with glued-on clothing. Dolls are unmarked.

Plate 803: Mattel. "Kiddle-Baby Rockaway," 1969. 2" tall. Vinyl head, painted features, tuff of black yarnlike hair coming out of glued-on cap. Sewn-on pink and white striped nightgown. All original with pink plastic cradle.

Plate 804: Mattel. "Dancerina" (1969–71). 24" tall. Vinyl head; hard plastic body; battery operated; poseable arms and legs; pirouettes and dances with operation of control knob in crown on head. Marks: c1968 MATTEL INC/MADE IN MEXICO, on head; c1968 MATTEL INC/MADE IN U.S.A./U.S. PATENT PENDING, body.

Plate 805: Mattel. "Baby Beans." 11½" tall. Soft viny head; molded, painted features; rooted black hair around forehead. Cloth body. Sewn-on clothes. Marks: c1970 MATTEL INC, on head; Tag sewn to body: A quality original/MATTEL/BABY BEANS/c1970 MATTEL, Inc./Hawthorne/Calif. 90250.

Plate 806: Mattel. "Dancerella," 17½". Very similar to previous doll, "Dancerina" except this doll is shorter and a lighter shade of brown. Battery operated. Vinyl head and arms, painted features and rooted dark brown hair; hard plastic body and legs. Doll dances like the earlier Dancerina with control knob in crown on head. All original in white tutu and tights with pink trim and ballet slippers. Marks: 1972 Mattel Inc., on head; Mattel Inc. 1968 1978 U.S.A., on body.

Plate 807: Mattel. "Li'l Drowsy Beans," 11" baby doll with vinyl head, molded painted hair, painted features, cloth body. Clothing is sewn on. Marks: MATTEL INC./1982 TAIWAN, on head.

Plate 808: Mattel. "Mama and Baby Beans." 10½" tall. Mama: soft vinyl head; painted features; rooted black hair; cloth stuffed body, velcro hands; sewn-on clothing. Marks: MATTEL INC. TAIWAN, head; Quality Originals by Mattel/Mama and Baby Beans/Mattel, Inc. 1975/Hawthorne, Calif 90250/Made in Taiwan...(tag sewn to body). Baby Beans: Soft vinyl head; painted hair and features; stuffed bunting for body. 3¾" tall. Tag sewn to body is identical to that on Mama.

Plate 809: Mattel. "Tippee Toes," 1980. 13". Vinyl head, painted eyes, open/closed mouth, rooted black hair, vinyl jointed toddler body. All original in red and white dotted sunsuit. Doll comes with push-powered 18½" stroller. No batteries required. Marks: c1980 MATTEL INC./MEXICO, on head.

Plate 810: Mattel. "Drowsy," baby doll. 15½" tall. Soft vinyl head; stuffed cloth body; rooted brown hair; dressed in sleepers. Doll talks with a pull string. Marks: DROWSY/C1964 MATTEL, INC./Hawthorne, Calif./made in Mexico, tag sewn to body.

Plate 811: Mattel. "Baby Skates," 15" tall, 1982. Vinyl head, painted features, open smiling mouth, rooted dark brown hair; hard plastic body and legs. Doll skates by herself, no batteries required, just wind the doll up. All original in pink and yellow striped outfit. Marks: 50/MATTEL INC. 1980/MEXICO, on head.

Plate 812: Mattel. "Saucy," the doll that makes faces, 16" tall. Soft vinyl head, hard vinyl arms and legs, hard plastic body, rooted black hair, open mouth with two teeth. When arm is raised, doll makes eighteen different faces. All original in bright pink dress with checkered trim. Marks: c1972 MATTEL INC, INC MEXICO, on head; c1972 MATTEL, INC./MEXICO/U.S. PATENT PENDING, on body.

Plate 813: Mattel. "Baby Come Back," c1976. 16" tall. She walks away, turns around and comes back. Batteries required. Vinyl head, painted eyes, closed mouth, rooted dark brown hair, jointed hard plastic body and limbs. Redressed. Original outfit was brown print and pink checked. Marks: 1976 MATTEL INC. USA., on head; MATTEL, INC 1976/U.S.A., on body.

Plate 814: Mattel. "Washington," 9". One of the Sweathogs from TV series "Welcome Back Kotter." Poseable vinyl with painted features and molded painted hair. All original in jeans, white cotton knit shirt, and orange windbreaker. Marks: WOLPER-KOMACK, on head; c1973/MATTEL INC./TAIWAN, on back. Role on TV was played by actor Lawrence Hilton-Jacobs.

Left – Plate 815: Mattel. "Stella" from the Rosebud series, c1976. 7" tall. Vinyl head, painted eyes, closed mouth, rooted brown hair, jointed vinyl bent leg baby body. All original in long yellow gown trimmed with white lace and matching bonnet. Marks: c1977 MATTEL INC, on head; cMATTEL INC. 1976/TAIWAN, on body.

Right – Plate 816: Mattel. "Baby Bettina" from the Rosebud series. 4½" tall. Vinyl head, long rooted dark brown hair, painted eyes, closed mouth, jointed vinyl body. All original in long blue baby gown. cMATTEL INC./1976, on head; cMattel, Inc. 1976/TAIWAN, on body.

Plate 817: Mattel. "Bye-Bye Diapers." 1981. Nursing doll who drinks from her bottle and then uses her potty. Vinyl head, painted eyes, rooted dark brown hair, vinyl arms, cloth body and legs. Blue flannel jammies are sewn on with a flap held by velcro in the back for using her potty. Marks: cMATTEL INC. 1981/MEXICO, on head.

Plate 818: Mattel. "Love 'n Touch Baby," 12". Soft vinyl realistic feeling head and arms, painted eyes, dark brown rooted hair, open/closed mouth, cloth body. All original in yellow and white hooded flannel sleepers. Marks: cMATTEL INC. 1979/Taiwan, on head. Courtesy of Dana Stith.

Plate 819: Mattel. "Indigo and Hammy Sprite," 9" tall, 1983, from the Rainbow Brite series. Vinyl head, painted features, black yarn hair with blue yarn streaks, cloth body and limbs. All original in sewn-on blue shirt, removable blue pants. Marks: c1983 HALLMARK CARDS INC./TAIWAN, on head.

Plate 820: Mattel. "Baby Small-Talk," 1968–69. 10½" tall. Talking doll that says eight different phrases in an infant voice. Vinyl head, painted eyes, rooted brown hair, open mouth with four teeth, vinyl arms and legs, hard plastic body with pull string in back and voice holes in front. All original in blue dotted dress. Marks: c1967 MATTEL, INC./JAPAN, on head; c1967 MATTEL, INC./U.S. & FOR./PATS. PEND/U.S.A., on body. Clothing is tagged "BABY SMALL-TALK."

Plate 821: Mattel. "Hush Little Baby." 15" battery operated crying and moving baby doll. Vinyl head, nursing mouth, painted eyes, hard plastic body, vinyl arms and legs. Hair restyled. Marks: c1975 MATTEL INC, head; cMATTEL INC 1975/U.S.A., on body. Courtesy of Jessica Randolph.

Plate 822: Mattel. "Baby Heather." 20½" tall. Vinyl head, arms, and legs; cloth body; rooted black hair. Talking doll says over three hundred and fifty different things. Battery operated. All original. Courtesy of Marge Betts.

Plate 825: Mattel. "My Child," 14" baby from the My Children collection of dolls. The skin on the doll looks like felt and feels something like real skin. It cannot be immersed in water but can be wiped clean. Hair is black rooted, eyes are unusual inset plastic and nose is a tiny attached covered button. Body is jointed five-piece baby body. All original in pink cotton dress with matching panties. Marks: Mattel Inc. 1985/Made in China, on tag sewn to body.

Plate 823: Mattel, c1980. "The Littles Family," Mr. and Mrs. Littles and their sweet little baby, 1" to 3" tall. Vinyl dolls with painted features. Mother has rooted brown hair, father and baby have painted hair. Mother and father are jointed, baby is one piece.

Plate 824: Mattel. "Baby Kickee," 14". Vinyl head, brown rooted hair, painted features, dimpled cheeks, vinyl arms, hard plastic body with wind-up mechanism in back that makes head move from side to side and legs kick. Redressed. Marks: Mattel Inc. 1984, on head.

Plate 826: Mattel. "Magic Nursery Newborn." 12" tall. Vinyl head, painted eyes, closed mouth, rooted hair on some of the dolls with some bald, cloth body. You won't know whether you have a girl, boy, or twins until the clothes doll comes in are put in water. Some dolls have brown hair, others have black. Marks: cMATTEL INC. 1989/CHINA, on head.

Plate 827: Mattel. Another all original "My Child" doll. This one is a boy dressed in blue and white sailor outfit with matching sailor hat.

Plate 828: Mattel. "Magic Nursery Newborn," girl, 13" tall. Vinyl head, rooted patch of sandy colored hair, painted features, cloth body. All original in pink dotted romper suit with yellow bow. Marks: MATTEL INC 1989/China, on head. Courtesy of Celeste Gates.

Plate 829: Mattel. "Magic Nursery Toddler," girl. Vinyl head with black rooted hair, painted features, cloth body. All original in denim skirt, white print blouse, and pink shoes. Marks: 1989, MATTEL, INC. on head. Courtesy of Michelle Coleman.

Plate 830: Mattel. "Magic Nursery Toddler," boy. Vinyl head, brown rooted hair, painted eyes, cloth body and limbs. All original in denim overalls with checkered pocket and bib, yellow print shirt. Marks: 1989, MATTEL INC., on head. Courtesy of Sherita Jackson.

Plate 831: Mattel. "Li'l Miss Dress Up," 13" tall. Vinyl head, painted features and painted-on earrings; rooted long black hair with blue streak; vinyl jointed toddler body. All original in pink and white striped dress. Marks: Mattel Inc. 1988, 1977, on head; Mattel Inc./China, on body. Collection of Celeste Gates.

Plate 832: Mattel. "Li'l Miss Magic Hair," 13" tall. Vinyl head, painted features, including earrings; rooted blond hair with pastel streaks that change colors; vinyl jointed toddler body. All original in pink sunsuit trimmed in green. Marks: Mattel Inc. 1988, 1977, on head; Mattel Inc./China, on body. From the collection of Candace Gates.

Plate 833: Mattel. "Li'l" Miss Make-Up," 13" tall. Vinyl head, painted features with white stars in her eyes and painted-on earrings; rooted black hair; vinyl jointed toddler body. All original in aquamarine pants and pink dress. Marks: Mattel Inc./China, on body. Collection of Charisse Gates.

Plate 834: Mattel. "Wee Li'l Miss." 1990. 7" tall. Vinyl head, painted eyes, open/closed mouth, very long rooted black hair; jointed vinyl body. All original in white and pink ballerina costume with pink plastic shoes. Marks: c1990 MATTEL, on head. Doll was also available as "Wee Li'l Miss" from playtime to bedtime.

Plate 835: Mattel. "P.J. Sparkles," 15" doll that sparkles with twinkling lights when hugged, dress transforms, too. Battery operated. All original in pink and white evening gown. Vinyl head, arms, and legs; painted features; rooted hair; hard plastic body. Marks: 1988 Mattel Inc./China, on head. Courtesy of Michelle Coleman.

Plate 836: Mattel. "Baby Sparkles," baby sister of P.J. Sparkles, 13". Baby lights up with love when she gets a kiss. The more she is loved, the more she sparkles. Vinyl head, arms, and legs; rooted brown glittering hair, painted eyes; open/closed mouth; white plastic baby body. All original in pink print nightie. Battery operated. Marks: 1989 MATTEL INC./China, on head.

Plate 837: Mattel. "Greta Grape" from the Cherry Merry Muffin series of dolls. 1990. Grape scented doll, 6½" tall, dressed in purple. Vinyl head, painted features, rooted hair; hard plastic movable body. Marks: Mattel Inc. 1988, on head; Mattel Inc. 1988/China, on body.

Plate 838: Mattel. "Apple Amy," 6½" from the Cherry Merry Muffin series of dolls. Doll is apple scented. Vinyl head, painted features, rooted dark hair; jointed hard vinyl body. All original. Marks: Mattel Inc. 1988, on head; Mattel Inc. 1988/China, on body.

Plate 839: Mattel. "Zizi," 18" doll in the "Hot Looks" models series of five dolls. The only black doll in the series, her nationality was Kenyan. Fully poseable with vinyl head, painted features, rooted black hair; stockinette covered wire frame body. All original. Marks: Mattel Inc. 1986, on head. Made in China.

Plate 840: Mattel. "Styla Blue." Outer space fashion leader from Spectra collection. 11½" tall. Vinyl head, rooted sky blue and silver hair, painted eyes, smiling mouth with painted teeth. Body and limbs are silver, fully jointed. All original in glittery pink lace dress. Marks: cMATTEL, INC. 1986, on head.

Plate 841: Mattel. "Suzie Cutie" from the Wee Wild Things collection. 2½" tall. Vinyl head, rooted blue hair, painted eyes, jointed hard plastic body with painted clothes. Marks: cM.I. 1987, on head.

Plate 842: Mattel. "Dancing Pretty Ballerina," 11". Soft vinyl head, hard vinyl body, painted eyes, brown rooted hair. Wind-up key in doll's back, no batteries required. All original. Marks: CHINA, on back. On box: 1990 MATTEL Inc.

Plate 843: Mattel. "Tapsie." 12½" tall. Vinyl head, painted eyes, rooted dark brown hair, open/closed mouth with painted teeth, hard plastic body and limbs. Tap dancing doll, no batteries required. All original in bright pink skirt with black dotted trim, white dotted blouse, black pants to knees. Marks: c1990, MATTEL/INC., on head; c1990 MATTEL, INC/MEXICO, on body.

Plate 844: Mattel. "Maiden Mistycurls" from the Lady Lovely Locks and the Pixietails Enchanted Island collection, 8" tall. Vinyl head, painted features, long rooted multicolored hair, hard vinyl jointed body. Marks: 1986 TCFC, on head. Made in China.

Plate 845: Mattel. "Big Jack," 1971. 9½" tall. Action doll. All vinyl; painted, molded features; fully jointed. Doll wears molded red shorts under removable red nylon shorts. Marks: c1971 MATTEL INC., on head; c1971 MATTEL, Inc./HONG KONG U.S. & /FOREIGN PATENTED, body. Courtesy of Todd Perkins.

Plate 846: Mattel. "Gold Medal Big Jack," 1974. Olympic champ. Identical to previous doll except this one wears molded red, white, and blue shorts and removable gold medal. Courtesy of Todd Perkins.

Plate 847: Mattel. "Rosemary Rock Flowers," 1971. 6½" tall vinyl doll with rooted black afro. Comes with 33⅓ rpm record and stand which fits into center of record. Marks: HONG KONG/ MATTEL/1970.

Plate 848: Mattel. "Jazz Performers, Mellie and Louis Harris," from Star Spangled Dolls series, dolls made to represent beautiful people from moments in our history. Historical couple are described on original box as follows: "We're Mellie and Louis Harris from the port city where life is music and music is jazz. Louis plays the trumpet with Jelly Roll Morton, the famous piano player. I sing the blues. We play in parks to people dancing on the grass, at cotillions or in cabarets 'till the night is

filled with swirling colors and a sweet jazz wail. Our favorite place to play is on street corners for the whole world to hear." Dolls are made from same mold as "The Happy Family."

Plate 849: Mattel. "The Happy Family," Hal, Hattie, and Hon. Father, 9½" tall; Mother, 9" tall; baby, 3" tall. All have soft vinyl heads, molded features; rooted black hair; brown stationary glassine eyes. Mother and father have jointed vinyl bodies, baby has one-piece bent leg vinyl body. Marks: 1973 MATTEL INC., head; 1973/ MATTEL INC./TAIWAN, body.

Plate 850: Mattel. "Happy Family Grandparents," 1976. Fully jointed vinyl dolls, stationary glassine eyes. Grandfather has gray rooted hair, full beard, and mustache; 9½" tall. Grandmother has white rooted hair, 9" tall. Marks: c1975 TAIWAN/MATTEL INC, head; c1973/MATTEL INC/TAIWAN, body.

Plate 851: Mattel. "Quick Curl Christie Beauty Center," 1975. 11½" tall. Cosmetics, barrettes, ribbons, brush, comb, etc., are included. Marks: 1971 MATTEL INC.

Plate 852: Mattel. Barbie makeup vinyl head with painted features; smiling mouth with painted teeth; rooted hair, reddish blond in front, the rest is dark brown; pierced ears. Marks: 1975 MATTEL INC. USA.

Plate 853: Mattel. "Barbie Color Change" makeup head. Her makeup appears when you add water. Painted features, rooted black curly hair. Marks: MATTEL, INC 1988, on head.

Left - Plate 855: Mattel. "Talking Julia," 1969. 11½" tall. Dressed in gold and silver one-piece jumpsuit, pull string at back of neck. Marks: 1967/MATTEL INC/U.S. FOREIGN/PATS. PEND/MEXICO, body. All vinyl jointed doll. Rooted brown hair has oxydized to red, rooted eyelashes, closed mouth. Doll made in the image of Diahann Carroll, singer and star of popular TV program.

Right – Plate 856: Mattel. "Julia," 1969. All original in two-piece nurse's uniform. Hair oxydized to bright maroonish red, was originally brown, real eyelashes, closed mouth. Marks: c1966/MATTEL, INC./U.S. PATENTED/U.S.PAT.PEND. /MADE IN/JAPAN, on body.

Plate 854: Mattel. "Carla," 1967, made for the European market. 6" tall. Vinyl head, painted eyes, closed mouth, rooted black hair with center part and bangs, one-piece vinyl body. All original in orange sundress, white vinyl shoes. White socks are missing. Marks: c1965/MATTEL, INC/HONG KONG, on body.

Plate 857: Mattel. "Julia," nurse, 1970–72. Doll now has new one-piece nurse's uniform. Rooted brown hair has oxydized, painted features, long rooted eyelashes, fully jointed bendable body. Marks are the same as previous Julia doll.

Plate 858: Mattel. "Talking Christie," 1970. All original in two-piece orange vinyl swimsuit with print overshirt with matching vinyl trim. Short black rooted hair, "real" eyelashes, closed mouth. Marks: c1967/MATTEL INC./ U.S. & FOREIGN/PATS. PEND/ HONG KONG, on body.

Plate 859: Mattel. "Live Action Christie," 1971. All original. Marks: 1968 MATTEL INC./U.S. & FOREIGN PATENTED/PATENTED IN CANADA 1967/OTHER PATENTS PENDING /TAIWAN.

Plate 860: Mattel. "Talking Brad," 1969, Christie's boyfriend. All original in print overshirt with orange vinyl trim and orange vinyl shorts, molded hair, closed mouth. Marks: 1969 Mattel Inc., on head; c1968/ Mattel Inc./U.S. & FOR. PAT'D/OTHER PAT'S./PENDING/HONG KONG, on body.

Plate 861: Mattel. "Brad," 1971 with the bendable legs. All original. Marks: 1968/MATTEL INC./U.S. & FOR.PATD./OTHER PATS/PEND-ING/HONG KONG, on back. Wrist tag: Genuine Brad By Mattel.

Plate 862: Mattel. "Quick Curl Cara," 1974. All original. Marks: 1966/Mattel Inc. U.S. & Foreign Patented/Other Pats./Pending/Made in /Taiwan, on body.

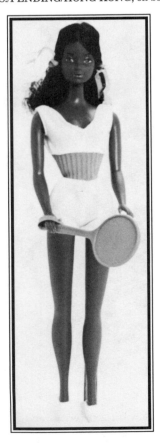

Plate 863: Mattel. "Free Moving Cara," 1974. All original. Marks: 1967 Mattel, Inc./TAIWAN/U.S. PAT. PEND., on body.

Plate 864: Mattel. "Ballerina Cara," 1975, one of Barbie's friends; 11½" tall; all vinyl, swivel waist. All original. Marks: Mattel Inc. 1966/U.S. Patent Pending/Tai-wan on back.

Plate 865: Mattel. "Deluxe Quick Curl Cara," 1976. All original in long yellow cotton dress with white fringe trim. Reddish brown rooted hair, mouth with lips slightly parted. Marks: cMATTEL INC. 1966/TAIWAN, on body.

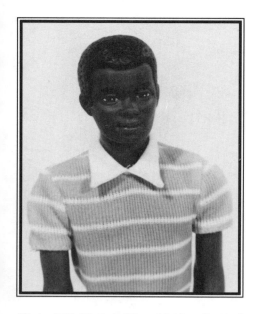

Left – Plate 867: Mattel. "Super Star Christie," 1976. Brown hair with reddish blond streaks, brown eyes, smiling mouth with painted teeth. All original in yellow gown with "diamond" ring, earrings, and necklace. Marks: Mattel Inc. 1966/Taiwan, on body.

Right – Plate 868: Mattel. "Super Size Christie," 1977. 18" tall. Vinyl head, sun streaked hair, brown and red; painted eyes; painted open mouth with teeth; jointed vinyl body. All original in long two-piece light blue gown with silver trim. Marks: TAIWAN/c1976 MATTEL INC, on head; cMATTEL, INC. 1976/U.S.A., on body.

Plate 866: Mattel. "Free Moving Curtis," 1974. 12" tall. All original in orange knit shirt with white stripes, white cotton shorts. Molded black kinky hair, closed mouth. Marks: 1969/MATTEL, INC, on head; 1968 MATTEL, INC./TAIWAN/U.S. PATENT/ PENDING, on body.

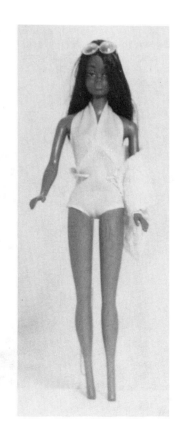

Plate 869: Mattel. "Malibu Christie," 1978. All original in yellow swimsuit. Marks: 1966/MATTEL, INC/U.S. PATENTED/U.S.PAT.PEND./MADE IN/KOREA.

Plate 870: Mattel. "Photo Fashion Christie," 1978. Reddish brown hair with highlights, open smiling mouth. All original in yellow pants, metallic top and yellow and pink net overskirt. Marks: cMattel, Inc. 1966/Taiwan, on body.

Plate 871: Mattel. "Kissing Christie," 1978. The doll who kisses and leaves her mark. Comes with her own special lipstick. Marks: Mattel Inc./1978 Taiwan, on head; Mattel Inc. 1966/Taiwan, on body. Doll's lips pucker up when button on back is pushed.

Plate 872: Mattel. "Sun Lovin' Malibu Christie," 1978. Dark brown vinyl with closed mouth, rooted black hair. All original in two-piece pink swimsuit. Marks: MATTEL INC/196? (cannot read)/PHILIPPINES.

Plate 873: Mattel. "Beauty Secrets Christie," 1979. Black hair, short, and curly on top, long and straight in the back, open smiling mouth. All original in blue bodysuit under long matching skirt and jacket. Marks: cMATTEL INC. 1979/TAIWAN 1966, on body.

Plate 874: Mattel. "Black Barbie," 1980. Short curly black hair, closed mouth with lips slightly parted, brown eyes and eye shadow, twisting waist. All original in long red gown with long sleeves, gold neck trim, red shoes, red earrings, and red ring on right hand. Marks: cMattel, Inc. 1966/TAIWAN, on body.

Plate 875: Mattel. "Golden Dream Christie," 1980. Two-toned hair, brown and blond, slightly parted lips. All original in gold glitter jumpsuit with overskirt. Marks: cMATTEL INC 1966/Taiwan, on body.

Plate 876: Mattel. "Magic Curl Barbie," 1981, curly dark brown hair, closed mouth with lips slightly parted. All original in long yellow dress. Marks: cMattel. Inc. 1966/TAIWAN, on body.

Plate 877: Mattel. "Pink & Pretty Christie," 1981. All original in pink glimmery top, furry-trimmed hat/peplum, slim skirt, and furry-trimmed overskirt. Closed mouth, long dark brown hair, clear plastic earrings, ring, and necklace. Marks: cMattel Inc. 1966/TAIWAN, on body.

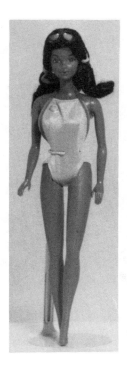

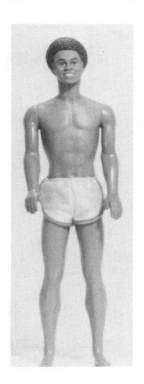

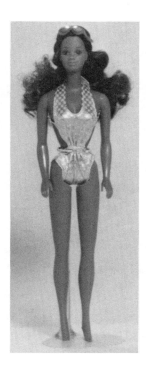

Plate 878: Mattel. "Sunsational Malibu Christie," 1981. Long black hair, closed mouth with lips slightly parted. All original in yellow swimsuit trimmed in orange. Marks: cMattel Inc./ 1966/Phillipines, on body.

Plate 879: Mattel. "Sunsational Malibu Ken," 1981, with rooted synthetic black hair, closed mouth. Marks: 1981 MATTEL INC, on head.

Plate 880: Mattel. "Sunsational Malibu Ken," 1983 with molded painted hair, smiling mouth with teeth showing. Marks: 1983 MATTEL INC, on head.

Plate 881: Mattel. "Sun Gold Malibu Barbie," 1983, long brown rooted hair, closed mouth, brown eye shadow. All original in gold swimsuit. Marks: cMATTEL, INC. 1966/ PHILIPPINES, on body.

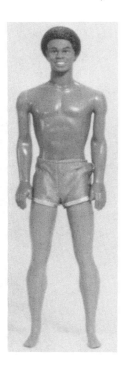

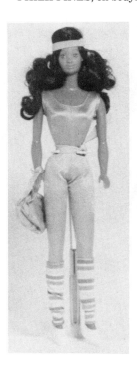

Plate 882: Mattel. "Twirly Curls Barbie," 1982. Below the hips dark brown hair, closed mouth, brown eye shadow. All original in long pink gown, comes with pink plastic chair and twirly curler. Marks: cMATTEL, INC. 1966/TAIWAN, on body.

Plate 883: Mattel. "Sun Gold Malibu Ken," 1983. Molded hair, smiling mouth with painted teeth. All original in blue swimsuit trimmed in gold. Marks: c1983 MATTEL INC, on head; c1968/MATTEL INC/HONG KONG, on body.

Plate 884: Mattel. "Great Shape Barbie," 1983. All original in aqua workout suit and multicolored leg warmers. Closed mouth, black hair, purple eye shadow. Marks: MATTEL, INC. 1966/PHILIPPINES, on body.

Plate 885: Mattel. "My First Barbie," 1984. All original in short white dress trimmed with pink ribbon. Closed mouth, long black hair with bangs, red eye shadow. Marks: cMATTEL, INC. 1966/PHILIPPINES, on body.

Plate 886: Mattel. "Peaches 'n Cream Barbie," 1984. All original in long peach chiffon gown with matching stole. Closed mouth, dark brown hair, earrings. Marks: cMATTEL, INC. 1966/ TAIWAN, on back.

Plate 887: Mattel. "Crystal Ken," 1984. All original. Marks: 1983 MATTEL INC, on head; MATTEL INC. 1968/TAIWAN, on body. Outfit is white with purple tie, buttons, and flower on lapel.

Plate 888: Mattel. "Crystal Barbie," 1984. All original in long white gown, crystal earrings, necklace, and ring on right hand, long dark brown hair, closed mouth, green eye shadow. Marks: MATTEL, INC 1966. MALAYSIA on back.

Plate 889: Mattel. "Day-to-Night Ken," 1985. All original in blue velveteen jacket, striped pants and vest, white shirt. Molded afro, open smiling mouth with painted teeth. Marks: c1983 MATTEL INC, on head; cMattel, Inc. 1968. TAIWAN, on body.

Plate 890: Mattel. "Day-to-Night Barbie," c1984. Long black hair, closed mouth, burgundy eye shadow, clear plastic stud earrings, ring. All original in pink suit with white hat. Marks: MATTEL INC. 1966/TAIWAN, on body.

Plate 892: Mattel. "Dee Dee, Barbie and the Rockers," 1985. All original in oversize green top, "leather" mini skirt, scarf, and tights. Orange t-shirt also came with the doll. Long dark brown curly hair, closed mouth, purple eye shadow, orange and yellow plastic earrings. Marks: cMATTEL INC. 1966/PHILIPPINES, on back.

Plate 891: Mattel. "Dee Dee," one of the Barbie Rockers, 1986. There were several editions of this doll. The one on the right was made in the Philippines, the one on the left was made in Taiwan. Both boxes are dated 1986. Eye shadow and lipstick on Taiwan doll are a brighter shade of orange, otherwise, they look identical. Marks: Mattel Inc. 1966/Taiwan (or Philippines), on body.

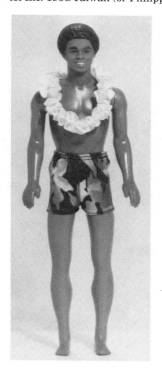

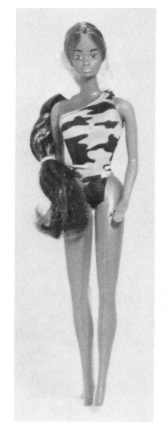

Plate 893: Mattel. "Tropical Ken," 1985. All original in print bathing trunks. Molded black hair, smile with painted teeth. Marks: c1983 MATTEL INC, on head; cMATTEL INC. 1968/Malaysia, on body.

Plate 894: Mattel, "Astronaut Barbie," 1985. Black curly hair pulled back, closed mouth, aqua eye shadow. All original in fuchsia astronaut suit, knee high fuchsia boots. Marks: cMATTEL. INC. 1966/MALAYSIA, on body.

Plate 895: Mattel. "Tropical Barbie," 1985. Almost to the knees long two-toned hair, reddish brown and black. Closed mouth, orange eye shadow. All original in print swimsuit. Marks: cMATTEL. INC. 1966, on body.

Plate 896: Mattel. "Magic Moves Barbie," 1985. When a switch on her back is pushed, she moves. Closed mouth, rooted dark brown hair. All original in pale aqua evening gown and matching cape. Marks: cMATTEL INC 1966/TAIWAN, on body.

Plate 897: Mattel. "Dream Glow Barbie," 1985. Long brown hair, purple eye shadow, closed mouth. All original in long two-toned pink gown, "crystal" earrings and matching ring. Marks: cMATTEL, INC. 1966/PHILIPPINES, on body.

Plate 898: Mattel. "Dream Glow Ken," 1985. Molded black afro hairstyle, heavy eyebrows, smiling mouth. All original in gray suit with glow in the dark pink vest. Marks: c1983 MATTEL INC, on head; cMattel, Inc. 1968/TAIWAN, on body.

Plate 899: Mattel. "My First Barbie," 1986. All original in pink ballet outfit. Closed mouth, dark brown curly hair. Marks: MATTEL INC. 1966/PHILIPPINES, on body.

Plate 900: Mattel. "Funtime Barbie," 1986. All original in pink shorts and matching top trimmed in blue. A real watch is included. Closed mouth, long brown hair, blue eye shadow. Marks: cMATTEL, INC. 1966/PHILIPPINES, on body.

Plate 901: Mattel. "Super Hair Barbie," 1986. Doll comes with a magic styling barrette. All original in white vinyl jumpsuit, closed mouth, long reddish brown hair, lavender eye shadow, "diamond" earrings and ring. Marks: cMATTEL, INC. 1966/PHILIPPINES, on body.

Plate 902: Mattel. "Jewel Secrets Barbie and Ken," 1986, sold separately. Marks on Barbie: MATTEL INC. 1966/Philippines, on body. Marks on Ken: 1983, Mattel Inc., on head.

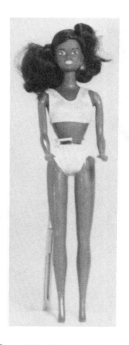

Plate 903: Mattel. "Island Fun Steven," 1987. Molded painted hair, open smiling mouth with painted teeth. All original in fuchsia print trunks and Hawaiian lei. Marks: cMATTEL INC. 1987, on head.

Plate 904: Mattel. "Fun-to-Dress Barbie," 1987. All original in two-piece pink and white swimsuit. Long dark brown hair, open smiling mouth with painted teeth. Marks: cMATTEL INC/1987, on head; cMATTEL, INC. 1966, on body.

Plate 905: Mattel. "Belinda," from group "Barbie and the Sensations" 1987. Dark brown hair with bangs, open mouth with painted teeth. All original in orange and gold dress, green jacket. Marks: MATTEL INC. 1966/China, on body.

Left – Plate 906: Mattel, "Island Fun Christie," 1987. Extremely long wavy hair, reddish brown on the top and black underneath; painted open mouth with teeth. All original in yellow swimsuit and orange print wrap skirt with lei. Marks: cMATTEL INC/1987, on head; cMATTEL, INC. 1966/PHILIPPINES, on back.

Right – Plate 907: Mattel. "California Christie," 1987. Black hair, blue eye shadow, open mouth with painted teeth. All original in yellow swimsuit under orange t-shirt and yellow striped shorts with orange earrings. Marks: cMATTEL INC/1987, on head; cMATTEL, INC. 1966, on body.

Plate 908: Mattel. "Super Star Barbie and Ken," 1988, sold separately. Barbie has long dark brown wavy hair, pink eye shadow, smiling mouth. Ken has molded black hair, mustache, smiling mouth. Marks on Barbie: cMATTEL INC/1987, on head; cMATTEL INC. 1966, on body. Marks on Ken: cMATTEL, INC. 1987, on head; cMattel, Inc. 1968/MALAYSIA, on back.

Plate 909: Mattel. "Perfume Giving Barbie," 1988. Long brown hair, open smiling mouth, blue and purple eye shadow, pink earrings and ring. All original in long pink gown with matching net wrap. Marks: cMATTEL INC./1987, on head; cMATTEL, INC. 1966/PHILIPPINES, on body.

Plate 910: Mattel. "Style Magic Christie," 1988. Long reddish brown hair, open smiling mouth with painted teeth. All original in short pink and blue swimsuit with print skirt and halter top. Marks: cMATTEL INC./1987, on head; cMATTEL, INC. 1966/MALAYSIA, on body.

Plate 911: Mattel. "Stacie," friend of Jazzie who is a teen cousin of Barbie. 1988. Long black hair, closed with lips slightly pursed, blue eyeliner. All original in hot pink outfit with white shirt. Marks: cMATTEL. INC. 1966/MALAYSIA, on back.

Plate 912: Mattel. "Perfume Giving Ken," 1988. Molded black hair, open smiling mouth, moustache. All original in gray and silver formal outfit. Doll has molded-on shorts. Marks: cMATTEL, INC. 1987, on head; cMattel, Inc. 1968/MALAYSIA, on body.

Plate 913: Mattel. "Fun-to-Dress Barbie," 1988. Dressed in pink teddy trimmed in white lace. Marks: MATTEL INC./1987, on head; MATTEL, INC. 1966/CHINA, on body.

Plate 914: Mattel. "Homecoming Queen Skipper," teen sister of Barbie. 1988. Long dark brown wavy hair, closed mouth. All original in below-the-knee white dress. Marks: cMATTEL INC/1987, on head; cMATTEL INC. 1987/CHINA, on body.

Plate 915: Mattel. "Cool Times Christie," 1988, open smiling mouth with teeth showing. Marks: MATTEL INC/1987, on head; MATTEL INC. 1966/China, on back.

Note: Mattel. "Dance Magic Barbie," 1989. Photograph not shown.

Plate 916: Mattel. "Dance Magic Ken," 1989. Molded black hair, smiling mouth with moustache. All original in white jumpsuit, vest, and sleeveless jacket with pink tie. Marks: cMATTEL. INC. 1987, on head; cMattel, Inc. 1968/MALAYSIA, on body.

Plate 917: Mattel. "Unicef Barbie," 1989. Mattel sends $0.37 of the price of this doll to the U.S. Committee for UNICEF. This was a special edition Barbie. All original in long gown with blue skirt, white bodice, red sash, blue earrings, blue ring on right hand. Long wavy dark brown hair, open mouth. Marks: cMATTEL INC/1987, on head; cMATTEL, INC. 1966/CHINA, on body.

Plate 918: Mattel. "Special Expressions Barbie," 1989. All original in silver and white dress. Woolworth special limited edition. Long black hair with bangs, lavender eye shadow, open mouth. Marks: cMATTEL INC./1987, on head; cMATTEL, INC. 1966, on body.

Plate 919: Mattel. "Flight Time Barbie," 1989, came with a black Barbie paper doll. Black hair, blue eye shadow, yellow gem-like ear posts and matching ring. All original in pink pilot's uniform. Marks: cMATTEL INC./1987, on head; MATTEL, INC. 1966/MALAYSIA, on body.

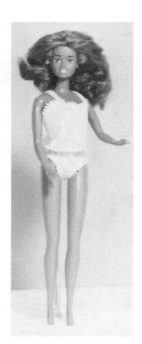

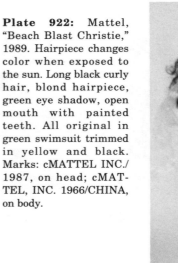

Plate 922: Mattel, "Beach Blast Christie," 1989. Hairpiece changes color when exposed to the sun. Long black curly hair, blond hairpiece, green eye shadow, open mouth with painted teeth. All original in green swimsuit trimmed in yellow and black. Marks: cMATTEL INC./1987, on head; cMATTEL, INC. 1966/CHINA, on body.

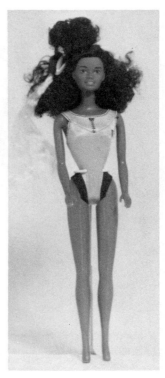

Plate 921: Mattel. "Fun-to-Dress Barbie," Long medium brown hair, dark pink eye shadow. Marks: MATTEL INC./1987, on head; MATTEL INC. 1966/CHINA, on body.

Plate 920: Mattel. "Animal Lovin' Barbie," 1989 with her own small plastic panda bear. Long black hair, pink eyeliner. All original in pink and gold three-piece outfit, pink plastic earrings and pink ring. Marks: cMATTEL INC./1987, on head; cMATTEL, INC. 1966/MALAYSIA, on body.

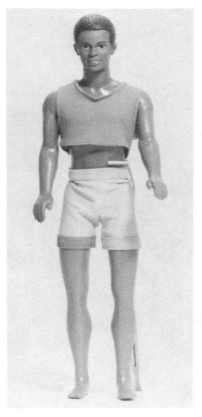

Plate 923: Mattel. "Lavender Surprise Barbie," Sears special edition, 1989. All original.

Plate 924: Mattel. "Wet'n Wild Christie." 1989. All original in orange and blue two-piece swimsuit. Marks: cMATTEL INC./1987, on head; cMATTEL INC. 1966/CHINA, on body.

Plate 925: Mattel. "Wet'n Wild Steven," c1989. The same mold for head as last year's black male in the Barbie line but doll does not have the mustache. Body is different, it does not have molded-on shorts. All original. Marks: cMATTEL, INC. 1987, on head; c1968/MATTEL, INC./MALAYSIA, on body.

Plate 926: Mattel. "All Star Christie," from the Barbie and the All-Stars collection, 1989. Below the waist black hair crimped at the ends, tan eye shadow, orange plastic earrings and ring. All original in orange and white outfit. Marks: cMATTEL INC./1987, on head; cMATTEL, INC. 1966/MALAYSIA, on back.

Plate 927: Mattel. "Cool Tops Skipper," teen sister of Barbie, 1989. Long dark brown hair, painted eyes, closed mouth. All original in short pink shirt over aqua shirt, white print skirt, pink pants. Marks: cMATTEL INC/1987, on head; cMATTEL INC 1987/CHINA, on body.

Plate 928: Mattel. "Wedding Fantasy Barbie," 1989. Open mouth, long dark brown hair, pearl-like earrings, pearl-like ring on right hand. All original in two-piece white satin gown with lace overlay. Marks: cMATTEL INC/1987, on head; cMATTEL INC. 1966/CHINA, on body.

Plate 929: Mattel. "Denim Fun Barbie, Ken, and Skipper" in cool city blues. 1989. Ken has molded hair, open mouth with painted teeth; Barbie has long brown hair, open mouth with painted teeth, fuchsia eye shadow; Skipper has long brown hair, pink eye shadow, closed mouth.

Plate 930: Mattel. "Christie and the Beat," 1989. Open mouth, long dark brown hair, lime green eye shadow, pierced ears. Marks: cMATTEL/1987, on head; cMATTEL INC. 1966/CHINA, on body.

Plate 931: Mattel. "Special Expressions Barbie," Woolworth's special edition, 1990. Dressed in pink with hot pink and orange chiffon trim. Marks: Mattel Inc. 1987, on head; Mattel Inc. 1966/Malaysia, on body.

Plate 932: Mattel. "Barbie Ready for a day of fun in Disney character fashions," 1990. Marks: Mattel Inc./1987, on head. MATTEL INC. 1966/CHINA, on body. Special Limited Edition Barbie.

Plate 933: Mattel. "Costume Ball Ken," 1990. Ken wears a tuxedo and comes with extra clothing to make changes to a genie and a pirate. Marks: Mattel Inc. 1987, on head; Mattel Inc. 1968/Malaysia, on body.

Plate 934: Mattel. "Costume Ball Barbie," 1990. Costume can be changed to three different looks. Long black hair, olive pink and blue eye shadow, open smiling mouth, pink stud earrings. All original in pink costume. Marks: cMattel Inc./1987, on head; cMATTEL INC 1966/MALAYSIA, on body.

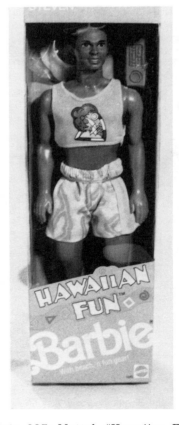

Plate 935: Mattel. "Western Fun Barbie," 1990. Dressed in the popular Sante Fe colors, turquoise and shades of pink. Marks: MATTEL INC 1987, on head; MATTEL INC 1966/MALAYSIA, on body.

Plate 936: Mattel. "Hawaiian Fun Christie," 1990. Long black rooted hair with brown streak, smiling mouth, dressed in two-piece green print swimsuit and comes with a green hula skirt. Marks: MATTEL INC./1987, on head; MATTEL INC. 1966/MALAYSIA, on body.

Plate 937: Mattel. "Hawaiian Fun Steven," 1990. Marks: Mattel Inc. 1987, on head; 1988/MATTEL INC./US & FOR.PATD./OTHER PATS/PENDING/MALAYSIA, on back.

Plate 938: Mattel. "Nigerian Barbie," special edition, 1990, part of the International collection, she wears a belted wrap dress done in an elegant print with an African flavor. Gele, earrings, and armband are representative of her proud heritage. Long black natural hairstyle. Marks: cMATTEL INC/1987, on head; cMATTEL, INC./CHINA, on body.

Plate 939: Mattel. "Happy Holidays Barbie," Special Edition, 1990. This was the first black Happy Holidays issued by Mattel. All original in long fuchsia gown. Dark brown hair, blue eyeliner, olive eye shadow, "gem" earrings, open smiling mouth. Marks: cMATTEL INC./1987, on head; cMATTEL INC. 1966/CHINA, on body.

Plate 940: Mattel. "All-American Christie," c1990. All original in two-piece orange cotton knit outfit and denim jacket. Included are two pairs of Reebok Hi-tops for Christie. Long brown wavy hair, green eye shadow, green earrings and ring. Marks: cMATTEL INC/1987, on head; cMATTEL INC 1966/MALAYSIA, on body.

Plate 941: Mattel. "Navy Barbie," 1990. First black doll in the Stars 'n Stripes series. All original in white navy outfit, short dark brown hair, open mouth with painted teeth, blue eye shadow. Marks: cMATTEL INC./ 1987, on head; cMATTEL INC. 1966/CHINA, on body. Doll came with high heel and flat shoes and a pair of long white pants.

Plate 942: Mattel. "Christie, United Colors of Benetton." c1990, on the market 1991. Long black hair in twist braids, open smiling mouth with painted teeth, brown eyes. Doll is dressed in pink tights; striped shirt in pink, green, orange and yellow; jacket in white with bands of multicolored strips; long yellow sash; and purse matching blouse. Marks: cMATTEL, INC./1987, on head; cMATTEL INC. 1966/CHINA, on body.

Plate 943: Mattel. "Babysitter Skipper," c1990. Skipper has on a two-piece dotted white, orange, and pink outfit; baby has on blue romper outfit. Marks on Skipper: cMATTEL INC./ 1987, on head; MALAYSIA/cMATTEL, INC. 1987, on body. Marks on baby: cM I 1985, on head; c1973/MATTEL, INC./MALAYSIA/7, on body.

Plate 944: Mattel. "Shani", 1991. New African-American fashion doll. Shani means "marvelous" in Swahili. Vinyl doll is 11½" tall and has painted eyes, long black wavy hair, open mouth with painted teeth. All original in long pink and blue print outfit. Marks: c1990/MATTEL INC., on head; cMATTEL, INC/MALAYSIA, on body.

Plate 945: Mattel. "Nichelle," from the Shani and Her Friends collection. 11½" tall. Vinyl fashion doll, painted eyes, long rooted black hair, closed mouth. All original in long fuchsia, pink, and gold gown that becomes a ballerina costume. Marks: c1990/MATTEL INC., on head; cMATTEL INC. 1966/MALAYSIA, on body.

Plate 946: Mattel. "ASHA," from the Shani and Her Friends collection. Vinyl fashion doll, 11½" tall, long curly auburn hair, painted eyes, open mouth with painted teeth. All original in long orange print gown with gold and net. Marks: c1990/MATTEL INC., on head; cMATTEL INC. 1966/MALAYSIA, on body.

Left – Plate 947: Mattel. "American Beauty Queen," 1991. Long dark brown hair, painted smiling mouth with teeth, pierced ears with "diamond" earrings, matching ring, blue and purple eye shadow. All original in silver bathing suit under long silver skirt with net overlay in blue print, ballet tutu at waist in the same print, banner, long silver gloves and crown. Marks: cMATTEL INC./1987, on head; cMATTEL, INC. 1966/CHINA, on body.

Right – Plate 948: Mattel. "M.C. Hammer," 1991. Rap music star personality doll. 12" tall. Vinyl head, molded hair, painted eyes, open mouth with painted teeth, vinyl jointed body with swivel waist. All original in purple outfit with removable glasses. Included with the doll is a taped message from M.C. Hammer. Marks: c1991 BUSTIN, on head; cMattel Inc. 1968/MALAYSIA, on body. Doll is also available in a deluxe edition dressed in a gold outfit.

Plate 949: Mattel. "The Heart Family, Mom & Baby," 1984. All original in pink print dress with white lace trim on both mom and baby. Marks: MATTEL INC. 1966/TAIWAN, on mom's body; Mattel Inc. 1975/Taiwan, on baby's body.

Plate 950: Mattel. "Heart Family, Dad & Baby," 1984. Dad is all original in blue shirt, white pants, pink tie. Baby also wears blue and white with pink trim.

Plate 951: Mattel. "The Heart Family Surprise Party Set." Mom, dad, boy, and girl. 1985.

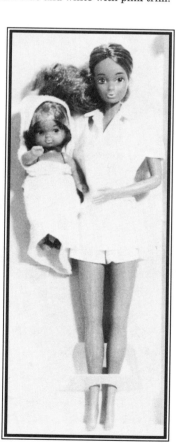

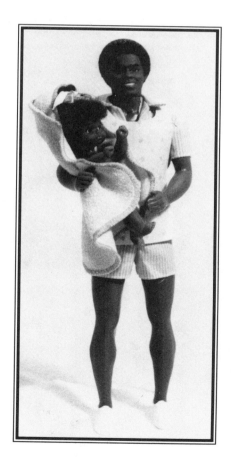

Plate 952: Mattel. "Heart Family Kiss & Cuddle Mom & Baby Boy," 1986. Also available were "Dad and Baby Girl," 1986; and all four dolls sold together in a deluxe edition.

Plate 953: Mattel. "Heart Family," bathtime fun, mom and baby boy. 1987.

Plate 954: Mattel. "The Heart Family, Bathtime Fun," dad & baby girl. 1987. Marks on dad: 1983 Mattel Inc., on head; MATTEL 1968, body. Baby: Mattel Inc. 1976, head; Mattel Inc. 1976, body.

Plate 955: Mattel. "The Heart Family, School Time Fun," coach dad and girl, 1988. Vinyl dolls with painted features. Dad has molded, painted black hair; girl has rooted brown long hair. All original.

Plate 956: Mattel. "Heart Family School Time Fun," Teacher mom and baby, 1988.

Plate 957: Mattel. "The Heart Family Visits Disneyland, Mom and Girl," 1989. Marks on mom: Mattel Inc. 1966, on body. Marks on girl: Mattel Inc. 1966, on head.

Plate 959: Mattel. "The Heart Family Kids on Parade," visits Disneyland. Minnie Mouse Car & Girl. 1990.

Plate 958: Mattel. "The Heart Family Visits Disneyland," 1989, dad and boy. Marks on dad: Mattel Inc. 1987, on head. Marks on boy: Mattel Inc. 1976, on head.

Plate 960: Mattel. "Kevin & Highchair," the Heart Family baby cousin, 5" tall. Vinyl head, rooted black hair, painted eyes, jointed vinyl body. All original in aqua and yellow. 1987.

Plate 961: Mego Corp. "Muhammad Ali," the Champ, 1976. 10" tall. Fully jointed vinyl action figure in likeness of boxing champion. Molded, painted hair; painted features. Doll comes with an Ali trigger mechanism that activates the champ. Marks: H.M. ENT/1975, head; box is marked: Manufactured exclusively for Mego Corp. New York, N.Y. 10010 in the British Colony of Hong Kong/c1976 – HERBERT MUHAMMAD ENTERPRISES INC.

Plate 962: Mego. "Muhammad Ali Opponent." 10" tall. Vinyl head, molded painted hair, painted eyes, moustache, jointed hard vinyl body. Which opponent the doll represents is not indicated on the package. Marks: c1975 MEGO CORP, on head.

Plate 963: Mego. "Action Jackson," 1971, 8" action doll. All original. Vinyl head; painted Negroid features, molded kinky hair. Fully jointed vinyl body. Action Jackson dog tag around neck, removable clothing. Marks: MEGO CORP/REG. U.S. PAT. OFF./PAT. PENDING/HONG KONG/MCMLXXI.

Plate 964: Mego. "Dinah-mite," 7½". All vinyl, rooted black hair, painted features; fully jointed and poseable. All original in purple jumpsuit. Marks: MEGO CORP./1972, on head; MEGO CORP/MCMLXXII/PAT. PENDING/MADE IN/HONG KONG, on body.

Plate 965: Mego. "Lt. Uhura," 1974, 8" fully poseable action figure based on TV show, "Star Trek." Rooted hair, painted features. All original. Role was played by Nichelle Nichols. Marks: 1974/PARAMOUNT/PICT CORP, on head; MEGO CORP/MCMLXXII/PAT. PENDING/MADE IN/HONG KONG, on body.

Plate 967: Mego. "Bubble Yum Baby." She looks like she blows a real bubble. 14" tall. Vinyl head, rooted black hair, painted eyes, open mouth, hard plastic body and legs. All original in red t-shirt and blue jeans. Doll comes with supply of pink balloons for blowing. Marks: PRESS HERE/LIFE SAVERS. INC., on head; PAT. PEND./MADE IN HONG KONG, on body. c 1978 Life Savers, Inc., on box.

Plate 968: Mego. "Diana Ross," 12¼" fully poseable vinyl personality doll. All original in long silver halter neck dress. Painted features, long rooted hair. Marks: MOTOWN RECORD/CORPORATION, on head; MEGO CORP. 1975/Made in Hong Kong, on body.

Plate 966: Mego Corp. "Buckwheat," 6½" character doll from Our Gang series. Vinyl head, molded painted hair, molded features; hard plastic fully articulated body. All original. Marks: 1975/MGM INC, on head; MEGO CORP.1975/REG. U.S. PAT. OFF/ PAT PENDING/HONG KONG, on body.

Plate 970: Mego. "Huggy Bear," left, and "Captain Dobey" from "Starskey and Hutch" TV program. All original. Marks: SPELLING/ GOLDBERG PROD., on head; MEGO CORP. 1974/REG. U.S. PAT. OFF./PAT. PENDING/HONG KONG, on back. Both dolls are marked the same.

Plate 971: Mego. "Nubia" from Wonder Woman series. 12" tall. Vinyl head, painted eyes, closed mouth, rooted long black hair with a streak of silver at right temple, fully jointed vinyl body. All original in metallic knit body suit under red cotton skirt and silver plastic breast shield, knee high silver boots. Marks: cD C COMICS/INC 1976, on head.

Plate 969: Mego. "Baby Princess," 11". Mechanical key wind walker. Vinyl head, rooted dark brown hair, inset brown glassine stationary eyes with lashes, closed mouth, vinyl arms, plastic body and legs. All original in black and white checkered dress and matching panties. No batteries required. Marks: MADE IN JAPAN, on head; KANTOYS (in circle)/Made in Japan, on body.

Plate 972: Meritus. "Kids Hair," girl sized beauty head. All vinyl with painted features and black rooted hair. Head turns on stand for easy styling. Marks: 1990 Meritus Ind. Inc.

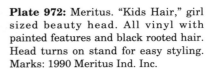

Plate 973: Metti. "Bindi," aborigine doll. 13½" tall. Vinyl head, rooted reddish brown hair, hazel sleeping eyes, open mouth with painted teeth; jointed vinyl toddler body. 1970's. Marks: Metti/AUSTRALIA, on head.

Plate 974: Miller Rubber Products, 22" walker doll; hard plastic body and limbs; vinyl head, brown sleep eyes, dark brown hair. Blue and white cotton pique dress may be original. Her feet are flat and hands widespread with separated fingers. Marks: MRP, on neck. Courtesy of Phyllis Houston.

Plate 975: Multi Toys Corp. "Wish-A-Bye," 7" doll in the Sleep Stars series of three dolls, two white, one black. Vinyl head and hands, painted eyes, rooted hair, cloth body with removable bib. Eyes and clothes glow in the dark. Marks: 1987 M.T.C., on head. Made in China.

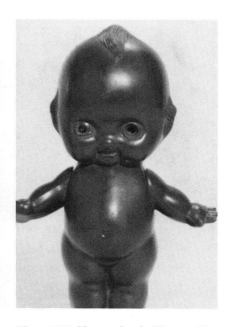

Plate 976: Nurseryland. "Kewpie-like plastic doll. 7" tall. Inserted blue glassine eyes, one is missing, movable arms, molded hair. Marks: NURSERYLAND/ CAT NO 3/59, on back.

Plate 977: Ohio Art Company. "Looking Pretty," 6" press-on, peel-off, dress-up doll. She is a unique combination of a doll and a paper doll. Her vinyl head is like a normal doll with painted features and rooted hair. Her body is like a paper doll made of thick rigid vinyl. Doll comes in two box sizes, one with extra fashions, a designer carrying case with mirror and one with just the doll. Made in China. Purchased new in 1990. Doll was available in a wide variety of outfits and hairstyles.

Plate 978: Olmec. "Queen Fatima," black girl from the Hip Hop Kids series. 12" tall. Head, arms and legs are vinyl, sleeping eyes, cloth body, rooted hair. Marks: GI-GO Toys. Fty Ltd, tag on body. Clothing tag: GiGo Toy/Made in China.

Plate 979: Olmec. "B-Boy Smart," black boy from the Hip Hop Kids series. Marks are the same as previous doll. Painted black hair, sleeping eyes, vinyl head, arms and legs, cloth body.

Plate 980: Olmec. "Cherisse," 14". Vinyl head, brown sleeping eyes with lashes, rooted black hair; vinyl arms and legs, cloth body. All original in lavender and white striped dress. Marks: OLMEC/1989, on head. Style No. 70002.

Plate 981: Olmec. "Cherisse," 18" toddler doll. Similar to previous Cherisse doll, only larger. All original. Marks: OLMEC/1989, on head. Made in China. Style No. 70005.

Plate 982: Olmec. "Naomi," 11½" fashion doll. Made only for 1988. Naomi dolls were sold in a variety of outfits, each with a swimsuit. The same doll was renamed Elisse for the 1989 market. It came with the same clothes as Naomi, but a second complete outfit replaced the swimsuit. Elisse also came in several new outfits not seen on Naomi. In 1990, the same doll was issued as Imani. She wore many of the same clothes as Elisse. Vinyl head, painted features, long black rooted hair, hard poseable vinyl body. Marks: 1987/OLMEC/CORP, on head. Made in China, on body.

Plate 983: Olmec. "Elisse," 1989. Identical to previous doll, Naomi. Doll was available in a wide variety of outfits and with various hairstyles.

Plate 984: Olmec. "Imani," issued for the 1990 market. Doll was also available in a variety of outfits, hairstyles, and box sizes.

Plate 985: Olmec. "Naomi Beauty Salon," 7" including stand. Vinyl head, rooted long black hair, painted eyes, open mouth with painted teeth. Nineteen-piece beauty salon with hair that takes a set and dryer that blows cool air. Batteries required. Marks: 1987/OLMEC/CORP., back of head.

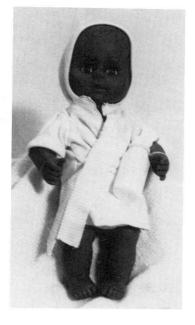

Plate 986: Olmec. "Amina," 12" drink and wet baby doll. All vinyl one-piece body, sleeping light brown eyes with lashes, molded hair. All original. Marks: CHINA/89, on head.

Plate 987: Olmec. "Amandla," 15" baby doll. Vinyl head, arms, and legs; sleeping brown eyes; rooted black hair; brown cloth body. All original. Marks: OLMEC/1989, on head.

Plate 988: Olmec. "Learning Kids," 14" tall, all cloth, painted features, yarn hair. Dolls have buttons, zippers, snaps, laces, etc., for teaching young children. Copyright 1989. Marks: GI-GO TOYS FTY LTD..., on tag sewn to body.

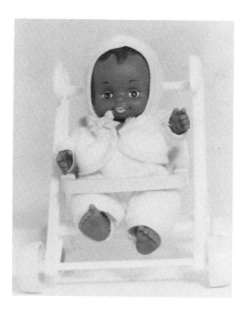

Plate 989: Olmec. "Baby Dumplin' with Stroller," 6". Vinyl baby with molded, painted hair, painted features, bent leg jointed baby body. All original in white suit trimmed in yellow. Marks: 1987 SPECTRA/CHINA, on head; 1988 SPECTRA/Made in China, on body.

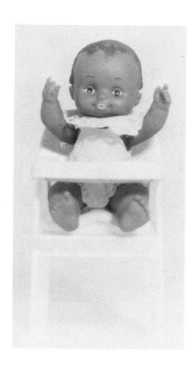

Plate 990: Olmec. "Baby Dumplin' with Chair," dressed in yellow sunsuit.

Plate 991: Olmec. "Baby Dumplin' with Crib," dressed in white print nightie.

Plate 993: Olmec. "Sun-man," action figure from Sun-man and the Sun People collection. Style no. 1001. Made in China, 1989. 6" tall. Marks: c1985 Olmec Corp., on back.

Plate 992: Olmec. "Butterfly Woman," 5½" poseable invincible heroine. All original in pink and glittered net with removable yellow plastic butterfly wings, rooted brown hair, painted features and molded-on pink boots. Doll is unmarked. Other dolls in the series were Felina, half cat, half woman vixen, and Amandla, super psychic.

Plate 994: Olmec. "Willie Pearl." 18" tall. Character doll that came with storybook with the same title. Vinyl head, sleeping dark brown eyes, closed mouth, vinyl arms and legs, cloth body. All original in white and pink print dress trimmed with pink bows. Marks: OLMEC/1989, on head. Courtesy of Marge Betts.

Plate 995: Dolls by Pauline. "Partytime," 10" baby doll. Hard vinyl head, arms, and legs; light brown in coloring; dark brown eyes; tight, curly rooted dark brown hair. Tan cloth body. Designed by Pauline Bjonness-Facobsen from Holland. Marks: PBJ (in heart)/91984, on head. Tag reads: International Design Corporation/A Schmid Company/Randolph, MA 02368. 1985.

Plate 996: Plastic Molded Arts Co. 7½" tall. Hard plastic head, sleeping amber eyes, glued-on mohair wig, hard plastic body jointed at shoulders, molded-on painted shoes. Marks: PLASTIC MOLDED ARTS/ CO./L.I.C. NEW YORK/PMA, on body.

Plate 997: Dolls by Pauline. "Georgette" V-105. 1970's. 18". Vinyl head, rooted black hair, painted features, open/closed mouth; vinyl hands, white cloth body and arms, brown cloth legs and feet. All original in white cotton dress with gold lace trim. Marks: Tiki Dolls/a/PAULINE/BJONNESS-JACOBSEN/ design, one side of tag sewn to body; TIKICRAFTS/INDUSTRIES INC./ MADE IN R.P..., other side of tag.

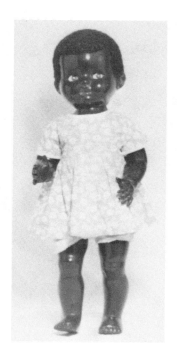

Plate 998: Dolls by Pauline. "George" V-106. Brother of previous Pauline doll. 18" tall. All original in brown cotton knickers and ecru cotton shirt trimmed with the same lace as that used on Georgette. Marks are the same as those on Georgette.

Plate 999: Pedigree. 20½" hard plastic walking doll, brown sleeping flirty eyes, glued-on black mohair wig, open/closed mouth, jointed hard plastic body. Doll's head turns when she walks. Red and white cotton print dress is original and is tagged Pedigree. Marks: Pedigree/ENGLAND, on head.

Plate 1000: Phoenix Toys, Inc. "Mr. T" as Clubberlang, 6½" action figure boxer from the "Rocky" movies. All vinyl, painted features and molded hair; hard vinyl articulated body, removable blue and white boxing shorts. Marks: HONG KONG on head; 1983/UNITED ARTISTS CORP., on body.

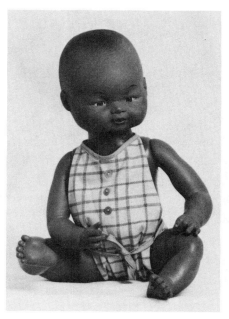

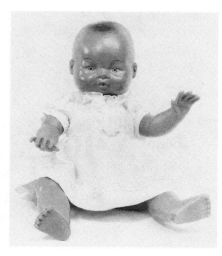

Plate 1003: Plated Moulds. 18". Vinyl head, molded painted hair, stationary light brown glassine eyes, nursing mouth, hard vinyl jointed toddler body. Redressed. Marks: PLATED MOULDS INC/c1961, on head. Courtesy of Ashley Anderson.

Plate 1002: Plated Moulds. "Baby," 19½" vinyl baby doll with glassine eyes, nursing mouth; molded, painted hair, jointed bent leg body. All original. Marks: PLATED MOULDS. INC./c1961, on head.

Plate 1001: Phoenix. "Appolo Creed," 6½" action boxing figure from the "Rocky" movies. Part of Appolo Creed was played by actor Carl Weathers. Vinyl head with painted features and hair; hard vinyl body. All original in red, white, and blue removable boxing shorts. Marks: HONG KONG, on head; 1983/United Artists Corp., on body.

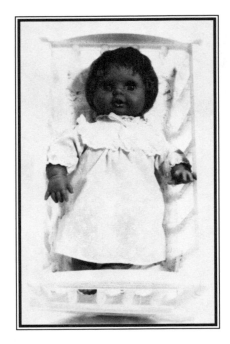

Plate 1004: Playgroup. "Cradle Time," 10" baby with vinyl head, brown sleeping eyes, brown rooted hair, vinyl arms and legs, pink cloth body. All original with cradle. Marks: P.G.I. TOYS LTD., tag sewn to body. Copyright 1989. Made in China.

Plate 1005: Playmates. "Sweet Tender Touch." 11" tall. Rooted black hair, brown sleeping eyes, nursing mouth, one-piece baby body. All original. Marks: 20. 8. 76/8110/PLAYMATES (in logo)/HONG KONG, on head; 01/112/PLAYMATES (in logo)/HONG KONG, 1977.7.21, on body.

Plate 1006: Playmates. "Cricket," 25" tall. Battery operated, she speaks for herself. Cassette player is inside her body, eyes and mouth move when she speaks. Vinyl head, inset movable eyes, rooted dark brown hair; vinyl arms and legs, cloth body. All original. Additional tapes and costumes are available. Marks: 9250/PLAYMATES/©1985, on head.

Plate 1009: Playmates. "Pixie," from the Precious Playmates series. 6" tall. All vinyl with molded, painted hair and small tuff of black rooted synthetic hair in top of head, painted features, fully jointed baby body. Doll was sold in a variety of outfits as shown in the photo. Marks: 13 9055 PLAYMATES, on head; CHINA, on body. Copyright 1987.

Plate 1007: Playmates. "Corky," Cricket's brother. 25" talking doll with moving mouth and eyes, comes with 30 minute cassette tape, battery operated. Vinyl head, arms, and legs; cloth body; rooted dark brown hair, open talking mouth with painted teeth, horizontal moving eyes, freckled cheeks. All original in red and yellow knit shirt, blue jeans, yellow corduroy cap and red plastic athletic shoes. Marks: 9251/PLAYMATES/©1986/37, on head.

Plate 1008: Playmates. "Baby Grows," 1987. 15" tall. Vinyl head, painted eyes, rooted brown hair, open mouth with four upper teeth, vinyl and cloth arms, vinyl legs, hard vinyl body. All original in pink sweatshirt and aqua tights. Marks: 8100/PLAYMATES/©1987, on head.

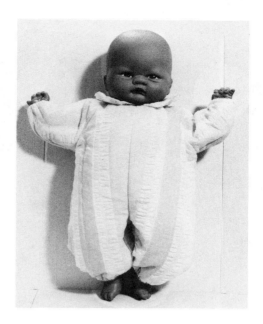

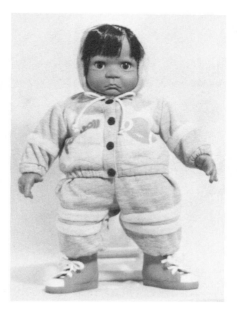

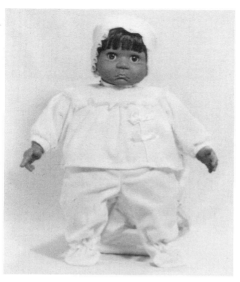

Plate 1012: Playmates. "Hug-A-Bye Baby," girl, from the Tiara Dolls collection. Identical to previous doll except for clothing. All original in white brushed flannel pajamas trimmed in pink with matching bonnet.

Plate 1010: Playmates. "Welcome Home Baby" from Precious Playmates, 18". Vinyl head, arms and legs, white cloth body with cry mechanism inside, painted features, slightly molded hair. All original in pastel striped sleeper, removable. Marks: PLAYMATES, on head. Copyright 1987, Made in China, on box.

Plate 1011: Playmates. "Hug-A-Bye Baby," boy, from the Tiara Dolls collection. 21" tall. Vinyl head, arms, and legs; cloth stuffed body; dark brown sleeping eyes, brown rooted hair, closed mouth. All original in gray knit sweatsuit, red athletic shoes. Marks: 3210/PLAYMATES/c1986 M-20, on head.

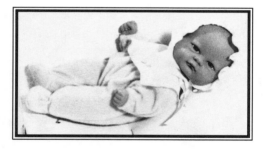

Plate 1013: Playmates. "Welcome Home Baby," 9" baby like the previous doll, only smaller. All original in blue flannel sleepers and white cap. Doll was available in other pastel colored sleepers. Marks: 23/4094/cPLAYMATES, on head; (logo)/CHINA/4093, on body.

Plate 1015: Playskool. "My Buddy," 22" vinyl and cloth doll dressed in overalls, polo shirt, socks, sneakers, and baseball cap. Vinyl head with painted features, closed mouth; rooted dark brown hair. The rest of the doll, including arms and legs, is cloth. Removable clothing, can wear infants clothes size 3-6 months. Marks: MY BUDDY 1001/Trademark MY BUDDY used under license from Buddy L. Corporation, 1986 Playskool Inc. (on tag sewn to cloth body). Made in Thailand.

Plate 1016: Playmates. "Water Babies Doll." 13" tall. When you fill her with warm water, she feels like a real baby. All vinyl with molded hair, painted eyes, closed mouth, one-piece body. Marks: c1990 LAUER TOYS, INC, on head. All original in flannel white print sleepers.

Plate 1014: Playskool. "Kid Sister," 22" companion doll for "My Buddy." Identical to "My Buddy," on right, except hair is longer and styled in two braids. She is dressed in blue and white overalls and matching visor, white print shirt, socks and sneakers. Tag sewn to body: Kid Sister 1008.

Plate 1017: Playskool. "Baby Dolly Surprise," 1988. 14" tall. Vinyl head, painted eyes, rooted growing hair, closed mouth, vinyl arms and legs, plastic body. All original in one-piece print romper. Marks: c1988 PLAYSKOOL, on head; U.S. PATENT NO. 4,801,286/MADE IN CHINA, on body. Child actress and model Raven-Symone from the "Cosby" TV show is the child model on the box.

Plate 1018: Playskool. "Head-to-Toe Dolly Surprise," 14". Vinyl head, painted eyes, long rooted hair that grows over 7" from her head to her toes, smiling mouth with painted teeth, jointed vinyl body. No batteries required. All original in short pink and lavender print jumpsuit. Marks: PLAYSKOOL INC, on head; U.S. PATENT NO. 4,801,286/MADE IN CHINA, on body.

Plate 1019: Playskool. "Prima Ballerina Dolly Surprise," 10½". Soft vinyl head, painted features; hard jointed vinyl body. Control in her right arm lengthens her ponytail, her left arm shortens. No batteries required. All original. Marks: U.S. PATENT NO 4801286/1987 PLAYSKOOL INC/MADE IN CHINA/H-22.

Plate 1020: Playskool. "Prairie Girl Dolly Surprise." 10½". All original in gray print dress and pink shoes. Painted eyes with lavender eye shadow, one growing ponytail. Marks: U.S. PATENT NO. 4,801,286/c1987 PLAYSKOOL, INC./MADE IN CHINA/H-22, on body. Head is unmarked.

Plate 1021: Playskool. "Rain Dancer Dolly Surprise." 10½" tall. All original in yellow print raincoat and hat, red tights. Vinyl head, painted eyes with tan eye shadow, painted smiling mouth with painted teeth, long brown wavy hair in two growing hair pigtails. Marks: c1988 PLAYSKOOL, INC., on head; U.S. PATENT NO. 4801286/c1987 PLAYSKOOL INC/MADE IN CHINA/H-22, on body.

Plate 1022: Playskool. "Pretty Princess Dolly Surprise," 10½". Vinyl head and jointed body, painted eyes, painted mouth with upper teeth, long brown rooted growing hair with purple and pink streaks. All original in aqua and pink long gown. Marks: c1988/PLAYSKOOL. INC, on head; U.S. PATENT NO. 4,801, 286/c1987 PLAYSKOOL, INC./MADE IN CHINA, on body.

Plate 1023: Playskool. "Dolly Surprise, Tea for Two," 10½", c1989. All original in yellow print dress with lavender trim. Two growing ponytails out of yellow plastic grow rings, orange-brown eye shadow. Marks: U.S. PATENT NO. 4,801,286/c1987 PLAYSKOOL INC./MADE IN CHINA/H-22, on body. Head is unmarked.

Plate 1024: Playskool. "Go Team Go Dolly Surprise," 10½". All original in cheerleader outfit with white shirt, aqua skirt, and yellow shoes. One growing ponytail out of pink plastic. Marks are the same as "Rain Dancer Dolly Surprise."

Plate 1025: Playskool. "Wedding Bouquet Dolly Surprise," 10½". All original in white wedding gown. Pink streak in one growing black hairpiece in pink plastic ring, no eye shadow, yellow-green highlights in eyes. Marks are the same as "Pretty Princess Dolly Surprise."

Plate 1026: Playskool. "Laurel Surprise," 10½", from the Pigtail Dolly Surprise series. Vinyl head, open smiling mouth with painted teeth, painted eyes, two ponytails. All original in lavender print dress with pink ribbon trim. Marks: U.S.PATENT PENDING/c1987PLAYSKOOL INC./MADE IN CHINA, on body.

Plate 1027: Playskool. "Sweet Dreams," 10½" from the Dolly Surprise series. All original in pink and white striped flannel nightshirt. One ponytail, open smiling mouth with painted teeth, orange eye shadow and orange tinted eyes. Marks: c1988 Playskool Inc., on head; U.S. PATENT NO. 4,801,286/c1987 PLAYSKOOL, INC./MADE IN CHINA/H-22, on body.

Plate 1028: Playskool. "Fun Time Little Miss Dolly Surprise," 6½". Vinyl head, painted eyes, painted open mouth, growing brown rooted hair, jointed vinyl body. All original in pink shirt, red print skirt, painted-on white panties and socks, painted red t-strap shoes. Marks: U.S. PATENT No. 4,801,286/1990 PLAYSKOOL, INC./MADE IN CHINA/H22, on back.

Plate 1029: Playskool. "Free Wheelin'", 6½", from the Little Miss Dolly Surprise collection. All original in yellow shirt and fuchsia shorts with painted-on white panties, socks, and orange tennis shoes. Marks are the same as "Fun Time Little Miss Dolly Surprise."

Plate 1030: Playskool. "Make-a-Wish Little Miss Dolly Surprise," 6½". 1989. All original in blue dotted synthetic dress with painted-on white tights and pink shoes. Marks are the same as "Fun Time Little Miss Dolly Surprise."

Plate 1031: Playskool. "Dancin' Romance Little Miss Dolly Surprise," 6½". All original in lavender ballet outfit. Painted-on lavender shoes and white tights. Marks are the same as "Fun Time Little Miss Dolly Surprise."

Plate 1032: Playskool. "My Very Soft Baby," 10". C.1990. Soft baby makes a giggle sound when squeezed. Girl is dressed in pink, boy in blue in sewn-on clothing. Vinyl faces, cloth head, body and limbs.

Plate 1033: Playskool. "Snuzzle and Friskers," 11". All cloth doll with soft vinyl covering on face from the Jammie Pies collection. Painted features, sewn-on clothing. All original. Marks: PLAYSKOOL BABY/5251, tag sewn to body; Jammie Pies, other side.

Plate 1034: Playskool. "Flat Folks," 3½". One-piece hard plastic figure with two snap-on outfits. Painted features and clothing. Doll is available with green, red, blue, or yellow painted shoes. Marks: FLATFOLKS, painted on front of shirt. Snap-on plastic clothes are marked: ALL RIGHTS/RESERVED/c1990/PLAYSKOOL INC./PAWT R I 02862/M-5755/6, on back.

Plate 1035: Playskool. "Pretty Cut 'n Grow," 13½". Vinyl head with opening in crown for inserting hair, painted eyes, closed smiling mouth, jointed vinyl body. All original in lavender print sundress. Marks: 1990 PLAYSKOOL, INC./PAWTUCKET R.I. 02862/ALL RIGHTS RESERVED/MADE IN CHINA, on body.

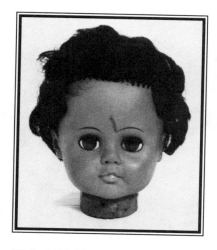

Plate 1036: Plaything. Head only of a doll that would have been approximately 27" tall. Vinyl with rooted black hair, sleeping brown eyes, closed mouth. Doll was made in the 1950's and originally wore an ivory wedding dress trimmed in ivory lace with matching headpiece. Marks on head: PLAYTHING/15. Courtesy of Cheryl Larry Perkins.

Plate 1037: Enesco. "Hi Babies" bride and groom, from the Precious Moments collection, 5½" tall. Vinyl head, body, and legs with movable head and arms, painted eyes, glued-on black yarn hair. All original in unremovable white wedding outfits. Marks: THE/ENESCO/PRECIOUS/MOMENTS/COLLECTION, left foot; HI BABIES/c1989 SAMUEL L. BUTCHER/ALL RIGHTS RESERVED WORLDWIDE/LICENSEE ENESCO CORPORATION/MADE IN PHILIPPINES, right foot.

Plate 1038: Enesco. "Hi Babies" from the Precious Moments collection dressed in a cap and gown. Marks are the same as previous "Hi Babies."

Plate 1039: Enesco. "Hi Babies" from the Precious Moments collection dressed in red. Both have removable hats, girl has on red shoes, boy has on black shoes. Marks are the same as previous dolls.

Plate 1040: Enesco. "It's a Boy" and "It's a Girl" Hi Babies from the Precious Moments collection. Marks are the same as previous dolls.

Plate 1041: Rainbow Classics. 1990. "Special Friends," three dolls sold together as a group, two of them 5½" tall and one 4" tall. The larger two have vinyl heads with inset stationary plastic eyes, rooted black hair and vinyl jointed bodies. The smaller doll has painted features, rooted black hair, and jointed vinyl body. All three dolls have freckles. All original and unmarked. Made in China. Stock #20022.

Plate 1042: Pressman. "Africa," 11½" "Small World Dolls" from Disney. Soft vinyl head, painted features; jointed vinyl body; original clothes but yarn wig is missing. Marks: Pressman Toys/Walt Disney Prod. 1965.

Plate 1043: Rainbow Classics. "Amina," 18" cloth doll. Painted features, black yarn hair styled in bangs and two braids. Sewn-on blue dress trimmed in white and red, blue and white hat, yellow stockings. Unmarked. Made in China. Stock #16000. Purchased new, 1990.

Plate 1044: Rainbow Classics. "Shauntee," 1990. 11½" fashion doll in "Today's Fashion." Vinyl head, painted features, rooted long black hair; hard vinyl body with poseable legs. All original. Doll is unmarked. Stock #11594. Made in China.

Plate 1045: Rainbow Classics. "Amber," 10" vinyl doll with sleeping eyes, nursing mouth, rooted black curly hair, jointed baby body. All original. Doll is unmarked, stock #10050. Made in China.

Plate 1046: Rainbow Classics. "Tenesha," 14" toddler. Vinyl head, sleeping dark brown eyes, open/closed mouth, rooted black hair, vinyl arms and legs, cloth body. All original in blue jumper and white synthetic blouse trimmed in red. Marks: ajena/8813 (not very clear). On head; RAINBOW CLASSICS, INC./Made in China, on tag sewn to body.

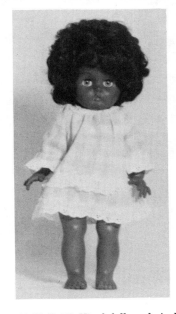

Plate 1047: Ratti. Vinyl doll made in Italy. 13" tall. Bright blue open/closed eyes, rooted black hair, closed mouth, jointed body. Marks: (logo on neck is too faint to read); RATTI (in logo)/MADE IN ITALY, on body.

Plate 1048: Regal Toy Limited, Canada. "Liza," all original. 1970's. 11" tall. Vinyl jointed doll, painted eyes, rooted black hair, closed mouth, pierced ears with earrings. Marks: REGAL/CANADA, on head; Regal, Canada, on body. Tag: Liza/A Kiddie's Joy is a Regal Toy/A Regal Doll/Made in Canada by/Regal Toy Limited, Toronto.

Plate 1049: Regal. Character doll, 12" tall. Vinyl head, rooted black hair, black eyes with black bead attached for pupil, smiling painted mouth; jointed vinyl body. Marks: REGAL/MADE IN CANADA, on head. Redressed.

Plate 1050: Remco. "Brown Eye Billy," 16½" tall. One of the Brown Eye series designed for Remco by black artist Annuel McBurrows. All vinyl; sleeping eyes; black rooted hair; fully jointed body. All original. Colorful, original box has picture of Annuel McBurrows along with his autograph. Marks: 3311/U13/REMCO IND. INC./1969.

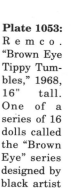

Plate 1051: Remco. Brown Eye "Baby Sister Grow-A-Tooth," 14½" tall. Designed by Annuel McBurrows. Soft vinyl head; sleeping glassine eyes; black rooted hair; open mouth with growing tooth feature. Hard plastic jointed body. All original. Marks: 2805/13/EYE/E2/REMCO Ind. INC/1968, on head; REMCO IND. INC./1966/3M, on body.

Plate 1052: Remco. Brown Eye Bunny Baby," a tricky whistle doll. Designed by Annuel McBurrows. 18" tall. Vinyl head, rooted black hair, stationary brown eyes with thick eyelashes, open/closed mouth, hard vinyl arms, hard plastic body and legs. Battery operated. All original in pink flannel pajamas. Marks: 2895/17 EYE E14/REMCO IND. INC./19c69, on head; c1969/REMCO INDUSTRIES INC./HARRISON, N.J./MADE IN U.S.A./PAT. PEND., on body.

Plate 1053: Remco. "Brown Eye Tippy Tumbles," 1968, 16" tall. One of a series of 16 dolls called the "Brown Eye" series designed by black artist Annuel McBurroughs for Remco. Dolls included in the series were "Twins," "Baby Grow-a-Tooth," "Billy," "Jumpsy," "Baby Whistle," "Tina," "Polly Puff," "Kewpie," "Tiny Tumbles," "Baby Laugh-a-Lot," "Li'l Winking Winny," "Growing Sally," and "Baby Know-it-All." All of these dolls were also made in white versions; however, black dolls were made from different molds and had ethnically correct features. Marks: 2-74/17 EYE (hair is rooted on top of these marks)/8M/E15/REMCO IND. INC./1968.

Saul Robbins   Annuel McBurrows

One of Mr. McBurrows' charcoal sketches that won management's OK.

Remco: Negro Girls Want 'Realistic' Dolls

PLANNING and producing on the premise that little Negro girls want dolls they can identify with more easily and quickly, Remco Industries brought to market at the March Toy Fair a quartet of "ethnically correct" Negro dolls.

All four carry the same names as their Caucasian counterparts in the line: Winking Winnie, Growing Sally, Tippy Tumbles and Baby Grow-A-Tooth. The first is a non-TV number, the others are all to be promoted heavily on television and in other media. Sally, in fact, now on the retail counters, was the subject of a six-week TV campaign begun in early April in 10 markets around the country.

The results of that spring promotion have been good, says Saul Robbins, Remco's board chairman, and bode well, he adds, for the big TV push that will get under way in August. Other promotional efforts will include store newspaper ads and Remco spots on Negro radio stations in September; in addition, the manufacturer will take space in the October issues of the Negro-audience magazines Ebony and Jet.

Because of the economics of network TV—i.e., the cost per viewer—only the white versions of the three televised dolls will appear in the commercials. Remco's expectation is that Negro customers will become familiar with the brand name, through exposure to the TV promotion, and then choose the Negro numbers when they confront them in the store.

The question naturally arises as to why Mr. Robbins and Remco's management feel they can succeed with a concept that has been sidetracked by other dollmakers for so many years. These other manufacturers have long held that the market potential is insufficient to justify the cost of special molds with Negro facial characteristics. Instead they have chosen to produce white and non-white dolls with identical features, using tinted plastic resins to achieve the desired color tone.

THE REASONING

In replying to the doubters, Mr. Robbins makes liberal use of a word that has always been significant in the product design thinking at Remco. The word is "realism."

"The key to the success of just about any item in the toy industry is the degree of its realism," says Mr. Robbins. "A girl playing with a doll is engaged in a mother-child fantasy. And if she's a Negro girl, we're certain she'll want a doll that most closely resembles Negro babies and toddlers.

"What we want the trade and public to realize," Mr. Robbins continues, "is that we didn't come out with these dolls as some kind of ges-

ture. There's no tokenism in our decision. . . . We're not looking for thanks, but for business. We're trying to fill what we believe is an unfilled market demand. If we're right in our assumptions, these four Negro dolls will turn a profit, which is why we're in business."

The company's spending plans are geared to the belief that the four colored dolls will be bought almost exclusively by Negroes, although, in Mr. Robbins' words, "we'll be delighted if some white shoppers buy them too . . . because it will be an indication that race attitudes are improving in this country."

Remco began exploring the possibility of making Negroid-feature dolls about two years ago. Last fall it retained a young Negro artist, free-lancer Annuel McBurrows, to develop some design ideas. The company liked his qualifications. He'd had seven years' experience sketching Negro youngsters, chiefly portraits, and several New York galleries had run showings of his work.

In the short span of two weeks, Mr. McBurrows was able to present Remco's management with a doll face that met the assigned standards. The most important of these, to quote Mr. Robbins again, was that it had to be "cute and appealing"; secondly, it had to have realistic elements that would find favor with as many members of the Negro com-

50

Side by side, the two versions of Growing Sally, one of four brand names in the new Remco line that is available with Caucasian or Negroid features.

Profile sketch in charcoal submitted by Mr. McBurrows.

munity as possible. (Editor's note: The four Negro dolls appear to have slightly larger lips, somewhat broader noses and higher cheekbones than the white versions. A midpoint in the possible range of natural color tones has been chosen.)

Mr. McBurrows then went on to create all four faces on which the molds were based. "The faces are representative of the way I 'see' Negro children. They're an expression of my own feeling," is the way Mr. McBurrows puts it.

SALES PROSPECTS

Remco is sure that Mr. McBurrows' design approach and design results have definite artistic—and commercial—validity. The proof, of course, will come at retail. If the dolls succeed on the counters, Mr. Robbins foresees the widening of the line in 1969 . . . and is also resigned to the inevitability of competitors following suit.

For now and for several months at least, competing dollmakers will watch and wait. Naysayers among them think Remco's market analysis is faulty. One argument: The sale of 500,000 pieces in a year is the sign of a strong selling doll (greater-volume numbers like a Barbie or Chatty Cathy are exceptions to the rule); if the Negro market can be said to represent 10-12% of the total, and if one subtracts a couple of percentage points to account for the Negro's lesser spending power, then the volume on a Negro doll would come to, possibly, 40,000 pieces. And, from this total, the argument goes on, one would have to subtract the number of white-version dolls that Negro consumers would have bought in the absence of the Negro version. The result? Too few sales to warrant the production and promotional expenses.

A counter-argument (not presented by Mr. Robbins, but it could have been) is that the offer of an alternative, ethnically correct Negro doll could push the total pieces sold of a successful brand-name doll well beyond the 500,000 or 600,000 norm. Another factor on the side of optimism would be that the Negro market is gaining in affluence at a faster rate than consumers on the whole and that its constituents are concentrated in urban areas that are heavily dotted with aggressive mass merchandising outlets such as discounters, popular-price department stores and large variety chain outlets.

Theoretical considerations to one side, buyers from all parts of the U.S. did respond favorably to the idea of ethnically correct dolls—and to the dolls themselves—at Toy Fair, according to Mr. Robbins. The final verdict, though, will be delivered by the public. In this instance, the Negro public.—TED ERICKSON

Tippy Tumbles goes into her act.

Duo: Baby Grow-A-Tooth in the highchair is regarded by Winking Winnie.

Plate 1054: Remco. "Brown Eye Baby Know-it-All," designed by Annuel McBurrows. 17" tall. Battery operated, comes with blue and yellow plastic feeding chair, magic slate and picture cards. When she loves something, she jumps up and down with joy. When she doesn't like something, she shakes her head no. Soft vinyl head; black rooted hair; sleep eyes; two lower teeth. Hard plastic jointed body and limbs. Shoes are not removable. All original. Marks: 2803 17 EYE/4/REMCO IND. INC./1969, on head.

Plate 1055: Remco. "Brown Eye Winking Winny," designed by Annuel McBurrows. Doll winks when you push the button on her tummy. 15" tall. All original, soft vinyl head and arms, sleep eyes, closed mouth, black rooted hair, hard plastic body. Marks: 2470/15 EYE (hair rooted on top of marks)/SE 17/REMCO IND. INC./1968.

Plate 1056: Remco. "Strolling Sweet April" walks and cries like a real baby. 5½" tall all vinyl with black rooted hair, stationary glassine eyes with tear holes in corners, open nursing mouth, jointed body with push button in back that raises arms. Doll came with bottle, walker-trainer and walking rod. All original in green sunsuit and bonnet. Marks: 3889/REMCO IND. INC./1971. Original box is marked copyright 1973.

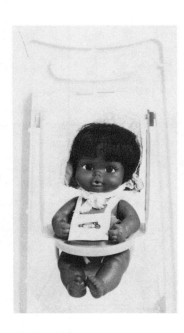

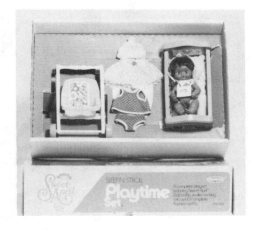

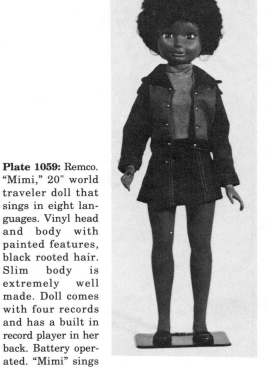

Plate 1058: Remco. "Sweet April Sleep 'n Stroll Playtime Set," 1972. A complete playset including doll, bottle, stroller, rocking crib, and three fashion outfits. Doll is identical to previous Sweet April dolls.

Plate 1059: Remco. "Mimi," 20" world traveler doll that sings in eight languages. Vinyl head and body with painted features, black rooted hair. Slim body is extremely well made. Doll comes with four records and has a built in record player in her back. Battery operated. "Mimi" sings in English, French, German, Greek, Polish, Hebrew, Spanish, and Italian. According to message on the box, "Mimi knows no boundaries...only the brotherhood of song." Marks: Hong Kong/Remco Ind./1972, on head. Sound Device/Made in Japan, on back. Lower on back: 1973 Remco Ind. Inc. Harrison, N.J.

Plate 1057: Remco. "Sweet April in Swing." Doll is identical to previous doll except sunsuit and bonnet are blue. All original.

Plate 1061: Remco Toys. "Little Bill," 22" character from the Fat Albert series. All original in blue jeans and striped shirt. Marked the same as "Fat Albert."

Plate 1062: Remco. "Pretty Penny Chatterbox," 17" talking doll. When you brush her hair, she talks automatically. Battery operated. Vinyl head, painted features, rooted dark brown hair, vinyl hands, cloth body and legs. All original in lavender print dress. Marks: 1988 REMCO IND/MADE IN CHINA/PAT. PENDING, on head. Tag sewn to body: PRETTY PENNY CHATTERBOX. Made in China.

Plate 1060: Remco. Toys Inc. "Fat Albert," 22" character from Bill Cosby's "Fat Albert and the Cosby Kids." Vinyl head, painted eyes, rooted black hair; cloth body, including arms and legs. All original. Marks: 1985 Wm. H Cosby Jr. Filmation Assoc/1985 Remco Toys Inc., on head.

Plate 1064: Remco. "Splashy," baby with pink plastic floating device. 11½" tall. Vinyl head, painted eyes, molded painted black hair, closed mouth, jointed vinyl baby body. Marks: REMCO 1980/MADE IN HONG KONG/PATENT PENDING, on body.

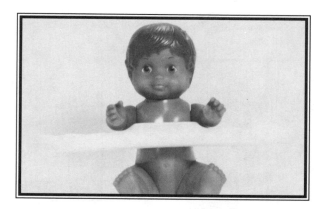

Plate 1063: Remco. "Sweet Baby This 'n That," 13½". Soft vinyl head and legs, hard vinyl arms, hard plastic body, rooted curly dark brown hair, painted eyes, open mouth. She can kiss, color with a crayon, sip through a straw, or brush her hair. No batteries required. Doll performs movement through the use of four air bellows in her feet. All original in pink dress and matching undies trimmed in lavender. Marks: cREMCO TOYS 1989, on head; c1989 REMCO TOYS/MADE IN CHINA, on body.

Plate 1065: Remco. 14" toddler doll with vinyl head, painted eyes, open nursing mouth, rooted black hair, hard vinyl arms and legs, plastic body, jointed at shoulders, wrists, and hips. Marks: cREMCO 1976/N.Y. N.Y. 10010, on head; c1976 REMCO TOYS, INC./NEW YORK, NY. 10010/MADE IN HONG KONG/PRO/PATENT PENDING, on body.

Plate 1067: Rose Mary Dolls Manufacturing Co. "Nurse Walking Doll," 36". Vinyl head, sleeping brown eyes, black rooted synthetic wig; closed mouth; jointed hard plastic body. All original in nurse's uniform, black and white cotton striped dress with white collar, white apron and red cross cap, white shoes and socks. Purchased in 1956 for Linda Hemingway on her 6th birthday. Marks: AE 5651/33, on head. Box marked: "Rose Mary Dolls Manufacturing Co., 500 West 180th Street. New York 33, N.Y., Nurse." Doll was probably manufactured by Allied Eastern, a company who made dolls in bulk and then sold them to various smaller companies to market. Courtesy of Linda Hemingway Perry.

Plate 1066: Rogark. "Rogark Character Doll," 6½" hard plastic jointed doll; sleeping eyes, glued-on wig. All original. Made in Wales, Gt. Britain. 1950–1960.

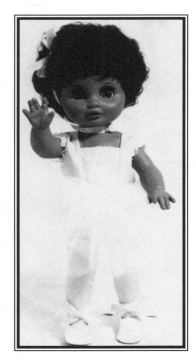

Plate 1068: Royal. "Tracy," 11" ballerina. Hard vinyl head and body, sleeping brown eyes, curly black synthetic rooted hair. All original. Marks: ROYAL HOUSE/OF DOLLS INC/1982, on head. Made in USA.

Plate 1069: Royal House. "Dallas Cowboys Cheerleader." 15". 1982. All vinyl, curly black rooted hair, brown sleep eyes, smiling mouth with painted teeth. All original blue and white costume. Marks: 1/ROYAL/c1982, on head.

Plate 1070: Royal. "Diana," ballerina. 15" tall. Vinyl head, sleeping brown eyes with one-piece lashes, rooted long black hair pulled back into a bun; hard jointed vinyl body. All original. Marks: AE 10, on head. Made in U.S.A. Style no. 1508.

Plate 1072: Sasha. "Caleb." No 4-309. 16". The first "Caleb" issued by Sasha dolls. His skin tone is very dark black rather than the brown skin tone issued later in the "Caleb" doll. Vinyl head, painted eyes, rooted black hair, hard vinyl body and limbs. Doll is unmarked. Printed on the box: Sasha serie/ Made in England/Trendon limited/Stockport, England/SK5 6DU. Doll is all original in yellow sweater, light colored pants and beige colored lace shoes. Wrist tag reads: MADE IN ENGLAND/SERIE.

Plate 1071: Russ Berrie and Company. "Toffee," 12". Head is stockinette fabric over styrofoam, stockinette body, glued-on black yarn hair, glued-on felt-like features. All original in blue and white gingham dress with white one-piece undies. Doll is marked "Toffee" on tag sewn to body.

Plate 1073: Sasha. "Cora," No. 4-109. 16" tall. Identical to "Caleb" except hair is longer and styled in looser fashion. All original in blue checked dress and white leather strap shoes. Doll is the same dark coloring as "Caleb."

Plate 1074: Sasha. "Baby Girl," No. 509, sexed. 12" long. All original in a two-piece white cotton suit with red, black, and white ribbon trim, and diaper. Doll has curly rooted black hair. Original wrist tag and box are printed the same as previous Sasha dolls except for doll name and number on the box.

Plate 1075: The first dark dolls in the Sasha family, early 1970. Dolls are shown individually in the three previous photographs. "Cora," "Caleb," and the baby. All originally dressed.

Plate 1076: Sasha. "Caleb." No. 4-309. 16" tall. All original with yellow knitted sweater, dark denim trousers, tan leather shoes. Metal wrist tag is the same as on the previous Caleb. This Caleb was purchased new in the early 1970's and is the same dark, almost black, coloring as the previous Caleb.

Plate 1077: Sasha. "Cora," all original No. 119 in the 1985 catalog issued for the Sasha dolls. 16½" tall. Doll is all original in blue corduroy dress. Her coloring is a lighter shade of brown than the previous Cora and doll is slightly taller. Unmarked.

Plate 1078: Sasha. "Cora," No. 118 in flowered dress. Made in England. All original, 16½" tall, and lighter in coloring than the earliest Cora dolls. Unmarked.

Left – Plate 1079: Sasha. "Caleb," No. 318. 16½" tall. All original in yellow knit sweater with black and white checked pants and white lace shoes. This Caleb is ½" taller and lighter in coloring than the earlier Caleb. Unmarked.

Right – Plate 1080: Sasha. "Cara," black baby 12", #519, one of the later Sasha dolls in the lighter brown coloring. All original in pink and gray plaid dress and panties in a natural-colored straw basket. Baby is not sexed like the earlier Sasha babies.

History Of Shindana

Shindana dolls are probably some of the most desired and collected modern black dolls today. The reasons for their desirability are numerous:

1. Formed in 1968, the first major manufacturer of black dolls.
2. The dolls were ethnically correct.
3. The dolls were of exceptionally high quality.
4. The dolls varied in a wide range of sizes, subject ages, personalities, etc.
5. Lastly, and most importantly, their scarcity. The dolls are no longer being produced as the company laid off its last dozen workers and shut its doors June 15, 1983.

The dolls were positively and readily accepted on the market when they were introduced. To give insight into the history of the company, following is a 1976 press release for Shindana Toys from Kirk Hallahan (Los Angeles office) of the Public Relations firm Harshe-Rotman & Druck, Inc.

SHINDANA TOYS:
BLACK DOLLS AND GAMES MADE BY A DREAM

Shindana Toys are black dolls and games made by a dream.

The dream was first envisioned in 1968 when Shindana was founded in the aftermath of the Watts riots in Los Angeles. Today, Shindana's dream remains just as viable – as the company grows and remains the world's largest manufacturer of black dolls and games.

Shindana's dream is simple – by manufacturing dolls and games that everyone can relate to, people of all races can learn to love those who are different from themselves. At the same time, the black community can prosper by the company providing jobs in the ghetto and by the firm's profits being used for community self-help projects.

Shindana was founded as a division of Operation Bootstrap, Inc., the nonprofit black community self-help organization in south central Los Angeles. Its founders were the late Lou Smith and Robert Hall. "We're turning our dream into a reality," says Robert Bobo, now president of the eight-year-old company. "We've shown that black businesses can be successful in what is still largely a white man's business world."

Shindana began by manufacturing a single black doll, "Baby Nancy." She was the first truly black doll made in contemporary America, with true black facial features, not merely white features painted black. Today, Shindana manufactures a line of thirty-two dolls, plus six black-oriented games and puzzles – making it the only full-line black toy company in America.

The company was founded without governmental subsidy, with initial capital and technical assistance provided by Mattel, Inc. Now totally independent from Mattel, Shindana is trying to live up to the meaning of its Swahili name – "competitor."

The idea for manufacturing black dolls and games is rooted in Operation Bootstrap's motto, "Learn, Baby, Learn!" – a paraphrase of the self-defeating cry heard during the riots, "Burn, Baby, Burn!"

Toys – especially dolls – are important in the self-images children learn, Bobo says. He cites the landmark findings of a black psychiatrist who found that black children, given a choice, usually chose white dolls over black. This is an expression of the lack of love and understanding these children had for themselves, Bobo explains.

"We believe that only by learning to love oneself can one learn to love others," Bobo concludes. "Shindana believes that by marketing black dolls and games that both black and white children can learn to relate to at an early age, the company can foster what the spirit of Shindana is all about – love."

As you can see, the history of Shindana is at the same time both interesting and intriguing. Going back a year in the history of Shindana, is the press release from 1975 from the same public relations company. It reports growth in 1974 and expectations for 1975. The president at this time was Lou Smith:

SHINDANA ENJOYS STRONG GROWTH IN 1974;
EXPECTS 1975 TO BE BEST YEAR IN HISTORY

Los Angeles – Shindana Toys, manufacturer of the world's leading line of black dolls and games, enjoyed strong sales in 1974, and is optimistic about black toy sales in 1975, according to President Lou Smith.

The company nearly doubled its annual sales in 1974, to approximately $1.3 million, Smith said. He cited growing consumer interest in ethnic toys and noted that black toy sales were almost totally unaffected by the recession.

In 1975, Shindana introduced eight new dolls and a new game at Toy Fair. The additions bring to 31 the number of items marketed by the black owned-and-operated firm, a division of Operation Bootstrap, Inc., the nonprofit community self-help organization in Los Angeles.

"Last year was a very significant one in terms of our overall growth," Smith said about the young company, which was founded in 1968 in the after-math of the Watts riots. "We not only expanded our product line significantly, but we also made major progress in improving our management and marketing efforts." Smith cited the following company highlights:

*In early 1974, Shindana acquired the Learning Tree and American Playmaker lines of black games and puzzles from Soular Systems, Inc. The acquisition made Shindana the first full-line black toy company in the U.S.

*Shindana opened a permanent showroom in Room 534 of the Toy Fair building – the first permanent display located in the facility devoted exclusively to ethnic toys.

*The company began international distribution of its products with the appointment of an exclusive distributor for East Africa, Mugawa Enterprises, Inc. The Nairobi-based firm distributes Shindana Toys in Kenya, Tanzania, Uganda, and Zanzibar.

*Shindana completed its nationwide sales network with the appointment of six sales representatives throughout the United States, headquartered in New York, Washington, D.C., Atlanta, Columbus, Houston, and Los Angeles. Others are expected to be added early in 1975.

*The company expanded its south central Los Angeles production facility with the addition of 15,000 square feet of nearby factory facilities, increasing its manufacturing and warehousing capability.

*Shindana began its first nationwide advertising effort with ads appearing in key black consumer magazines such as *Ebony* and *Essence*. The company was also featured in major newspaper stories and on television and radio shows in nine key markets.

"We are very optimistic about 1975 and hope to double our sales again this year. We've come a long way toward making our dream a reality and have shown that a black toy company can be competitive in today's tough toy market," Smith concluded.

Following is another press release from Harshe-Rotman & Druck, Inc., Los Angeles office, on Shindana in 1976 following the Toy Fair in New York. This release provides interesting information from the then president of Shindana, the late Robert Bobo.

GROWING INTEREST IN BLACK TOYS
REPORTED AT 1976 TOY FAIR

New York, February 16 – The nation's largest black toy manufacturer reported that more American parents than ever before are exposing their children to ethnic playthings, making black dolls and games one of the fastest-growing segments of America's $6 billion toy industry.

Robert Bobo, president of Los Angeles-based Shindana Toys, said that more than a half-million black dolls were sold in the U.S. last year, up from near-zero sales a decade ago. Of these, more than half were produced by his eight-year-old firm, with the balance sold by some of the nation's largest toy manufacturers.

"If you went into a toy store ten years ago and told the salesman you wanted a black doll, he would think you were crazy," said Bobo on the eve of the industry's major trade show, American Toy Fair. "Now that request is commonplace, and retailers are stocking larger quantities all the time."

Bobo cites a recent study conducted by *Toys Magazine* that showed black dolls represent approximately five percent of all doll sales in the U.S. He anticipates that the figure will double by 1980, bringing sales close in line with the portion of the black population.

Shindana was the first black owned-and-operated toy company in the U.S., founded in 1968 in the ashes of the Watts riots. It was the first to manufacture dolls expressly for blacks, and began by manufacturing a single black baby doll, known as "Baby Nancy."

At the 1976 Toy Fair, Shindana will exhibit a total of thirty-two dolls and six game-puzzles. Among its new items are an O.J. Simpson doll, patterned after the Buffalo Bills running back and a CIA-type agent named Slade, The Super Agent. The firm already markets the J.J. Talking Character doll and a wide range of other dolls.

Bobo says that Shindana began by directing its line primarily toward the 23 million black consumers in the U.S., stressing that its dolls were ethnically correct – featuring true Negroid features, not just white dolls painted black.

Surprisingly, however, the company discovered that more than half of its output was being purchased by white parents.

"Many white parents will tell you point blank that they don't want their children growing up with the same hangups that they did," Bobo says in explaining the phenomenon. According to Bobo, that trend is healthy, but there are some other very good reasons.

"There simply are more whites – and they generally have more money than blacks," he says, pointing out that white parents also tend to buy their Christmas gifts earlier than blacks. "Often by the time black parents get to the store, all the black dolls are sold out," he explains.

Bobo, who says Shindana's sales topped $1.4 million in 1975, reports that toy buyers have been slow to recognize the growth of ethnic playthings, partly because they underestimate the black consumer market. Yet, the 9½ million black families in the U.S. account for 10% of U.S. toy and game purchases – amounting to some $350 million annually.

"The competition this year is fiercer than ever," says Bobo, who notes that almost every major doll manufacturer will be offering a black doll line in 1976. However, he feels that Shindana has an advantage, having pioneered in the field and having already established strong consumer identification, particularly within the black community.

As mentioned earlier, Shindana Toy Co. closed its doors June 15, 1983. The dream of the 60's had collapsed under the economic realities of the 80's. It had grown to become one of the longest enduring enterprises to rise from the ashes of the Watts riot. Afterwards, everything from lace to plastic to doll parts to molds were auctioned off after the company failed to meet payments on a $325,000 loan from the Federal Economic Development Administration. Quoting from the Los Angeles *Herald Examiner*, Friday, August 26, 1983, the then President Herman Thompson said: "I was there at the (company's) inception, in February of 1968," he said. "We always felt it was a permanent thing."

The company had never been able to get local financing and had turned to Eastern Banks and finally the U.S. government to meet cash flow needs before failing.

In order to get the most complete history of Shindana as possible, many of the product catalogs were examined. Following is a listing of dolls shown in catalogs for the following years: 1973, 1975, 1976, 1977, 1978, and 1979. The search is ongoing for catalogs from 1968–1972, 1974, and 1980–1983. It is hopeful that they were issued for these years as this would give a complete history of Shindana.

1973 Catalog. Watts Towers is shown on the cover.

"Rhonda" #2010. Rag doll 22" tall, dressed in unremovable big apple hat, mod dress with knee socks, and sneakers.

"Lea" #3050 black; #3150, white. Vinyl and cloth from "Hug and Hold" line. 11" tall. Dressed in unremovable pink pajamas.

"Baby Zuri" #3000 black; #3100, white. Jointed vinyl doll in yellow two-piece sunsuit. 13" tall.

"Wanda Career Girl" #2050, black; #2150, white. Vinyl fashion doll. 9" tall. Dressed in green tunic with matching shoes.

"Wanda Ballerina" #2060, black; #2160, white. Vinyl fashion doll. 9". Dressed in pink tutu and tights. With doll comes ankle-length peasant dress in dark print.

"Wanda Stewardess" #2070, black; #2170 white. Vinyl fashion doll. 9". Dressed in pink hot pants, boots, and maxi with flightbag included. Extra clothing included are a hot pantsuit with bolero and sweater and knee-high boots.

"Wanda Nurse" #2080; #2180, white. Vinyl fashion doll. 9". She wears white nurses pantsuit and cap. Extra clothing includes a mini skirt and sweater with a maxi wrap plus boots.

"Jo-Jo Li'l Soul" #2131. Cloth doll 16½" tall dressed in long print granny dress. Jo-Jo comes with a 12-page storybook to color and read.

"Li'l Souls Sis" #2020. Cloth doll 10" tall. Doll is wearing blue shirt with "Say It Loud," "Right On," "I'm Proud," "Learn Baby Learn," and "Peace" printed on and green skirt.

"Li'l Souls Wilky" #2021. Cloth doll 10" tall wearing a yellow shirt with the same sayings as previous doll and blue shorts.

"Li'l Souls Coochy" #2023. Cloth doll 6" tall with pink sewn-on pajamas and yellow bib.

"Li'l Souls Natra" #2022. Cloth doll 6" tall in multicolored dress.

"Talking Tamu" #1020. Vinyl and cloth dressed in removable orange sleeveless dress. Tamu has yellow cloth body and limbs. 16" tall.

"Flip Wilson/Geraldine Jones" #1030. Cloth talking doll. 15¾" tall.

"Dreamy Dee Bee" #1002. Vinyl and cloth. Dressed in removable pink flannel pajamas with matching blanket. 16" tall.

"Baby Nancy" #2002. All vinyl drink and wet doll. Dressed in yellow and white print party dress with matching panties and booties. She has rooted hair with two ponytails. 13" tall.

1975 Catalog. Cover has Shindana Logo (two abstract drawings of children holding hands).

"Dreamy Walker" #8050. All vinyl 32" Walker. She is dressed in red blouse and light blue coveralls. She has a shag hairdo.

"Kesha" #7050. Vinyl and cloth baby doll. 22" tall. She is dressed in a sheer batiste baby dress with long puff sleeves, matching pantaloons and a sheer nylon, lace trimmed overlay.

"Tamu" #1015. Vinyl and cloth talking doll. 16" tall. She is dressed in white sleeveless dress printed with hot pink flowers. Her body and limbs are hot pink cotton.

"Rodney Allen Rippy" #1050. Cloth talking doll. 16¾" tall.

"Wanda Assortment" #2065. Action career doll that comes in three new careers this year. The first is "Wanda Singer-Performer" in long green and gold gown. Included with her is a microphone and casual outfit consisting of cutoffs, halter top, and shoes. The second new Wanda is "Wanda Sky Diver-Racing Car Driver" dressed in one-piece red and silver jumpsuit with parachute, helmet, and sky diving boots. The third new Wanda is "Wanda Tennis Pro" in white shorts outfit trimmed in red with tennis accessories. Dolls were packaged and sold separately.

"Wanda Assortment" #2055 includes the three Wanda dolls from 1973, "Wanda Doctor," "Wanda Stewardess," and "Wanda Ballerina."

"Baby Zuri Swimsuit" #3004. Vinyl doll with molded hair. Comes in a two-piece swimsuit and overskirt in a bright nautical print with her own inflatable swan. 13" tall.

"Baby Zuri" #3000. Same doll in removable two-piece yellow cotton playsuit.

"Baby Nancy Ponytail" #2002. All vinyl doll with rooted hair styled in two ponytails. Comes in yellow cotton dress covered with a layer of nylon chiffon and matching panties. 13" tall.

"Baby Nancy Natural" #2003. The same doll as previous one with short curly hairstyle.

"Kimmie Basic Set" #3010. Vinyl nursing doll wearing diapers with a soft pink blanket tied around her with a pink ribbon. 13" tall.

"Kimmie Gift Set" #3210. The same doll dressed in a bright pink baby dress with her own complete layette which includes terry cloth robe and matching towel, underpanties, flannel sacque, diaper, and bib.

"Dreamy Dee Bee" #1000. Vinyl and cloth with different clothing from 1973. This one is wearing a pink tricot nightgown and has a matching pink satin pillow, trimmed in white lace. 16" tall.

"Lea" #3050. Vinyl face and hands, cloth covered foam body. Dressed in unremovable bright pink sleepwalker with cap, all trimmed in white lace. 11" tall.

"Li'l Soft Soul" #8000. Doll was the feel of a real baby because she is made of velvety foam. Dressed in blue polka dot cotton smock and matching pantalettes. 11" tall.

"Kim Bride" #6005. Vinyl doll with jointed body in white floor-length gown and bridal train. 15¾" tall.

"Kim Formal" #6000. The same doll in a long elegant gown with yellow seersucker bottom skirt and yellow broadcloth bodice with raglan sleeves and matching broad-brimmed hat.

"Li'l Souls Sis" #2020. Clothing has changed since 1973. Doll is now wearing sewn-on mod yellow cotton broadcloth hiphuggers with a belt and buckle, a gingham blouse with floral designs and a long sleeve midriff bodice, and a fitted cap.

"Li'l Souls Wilky" #2021. Wilky's clothes have been changed to red bell-bottom pants with belt and buckle, a blue and white striped long sleeve shirt with a blue gingham hat.

"Lisa Long Hair" #2015, new for 1975. Vinyl head, cloth body and limbs with velcro hands for holding things. Sewn-on clothing includes a pink pinafore with puff sleeves and a pique top. Her rooted hair is styled in a curly bun hairdo and corkscrew curls.

"Lisa Curly Hair" #2017. The same as previous doll except clothing and cloth body. Her body consists of a cotton red print calico outfit with yellow apron with patch pocket. Her hair is styled in a short curly hairdo.

"J.J. Talking Character Doll" #1040, listed on a supplementary sheet in the catalog. He is an all cloth talking doll 23" tall with sewn-off arms and legs. He is wearing fuchsia shirt and blue jeans.

1976 Catalog.

"Little Karee Long Hair" #8015. All vinyl baby doll with rooted hair tied back with ribbon in two braids. Doll is wearing pink nightgown. 10½" tall.

"Little Karee Gift Set" #8020. The same doll with a short curly hairdo, dressed in panties and bib, and wrapped in a blue blanket with a bright pink ribbon.

"Little Karee Short Hair" #8010. Identical to "Gift Set Karee" except the clothing. Doll wears a white fleece beret, jacket, matching panties, and booties.

"Baby Nancy Natural" #2003. Doll has short natural hairstyle and comes in either an aqua and white dress or a pink with print dress. 13" tall.

"Baby Nancy Ponytail" #2002. Doll has center part with short bangs and two ponytails tied with white ribbons. Doll comes in either of the dresses described for previous Nancy.

"Kimmie Gift Set" #3210. Identical to 1975 "Kimmie Gift Set."

"Kimmie Basic Set" #3010. Identical to 1975 basic set.

"Baby Zuri Swim Set" #3004. Identical to 1975 doll except swimsuit is made of smaller print in red, white, and blue.

"Baby Zuri" #3000. Doll is now available in a playsuit in either blue denim or a bright yellow.

"Lisa Long Hair" #2017. Doll is identical to last year's version.

"Lisa Short Hair" #2017. Hair is styled in short curly natural hairdo like last year but clothing has changed. Doll is now wearing pink print pinafore like "Lisa Long Hair."

"Janie" #8040. New for this year. Catalog says she is made of velvety foam but she looks all vinyl, is bathable. 11" tall, dressed in pink dress with matching panties.

"J.J. Talking Character Doll" #1040. Identical to last year.

"J.J. Fun Pal" #1045. New for this year, vinyl head and hands. Sewn-on red jumpsuit, removable denim cap. 14" tall.

"Talking Tamu" #1015. Like last year's outfit with the following exceptions, pink rickrack is added to waist and hem of dress, pink collar is added, and lace is now around the top of the shoes.

"O.J. Simpson" #9000, new for 1976, vinyl action figure. 9½" tall, dressed in blue and white football outfit.

"O.J. Simpson" #9005, also new. The same doll as previous one with complete assortment of athletic accessories. Included are a tank top and shorts set, a running suit, and a tennis outfit.

"Slade, The Super Agent" #9010. New for 1976. All vinyl action figure, 9½" tall. Dressed in simulated leather suit with a turtleneck sweater and shoes. Also included is a backpack with a special signaling device.

"Slade, The Super Agent" #9020. Same as the basic doll above plus many more play accessories, including a silver colored protective suit with hood, front wrap, and gloves.

"Kim Jeans 'n Things" #6050. Doll is identical to last year's but clothing has changed. Doll is available in three tie-dye denim and mod print outfits, pants, and mod print outfits, pants, ankle-length dress and knee-length skirt and jacket.

"Kesha" #7050. Identical to last year's in pink baby dress.

"Dreamy Walker" #8050. Doll is now dressed in bright pink print blouse and mod pink coveralls.

"Wanda" #2065. Available in three careers for 1976, "Sky Diver-Racing Car Driver," "Tennis Pro," and "Singer-Performer." All of these were available in 1975. "Doctor," "Stewardess," and "Ballerina" have been dropped from catalog.

"Kim Formal" #6000. Identical to 1975.

"Kim Bride" #6005. Identical to 1975.

"Dreamy Dee Bee" #1000. Dress is now a white rosebud print instead of pink print of 1975.

"Li'l Souls Sis" #2029. Identical to 1975.

"Li'l Souls Wilky" #2029. Clothing has changed since 1975. He is now wearing red pants; red, black, yellow, and white striped shirt; and print hat in the same colors.

1977 Catalog with Janie and Baby Zuri on the cover.

"Little Friends Asian Girl" #4005. Vinyl head and jointed body, rooted hair. Dressed in yellow and blue. 13" tall.

"Little Friends Asian Boy" #4010. Dressed in yellow shirt, denim shorts. 13".

"Little Friends Hispanic Girl" #4015. Blue and white striped dress with red dotted bodice, yellow bandana. 13".

"Little Friends Hispanic Boy" #4020. Dressed in yellow shirt, denim shorts.

"Little Friends Black Girl" #4025. Dressed in red and white romper suit.

"Little Friends Black Boy" #4030. Dressed in red shirt with yellow sleeves, denim shorts.

"Little Friends White Girl" #4035. Dressed in white and blue print rompers with blue headband.

"Little Friends White Boy" #4040. Dressed in red shirt with yellow sleeves, denim shorts.

"Kim Jeans 'n Things" #6050. Identical to 1976.

"Dear Friends" #3055, new for 1977, Shindana's first basic white baby doll. 13" tall, all vinyl with movable arms and legs. Available in three hairdos – black, auburn, and brunette in yellow print, blue print, and pink print dresses.

"Baby Nancy Natural" #2003. Doll is now wearing the pink dress that "Baby Nancy Ponytail" wore last year.

"Baby Nancy Ponytail" #2002. Now wearing the same blue print dress that auburn haired "Dear Friends" #3055 is wearing.

"Baby Zuri" #3000. Dressed the same as last year in blue sunsuit except that ribbon ties on shoes are now white instead of yellow.

"Little Karee Long Hair" #8010. Long pink dress is similar to last year's dress with the following exceptions. Lace has been added to hemline and lace down the front is off-white and not gathered.

"Little Karee Gift Set" #8020. Identical to 1976.

"Little Karee Long Hair" #8015. Identical to 1976.

"Janie" #8040. Identical to 1976.

"Li'l Souls Sis and Wilky" #2029. Identical to 1976.

"Kimmie Gift Set" #3210. Identical to 1976.

"Kimmie Basic Set" #3010. Identical to 1976.

"Redd Foxx Talking Character Doll" #1060. New for 1977.

"J.J. Talking Character Doll" #1040. Identical to 1976.

"J. J. Fun Pal" #1045. Identical to 1976.

"O. J. Simpson Super Pro" #9000. Identical to 1976 except jersey now has number "32" in white instead of red.

"O. J. Simpson Super Pro Set" #9005. Changes for 1977 are the same as in above doll.

"Slade Super Agent" #9010. Identical to 1976.

"Slade Super Agent Set" #9020. Identical to 1976.

"Slade Super Agent With Beard" #9015, new for 1977. Set includes the basic Slade doll with a beard, dressed in a yellow suit instead of the black one.

"Wanda Action Career Dolls" #2065. Assortment is identical to 1976: "Sky Diver-Racing Car Driver," "Singer-Performer," and "Tennis Pro."

"Talking Tamu" #1015. Identical to 1976.

"Dreamy Dee Bee" #1000. Identical to 1976.

"Kesha" #7050. Clothing is changed. She is now wearing a pink batiste baby dress with white sheer nylon, lace trimmed overlay.

"Dreamy Walker" #8050. Clothing is changed. She now is available in five different costumes. Catalog pictures a two-piece tie-dye denim pantsuit similar to that on "Kim in Jeans 'n Things."

"Jump 'n Sweet" #6060, new for 1977. 11½" tall, available in three pants outfits, all of them in white denim trimmed in red.

"Promotional Doll" #7035, new for 1977. All vinyl drink and wet doll, rooted hair, painted eyes, jointed baby body. Dressed in blue print sleeveless dress. 14" tall.

"Promotional Doll" #7030, new for 1977. Similar to previous doll except smaller. Mouth does not appear to be open. Dressed in orange dotted dress. 12" tall. Except for shorter hairstyle, doll's head looks like Janie's, 1976.

"Baby Janie" #7072, new for 1977. Doll is totally different from "Janie," 1976 #8040. Doll is 16½" tall. Vinyl head, sleeping eyes, rooted hair, jointed vinyl baby body. Dressed in pink lace trimmed dress with white panties and booties.

"Rhonda" #7025, new for 1977. 18½" tall. Vinyl head and jointed toddler body, sleeping eyes, rooted hair. Doll is wearing denim A-line jumper, red print blouse, and red tights.

1977 Catalog Supplement.

"Shindana Promotional Dolls" #7040, black; #7140 white. 12" doll with sculptured hair, moving eyes, arms, legs, and head; nursing mouth. Doll comes dressed in assorted pajama outfits.

"Dreamy Walker" #8150, white doll 32" tall. Identical to black "Dreamy Walker" except for blond hair. Dressed in long print dress.

"Rag Doll Assortment" #2035. Two of the dolls are identical to "Sis and Wilky," 1976, only they are now 16" tall. The third doll is "Jo-Jo" from 1973 with the fabric in her blue print dress slightly different. It now looks more like patchwork fabric.

"Little Karee Short Hair" #8110, white doll, new for 1977. Identical to black doll, wearing the same white outfit.

"Jump 'n Sweet" #6160, white doll, new for 1977. Similar to black "Jump 'n Sweet" dolls in 1977 catalog, wearing same clothing.

"Little Stepper" #8055, black; #8155 white, new for 1977. A big 24" walker with sleeping eyes, jointed body. Black doll is dressed in blue denim jumpsuit with red print pockets and sleeves. White doll has denim pants and white shirt. Both dolls have "Little Stepper" written on front of clothing.

"Promotional Doll" #7130, new for 1977. White doll, 12" tall. Similar to black promotional doll #7030 in 1977 catalog. All vinyl, sleeping eyes, jointed body, rooted blond hair. Dressed in print dress, white socks.

"Promotional Doll" #7135, new for 1977. White doll, 14" tall. Similar to black promotional doll #7035 in 1977 catalog. Dressed in patchwork print dress.

"Dr. J. Super Pro" #9025, new for 1977. Basketball star Julius Erving. 9½" tall. All vinyl. Dressed in white uniform with "Dr. J" in red letters.

"Dr. J. Super Pro Set," new for 1977. Same as basic doll above with additional accessories.

1978 Catalog.

"Disco Wanda" #2058, new for 1978. 11½" tall, fully articulated vinyl doll. Available in three different outfits, long orange gown, off-one-shoulder blue top with striped skirt and green pants outfit with striped wrap-around blouse.

"Marla Gibbs" #1048, new for 1978. 15½" tall all vinyl personality doll from popular TV show. Doll is dressed in "homemaker" outfit with "Superstar" long yellow and gold gown included.

"Little Friends Asian Girl" #4005. Identical to 1977.

"Little Friends Hispanic Girl" #4015. Doll is now wearing a red plaid dress with yellow bandana on her head.

"Little Friends Black Girl" #4025. Identical to 1977.

"Little Friends White Girl" #4035. Identical to 1977.

"Little Friends Indian Girl" #4060, new for 1978. Dressed in suede-like brown dress with matching headband.

"Rag Doll Assortment" #2035. Identical to 1977 catalog supplement.

"Little Stepper" #8055. Now dressed in the same outfit as white "Little Stepper" in the 1977 catalog supplement, a white shirt with blue bell-bottom jeans. The words "Little Stepper" on shirt are now outlined in red instead of blue as in the 1977 version.

"White Little Stepper" #8155. Dressed as above "Little Stepper" #8055.

"Dreamy Walker" #8050. Dressed in dark pink coveralls with white print blouse in the catalog. Doll also comes in a variety of other costumes although they are not described.

"Kim Jeans 'n Things" #6050. Identical to 1977.

"Kim Jeans 'n Things" #6150, new for 1978, white doll. Dolls are identical to above dolls except for blond hair, blue eyes, and skin coloring. Dolls are dressed in white denim outfits, a long dress trimmed in blue gingham, an above-the-knee overall outfit, and a two-piece pantsuit.

"Kim Jeans 'n Things Costume Pack" #6500. Six different outfits sold separately, three in blue jean material, three in white jean material.

"Dr. J. Super Pro" #9025. Identical to 1977.

"Dr. J. Super Pro Set" #9030. Identical to 1977.

"O.J. Simpson" #9000. Identical to 1977.

"O.J. Simpson Super Pro Set" #9005. Identical to 1977.

"Redd Foxx Talking Character Doll" #1060. Identical to 1977.

"Baby Zuri" #3000. Identical to 1977.

"Janie" #8040. Redressed this year in white party dress trimmed in lace.

"Baby Nancy Ponytail" #2002. Redressed this year in the pink and striped dress worn by "Baby Nancy Natural" last year. "Baby Nancy Natural" is not in the 1978 catalog.

"Jump 'n Sweet" #6160, white. Identical to 1977 catalog supplement.

"Jump 'n Sweet" #6060. Identical to 1977.

"Little Karee Long Hair" #8015. Dressed in long pink dress similar to 1977 except for different lace trim.

"Little Karee Short Hair" #8010. Dressed in white skirt and blue and white jacket with matching headscarf and booties.

"Deluxe Baby Tasha" #7037, new for 1978. 12" drink and wet vinyl baby with rooted hair and sleeping eyes. Dressed in long red print two-piece blouse and skirt.

"Promotional Doll Baby Elisa" #7040. Doll is shown in 1977 catalog supplement, but is only called a promotional doll. Flannel pajama outfit is now blue.

"Promotional Doll Baby Elisa" #7140, white doll. Identical to 1977 catalog supplement.

"Promotional Doll Baby Kimmie" #7030. Doll is shown in 1977 catalog but just called a promotional doll. Clothing is now changed to white print with yellow flowers.

"Promotional Doll Baby Kimmie" #7130, white doll. Shown in 1977 catalog supplement as a promotional doll in the same dress doll above is now wearing.

"Mi Nina" #7400, new for 1978. 18" Hispanic vinyl baby doll dressed in long white dress and booties.

"Baby Janie" #7020. Identical to 1977.

"Playmates Baby Kesha Assortment" #7047, different from Kesha doll of previous years. Doll is now 18" tall, all vinyl, movable arms and legs, sleeping eyes, drink and wet. Assortment comes in long gown outfits and includes dolls with rooted hair, dolls with sculptured hair, and dolls with a new lighter skin color.

1979 Catalog.

"Little Friends Asian Girl" #4005. Identical to 1978 and 1977.

"Little Friends Hispanic Girl" #4015. Identical to 1978.

"Little Friends Black Girl" #4025. Identical to 1978 and 1977.

"Little Friends White Girl" #4035. Identical to 1978 and 1977.

"Little Friends Indian Girl" #4060. Identical to 1978.

"Little Karee Long Hair" #4060. Identical to 1978.

"Little Karee Short Hair" #8010. Identical to 1978.

"Deluxe Baby Tasha" #7037. Identical to 1978.

"Baby Elisa" #7140, white. Identical to 1978.

"Baby Elisa" #7040. Identical to 1978.

"Baby Kimmie" #7130, white. Identical to 1978.

"Baby Kimmie" #7030. Identical to 1978.

"Deluxe Baby Tasha" #7137, white. Except for skin coloring, identical to black "Baby Tasha" #7037. Doll is dressed in the same red print outfit.

"Janie" #8040. Dressed in blue party dress with white overlay.

"Baby Nancy" #2002. Identical to 1978.

"Mi Nina Baby Kesha Assortment" #7047. Identical to "Mi Nina and Playmates Baby Kesha Assortment" of 1978.

"Asian Baby" #7310, new for 1979. All vinyl baby doll with Asian features. 18" tall, drinks and wets. Dressed in long white dress with booties.

"Kim Jeans 'n Things" #6050. Identical to 1978.

"Kim Jeans 'n Things" #6150, white. Identical to 1978.

"Disco Wanda" #2058. Identical to 1978.

"Marla Gibbs" #1048. Identical to 1978.

"Li'l Souls Assortment" #2095, new for 1979. 16" rag dolls, Hispanic, Asian, and American Indian; all with black yarn hair.

"Li'l Souls Assortment" #2035. Identical to 1978, includes three black dolls.

1980 Catalog.

"Little Friends Asian Girl" #4005. Identical to 1979, 1978, and 1977.

"Little Friends Hispanic Girl" #4015. Identical to 1979 and 1978.

"Little Friends Black Girl" #4025. Identical to 1979, 1978, and 1977.

"Little Friends White Girl" #4035. Identical to 1979, 1978, and 1977.

"Little Friends Indian Girl" #4060. Identical to 1979 and 1978.

"Little Karee Long Hair" #8015. Identical to 1979 and 1978.

"Little Karee Short Hair" #8010. Identical to 1979 and 1978.

"Deluxe Baby Tasha" #7037. Identical to 1979 and 1978.

"Baby Elisa" #7140, white. Identical to 1979 and 1978.

"Baby Elisa" #7040. Identical to 1979 and 1978.

"Baby Kimmie" #7130, white. Identical to 1979 and 1978.

"Baby Kimmie" #7030. Identical to 1979 and 1978.

"Deluxe Baby Tasha" #7137, white. Identical to 1979.

"Janie" #8040. Identical to 1979.

"Baby Nancy" #2002. Identical to 1979 and 1978.

"Mi Nina Baby Kesha Assortment" #7047. Identical to 1979.

"Asian Baby" #7310. Identical to 1979.

"Kim Jeans 'n Things" #6050. Identical to 1979 and 1978.

"Disco Wanda" #2058. Identical to 1979 and 1978.

"Marla Gibbs" #1048. Identical to 1979 and 1978.

"Li'l Souls Assortment" #2095, Hispanic, Oriental, and Indian. Identical to 1979.

"Little Friends Asian Girl" #7315, new for 1980. 18" tall. Fully jointed vinyl doll with rooted black hair and sleep eyes, dressed in blue jumper and yellow shirt like smaller Asian Li'l Friend.

"Little Friends Hispanic Girl" #7400, new for 1980. 18" tall. Fully jointed vinyl doll with rooted brown hair, sleep eyes, dressed in red plaid jumper and white shirt like smaller Asian Li'l Friend.

"Little Friends White Girl" #7048, new for 1980. 18" tall. Fully jointed vinyl doll with rooted blond hair, sleep eyes, dressed in blue print rompers like smaller white Li'l Friend.

"Little Friends Black Girl" #7046, new for 1980. 18" tall. Fully jointed vinyl doll with rooted black hair, sleep eyes, dressed in red and red rompers like smaller black Li'l Friend.

"Little Friends Indian Girl" #7060, new for 1980. 18" tall. Fully jointed vinyl doll with rooted black hair, sleep eyes, dressed in brown suede-like dress like smaller Indian Li'l Friend.

"Little Souls Assortment" #2035. Three 16" black rag dolls. Identical to 1979 and 1978.

Plate 1081: Shindana. "Nancy." 1968. 13". The first doll of Shindana Toys. All vinyl, short black rooted hair, painted features, nursing mouth, five-piece vinyl bent legs baby body. Another "Nancy" doll was copyright in 1972 with different face, this Nancy was no longer available. Marks: DIV OF/OPERATION BOOTSTRAP, INC. U.S.A./c1968 SHINDANA, on head.

Plate 1082: Shindana. "Kim." 1968. Sold along with Baby Nancy in a set promoted as "We Have a Dream." White Baby Kim was made from the same mold as Nancy, with blue eyes and blond hair. Redressed. Marks are the same as for Nancy.

Plate 1083: Shindana. "Baby Janie," 1968. 13" tall. Painted eyes, rooted long black hair, drinks and wets. Head and body are good quality vinyl, fully jointed. Marks: DIV OF/OPERA-TION BOOTSTRAP, INC, USA/c1968 SHINDANA. Courtesy of Phyllis Houston.

Left – Plate 1084: Shindana. Another version of the previous doll only this one has bangs and longer hair. Marks are the same.

Right – Plate 1085: Shindana. "Baby Nancy" paper doll. 9½" paper doll marketed by Whitman, printed in U.S.A. by Western Publishing Company. Along with doll comes 23-piece pressout wardrobe, no scissors necessary. "Baby Nancy" is the trademark of OPERATION BOOTSTRAP, INC. for its doll.

Plate 1086: Shindana. "Dreamy Walker," 1975. Shindana's first walker doll, 32" tall. Sculptured vinyl face with big brown sleeping eyes, rooted curly shag styled hair, vinyl body with movable arms and legs. Dressed in a bright red blouse trimmed in lace and mod light blue overalls. She also came wearing yellow pants. Marks: SHINDANA TOYS 1975/DIV OPERATION BOOTSTRAP INC., on head. Photograph courtesy of Shindana Toys.

Plate 1087: Shindana. "Dreamy Walker." "Whether playing in the backyard or taking a walk down the street, Shindana's new Dreamy Walker goes everywhere. She's Shindana's first walking doll, measuring 32" tall, with movable vinyl arms, legs, and eyes. She's dressed in a bright red blouse, trimmed in delicate white lace and comes with mod light blue coveralls. She's the perfect doll to step out with in style!" Suggested retail price in the mid-1970's was $21.99. Photograph and description courtesy of Shindana Toys.

Plate 1088: Shindana. "Baby Zuri," 1972. Zuri means beautiful in Swahili. Soft and poseable vinyl; molded, painted hair; painted features, nursing mouth. Doll wears two-piece sunsuit and is also available in swimsuit as shown in the following photograph. Marks: SHINDANA TOYS 1972/DIV. OPERATION BOOTSTRAP INC. Photograph courtesy of Shindana Toys.

Left – Plate 1089: Dreamy Walker in a slightly different original outfit, print is different on blouse, belt was added. Original shoes are missing.

Right – Plate 1090: Shindana. #3004. "New! Baby Zuri Swimsuit – Shindana's 13" soft vinyl doll comes ready for hours of bathtub fun, dressed in a two-piece swimsuit and overskirt in a bright nautical print. She's fully bathable and comes with her own inflatable swan for hours of splashing fun. c1975." Photograph and description courtesy of Shindana Toys.

Plate 1092: Shindana. "Jo Jo," 1972, 16" tall member of Shindana's Li'l Souls family, along with the following dolls: "Sis," "Wilky," "Coochy," and "Natra." "Jo Jo" is all cloth with yarn hair; painted features; removable mod dress. Li'l Souls family story, coloring book is included with doll. Marks Li'l Souls/Jo Jo/1972/SHINDANA TOYS/DIV OF OPERATION/BOOT-STRAP, INC./L.A. CALIFORNIA/MADE IN TAIWAN...on tag sewn to body. Photograph courtesy of Shindana Toys.

Plate 1091: Shindana. "Lea," 1972. 11" tall. Soft vinyl face and hands, sculptured painted features, soft cloth body in sewn-on clothing. Doll was discontinued in 1976. Marks: Lea/1972/Shindana Toys, Div. of/Operation Bootstrap Inc., tag sewn to body. Doll was made in Taiwan. Photograph courtesy of Shindana Toys.

Left – Plate 1093: Shindana. #2050. "Wanda The Career Girl. Shindana's all new career girl. Her shag hairdo gives her that 'in look' for work 'n play. She is 9" tall with a twist waist, movable arms and legs, and real rooted hair 'n lashes. Wanda is dressed in a basic green tunic with matching shoes." c1972. Photograph and description courtesy of Shindana Toys.

Right – Plate 1094: Shindana. #2060. "Wanda, Career Girl Ballerina," 1972. All vinyl 9" action career doll dressed as a ballerina. Comes with granny-type dress with accessories included. Doll has twist waist; movable arms, bendable legs; rooted eyelashes and hair. Each Wanda doll comes packaged with a folder containing career information on the career depicted and instructions on how little girls can join Shindana's unusal Wanda Career Club. Marks: 1972/Shindana Toys/Hong Kong. Photograph courtesy of Shindana Toys.

Plate 1095: Shindana. #2065. "Wanda Assortment," 1975. Wanda Action Career doll comes ready for three new careers in 1975: "Wanda Singer-Performer," "Wanda Sky Diver-Racing Car Driver" and "Wanda Tennis Pro." Marks are the same on all Wanda Career Girl dolls. Photograph courtesy of Shindana Toys.

Plate 1096: Shindana. #2070. "Wanda The Career Girl Stewardess," 1972–1975. Her after-hours costume is a hot pantsuit with bolero, sweater, and boots. Photograph courtesy of Shindana Toys.

Plate 1097: Shindana. #2080. "Wanda The Career Girl Nurse" dressed in traditional uniform and cap with stethoscope. For after-hours dress, Wanda has a mini skirt, sweater, and boots. Photograph courtesy of Shindana Toys.

Plate 1098: Shindana. "Wanda — An exciting career is a part of every girl's dreams, and with Shindana's Wanda doll, dreams can begin to become a reality...All Wanda dolls sport appropriate career costumes and come packaged with a folder about the career depicted and information on how little girls can join Shindana's Wanda Career Club. Suggested retail price $6.29." Photograph and description courtesy of Shindana Toys.

Plate 1099: Shindana. "Natra," member of Li'l Souls Family, 1970. All cloth, removable dress, yarn-like hair, headband fastened across forehead. 7". Marks: Li'l Souls/c1970/Shindana Toys/Div. of Operation/Bootstrap, Inc./L.A. California..., tag sewn to body.

Plate 1100: Shindana. "Coochy," baby in Li'l Souls Family, 1970. 6" all cloth, legs are sewn in bent baby style, black yarn "natural" hairstyle. Sewn-on clothes. Marks: same as previous doll "Natra."

Plate 1101: Shindana. "Sis," Similar to previous "Sis" only this one is larger, 15". Courtesy of Margaret Betts.

Plate 1102: Shindana. #2020 "Sis" and #2021 "Wilky." Cloth dolls called rag pals by Shindana. 10" tall. Printed features, black yarn hair for Sis, sewn-on clothing. They are both dressed in the mod dress of the 70's. c1974. Photograph courtesy of Shindana Toys.

Plate 1103: Shindana. "Sis." Public relations release, 1975: "Li'l Souls – Rag dolls are perennially popular Christmas gifts for small children, and this year Shindana introduces two new members of its Li'l Souls collection, Sis and Wilky. Both are fun-filled rag dolls that measure only 10" tall and come dressed in the latest mod fashions. Sis (shown above) sports cotton broadcloth hiphuggers with a blue belt, gold buckle, red and white checked gingham blouse with floral designs, a longsleeve midriff bodice and fitted hood made from the same fabric. Her distinctive hairdo is made of black yarn with twin pompons. Suggested retail price for both Sis and Wilky: $3.95."

Plate 1105: Shindana. "Li'l Souls" boy. All cloth with yarn hair in big "Afro," painted features, 9½" tall. Removable shirt with sayings popular in the early 70's printed on. Tag sewn to body is the same as previous doll.

Plate 1106: Shindana. "Li'l Souls" girl. Identical to previous Li'l Souls boy except for removable dress, sewn-on shoes and painted smile.

Plate 1104: Shindana. "Li'l Soul Sis." 10". All cloth, sewn-on clothing, red pants, blue and white striped shirt, aqua gingham cap. Marks: Li'l Souls/c1970/Shindana Toys/Div. of Operation/Bootstrap, Inc...,tag sewn to body.

Plate 1107: Shindana. Collection of previous Li'l Souls dolls for size comparisons.

Plate 1108: Shindana. #1040. "New! J.J. Talking Doll – Kids think he's 'Dyn-O-Mite!' He's Shindana's new talking novelty doll, based on J.J. Evans, the comical older son seen on TV's hit show "Good Times." J.J. measures 23", with floppy, poseable sewn-off arms and legs. He comes dressed just like the real J.J. and says any of nine sayings in the real J.J.'s voice when kids pull his talking ring. No batteries required. c1975, Tandem Productions, Inc." Photograph and description courtesy of Shindana Toys.

Plate 1109: Shindana. Another photograph of J.J. Talking doll. He says the following sayings: Don't squeeze me too tight, I'm Dyn-O-Mite; You're talking to kid Dyn-O-Mite; Easy now, you're playing with kid Dyn-O-Mite; It's always right with kid Dyn-O-Mite; Hello, this is J.J. the light of your life; Boy you're lucky, now you've got your own kid Dyn-O-Mite; Hello, this is the ebony genius of the ghetto; Hello this is the Cassanova of the ghetto; There is nothing as bright as kid Dyn-O-Mite. Marks: c1975/TANDEM/Productions, Inc./Shindana Toys, Div. of/Operation Bootstrap Inc./Los Angeles, Calif. 90001...tag sewn to body. Photograph courtesy of Shindana Toys.

Plate 1110: Shindana. "J.J. Fun Pal. Joining talking J.J. for 1976 is the new J.J. Fun Pal, a cuddly 14" handsize version of 'Kid Dyn-O-Mite.' Kids can carry him anywhere for hours of fun. The smaller J.J. features a self-dressed body made of soft, trico fabric and has a finely sculptured head and removable denim hat. He's also poseable, with long, floppy, sewn-off arms, legs and hands." Marks: tag sewn to body is same as previous talking J.J. Photograph and description courtesy of Shindana Toys.

Plate 1111: Shindana. "O.J. Simpson Super Pro. Any boy can be a football superstar in 1976 with Shindana Toy's new O.J. Simpson male action figure, patterned after the All-American running back making the big plays for the Buffalo Bills. Shindana's O.J. measures 9½" tall and features movable vinyl arms, legs, and head and is available in both basic and deluxe sets. His basic outfit (shown here) features O.J. dressed in his now-famous #32 football jersey, complete with helmet, shoulder pads, pants, two-toned football shoes, and striped socks. Football also included." Photograph and description courtesy of Shindana Toys.

Plate 1112: Shindana. O.J. in original box purchased in 1976. Marks on doll: SHINDANA TOYS/ c1975, on head; HONG KONG, on body.

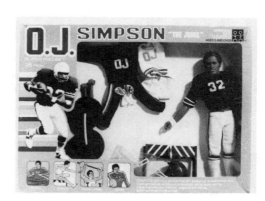

Plate 1113: Shindana. "Slade, The Super Agent." "Slade, The Super Agent is Shindana's new undercover spy. Slade grew up in the ghetto, where he learned to survive. He went to war and was taught to fight. Now, following college, he puts it all together as he sets out to fight corruption and crime. The basic Slade Super Agent outfit (shown above) features the 9½" male action figure dressed in a sharp, simulated leather outfit, topped off with a turtleneck sweater and shoes. Also included is Slade's own special signalling device." Marks: SHINDANA TOYS/c1976. Photograph and description courtesy of Shindana Toys.

Plate 1114: Shindana. "Kim Bride," 1975. #6005. "A bride doll is a very special doll, and Kim is a very special bride, measuring 15¾" tall. With fully jointed body and real rooted hair. Her elegant white floor-length gown features a scalloped hemline, complete with floral appliques, nylon basket-woven lace trim and floor-length bridal veil train. Accessories include a white taffeta underskirt, a netted petticoat and pantalettes." Photograph and description courtesy of Shindana Toys.

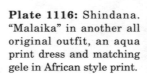

Plate 1115: Shindana. "Malaika," angel in Swahili. An afro fashion doll, 15" tall, 1969. All original with vinyl head and jointed body; rooted black "Afro" styled hair; painted features. Doll is wearing Afro-American fashions designed by Aajib. Original box has painted African bush scene as background for doll. Marks: 41/c1969/SHINDANA TOYS/DIV. OF OPERATION/BOOT-STRAP INC. U.S.A. Malaika, Kim Bride, and Kim Formal are much darker in coloring than Kim Jeans 'n Things dolls.

Plate 1116: Shindana. "Malaika" in another all original outfit, an aqua print dress and matching gele in African style print.

Plate 1117: Shindana. "Kim Jeans 'n Things." Promotional literature from Shindana, 1976: "Stepping out in high fashion for 1976 is Shindana's Kim, who this year comes in a new Jeans 'n Things collection. Each of Kim's three assorted 'in' outfits are specially tailored for today's look, made of tie-dye denims and mod prints. Kim measures 15" tall, with movable arms, legs, and head and is sure to delight older fashion-conscious girls as they style Kim's long, real rooted hair or mix and match her outfits. (Wardrobes are not sold separately.)" Marks: 17/c1969/Shindana Toys/Div. of Operation/Bootstrap Inc. U.S.A./K, on head. Photograph and description courtesy of Shindana Toys.

Plate 1118: Shindana. "Kim Jeans 'n Things." All original in jeans jumpsuit and matching striped cap. Marks: 17/c1969/SHINDANA TOYS/DIV. OF OPERATION/BOOTSTRAP INC. U.S.A./K, on head. Extra outfit, like the one shown on previous doll, was included with dolls.

Left – Plate 1119: Shindana. "Kim Jeans 'n Things" in the third outfit in the Jeans 'n Things collection. All original in ankle-length denim skirt and pink print blouse and headscarf that matches trim on skirt. Marks: 4/c1969/SHINDANA TOYS/DIV OF OPERATION/BOOTSTRAP INC. U.S.A./K., on head.

Right – Plate 1120: Shindana. "Kim" from new mold. This Kim was made from the same mold that was used for white Kim #6150, shown only in 1977 and 1978 catalogs. The features are more caucasian on this Kim than the previous one. 15" tall. Painted eyes, long black rooted hair, closed mouth, jointed body. All original in white three-piece denim outfit. This is the same outfit white Kim wore in 1977–78. Marks: cSHINDANA TOYS 1978/HONG KONG, on head; HONG KONG, on body.

Plate 1121: Shindana. The new "Kim" in another all original outfit, white denim bibbed shorts and cap with red, white, and blue striped knit shirt and knee highs. Marks are the same. White Kim also wore this outfit in the 1977 and 1978 catalogs.

Plate 1122: Shindana. "Kim" in another all original outfit, white denim pants with blue gingham top and headscarf. White doll Kim #6150 also wore this outfit in the 1977 and 1978 catalogs. Black Kim in the same catalogs was shown from the earlier Kim mold in blue denim clothing.

Plate 1123: Shindana. The back of a package of Jeans 'n Things Fashions for Kim showing all six of the Kim dolls available. Box is c1978. All six outfits were sold separately.

Plate 1124: Shindana. "Rodney Allen Rippy Talking Doll," 1973. All cloth talking child doll of T.V. personality. 16¾" tall. Body is four-color silk-screened foam filled, imprinted with monogram t-shirt, blue jeans, black and white easy walkers, and Rodney's natural hairstyle. Doll says ten different phrases in the real Rodney's voice when talking string is pulled. Phrases are as follows: Pull my string (laughter) that tickles; I pray for the whole world. Will you pray with me?; Laughter; I don't know about kissing, but I know about honey; Take life a little easier; Let's go walking and get some energy; Know who I really love? You. (kiss); My name is Rodney Allen Rippy R-I-P-P-Y. Marks on tag sewn to body: c1973/Target Marketing, Inc./Shindana Toys, Div. of /Operation Bootstrap, Inc./...Photograph courtesy of Shindana Toys.

Plate 1125: Shindana. "Rodney Allen Rippy." Rodney Allen Rippy with the doll Rodney Allen Rippy. Photograph courtesy of Shindana Toys.

Left – Plate 1126: Public Relations release in 1973 from Harshe-Rotman & Druck for Shindana Toy Company: Photograph courtesy of Shindana Toys.

Right – Plate 1127: Shindana. "Dee Bee," 16". Vinyl head, rooted black hair, painted features with white glisten dot in lower left corner. In similar "Tamu," dot is in upper left corner. Cloth body and legs, vinyl hands. All original in animal print sleeper. Marks: 1969 SHINDANA/DIV. OF OPERATION BOOTSTRAP INC, on head; tag sewn to body: DEE BEE/1969 Shindana Toys/Division of Opera-tion/Bootstrap Inc.

Plate 1128: Shindana. "Dreamy Dee Bee" #100, 1975. 16" all-rag body with vinyl hands and face, rooted hair, painted eyes. All original in pink tricot nightgown with her own matching pink satin pillow, trimmed in white lace. Earlier "Dee Bee" as shown in previous photo in leopard print flannel has a brown cloth body. This later "Dreamy Dee Bee" has a pink cloth body or a salmon colored cloth body. Both heads are marked the same. Clothing is tagged "Dee Bee." Photograph courtesy of Shindana Toys.

Plate 1129: Shindana. #7050. "Kesha – Shindana's new half-rag, half-foam baby doll has the feel and weight of a real baby. She is 22" tall, with short baby curl hair, movable hazel eyes, movable arms and legs, and cute baby dimples. She's dressed in a sheer batiste baby dress, with matching pantaloons and a sheer nylon, lace-trimmed overlay." c1975 Shindana Toys. Marks: SHINDANA TOYS c1975/DIV. OPER. BOOTSTRAP, INC. Photograph and description courtesy of Shindana Toys.

Left – Plate 1130: Another photograph of the previous doll. Except for slight variation in painted eyebrows, head on Keesha is identical to head on Shindana's "Dreamy Walker." Marks are also the same on the back of the head. Suggested retail price in 1975 was $21.99. Photograph courtesy of Shindana Toys.

Right – Plate 1131: Shindana. #2002. "Baby Nancy." This doll has the same name as the first Shindana doll, but now has a completely new sculptured face. 13" tall. Vinyl head, rooted black hair, painted eyes, nursing mouth, jointed vinyl bent leg body. All original in yellow party dress with lace overlay and matching panties. Marks: SHINDANA TOYS c1972/Div. Oper. Bootstrap, Inc., on head; HONG KONG, on body. Photograph courtesy of Shindana Toys.

Left – Plate 1132: Shindana. #2003. "Baby Nancy" (natural hairstyle). Except for black natural curly hairdo, doll is identical to previous "Baby Nancy." Photograph courtesy of Shindana Toys.

Right – Plate 1133: Shindana. #2010. "Rhonda," 1973, all cloth doll, painted features and hair, sewn-on clothing including a big apple hat. 22" tall. Printed on original box is this statement from Shindana: "Shindana, Swahili for 'competitor,'" is owned, managed, and staffed by black people – as part of Operation Bootstrap, we share the slogan "Learn Baby, Learn." Our goal is to develop the jobs and skills necessary to build a profitable black business which will become a permanent part of the community." Marks: RHONDA/c1973/SHINDANA TOYS/DIV. OF OPERATION/BOOTSTRAP, INC., tag sewn to body. Photograph courtesy of Shindana Toys.

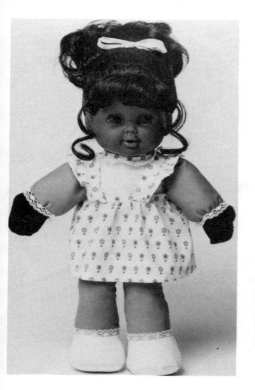

Left – Plate 1134: Shindana. #2015. "Lisa (long hair) – Learning can be fun for a little girl – if she has someone to learn with, such as Lisa. She's Shindana's new self-dressed doll that features velcro hands, permitting her to hold things. Lisa with long hair comes dressed in a bright pink pinafore, with puff sleeves and a pique top. She's smartly coiffured with a curly bun hairdo and corkscrew curls." c1975 Shindana Toys. Photograph and description courtesy of Shindana Toys.

Right – Plate 1135: Shindana. #2017. "Lisa (curly hair)…Lisa with curly hair comes dressed in a bright cotton calico-print outfit, with a solid-color apron featuring patch pockets. She wears a short curly natural hairdo." c1975 Shindana Toys. Marks: SHINDANA TOYS c1972/DIV. OPER. BOOTSTRAP, on head. Photograph and description courtesy of Shindana Toys.

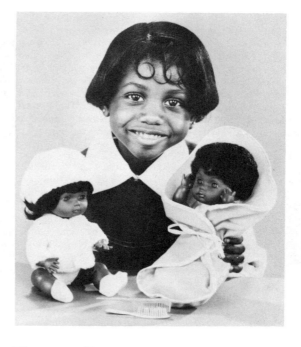

Plate 1136: Shindana. #8040. "Little Soft Janie," 1976. 11" tall. Shindana has two dolls named Janie, this one, and a larger doll issued in 1977, "Baby Janie." This Janie has a vinyl head, painted eyes, rooted black hair, closed mouth, one-piece vinyl baby body. All original in bright pink cotton dress trimmed in white lace. Janie wore the same outfit in 1977. In 1978, she wore a white party dress with white organdy overlay. In 1979 and 1980, she was shown in the catalogs in a blue party dress with white organdy overlay. Marks: SHINDANA TOYS/c1975 HONG KONG, on head. Photograph courtesy of Shindana Toys.

Plate 1137: Shindana. "Little Karee." Joining the Shindana family in 1976 is Shindana's petite vinyl doll, Little Karee, 10½" tall. Fully jointed, rooted black hair, sleeping hazel eyes, closed mouth. She is available in three hairdos, each dressed in a different outfit. #8015 – long hair in two braids and bangs, dressed in a long pink gown trimmed with a bow and lace. #8020 – short curly hairdo, doll on the right in photo above. #8010 – short straight hairdo, doll on the left. Marks: c1975 SHINDANA/TOYS, on head. Photograph courtesy of Shindana Toys.

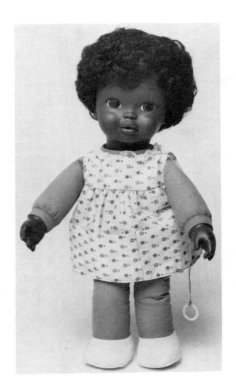

Plate 1138: Shindana. "Flip Wilson/Geraldine," 1970. All cloth talking character doll of comedian Flip Wilson. 16½" tall. One side is printed with Flip Wilson, the other side is Geraldine. When string is pulled, Flip says the following phrases, at random, in his own voice: "Easy on that string. I'm only going to tell you one more time"; "I smell a rat and the wind is coming from your direction"; "The ugly people know who they are, don't they"; "Oh yeah, and I'll punch you right in the fist with my face"; "I like the blues 'cause when the record wears out it still sounds the same"; "Help y'all, they got me trapped inside this doll." The following phrases are said in the voice of Geraldine: "What you see is what you get honey – ooh"; "If I had known you were coming, I'd have stayed at home;" "Don't touch me, you don't know me that well." Marks: c1970/Street Corner/Productions Inc./Operation Bootstrap, Inc..., on tag sewn to body.

Plate 1139: Shindana. #1015. 1975. "Tamu – Her name means sweet and kids will delight to the 18 sweet things that Tamu says when they pull her talking ring. She measures 16" tall, with an all-soft rag body and vinyl face and hands. She comes dressed in a smart hot pink sleeveless print dress. No batteries required." Tamu for 1976 has the same dress with the following changes: a pink collar replaced the white lace at the neck; a strip of pink rickrack was sewn around waist and hem of dress. Photograph and description courtesy of Shindana Toys.

Plate 1140: Shindana. "Talking Tamu," 1970. Earlier Tamu doll with short straight hair. The cloth body is different also. Previous doll had a hot pink cloth body with white cloth feet. The body on this doll is yellow with black cloth feet. Marks: c1969 SHINDANA/DIV OF BOOTSTRAP INC., on head. Tag sewn to body: Tamu/c1970/ Shindana Toys/Div. of Operation/Bootstrap Inc. Doll is all original in orange dress with yellow collar trimmed with yellow rickrack. Phrases Tamu says at random when string is pulled: "Pick me up," "Cool it baby," "I love you," "Give me a kiss," "It's your thing," "Tell me a story," "Are you hip to the facts," (Giggling), "I'm proud like you," "What's happening sister," "Lay me down," "I'm sleepy," "Hold me tight," "My name is Tamu."

Plate 1141: Shindana, "Talking Redd Foxx." Two dolls in one, "The Man" on one side, "The Entertainer" on the other side. All cloth with floppy arms and legs, 16" tall. Pull string doll with nine sayings in Redd's voice, no batteries required. Tag sewn to body: c1976/Redd Foxx Enterprises/Shindana Toys Inc./Los Angeles, Calif. 90001...

Plate 1143: Shindana. "Kimmie." #3010. Kimmie is made from the same mold as "Baby Nancy" #2002. The differences are that Kimmie is a slightly lighter shade of brown and has dark brown hair instead of black hair. 13" tall. Vinyl head, painted eyes, nursing mouth. All original in a soft pink flannel diaper with matching blanket. Marks: Shindana Toys c1972/Div. Oper. Bootstrap Inc., on head. Photograph courtesy of Shindana Toys.

Plate 1142: Shindana. "Baby Janie." #7020. 18" bent leg vinyl baby doll. Hazel sleeping eyes, short curly, rooted black hair, five-piece jointed body, nursing mouth. All original in pink dress with white yoke and white socks. Marks: ©Shindana Toys/1976 HONG KONG, on head; HONG KONG, on body.

Plate 1144: Shindana. "Kimmie Baby Gift Set" in the original box. Advertised as "Dolls Made By a Dream." The gift set sold for $15.50 in the mid-1970's. Marks: Shindana Toys c1972/Div. Oper. Bootstrap, Inc., on head.

Plate 1145: Shindana. #3210. "Kimmie Baby Gift Set," 1974. "Kimmie is dressed in a pink taffeta kimono. The set includes a pink terry cloth robe, matching towel, a white flannel sacque with matching diaper, a bib, miniature comb, brush, and bottle." Photograph and description courtesy of Shindana Toys.

Plate 1146: Shindana. "Kimmie." Photograph courtesy of Shindana Toys, 1976.

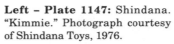

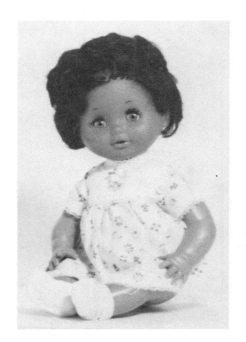

Left – Plate 1147: Shindana. "Kimmie." Photograph courtesy of Shindana Toys, 1976.

Right – Plate 1148: Shindana. "Promotional Dolls Baby Kimmie." #7030. This Kimmie is different from earlier Kimmie as she has hazel sleeping eyes, is made of lighter weight vinyl, and has less Negroid facial features. 12" tall. Vinyl head, rooted black hair, nursing mouth, jointed vinyl bent leg baby body. All original in white print cotton dress and white socks. Doll is shown for the first time in 1978 catalog. Marks: K/SHINDANA TOYS c1976, on head; MADE IN/HONG KONG, on body.

Plate 1150: Shindana. "Little Friends Asian Boy and Girl." 13" tall. All vinyl, molded painted hair, painted eyes. Boy is all original in red and white shirt, denim pants. Girl has yellow dress with red trim. Although these dolls and some following are not black, they are included because they were made by the first major black doll company in the United States, Shindana Toys. Marks are the same for both dolls: SHINDANA TOYS c1976, on head; HONG KONG, on body.

Plate 1149: Shindana. "Promotional Dolls Baby Kimmie." White. #3130. Except for clothing, blue eyes, and blond hair, this Kimmie is identical to previous Kimmie. All original in pink dress and white socks. Marks: K/SHINDANA TOYS c1976, on head; MADE IN HONG KONG, on body.

Plate 1151: Shindana. "Asian Baby," 18", from Our Friends collection. Vinyl head, sleeping dark brown eyes with lashes, black rooted hair, nursing mouth, bent leg baby body. Redressed. Marks: 1978 SHINDANA TOYS/ Hong Kong, on head; Hong Kong, on body.

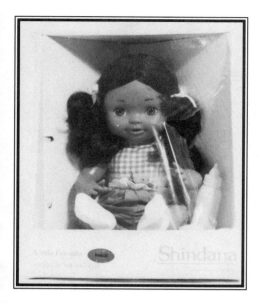

Plate 1152: Shindana. "Little Friends Black Girl," 13". Vinyl head, painted eyes, rooted long black hair, nursing mouth, jointed vinyl body. All original in red and white sunsuit. Marks: SHINDANA TOYS c1976, on head; Hong Kong, on body.

Plate 1153: Shindana. "Little Friends Black Boy." 13" tall. Vinyl head, painted eyes and hair, open nursing mouth; jointed vinyl bent leg body. All original in yellow numbered football t-shirt and black shorts. #4020. Marks: SHIN-DANA TOYS c1976. Courtesy of Marge Betts.

Plate 1154: Shindana. "Little Friends Indian Girl." 13" tall. Vinyl head, rooted black hair, painted eyes, nursing mouth, jointed vinyl body. Dress is original, matching headband and shoes are missing. Marks: SHINDANA TOYS c1976, on head.

Plate 1155: Shindana. "Little Friends Hispanic Boy and Girl. 13" tall. Vinyl with molded painted hair, painted eyes, nursing and wetting dolls. Boy is all original in red and yellow shirt, denim short pants. Girl is all original in red plaid dress, panties, yellow bandana. Marks: SHINDANA TOYS c1976, on head; Hong Kong, on body.

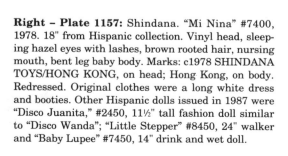

Left – Plate 1156: Shindana. "Little Friends White Girl," 13". Vinyl head, painted eyes, rooted blond hair, nursing mouth, jointed vinyl body. Marks: SHINDANA TOYS c1976, on head; Hong Kong, on body. Courtesy of Dr. Margaret Betts.

Right – Plate 1157: Shindana. "Mi Nina" #7400, 1978. 18" from Hispanic collection. Vinyl head, sleeping hazel eyes with lashes, brown rooted hair, nursing mouth, bent leg baby body. Marks: c1978 SHINDANA TOYS/HONG KONG, on head; Hong Kong, on body. Redressed. Original clothes were a long white dress and booties. Other Hispanic dolls issued in 1987 were "Disco Juanita," #2450, 11½" tall fashion doll similar to "Disco Wanda"; "Little Stepper" #8450, 24" walker and "Baby Lupee" #7450, 14" drink and wet doll.

Plate 1158: "Dr. J., Julius Erving," 9½" tall basketball playing doll. Fully jointed, all vinyl with painted features. All original with basketball. Marks: SHINDANA TOYS/c1977, on head; HONG KONG, on body.

Plate 1159: Shindana, "Marla Gibbs" as Florence, the maid on the TV show "The Jeffersons." 15½". Vinyl head, rooted hair, poseable arms and legs, painted eyes and mouth. Doll came with two outfits, "Super Star" evening gown and "Homemaker" with apron. Marks: c1978/SHINDANA TOYS/HONG KONG, on head; HONG KONG, on body.

Plate 1160: Shindana. "Disco Wanda" #2058, 1978. 11½" tall. Fully articulated, bendable legs, twisting waist, movable arms and legs; long rooted black hair, painted eyes and open painted mouth. Doll was sold in three different disco outfits. This Wanda is all original in long gold satin gown with black print shawl. Marks: HONG KONG, on back.

Plate 1161: Shindana. "Disco Wanda" in all original pant outfit. Pants are lime green, tie front shirt is printed in various bright colors with matching headscarf.

Plate 1162: Shindana. "Disco Wanda" all original in short striped skirt and off-one-shoulder blue blouse with matching headband.

Plate 1163: Shindana. One of the early dolls. 13". Vinyl head, sleeping brown eyes, long black rooted hair, open nursing mouth, jointed vinyl arms and bent legs, plastic body. Redressed. Marks: c1969/SHINDANA TOYS/DIV. OF OPERATION/BOOTSTRAP INC. U.S.A., on head. This is one of the few early Shindana dolls with sleeping eyes. Most of the early dolls had painted eyes.

Plate 1164: Shindana. "Jumpin' Sweet," 11½". Vinyl head, long rooted black hair, sleeping brown eyes with eyelashes, jointed vinyl body. All original in one-piece off-white cotton jumpsuit top-stitched with red thread. Marks: c1975 SHINDANA/TOYS, on head.

Plate 1165: Shindana. This doll has a face like Kesha and a Tamu body, both earlier Shindana dolls. 16" tall. Vinyl head, sleeping hazel eyes, rooted black hair, vinyl hands, cloth body and legs. Marks: SHINDANA TOYS c1975/DIV. OPER/BOOTSTRAP INC., on head. Courtesy of Marge Betts.

Plate 1166: Shindana. "Li'l Souls Oriental." 16" tall. Painted-on facial features, black yarn hair. All original. Courtesy of Marge Betts.

Plate 1167: Shindana. "Li'l Souls," Indian. 16" tall cloth doll with painted features, sewn-on clothing, black yarn hair. Tag sewn to body: c1970/Shindana Toys, Div. of /Operation Bootstrap, Inc...

Plate 1168: Shindana. "Li'l Souls," Hispanic. 16" tall. Cloth doll with painted features, sewn-on clothing and black yarn hair. Doll is marked the same as previous doll.

Plate 1169: Shindana. "Baby Tasha" 7037. 12" tall. Vinyl head, sleeping brown eyes, long rooted black hair, open nursing mouth, jointed bent leg plastic body. All original in long red print dress with white sleeves trimmed in rickrack. Marks: x/SHINDANA TOYS c1976, on head. Baby Tasha was presented for the first time in the 1978 Shindana catalog.

Plate 1170: Shindana. "Little Stepper" #8055, black; #8155, white. Walking doll 24" tall. Vinyl head, rooted hair, sleeping eyes, jointed body. 1978. Shown with Shindana doll Kesha in the center. Shindana catalog, 1978.

Plate 1171: Shindana. All original doll with a head identical to that of Kimmie and Kim's body. 15" tall. All vinyl, nursing mouth, rooted short curly brown hair, painted eyes, jointed body. All original in two-piece sunsuit made of the same fabric and very similar to that worn by Baby Zuri in 1976. Marks: SHINDANA TOYS c1972/DIV. OPER. BOOT-STRAP INC., on head; MADE IN/ HONG KONG, on body.

Plate 1172: Tanline. "Baby Chubby," 18" baby doll. Vinyl head with open/closed mouth, dark brown sleeping eyes, real lashes, brown rooted hair; vinyl arms and legs, cloth body. All original. Marks: China, on head. Tag sewn to body:...made in China by H.K. City Toys FYT. LTD. Box marked: Made in China/TLHK LTD, Marketed by TANLINE ASSOCIATES, USA., No. 2090. Purchased new in 1990.

Plate 1174: Tanline. "Baby Peaches." 14" soft, huggable baby doll. Product No. 2030. "Baby Peaches" has the same coloring as many of the Tanline dolls, a very reddish medium brown, not often seen naturally on black children. Sleeping brown eyes, rooted hair, brown cloth body, vinyl limbs. All original in overalls and striped knit shirt. Marks: China, on head.

Plate 1173: Tanline. "Little Cheryl," 12" doll with vinyl head, sleep eyes, rooted brown hair, vinyl arms and legs, brown cloth body. All original in light blue dress and matching bloomers. Marks: China, on head. Box is marked No. 2045. Purchased new in 1990.

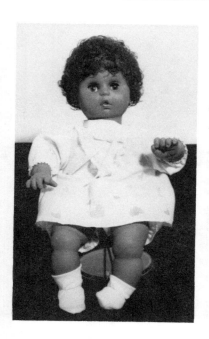

Left – Plate 1175: Another "Baby Peaches" by Tanline. All original in a pink and white dress with white undies, white booties. Doll is identical to previous doll except for shorter hair and lips are painted a slight shade lighter in coloring. Marks: China, on head. Sticker on cloth body: Made in China by HK City Toys FTY LTD. Box is marked: TANLINE PRODUCTS/DETROIT MICHIGAN 48235.

Right – Plate 1176: Another 14" "Baby Peaches." Although this doll was made from the same mold, her coloring is very different from the previous Baby Peaches dolls. As she was purchased one year earlier than the others and on clearance, she was probably the earliest issue. Her brown skin coloring has much less of a red tint, lips are painted brighter coral rather than darker shade as on the other dolls. All original in matching blue dress and underpants. Marks: Tanline Products/Hong Kong, on head. She is the prettiest of the Baby Peaches dolls.

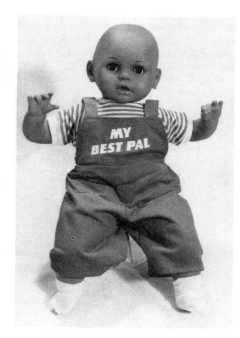

Left – Plate 1177: Tanline. "Softie Cortney," 13" baby doll with vinyl head, painted features and molded, painted hair. She has vinyl arms and legs with brown soft cloth body. Doll is all original with long pink nightgown and cap. Doll is unmarked. Box is marked: No. 1015. Tanline Products Detroit, Michigan 48221. Doll was purchased at K-Mart in 1983.

Right – Plate 1178: Tanline. "My Best Pal," 18" tall. All original with sleeping brown eyes; soft vinyl head, arms and legs; soft brown cloth body. Doll was available in either red or blue corduroy overalls. Marks: Tanline Products/c1986, on head. Tanline/Tanline Products Inc/Detroit, Michigan 48235, tag sewn to body.

Left – Plate 1179: Tanline. "Two Best Friends." Two 4½" dolls sold together. All vinyl with painted features; rooted hair, fully jointed bent leg bodies. All original. The dolls were available in several different original outfits. Marks: China, on back. Box is marked: Tanline Toys Inc., Detroit, Michigan 48235. One doll has long hair, the other has short hair.

Right – Plate 1180: Tanline. "Just Duckie," 6" all vinyl bathtub doll with movable head, arms, and legs; painted features, molded hair. All original. Doll was available in robe as shown in white, blue, pink, or yellow. Marks: Made in China/1985 CITITOY, on head; Made in China, on back.

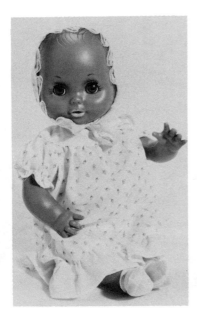

Plate 1181: Tanline. "Baby Susie." 12" drink and wet baby doll. Soft vinyl head with sleeping brown eyes, nursing mouth, fully jointed five-piece vinyl body. All original in white and pink dress and matching bonnet. Doll came with bottle, comb, and brush even though hair is molded on head. Marks: K, on head; Made in/Hong Kong, on body.

Plate 1182: Tanline. "Crystal," 14" slender collectible doll. All original, she came in a variety of outfits. Reddish brown vinyl head, painted features, reddish brown rooted hair. Crystal has fully developed figure. All vinyl, movable limbs. Marks: Tanline Products/Hong Kong, on head.

Plate 1183: Tanline. "Baby Ashley," 9" wet and drink baby doll with a bottle. Doll is all vinyl with painted features, rooted hair, and jointed limbs. All original, she was available in assorted dresses. Marks: 6008, on head; Made in China, on body.

Left – Plate 1184: Tanline. "My Friend Wanda," 32" walking doll. All vinyl with sleeping brown eyes and rooted hair. All original, she was available in the same outfit in red print or blue print. Marks: China, on head; Made in China, on body. On the market in 1990.

Right – Plate 1185: Tanline. "Crystal's Uptown Fashion Party," 11½" fashion doll with six color coordinated outfits and accessories. Doll is all vinyl with long rooted hair and painted features. Marks: China, on head.

Plate 1186: Tanline. "Crystal Rocker," 11½" fashion doll. All vinyl with painted eyes, rooted hair, bendable legs, twisting waist. All original. Product No. 3080. Marks: TANLINE PRODUCTS, on head. Tanline Products/Detroit, Michigan 48235/Made in China, on box. Doll was available in several different outfits.

Plate 1187: Tanline. "Crystal." 11½" tall. Identical, except for clothing, to Crystal Rocker. All original in long red metallic gown. Doll was available in several different outfits.

Plate 1188: Tanline Toys. "Little Tina," 10" all vinyl jointed baby doll, sleeping eyes, rooted dark brown hair. All original in white cotton dress and bonnet. Marks: 4101/A52, on head.

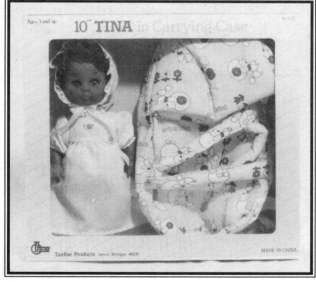

Plate 1189: Tanline. "Little Tina," 10" bathtime fun baby doll. All vinyl, sleeping brown eyes with lashes, rooted brown hair, bent leg jointed body. Doll comes with clothes and bathtub. No. 1020. Marks: 42/CHINA, on head.

Plate 1190: Tanline. "Tina in Carrying Case," 10". All original in pink and white cotton gown with matching bonnet. All vinyl jointed baby, rooted reddish brown hair, sleeping brown eyes, closed mouth. Marks: Made in/China, on sticker on back of doll. Head is unmarked. Carrying case is tagged Tanline Toys.

Left – Plate 1191: Tanline. "Gift Set," 11½" set of three dolls. Except for clothing, dolls are identical to "Crystal" by Tanline. Available late 1980's.

Right – Plate 1192: Tanline. "The Happy Family," 11½" and 4½". Late 1980's. Mother and two children have rooted dark brown hair, father has molded painted black hair; all have painted eyes; mother and father have open mouths, children have closed mouths. All original. No. 1145.

Plate 1193: Tanline. "Little Jeanette." 1980's. #1570. 7" tall. Vinyl head, painted eyes, rooted dark brown hair, nursing mouth, jointed vinyl bent leg baby body. All original in print nightgown trimmed in blue with blue bonnet. Doll comes with extra clothing. Marks: Made in China, on label stuck to back.

Plate 1194: Thomas. "Cabbage Patch type doll," 10". Hard vinyl head, painted eyes, dimple in each cheek, black yarn looped hair, cloth body. This type of head was sold in fabric and crafts shops and you made the body and clothes at home. Patterns were available for the latter. Marks: COPR 1984 M N THOMAS, on head.

Plate 1195: Tiger Toys, Inc. "Your Loving Babies," a series of twelve dolls, 5½" tall. Only one of the twelve was black. All vinyl, fully poseable, painted features, rooted dark hair. All original. Marks: B/ c1988/TIGER/CHINA, on head.

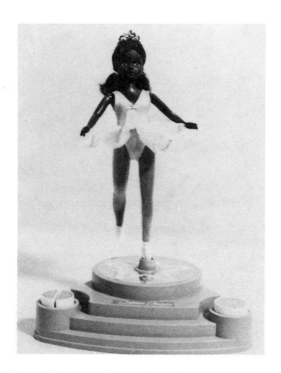

Plate 1196: Tiger Toys. "Modilyn," 17" flashy fashion doll. Soft vinyl head, painted features, rooted black hair; hard vinyl jointed body. All original. Marks: 1990 TIGER/MADE IN CHINA, on head and body.

Plate 1197: Tomy. "Dream Dancer," 10" high-fashion dancing doll. Battery operated with her own stage. You control all of the movements on stage. When she is removed from the stage, she's a high-fashion doll. Doll comes with two outfits, workout and ballet. All vinyl with painted features and rooted hair, closed mouth. Marks: TOMY/CHINA, Copyright: 1984.

Plate 1198: Tomy. "Dream Skater," 10" high-fashion ice skating doll. Battery operated with her own skating rink. Similar to "Dream Skater" except that painted mouth is smiling with teeth showing. Marks: TOMY/CHINA, copyright: 1985.

Plate 1199: Tomy. "Kimberly," 17". Vinyl head and jointed body, rooted dark brown hair, painted eyes. All original in pink and white "Hang Ten" outfit and roller skates. Marks: (boy and girl figures incised) TOMY, on head; TOMY, on body. Copyright 1982. Courtesy of Xzena Moore.

Plate 1200: Tomy. "Kimberly Cheerleader." All original. Marks are the same as previous Kimberly.

Plate 1201: Tomy. "Getting Fancy Kimberly," 1984. 17" tall. Vinyl head, rooted long dark brown hair, painted eyes, open smiling painted mouth with teeth, jointed vinyl body. All original in white net dress with pink sateen lining, pink slipper shoes. Marks: cTOMY, on body.

Plate 1202: Tonka. "Star Fairies Nightsong," 6" tall, 1985. Vinyl head, rooted brown hair, painted eyes, closed mouth, jointed vinyl body. All original in blue and white dress with matching fairy wings. Marks: HORNBY/c1983, on head.

Plate 1203: Tonka. c1990. "Sweet Sue," 6", from "Sugar & Sparkle Cupcakes." Magical doll that changes from a cupcake to a doll. Vinyl half-doll, painted eyes, smiling mouth with painted teeth, rooted brown hair with glitter strands. All original in lavender dress trimmed in pink. Marks: TONKA/TONKA CORP./MADE IN CHINA, on bottom of cupcake. Other dolls in the series are "Honey Drop," dressed in aqua; "Sugar," dressed in pink; and "Crystal," dressed in silver. Except for color of dress, they are identical.

Plate 1204: Tonka. "Sara," 13½", from the Bathing Beauties collection. Her hair changes from a light dusty brown to a warm pink color with the warmth of your hand or warm water. Vinyl head, and jointed baby body, decal eyes, rooted hair, closed mouth, dimple in the chin. Marks: cTONKA 1985/ MADE IN CHINA, on body.

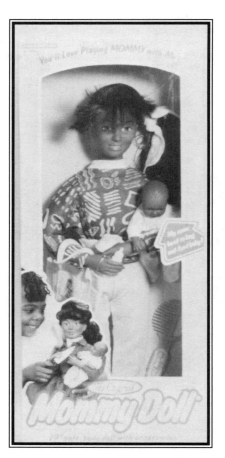

Plate 1205: Tootsie. Two other "Mommy Dolls" in original outfits.

Plate 1206: Tootsie. "Mommy Doll," 19" soft-body doll with her own baby. Her arms bend to hug and feed baby. Vinyl head with painted features, dark brown rooted hair, vinyl arms and legs, cloth body. All original. Marks: 1990 CJ DESIGNS, INC./TOOTSIE TOY. Baby is 6½" all vinyl with painted features, jointed body. Marks: CJ DESIGNS INC./1987.

Plate 1207: Deluxe Topper. "Baby Catch-A-Ball." Battery operated doll catches a ball and throws it back. Special metal ball comes with doll. 19" tall. Soft vinyl head; rooted black hair; brown glassine eyes, closed mouth with molded tongue sticking out slightly. Jointed hard plastic body with pre-set arms. Unremovable bracelets on each arm are part of the mechanism. Tag on wrist warns: Do not force arms up or down or mechanism will be damaged. Marks: PB 2/97/Deluxe Topper/19c68, on head.

Plate 1208: Deluxe Topper. "Baby Luv 'n Care." Battery operated doll gets a fever just like a real baby. 19" tall. Comes with nursing bottle, hot water bottle and thermometer. Soft vinyl head, curly black hair, stationary glassine eyes, nursing mouth. Jointed hard plastic body and limbs. All original. Marks: DELUXE TOPPER/19c66/E5, on head.

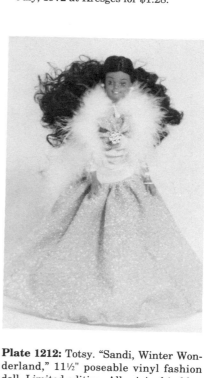

Plate 1209: Topper. "Dale," 6" tall. All original. Vinyl head, painted features, rooted black hair, jointed waist, snapping knees. Marks: 4/H149, on head; 1970/TOPPER CORP./HONG KONG/11 2, on body. Purchased new July, 1972 at Kresges for $1.28.

Left – Plate 1210: Topper Corp. "Van," 6½" tall. Vinyl head, painted features, molded black hair. Jointed body with snapping knees. All original. Marks: 1970/Topper Corp/Hong Kong/P., on body.

Right – Plate 1211: Totsy. "Ms. Flair," 11½" fashion doll. Vinyl head, painted features, black rooted hair, pierced ears, plastic body. All original in blue swimsuit. Doll is also available in brown or tan swimsuit. Marks: cTOTSY 1988, on head; Made in/Hong Kong, on body.

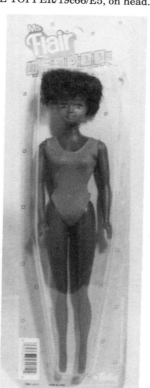

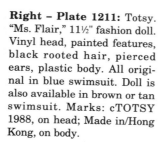

Plate 1212: Totsy. "Sandi, Winter Wonderland," 11½" poseable vinyl fashion doll. Limited edition. All original in blue and white gown with silver threads and white feather boa. Marks: TOTSY 1987, on head.

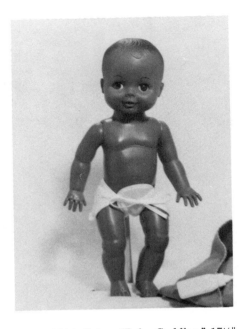

Plate 1213: Totsy. "Sandi, Magic Moments." Special edition. All original in white wedding gown. Doll is identical to previous Sandi. Marks: TOTSY 1987, on head. Box marked c1990.

Plate 1214: Totsy. "Baby Cuddles," 17½" tall. Vinyl head, molded hair, sleeping dark brown eyes, nursing mouth; jointed plastic bent leg baby body. All original with diapers and turquoise cotton flannel wrapper. Marks: 6/17ME/S, on head.

Plate 1215: Totsy. "Debbie," 18½". Vinyl head, sleeping dark brown eyes, rooted black curly hair, closed mouth; jointed hard plastic body. All original in blue cotton dress, gingham on skirt part. Marks: TOTSY c1988/Made in China. Mold looks identical to Beatrice Wright mold from 1960–70.

Plate 1217: Toy Time. "Miss Sergio Valente," 11½" fully poseable fashion doll. 1982. Made in Hong Kong.

Plate 1216: Totsy. "Christopher," 18½". Identical to previous doll except for clothing. All original in white cotton shirt that snaps up the back and red cotton bibbed pants. This doll is identical to Beatrice Wright's "Christopher." Marks: by TOTSY c1988/Made in China.

Plate 1219: Tyco Industries, Inc. "Quints," five tiny baby dolls with bottles and bunting, 2½" tall. Hard vinyl with painted features, rooted hair, fully jointed. Each baby has its number, 1 to 5, on the back of its molded-on diaper. Marks: Tyco 1990, on head.

Plate 1218: Toy Time. "Sergio Valente," 12" fashion doll. 1982. Vinyl head, molded hair, painted features. Although doll is brown in coloring, it has Caucasian features.

Plate 1220: Toys 'n Things. "Mermaid Princess." 12" tall vinyl doll with long black rooted hair, painted brown eyes, open mouth with painted teeth, twisting waist, movable arms and legs. All original in two-piece blue metallic mermaid outfit. Marks: BARTER, on head; MADE IN CHINA, on body. Available 1991.

Plate 1221: Tyco. "My Pretty Ballerina." 16". Vinyl head doll with painted features, dark brown rooted hair; hard plastic fully jointed body. Doll dances on her toes forward and backward. Her head and arms move. Rose in her right hand controls her movements. Batteries required. Marks: cTYCO, 1989. Real ballet music cassette comes with doll as well as plastic barre. All original.

Plate 1222: Tyco. "Oopsie Daisy," 16" tall. Vinyl head and body, rooted hair. She is just learning to crawl. She crawls, falls down, cries for mommy, and gets back up. Battery operated, comes with pacifier. All original in pink cotton knit rompers with white knit shirt. Marks: OOPSIE DAISY/IRWIN TOY LIMITED 1988, on body. Courtesy of Celeste Gates.

Plate 1223: Tyco. "Drink and Wet Quints" with Magic Diapers. c1990. The numbers on their diapers, 1 to 5, magically appear when wet. Dolls are the same size as previous quints, rooted dark brown hair, painted eyes, open nursing mouth, jointed bodies. Diapers are removable and are in assorted pastel colors. Marks: cTYCO/1990, on head.

Plate 1225: Tyco. "Playful Quints." Similar to previous quints except for smiling faces with upper teeth showing. Dolls have playful motions and have molded-on diapers in the following colors: pink, blue, yellow, green and lavender. The doll's motions are controlled by a lever in the doll's back. Marks: cTYCO/1990, on head.

Plate 1226: Tyco. "Patty," 3½", from the Dixie's Diner Kids. Poseable vinyl, painted eyes, molded painted black hair, jointed body. All original in removable pink satiny dress with aqua jacket. Doll comes with a Dixie's Diner button that can be worn or used as a doll stand. Marks: 1988 EPOCH/MADE IN/TAIWAN, on body.

Plate 1224: Uneeda. "Lovable Lynn," 11" all original jointed vinyl toddler doll, light brown sleeping eyes, rooted black hair. Marks: UNEEDA DOLL CO. INC./MCMLXX/Hong Kong, on head and body.

Plate 1227: Uneeda Doll Co., 15" tall, 1970's. Soft vinyl head, rooted black hair, light brown sleeping eyes; hard plastic jointed toddler body. Redressed. Marks: 13/UNEEDA/DOLL CO./INC/N.F., on head.

Plate 1228: Uneeda. 1970's. 15" tall. Soft vinyl head, sleeping glassine eyes, rooted hair, molded smiling mouth, dimpled cheeks, vinyl jointed toddler body. Redressed. Marks: UNEEDA/DOLL CO/INC (in circle on head)/N.F.

Plate 1229: Uneeda. Walking doll, 32" tall. Vinyl head, brown sleep eyes, rooted black short hair styled in a bob. Marks: TAIWAN/3178 ME/Uneeda Doll Co. Inc./MCMLXXVI/40, head.

Plate 1230: Uneeda. "Tricki Miki," 6½" fashion doll with ten movable joints, poses like the human body. Soft vinyl head, painted features, long straight black rooted hair, vinyl body. All original. Doll was advertised on TV. Printed on box: Available only at Woolworth/Woolco. Marks: UNEEDA, on head; LITTLE MISS/DOLLIKIN/U.S. PAT./No. 3,010,253/OTHER U.S. &/FOR. PAT. PEND./Made in Hong Kong, on body. 1971.

Plate 1232: Uneeda. 32". Vinyl head, black rooted hair cut short in back with long bangs and two long ponytails, large brown sleep eyes, closed mouth, rosy cheeks, lightweight vinyl body with outline of opening that looks like it could be an opening for a battery case on the back of the doll. Opening was not cut out. Long print dress that looks original. Marks: 27/3176 ME/cUNEEDA DOLL CO. INC./MCMLXXVI, on head.

Plate 1231: Uneeda. Fashion walking doll, 23" tall. Vinyl head, sleeping brown eyes, rooted black hair, jointed hard plastic body. All original in white vinyl dress with aqua trim. Marks: 9/UNEEDA DOLL CO. INC./19c69/2469, on head. Courtesy of Sandra Johnson Taylor.

Plate 1233: Uneeda. Cabbage Patch Kids type of doll, 14" tall. Bald vinyl head with brown sleeping eyes with lashes, open nursing mouth, two dimples, cloth body. Redressed in Cabbage Patch Kids marked clothing. Marks: UNEEDA DOLL CO INC/MCMLXXX (the remainder is blurred), on head.

Plate 1234: Uneeda. "Toddles," 36" life-size walking doll. Vinyl head, sleeping brown eyes with lashes, rooted black hair; jointed hard plastic body. All original. Style no. 83660. Marks: Taiwan/UNEEDA, on head. Box is marked MCMLXXXI. (1981)

Plate 1235: Uneeda. "Samantha," 14". Vinyl head, long black rooted hair, brown sleeping eyes, open mouth with hole so that doll can "suck her thumb," vinyl hands, cloth body and legs. All original in green and white striped pajamas. Marks: 1984 UNEEDA DOLL COMPAY ("N" is missing) INC./Made in China, on head.

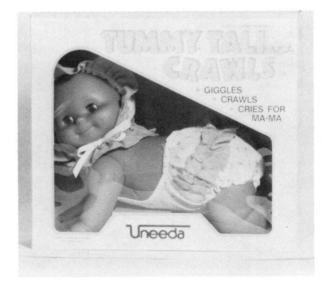

Plate 1236: Uneeda. "I See You Dolly," 15". Vinyl head, black rooted hair, dark brown eyes that follow you in any direction, vinyl hands, cloth body and legs. All original in pink print sleepers. Marks: U.D. CO. INC./MADE IN CHINA, on head. c1988.

Plate 1237: Uneeda. "Tummy Talks Crawls." Doll giggles, crawls, and cries for ma-ma. Vinyl head, molded hair, sleeping brown eyes, closed mouth, dimples in cheeks, vinyl arms and legs, hard plastic body. Battery operated. All original in white print sunsuit trimmed in blue and matching bonnet. Marks: U.D. CO., INC./MADE IN CHINA, on head; U.D.CO., INC./MADE IN CHINA, on body.

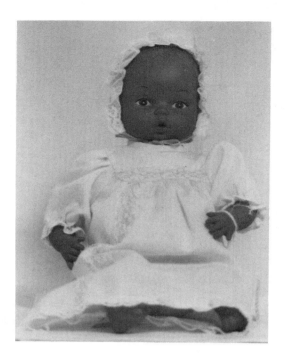

Plate 1238: Uneeda. "Musical Soft Luv," 1983. 14" tall. Vinyl head, painted eyes, open/closed mouth, molded hair, vinyl arms and legs, white cloth body. Music box is attached to doll's dress, not body. All original in white cotton gown trimmed in pink. Marks: cU.D. CO. INC/MCMLXXVII/MADE IN HONG KONG, on head.

Plate 1239: Vogue. "Miss Ginny." 15" tall. 1975. Vinyl head, sleeping eyes, rooted hair, jointed vinyl body. Photograph courtesy of Vogue Dolls.

Plate 1240: Vogue. "Miss Ginny," dressed in casual clothing. 15". All original in green polyester pantsuit trimmed in yellow. This was the latest fashion in the mid-1970's. Marks: VOGUE DOLL/1974, on head. Clothing: VOGUE DOLLS, INC./Made in USA.

Plate 1241: Vogue. "Miss Ginny." All original in bridal gown. 15" tall. Vinyl head, sleeping brown eyes with lashes, closed mouth, rooted brown hair, pierced ears, jointed vinyl body. Doll is unmarked.

Plate 1242: Vogue. "Miss Ginny," all original 15" doll. Vinyl head, rooted brown hair, brown sleep eyes with lashes, painted open mouth, fully jointed vinyl body. All original in well-made gown of green dotted swiss with lots of white lace trim. Marks: Vogue Doll/1974.

Plate 1243: Vogue Dolls. "Ginny Baby," 1975. 16" tall. Drink and wet doll, rooted hair, sleeping eyes. Marks: GINNY BABY/VOGUE DOLLS INC, on head. Photograph courtesy of Vogue Dolls.

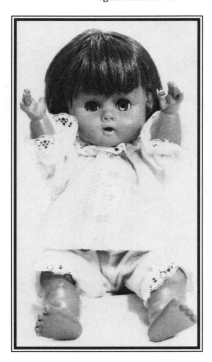

Plate 1244: Vogue. "Ginny Baby," 1970's. 11". Vinyl bent leg baby doll, sleeping brown eyes, rooted dark brown hair, nurser mouth, jointed body. All original in pink flannel pajamas. Marks: GINNY BABY/VOGUE DOLLS INC, on head; 12-5, on body.

Plate 1245: Vogue. "Ginny, Africa," 8" doll from Far-Away Lands series. Hard vinyl with brown sleeping eyes, black hair, jointed body. All original. Marks: Ginny, on head. Vogue dolls 1972/Made in Hong Kong, on back.

Plate 1246: Vogue. "Jamaican" from Far-Away Lands series. 8" tall. Vinyl head, painted eyes, dark brown rooted hair done up in bun on top, closed mouth, jointed vinyl body and limbs. All original in yellow and white dress trimmed with orange and green rickrack and ribbons. Marks:VOGUE DOLLS/cGINNY TM/1977, on head; VOGUE DOLLS c1972/MADE IN HONG KONG/3, on body.

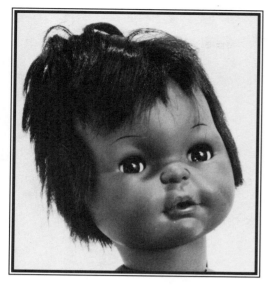

Plate 1247: Vogue. "Dearest One." 18" tall. Vinyl baby doll, brown sleeping eyes, real lashes; rooted brown hair; nursing mouth. Marks: VOGUE DOLLS INC./1967, on neck. VOGUE DOLLS INC./1967/PAT.PEND., on back of doll.

Right – Plate 1248: Vogue. "Lil Imp," 10½" doll. Soft vinyl head and jointed body, long rooted black hair, sleep eyes, closed mouth. Cute dimples on elbows and knees. Redressed. Marks: 1964/Vogue Doll, on head.

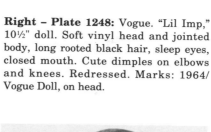

Plate 1250: Vogue. "Dear Baby," 1975. 12". Vinyl head, arms, and legs; soft foam body; sleep eyes, molded hair. Photograph courtesy of Vogue Dolls.

Plate 1249: Vogue. "Wash-A-Bye Baby," 1975. 16" tall. All vinyl, molded hair, painted eyes. Photograph courtesy of Vogue Dolls.

Plate 1251: Vogue. "Baby Dear-One," 1975. 18" tall. Vinyl head, arms, and legs, cloth body; rooted hair; sleeping eyes. Photograph courtesy of Vogue Dolls.

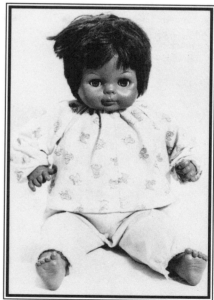

Plate 1252: Vogue Dolls Inc. "Baby Dear-One," 25" doll, big enough to wear clothing from a one-year-old child. Head, arms, and legs are soft vinyl, rooted dark brown straight hair, sleep eyes, closed mouth. Body is brown cloth stuffed with soft foam, cry box inside body. All original. Marks: Vogue Doll/1965. Doll was purchased new in mid-1970's.

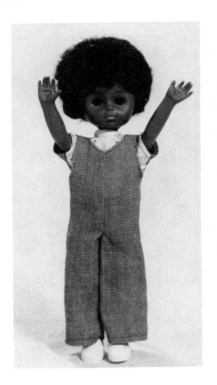

Plate 1254: Vogue. "Littlest Angel," 1975. 15" tall. All vinyl with sleeping eyes, rooted black hair. Photograph courtesy of Vogue Dolls.

Plate 1253: Vogue. "Littlest Angel," 15". Fully jointed vinyl toddler, brown sleep eyes, brown rooted hair in two braids with bangs, closed mouth. All original in pink gingham nightgown trimmed in white lace. Marks: VOGUE DOLL/1963, on head. Available on the market in 1974. Made in U.S.A.

Plate 1255: Vogue. "Ginnette," 8". Vinyl head, sleeping brown eyes, rooted black hair, five-piece jointed hard vinyl body. All original in green jumpsuit with white print trim. Marks: GINNY/VOGUE DOLLS/1977, on head; 1978 VOGUE DOLLS INC/MOONACHE N.J./Made in Hong Kong, on body.

Plate 1256: Vogue. "Ginnette." All original in red polyester dress with white trim, red hat and white tights. Marks are the same as previous "Ginnette."

Plate 1257: Vogue. "Ginny, Tropical Adventure," 8". All hard vinyl with black rooted curly hair, brown sleep eyes, jointed body. All original. Marks: Vogue Dolls/1986 R. Dakin Co./Made in China, on back. Hang tag: Vogue Dolls/Made with love. Reverse side: 71-3550/Tropical Adventure/International/Collection/1990/Vogue/Dolls.

Plate 1258: Vogue Dolls. "Black Curls," bride from the Special Days collection. #71-3580. 8" tall. Vinyl head, sleeping brown eyes with lashes, rooted brown hair, jointed hard vinyl body. Marks: VOGUE DOLLS/c1986 R. DAKIN & CO./MADE IN CHINA, on body.

Plate 1259: Vogue. "Ginny, Sunday Best, Girl and Boy." 8". All original, 1989. Marks: VOGUE DOLLS/c1986 R. DAKIN & CO./MADE IN CHINA, on body of both dolls. Shirley's Dollhouse exclusive editions.

Plate 1260: Vogue. "Ginny at the Beach," 1987, 8" tall. A Shirley's Dollhouse exclusive. Vinyl head, jointed hard vinyl body; sleeping brown eyes, rooted black hair. All original in white and red striped swimsuit and matching cover-up. Marks: VOGUE DOLLS/c1986 R. DAKIN & CO./MADE IN HONG KONG, on body.

Plate 1261: Vogue. "Dress Me Ginny," 8", c1988. All original in pink undies trimmed in lace with white socks and shoes. Marks: VOGUE (R in circle) DOLLS/c1984 DAKIN INC./MADE IN CHINA, on head.

Plate 1262: Vogue. "Ginny, Queen of the Mardi Gras" from the Make Believe collection, 8" tall. All original in bright fuchsia, green, and orange five-piece outfit with orange and green feather accessories. #71-4010, 1991. Marks: VOGUE DOLLS/c1986 R. DAKIN & CO./MADE IN CHINA, on body.

Plate 1263: Vogue. "Ginny, Sweet Dreams" #71-3850 from the Ginny and Friends collection. Vinyl head, brown sleep eyes, rooted dark brown hair, jointed vinyl body. All original in white cotton nighties and includes jointed teddy bear. Marks: R/VOGUE DOLLS/ c1984 DAKIN INC./MADE IN CHINA, on head. 1991.

Plate 1264: Wanna Be. "Doctor," male, 17" tall from the Wanna Be Career collection. These were the only dolls made by Wanna Be, Inc. before they went out of business. Vinyl head, sleeping brown eyes, rooted brown hair, closed mouth; vinyl arms and legs, white cloth body with Wanna Be logo sewn on chest. Marks: (Wanna Be logo, rainbow and sun)/1986 Wanna Be Inc., on head. The Wanna Be dolls were extremely well made. Included in the line were the following dolls: Doctors, male and female; Teachers, male and female; Executives, male and female; Pilots, male and female; Firefighters, male and female; Soldiers, male and female, Football player, male and Cheerleader, female.

Plate 1265: Wanna Be. "Teacher," male.

Plate 1266: Wanna Be. "Executive," male.

Plate 1267: Wanna Be. "Pilot," male.

Plate 1268: Wanna Be. "Firefighter," male.

Plate 1269: Wanna Be. "Football Player."

Plate 1270: Wanna Be. "Pilot," female. The female has longer hair than the male. That is the only difference between the two dolls.

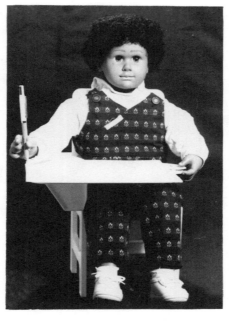

Plate 1271: Well Made Toy Mfg. Corp. "Giggles," the Happy Doll, laughs and giggles when tossed around. 15" tall. Brown stockinette cloth body, black yarn hair, black button eyes, pink button nose, embroidered mouth. All original in pink and aqua sewn-on clothes, removable white bib. Batteries required. Distributed by F.W. Woolworth Co. Tag sewn to body: Dolly Mine, on one side; MAINE LIC #67 PENN REG #194/MASS LIC 0134 OHIO LIC #4193/COPYRIGHT c 1989..., other side.

Plate 1272: Wonderama. "Susie Scribbles," 26" talking and writing doll. She can write anything she says. Battery operated, she comes with cassette tapes inserted into her back, plastic desk, and removable pen. Vinyl head, arms and legs, stationary brown eyes with lashes, rooted black curly hair, cloth body. All original in blue print overalls, pink sweater, and pink shoes. Marks: H. GARFINKEL, on head.

Plate 1273: World. "Mammy," 19" limited edition portrait doll from 50th Anniversary of Gone With the Wind. Vinyl head, painted features, rooted short black hair; vinyl lower arms and legs; brown cloth body. All original. Marks: World Doll, on head. Made in China/By World Doll, tag sewn to body. Style 61900. Box marked same as below Mammy. Doll has on black dress with red petticoat. This same doll also came in gray dress with white apron, like the smaller size Mammy.

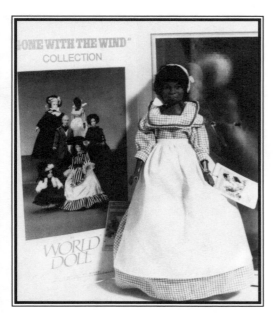

Plate 1275: World. "Mammy," 11" limited edition portrait doll from 50th Anniversary of Gone With the Wind. Role of Mammy was played by actress Hattie McDaniel. Doll has vinyl head, painted features and hair; vinyl lower arms and legs, molded-on shoes; brown cloth body. All original in gray dress, white apron. Marks: 1939 SELZNICK REN/ 1987 MGM, on head. Made in China/By WORLD DOLL, tag sewn to body. Box marked: 1939 Selznick, Ren, 1967 MGM/1989 Turner Entertainment Co. Style 61062.

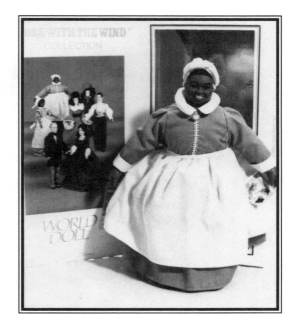

Plate 1274: World. "Prissy," 11" portrait doll from Gone With the Wind collection. Doll bears a close resemblance to actress Butterfly McQueen who played the part of Prissy in the movie. Hard vinyl head, painted features, rooted black hair; five-piece hard vinyl, swivel waist body. Marks: World Doll, on head. Made in China, on back. World Doll issued this Prissy along with Scarlett, Bonnie Blue, Mr. O'Hara, Mrs. O'Hara, and Pitty Pat. Style 71072.

Plate 1276: World. "Prissy," 11". All original, dress is different from previous Prissy. The doll was part of the third issue in the Gone With the Wind mini series. Sculpture and decorating was done by Neal Estern. Costume is an authentic recreation. This issue was limited to 25,000 pieces. Other GWTW dolls in this series are Scarlett, Melanie, Ashley Rhett, Mammy, and Bonnie Blue. Marks:World Doll, on head; Made in China, on back.

Plate 1277: World. "Prissy," 17". Vinyl head, painted features, rooted black hair, vinyl lower arms and legs, cloth body. All original. Marks: 400-61720 PRISSY/ WORLD DOLL/MADE IN CHINA, on head. Costume similar to previous Prissy except basket was added.

Plate 1278: World. "Mammy," 19". All original in gray dress with white apron. Doll is identical to 19" Mammy in black dress.

Plate 1279: Worlds of Wonder. "Ashley," one of the "Rockin' Boppers," 9½". Vinyl head, painted features, rooted dark brown hair vinyl arms, hard plastic body and legs. Doll can really dance to any beat. Batteries required. All original in yellow knit dress with red legwarmers. Marks: Rockin' Bopper/WOW/WORLDS OF WONDER, on bottom of right shoe; Fremont, CA 94538/Made in China/1990 Worlds of Wonder, Inc./All Rights Reserved, on bottom of left shoe.

Plate 1280: World. "Kristina." 24" toddler doll with vinyl head, arms and legs, dark brown sleeping eyes, open/closed mouth with painted teeth, rooted black curly hair, white cloth body. All original in floral cotton dress with matching bloomers and stuffed animal. Limited quantity for one year only. Shown in J.C. Penney Christmas catalog 1991. Marks: c1983 WORLD DOLL, INC./96-62850, on head.

Mrs. Beatrice W. Brewington the Creator, founder and president of The First Negro Toy Co. to manufacture dolls and stuffed toys.

B. WRIGHT'S
TOY
COMPANY, INC.

165 NORTH MAIN STREET
FREEPORT, NEW YORK 11520
TEL: 516 FR 9-5270

I was born on a county farm in North Carolina and received my elementary and high school education in Faison, N.C. I majored in elementary education and art, received my B.A. Degree from Shaw University, Raleigh, N.C. The following are schools I have attended: Hampton Institute in Hampton, Va.; Winston Salem Teachers College, Winston, N.C.; Fayettesville State Teachers College, N.C.; Columbia University, New York, N.Y.; Bank Street College, New York, N.Y.

I was licensed in "Early Childhood Education," at Bank Street College. My teaching in art took me to North Carolina, New York and New Jersey. In Kingston, N.C., I introduced the first art exhibit in 1946 which was then programmed for all schools in the city under the supervision of School Sup't. of Lenoir County, Mr. H.H. Bullock and principal Mr. R.L. Flanagan. This exhibit was continued annually for 2 weeks prior to Easter and is enjoyed by many viewers. At this time, I was elected to be County Chairman of the Art Program.

During 1955 I instructed 19 girls in the art of making dolls. The idea was very well received and has been improved and grown into the business I now operate. As a youngster I played with the dolls of that day which were made of rags by the mothers for their children. I started by making my own, stuffing and coloring them until I developed some that were very life-like. This was the beginning of my interest in creating a Negro doll. I then took courses in doll making and discovered that there wasn't a truly representative Negro doll. This encouraged me to create a doll that trully reflects all the Negro features. I then sought a factory that produces Negro dolls and didn't find any in existence in the U.S.A., up until then dolls were imported from abroad. The first doll company was set up here in 1910. It was thought that colored dolls would not appeal to Negro children. This was a misconception that I have since disproven. In many areas poor children could not afford real dolls only the wealthy children had them. Today, dolls produced at very reasonable rates which are accessible to all children. Children relate to dolls very well and they help to develope the childs mental and social areas as children are very imaginative. Dolls are a symbol of love and beauty.

I pride myself in having developed many natural looking dolls and stuffed toys which have been copyrighted. I trust they will be perpetuated for a long time to come.

Dedicated to my son, Verden

Plate 1281: Biography of Beatrice W. Brewington, creator of Beatrice Wright Dolls. Courtesy of Beatrice Wright Brewington.

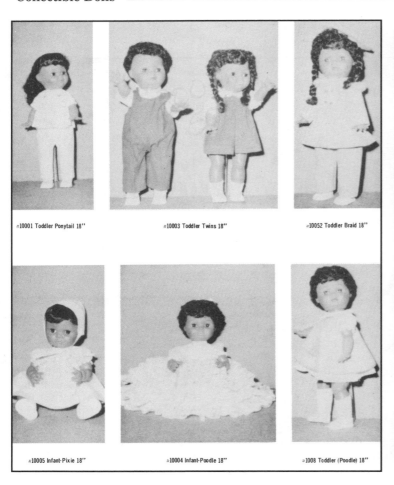

#10001 Toddler Ponytail 18"   #10003 Toddler Twins 18"   #10052 Toddler Braid 18"

#10005 Infant-Pixie 18"   #10004 Infant-Poodle 18"   #1008 Toddler (Poodle) 18"

THE ETHNIC DOLL PEOPLE

No. 1008   No. 1001   No. 1002   No. 1003

No. 1007   No. 1054   No. 6002   No. 6001

No. 1004   No. 1005   No. 2001   No. 2002

Plate 1282: Promotional literature on B. Wright dolls. Literature is hand-dated 1969.

Plate 1283: Additional promotional literature on Wright dolls. Courtesy of Beatrice Wright Brewington.

Left – Plate 1284: B. Wright Toy Co. "Jacqueline," 19" tall Beatrice Wright doll. Soft lyka head, sleep eyes, rooted black curly hair, hard jointed vinyl body. All original in white cotton dress with blue and yellow smocking. Marks: 1967/BEATRICE WRIGHT, on head. This is the same dress that Wright's doll "Christine," named after her granddaughter, wore. Photograph of Christine is not available; however, the only difference in dolls was that Christine had long braids. Beatrice Wright dolls are currently made by Totsy and are marked: Totsy c1988/Made in China.

Right – Plate 1285: Wright. "Debbie," 18" toddler doll with dimpled knees. Hair is short and curly. All original in two-piece blue outfit. Marks: 1967/Beatrice Wright, on head.

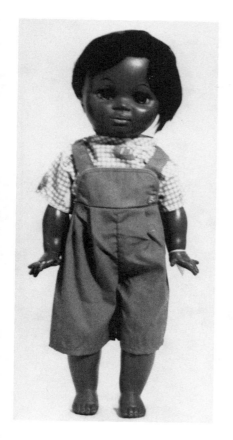

Plate 1288: Zapf Creation. Baby girl, 19" tall. Vinyl head, sleeping light brown eyes, rooted short black hair, open/closed mouth; vinyl arms and legs, brown cloth body. All original, 1983. Marks: Z (in logo)/50-18, on head. Made in Germany.

Plate 1286: Wright. "Alfie." 19" tall. Vinyl head, sleeping brown eyes, rooted black hair, jointed hard plastic straight leg body. Redressed. Marks: 2602 (under rooted hair)/17 EYE/18F/2/B. Wright, on head.

Plate 1287: Zapf. "Friends of the 4 Continents" boy doll. 21" tall. Vinyl head, brown sleeping eyes with lashes, rooted black curly hair, pierced ears with gold stud earrings. Well-made brown cloth body with vinyl limbs. All original. Marks: (Z in a circle with ten small circles surrounding with the number 2017 written below.) Clothing is labeled. Made in Western Germany. There was also a black girl in Friends of the 4 Continents series. No photo available of her.

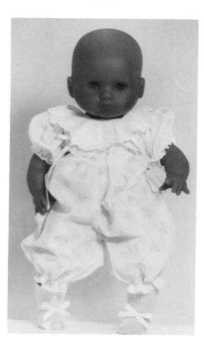

Plate 1289: Zapf. Fully articulated 11½" action figure. Vinyl head, painted features, black flocked hair; hard plastic body. Marks: MAX (ZAPF logo) ZAPF, on back.

Plate 1290: Zapf. "Colette." 19½" tall. Vinyl head, brown sleeping eyes, closed mouth, rooted black curly hair, cloth body, vinyl limbs. All original. Marks: Z (in circle)/50-17, on head. Courtesy of Marge Betts.

Plate 1291: Zapf. "Lisa," 17" from the Balica Dolls collection, designed by Brigitte Zapf. Vinyl head, arms and legs, cloth body, sleeping brown eyes, bald head, closed mouth. All original in pink print cotton rompers trimmed in white lace with white print blouse. Marks: 30/1988/MAX ZAPF/ W. Germany/All rights reserved/40 Z (in circle) 16, on head. Balica Dolls is a division of Tiger Toys. Doll was made in Yugoslavia, copyright 1989 by Tiger Toys.

Plate 1292: Zapf. Toddler girl, 19½" tall. Vinyl head, arms and legs, cloth body; brown sleeping eyes, closed mouth. All original in red cotton pants, aqua vest, white pastel striped shirt. Marks: Z (in circle)/5511, on head. Courtesy of Marge Betts.

Plate 1293: Zapf. "Malcolm." 26" tall. Vinyl head, arms, and legs; cloth body; open/closed mouth, sleeping brown eyes. All original lavender knit sweater vest, lavender shorts, white shirt. Marks: 1986 4/MARZ ZAPF W. GERMANY, on head. Courtesy of Marge Betts.

Plate 1294: Zapf. Toddler, 19½" tall. Vinyl head, sleeping brown eyes, short black rooted hair. All original in brown print rompers with blue piping trim. Marks: MAX Zapf 1986/ALL RIGHTS/RESERVED/17 Z (in circle), on head. Courtesy of Marge Betts.

Plate 1295: Character toddler doll, 19" tall. 1970's. Vinyl head, rooted black hair, brown sleeping eyes with lashes, smiling mouth, vinyl arms, hard plastic jointed body and legs. Redressed. Marks: AEG 18, on head. (Backward) EA on body.

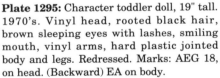

Plate 1296: "Junior Miss." 2" tall. 1970's. Child's necklace with doll used as pendant. Oversized soft vinyl head; black rooted hair; painted features; one-piece vinyl body. All original. Marks: Hong Kong. Included is blue butterfly ring.

Plate 1297: All original 11" baby doll. 1970's. All soft jointed vinyl; painted features; rooted black hair. Marks: HONG KONG, on head; 8/8121/11 74/(very faint logo, unable to identify)/Hong Kong, on back.

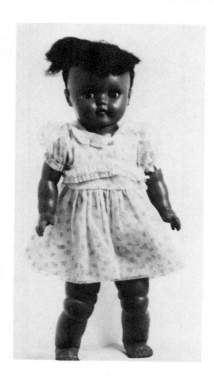

Plate 1299: 12½" doll from the 1960's. Vinyl head, rooted black hair, sleeping light brown eyes; hard plastic body. Marks: K27, on head.

Plate 1298: 18" doll from the 1960's. Vinyl stuffed head; sleeping brown eyes, rooted black hair. Body is soft stuffed vinyl, one piece. Doll is very heavy for its size. Marks: 24, on head.

Plate 1300: 11" doll from the early 1970's. Vinyl head; dark brown sleeping eyes; rooted black hair; jointed vinyl body. All original. Very inexpensive doll. Marks: MADE IN/HONG KONG, on back.

Plate 1301: 14" toddler doll. 1960's. Vinyl head, black sleeping eyes with lashes, rooted black hair; hard vinyl jointed body. All original. Marks: Made in Hong Kong, on back.

Plate 1303: "Playful Twins," 7" tall. 1975. Soft vinyl heads, painted features, rooted black hair, jointed vinyl bodies. Faces are not identical, boy has wider smile, smaller eyes. Manufacturer not marked on box or dolls. Only marks: Made in/Hong Kong, on body.

Plate 1302: Girl, 8" tall. Vinyl head, painted eyes, rooted hair in afro style; plastic body and limbs, fingers are curled under except forefinger on right hand. Shoes and socks painted on over toes. Original dress. Marks: Turtle in diamond, on head; same on shoulders over 16/18. Hair is molded under wig. Courtesy of Phyllis Houston.

Plate 1304: "Bride Doll," 29" tall. Vinyl head, brown sleep eyes, rooted black hair. One-piece body and limbs, fully stuffed; fingers are separated; high heel feet. Overskirt and veil new, top of dress is original. Marks: 64, on head. 1950's. Courtesy of Phyllis Houston.

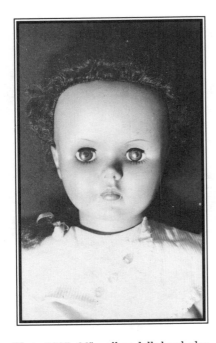

Plate 1305: 36" walker doll; hard plastic body and limbs, vinyl head, black rooted hair, brown sleep eyes. Doll's hands resemble those of "Patti Playpal" by Ideal, about 1959–60. Doll is unmarked. Courtesy of Phyllis Houston.

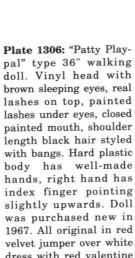

Plate 1306: "Patty Playpal" type 36" walking doll. Vinyl head with brown sleeping eyes, real lashes on top, painted lashes under eyes, closed painted mouth, shoulder length black hair styled with bangs. Hard plastic body has well-made hands, right hand has index finger pointing slightly upwards. Doll was purchased new in 1967. All original in red velvet jumper over white dress with red valentine print. Tights replace original white socks. Doll's head appears identical to that made by Rose Mary Dolls. Marks: U 6, on head. Courtesy of Linda Reynolds Young.

Plate 1307: Another Patty Playpal type doll, 36" tall. Doll was purchased in 1960 or 1961. All original in white cotton print dress, white slip and matching pantaloons, pink socks and black shoes. Marks: u/19 on head. Courtesy of Joycelyn W. Parker.

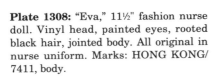

Plate 1308: "Eva," 11½" fashion nurse doll. Vinyl head, painted eyes, rooted black hair, jointed body. All original in nurse uniform. Marks: HONG KONG/7411, body.

Plate 1309: "World Championship Boxer," 9", issued while Cassius Clay (now Muhammad Ali) was World Heavyweight Champion. All plastic with painted eyes, molded hair. Controls in back makes arms throw punches. Marks: SMC9 (in circle)/Made in/Hong Kong. Early 1970's.

Plate 1310: Patty Playpal type 36" walking doll. Vinyl head, rooted black hair, sleeping brown eyes, closed painted mouth, hard plastic jointed body. Redressed. Purchased new in 1963. Doll is unmarked. Courtesy of Karen Ewing.

Plate 1311: Walking doll, 17½" tall. 1950's. Vinyl head, rooted black hair; sleeping brown eyes, closed painted mouth, hard plastic jointed body. When doll walks, her head moves from left to right. All original in two-piece lavender print swimsuit and green grass hula skirt. Marks: P24, on head.

Plate 1312: Lady fashion doll, 21" tall. 1950's. Vinyl head, sleeping brown eyes with top lashes missing, rooted black hair, stuffed vinyl one-piece body with high heeled feet. Clothing could be original as it is commercially made and appropriated with the period. Doll is unmarked.

Plate 1313: High-heeled fashion doll from the 1950's. 24" tall. Vinyl head, short rooted black hair, brown sleeping eyes, closed mouth, jointed hard vinyl body. Redressed. Marks: 148, on head.

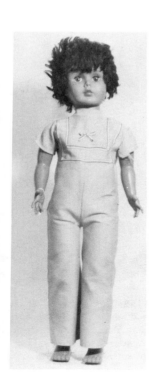

Left – Plate 1314: Walking doll 36" tall. 1970's. Vinyl head, sleeping brown eyes, rooted black hair, closed mouth, jointed vinyl body. All original in one-piece aqua jumpsuit. Marks: AE3651/34, on head. Allied Eastern is known to have manufactured dolls with this mark.

Right – Plate 1315: Walking doll from 1965–75, 36" tall. Vinyl head with sleeping brown eyes with lashes, short rooted black hair; hard plastic body and legs. Redressed. Marks: AEG, on head.

Plate 1316: Hard plastic 19" doll from the 1950's. Doll is unmarked but looks very much like an Arranbee "Nanette." Long black rooted hair in original set, sleeping brown eyes with lashes, closed mouth, jointed hard plastic body. All original in red and white checked taffeta dress and matching long pantaloons.

Plate 1317: Saucy Walker-type hard plastic walking doll. 22" tall. Hard plastic head and jointed body, open mouth, two upper teeth, red felt tongue, brown sleeping eyes, glued-on mohair-like wig. Doll is unmarked. Clothing could be original, replaced shoes.

Plate 1318: Unmarked Ginny or Muffie-type hard plastic doll. 8" tall. Sleeping brown eyes, glued-on long black wig, closed mouth, jointed hard plastic body with molded-on shoes painted black. Doll has been redressed and is wearing an old hand crocheted dress.

Plate 1319: Souvenir doll from New Orleans, Louisiana, circa 1960, 7½" tall. All original with basket of cotton. Hard plastic head, sleeping brown eyes, glued-on mohair-type wig, jointed hard plastic body. Doll is unmarked.

Plate 1320: Souvenir doll from South Africa circa 1960, 7½" tall. All original. Hard plastic head, sleeping brown eyes, glued-on mohair wig, hard plastic jointed body.

Plate 1321: Souvenir doll from the islands, could date 1930–1950. Ceramic head, painted features, cloth body and limbs, sewn-on clothing.

Plate 1322: Holcombe, L. Zena. "Market Woman," 10½" souvenir doll made in Monrovia, Liberia by L. Zena Holcombe, early 1970's. Courtesy of Dr. and Mrs. William Chavis.

CHAPTER 8
DOLL ARTIST AND
REPRODUCTION DOLLS,

Doll artist dolls are dolls manufactured for, and/or marketed to, adult collectors. They were seldom intended to be playthings for children. They are generally made in the same materials used to make dolls of the past: porcelain, papier-maché, wood, cloth, vinyl, etc. At times, new terminology is used however. Some cloth dolls when made by artists are now called "soft sculpture."

Doll artists dolls are readily available for collectors today. They are sold mail order in Sears and J.C. Penneys Christmas catalogs, on television through home shopping, through advertisements in weekly and monthly magazines, through magazines devoted to doll collecting, at national and local doll shows, and in specialty toy shops around the country.

These dolls can be mass-produced from original artists molds or are sometimes reproduction molds from highly collectible antique dolls. Some artists even specialize and make "one-of-a-kind" dolls. These can be very expensive. At times, costing more than antique porcelain dolls.

Following are photographs and descriptions of dolls marketed to adult collectors.

Plate 1323: ArtChees. "Madam C.J. Walker." First black millionaire. Courtesy of ArtChees.

ArtChees Historical Dolls are soft sculptured dolls varying in size from 20" to 21" tall. The dolls are authentic in weight, height, skintone, and attire. ArtChees, founded in 1989, is primarily a doll company that manufactures African Tribal dolls and African American dolls. The company was founded out of a need to enhance the delivery of presentations on Africa, African-American History, and African Folktales by displaying three dimensional forms. They also wanted to build pride and self-esteem.

The name ArtChees is a "play off" on the maiden name of the founders, Bertha B. Archie-Cook and Betty J. Archie-Smith, two sisters. The company is operated through the collaboration of family efforts. Eight family members are listed as partners in the business. All of the products are manufactured by family members.

Plate 1324: ArtChees. "Mary McLeod Bethune." Founded Daytona School for Girls in 1904 which later merged with Cookman College forming Bethune-Cookman College. Doll is all original.

Plate 1325: ArtChees. "Carter G. Woodson." Historian, founder of Black History Month.

Plate 1326: ArtChees. "Prince Hall." Courtesy of ArtChees.

Plate 1328: ArtChees. "Harriet Tubman." Leader in the underground railroad, she led over 300 slaves to freedom. Courtesy of ArtChees.

Plate 1327: ArtChees. "George Washington Carver." Scientist. Courtesy of ArtChees.

Plate 1329: ArtChees. "Louis Armstrong." Musician. Courtesy of ArtChees.

Plate 1330: ArtChees. "Mary Edmonia Lewis." Artist. Courtesy of ArtChees.

Plate 1331: ArtChees. "Marcus Garvy." Leader of the Back to Africa movement. Courtesy of ArtChees.

Plate 1332: ArtChees. "Matthew Henson." First person to reach the North Pole. Courtesy of ArtChees.

Plate 1333: ArtChees. "Frederick Douglass." Courtesy of ArtChees.

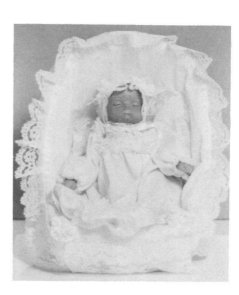

Plate 1334: Art Mark. "Musical Moving Baby." 10". Porcelain head and hands, cloth body and legs, closed eyes, mouth turned down at corners. When doll is wound up, it plays "Love Makes the World Go Round" and moves its head and body in circular sleeping motion. All original in long white gown and bonnet in its own lace trimmed cradle. Tag sewn to body: ART MARK 1989.

"Bertabel's Dolls." Porcelain likeness of famous black Americans, designed and hand-crafted by artist I. Roberta Bell of Chicago, Illinois. Mrs. Bell was the first black person elected to the "National Institute of American Doll Artists." The dolls have head and hands of porcelain, bodies are cloth stuffed with sawdust. The dolls are all dressed in a manner appropriate to the character. All dolls are approximately 18" tall.

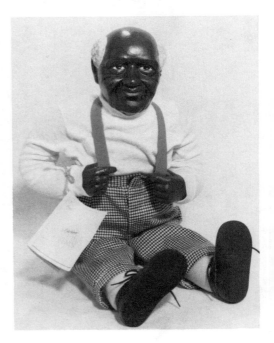

Plate 1337: Billie Pepper. "The Checker Player," 30". Head and arms are made of fibre-craft, body is cloth, painted features and white hair. All original. Billie Peppers' Old Friends is a Trademark of Fibre-Craft Materials Corp. Marks: cBillie Peppers 1987, on head.

Plate 1335: Bell. "Jean Point De (Du) Sable," first citizen of Chicago. Made in the early 1970's. Marks: DeSable/ "Bertabel"/c1971, on back of shoulder plate head.

Plate 1336: Bell. "Sojourner Truth," abolitionist-Suffragette.   Marks: Sojourner Truth/"Bertabel"/c1969, on back of shoulder plate head.

Left – Plate 1338: Bell. "Paul Laurence Dunbar," poet of the people. From "Bertabel's Dolls" catalog. Courtesy of I. Roberta Bell.

Right – Plate 1339: Brinn's. "Fran," 16" collectible doll. Porcelain head, dark brown inset eyes, glued-on black wig, porcelain arms and legs, cloth body. All original in white print dress and red print blouse. Marks: Brinn's 1989, on head. Made in Taiwan.

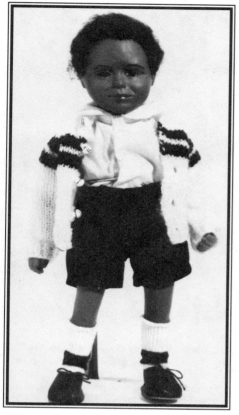

Plate 1340: Bro. "Todd," an original handcrafted portrait doll by doll artist Lois Bro. c1982. 14" tall. Porcelain head, stationary brown glass eyes, closed mouth, black mohair wig; porcelain arms and legs; cloth body. All original in navy short pants, white shirt, handknitted white sweater with blue stripes, and white and blue socks. Doll was sculpted from a photograph of Todd Perkins when he was four years old but was marketed as a girl doll by Lois Bro. When sold as a girl, the doll had a longer wig and was dressed differently. The doll was named Julie. Marks: (Incised heart)L. Bro/JULIE/#2/C1982, on head.

Plate 1341: Barbara Buysse. "Memory." Cloth one-of-a-kind dolls, flat faces, oil painted. Man is 25" tall, lady is 24" tall. The dolls were "gleaned" from black literature, specifically Toni Morrisons' book *Beloved*. In designing the dolls, Buysse wanted to say something and not just create sterotyped black images. "Memory" has tin types in the base, broken pottery, pieces of old letters, such as old african wooden statue, etc. The clothing is interlaced with fragments of the past – some pleasant, some not. Courtesy of Barbara Thiery Buysse.

Left – Plate 1342: Barbara Buysse. "The Conjurer." Another one-of-a-kind cloth doll with oil painted flat face. 25" tall. The inspiration behind this doll came from the book, Lady's Time, the beginning era of jazz in Louisiana. Made in 1990. Courtesy of Barbara Thiery Buysse.

Right – Plate 1343: Barbara Buysse. "Mukkie," character doll in oversized clothing. 10" tall. All cloth, oil painted flat face. Made in 1989. Courtesy of Barbara Thiery Buysse.

Plate 1346: Doll Collectors. "Amanda," 15". Porcelain head, glass eyes, glued-on wig, porcelain arms and legs, cloth body. All original in long pink gown trimmed in lace with matching bonnet. Doll is unmarked.

Plate 1344: Barbara Buysse. Oil painted cloth girl doll. 15" tall. 1989. Buysse's dolls are known as "Johnna Art Dolls." Courtesy of Barbara Thiery Buysse.

Plate 1345: Camelot. "Courtney-Anne," 13". 1980's. Porcelain head, arms and legs, cloth body; inset brown glass eyes, glued-on mohair wig. All original in red pinafore and white blouse. Marks: Camelot, on head.

Plate 1347: Dynasty. "Alexis at the Fair" from the Alexis series. 15". 1990. Porcelain shoulder head, arms and legs, cloth body, brown glass eyes, open smiling mouth, black wig. All original white print dress with white bow trim and natural straw hat. Marks: DYNASTY/DOLL/COLLEC-TION/Design copyright/Cardinal Inc., on head.

Plate 1348: Dynasty. "Holiday Alexis," 1990. Identical to previous Alexis except brown skin coloring is a darker shade and clothes were changed. Dressed in pink satin party dress. Marks are the same as previous doll.

Plate 1349: Dynasty. "Alexis," 16". 1988. Porcelain head and limbs, cloth body, black kanekalon wig, inset brown eyes, open/closed laughing mouth. All original in blue corduroy jumper with white print blouse, white shoes and socks, white bloomers. Marks: DYNASTY/Doll/Collection/Design Copyright/Cardinal, Inc., on shoulder plate back. Made in Taiwan.

Plate 1350: Dynasty. "Felicia," 15" collectible doll designed exclusively for Welcome Home. Porcelain head, inset brown glass eyes, glued-on long black crimped kanekalon wig, porcelain arms and legs, cloth body. All original in pale green silk-like dress trimmed with lace and matching head bow. Marks: WELCOME HOME/CARDINAL INC./1989, on head. Dynasty is a division of Cardinal Inc.

Plate 1351: Dynasty. "Thelma", 1990. 15" from the Anna collection. Porcelain head, arms and legs, stationary glass eyes, black wig. All original in red and white striped cotton dress with white straw hat. Marks: DYNASTY/DOLL/COLLECTION/Design Copyright/Cardinal Inc., on head.

Plate 1352: Dynasty. "Whitney," 14" musical doll from the Anna collection. All original in rose satin dress with lace trim. Doll plays "You've Got a Friend." Marks: DYNASTY/DOLL/COLLECTION/Design Copyright/Cardinal Inc. (stamped on); CARDINAL, INC./1989, incised on head. Whitney is also available as a nonmusical doll dressed in the same outfit.

Plate 1354: Dynasty. "Muhammed," 27", from United Children of Our World collection representing Egypt. Vinyl head, arms, legs and shoulder plate, cloth body. All original in Egyptian styled clothing, a pajama striped coat in shades of brown, and a "gelabil." This doll is number 44 out of a limited edition of 1,200 dolls. Muhammed appears to have been made from the same mold as Tala, facial features are identical. Marks: cJohn Nissen, on head; R/UNITED/CHILDREN/OF OUR/WORLD/No. 344143/44 of 1200/ MADE IN DENMARK/BY DAN HILL PLAST, on back.

Plate 1353: Dynasty. "Annie," 12½" seated. Doll was designed for Dynasty by black doll artist Karen Henderson. Porcelain head and hands, cloth body with movable arms and legs, brown stationary eyes with real eyelashes, closed mouth. All original in pink dress. Marks: DYNASTY/DOLL/COLLECTION/DESIGN COPYRIGHT/CARDINAL INC., (stamped on head); Cardinal Inc. (incised on head).

Plate 1355: Dynasty. "Tala," 27" tall doll in the United Children of Our World series, made in Denmark. Tala represents Nigeria. Vinyl head, arms, legs, and shoulder plate; cloth body; stationary glassine eyes with lashes; glued-on black, curly wig; closed mouth. Doll is wearing typical Nigerian styled dress and matching head wrap in gray, lavender, and green print with beads around neck, wrists, and ankles. Tala was designed by John Nissen, a Danish sculptor in the Dan Doll Studios, founded by Else and Einar Madsen in eastern Denmark. Else worked with Nissen to create the series of dolls which includes the following countries: Mexico, Egypt, China, Pakistan, Greenland, Ecuador, Japan, and Holland. They are all produced in limited editions of 1,200 pieces each worldwide and come with signed and numbered certificates. Marks on Tala: JOHN NISSEN, on head; R/UNITED/CHILDREN/OF OUR/WORLD/No. 342243/223 of 1200/MADE IN DENMARK/BY DAN HILL PLAST, on back.

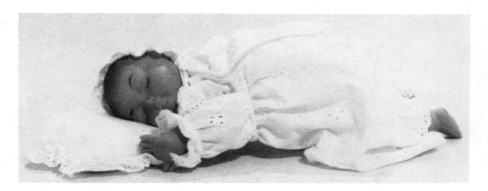

Plate 1356: Dynasty. "Mindy," 10" musical moving doll. When doll is wound up, it plays soft music and moves head, arms, and body in circular motion, imitating a baby waking up. Porcelain head with painted closed eyes, porcelain arms and legs, cloth body. All original in long white eyelet gown and matching cap. Doll comes with a white baby pillow. Marks: 1989, on head. Made in Taiwan, sticker on foot.

Left – Plate 1357: Dynasty Doll Division, Cardinal, Inc. "Rosemarie" from the Sweetheart collection, 15" tall, porcelain head, stationary brown glass eyes, closed mouth, black glued-on wig, porcelain arms and legs, cloth body. All original. All sweetheart dolls come with a red sweetheart pin which she is wearing. Doll is unmarked and is pictured in the 1990 Dynasty Doll Collection catalog.

Right – Plate 1358: Esteban. "Sabine," artist doll representing a Louisiana Creole. 27" tall. Vinyl shoulder head, rooted long curly brown hair, brown stationary glassine eyes, real eyelashes, pierced ears, closed mouth, vinyl arms and legs, brown cloth body. This is doll #64 in a numbered edition from the Ultimate collection by Jennifer Esteban. All original in a lavender dress with white collar and blue waist bow. Marks: Sabine/c1990/ THE ULTIMATE COLLECTION, on head.

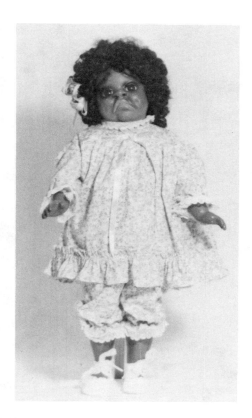

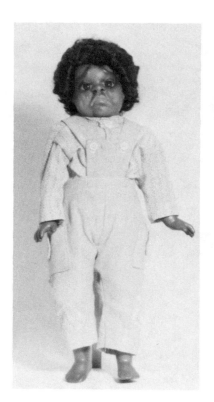

Plate 1359: Formaz. "Ruby", porcelain head girl made by Betty Formaz. 18½" tall. Stationary brown eyes, molded tears, closed mouth, pierced nostrils, black synthetic wig, jointed body. All original. Marks: B. Formaz, on head.

Plate 1360: Formaz. "Leo," porcelain head boy doll. Except for style of wig and all original clothing, identical to previous doll. Betty Formaz brought the Leo Moss dolls to the attention of doll collectors.

Plate 1361: Goebel. "Jalisa," numbered limited edition musical doll, plays "Everything is Beautiful." Designed by Bette Ball for the Betty Jane Carter Doll collection. 18" tall. Porcelain head, arms and legs, brown stationary glass eyes, curly dark brown snythetic wig, closed mouth, cloth body. All original in white cotton lace dress with salmon ribbon trim. Marks: Betty Jane Carter Dolls/Designed By Bette Ball/Limited Edition 196 (of)1000/cGoebel, Inc. 1989.

Left – Plate 1362: Gorham. "Sweet Marini," 10", African from Gorham Around the World collection. Head, arms, and legs are porcelain with painted features. Body is white cloth. Sandals are molded on the feet. Doll is wearing a turban with no hair underneath and a beautiful African dress in shades of mauve, rose, and blue in various prints and stripes with beads around the neck. Unmarked. Courtesy of Xzena Moore from the Cubby Hole.

Right – Plate 1363: Head. "Old Man," 11½" collectors doll made by Maggie Head Kane, member of National Institute of American Doll Artists. Head, arms, and legs are made of ceramic base; cloth body. Shoulder head with flocked gray hair, flocked eyebrows, closed mouth, painted eyes. Doll is unmarked.

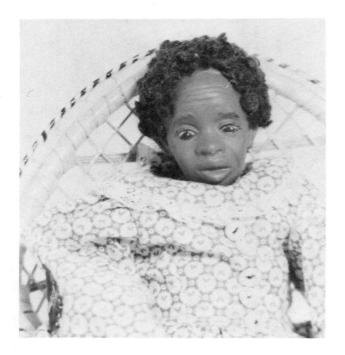

Plate 1365: Himstedt. "Ayoka," 27" from "Reflections of Youth," a collection by Annette Himstedt. No. 4848, modeled and scaled after a real child. Vinyl head, human hair wig and eyelashes, upper and lower; vinyl arms and legs, cloth body. All original in aqua and yellow dress. Marks: Ayoka/Annette Himstedt, on head.

Plate 1364: Maggie Head Kane. "Old Lady," 15½" tall. Porcelain shoulder head, arms and legs, cloth body, painted features, open/closed mouth, glued-on wig, looks like caracul. All original in long print dress. Marks: 1967/MAGGIE/HEAD/KANE/something that looks like T.T A in a circle, incised on shoulder head.

Plate 1366: Himstedt. "Fatou," 26", from The Barefoot Children series by Annette Himstedt, No. 3809. Vinyl head, arms and legs, cloth body; human hair wig and eyelashes, realistic looking stationary eyes, closed mouth. All original in mauve colored linen dress with pinafore made of soft cotton, embellished with double ruffles, pin tucks, and lace. Doll was modeled after an Ethiopian child. Marks: Fatou/Annette Himstedt, on head. 1987. Made in Spain. Himstedt dolls are distributed by Timeless Creations, a division of Mattel, Inc.

Plate 1367: Himstedt. "Mo," 1990, 22", from the series "Mo and the Barefoot Babies" by Annette Himstedt. Vinyl head and limbs, cloth body stuffed with pellets. Mo is a boy from USA, designed in Germany, manufactured in Spain. All original with human hair and mohair wig and eyelashes, white cotton rompers. Marks: Mo/Annette Himstedt, on head. Himstedt signature is also engraved on each limb.

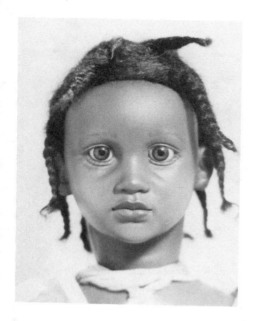

Plate 1369: Jo Hunt. "Louis Armstrong" porcelain doll making kit. Shoulder head, 2½" tall, painted features; porcelain limbs with painted-on shoes and socks. Making a cloth body, this would make up into an 11" or 12" doll. Marks: Satchmo/Jo Hunt/1971, incised on shoulder head back.

Plate 1368: Himstedt. "Fatou" with cornrow hairstyle and bigger eyes than previous Fatou doll. This doll was made in Germany for the European market, circa 1985. The body is identical to previous doll. All original in striped cotton dress in blue, green, pink, and white. Marks: Fatou, on head. Courtesy of Marge Betts.

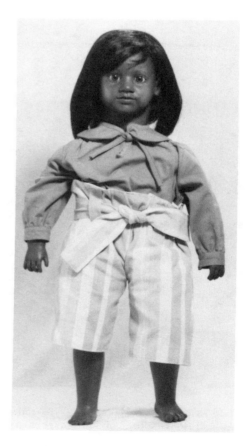

Plate 1370: Lenox. "Amma," The African Drummer Girl from the Lenox Children of the World doll collection. 14½" tall. Porcelain shoulder head, arms and legs, cloth body, stationary brown eyes, closed mouth. All original in bright red print blouse and traditional wrapped style striped skirt, print hat, leather sandals, and beads. Marks: LENOX TM/1991 (stamped on)/cLENOX (incised on).

Plate 1371: Jerri. "Uncle Remus," 19½". Porcelain shoulder head with glass eyes, glued-on white hair and beard, porcelain arms and legs with molded-on shoes, cloth body. All original in tweed coat, black wool pants and blue shirt. Limited edition. Marks: Jerry McCloud/4-1989 (written in pen); 8703 Jerry/copyright 1987, incised on back.

Plate 1372: Himstedt. "Bekus." Dark doll made for the European market, 1985. 26½" tall. Vinyl head, stationary brown eyes with lashes, dark brown wig, vinyl arms, legs and shoulder plate, cloth body. All original in striped pants in earth tones and brown shirt. Doll is barefoot. Marks: Bekus, on head.

Left – Plate 1373: "Little Luvables" collector edition, 14½" tall boy and girl. Porcelain heads, arms and legs, cloth bodies; inset glass eyes, glued-on black curly wigs. All original in gray and pink checked for girl, gray and blue checked for boy. Dolls are unmarked.

Right – Plate 1374: Mann. "Lavonne," 16" collectors bride doll. Porcelain head, inset brown glass eyes, glued-on dark brown wig, porcelain arms and legs, cloth body. All original in white wedding gown. Marks: 363 MANN/Handmade/Porcelain MCMLXXXIX, on head. Limited edition of 3,500 dolls.

Plate 1375: Seymour Mann. "Zena," 16" collectors doll. Porcelain head, stationary brown glass eyes, long dark brown glued-on wig; porcelain arms and legs; cloth body. All original in ivory wedding gown with ivory lace and ribbons. Edition was limited to 3,500 dolls. Marks: #383/MANN/Handmade/Porcelain/MCMXC, inside Mann logo on head.

Plate 1376: Mann. "Liz," 17" Christmas doll, 1989. Porcelain head, stationary brown glassine eyes, dark brown wig, closed mouth, porcelain lower arms and legs, cloth body. All original in white taffeta lace trimmed dress with red and green ribbons and silk-like flowers. Marks: #383/MANN/HANDMADE/PORCELAIN/MCMLXXXIX, on head.

Plate 1377: Mann. "Doreen," 12½" collectors doll. Porcelain head, inset glass eyes looking to the left, black glued-on wig; porcelain hands and legs, cloth body. All original in pink dress trimmed with lots of white lace. Marks: #383/MANN/Handmade/Porcelain/MCMLXXXIX, inside Mann Logo on head.

Plate 1378: Mann. "Michelle," 15½". Porcelain head, legs and arms, stationary glass eyes, glued-on black synthetic wig, closed mouth, cloth body. All original in cotton print dress under cotton ecru pinafore. Limited edition of 2,500. Marks: #383/MANN/HANDMADE/PORCELAIN/MCMLXXXIX, on head. Dress tagged MCMXC.

Plate 1379: Mann. "Lionel," 14". Porcelain head, stationary brown glass eyes, glued-on black wig, porcelain arms and legs, cloth body. All original in blue and white striped pants, bow tie and cap with white shirt. Doll is unmarked. Clothing marked: MANN 1987.

Plate 1380: Mann. "Tabitha," 15". Porcelain head, stationary brown glass eyes looking to her left, black synthetic wig, porcelian lower arms and legs, cloth body. All original in blue and white striped dress with blue pantaloons. The face on this doll is similar to that on "Doreen," only larger. Marks: #383/MANN/HAND-MADE/PORCELAIN/MCMLXXXIX, on head.

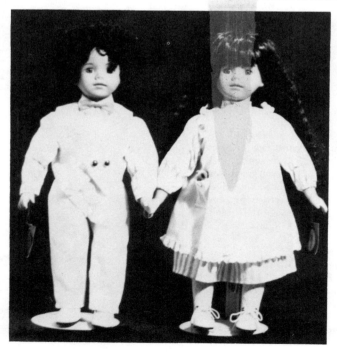

Plate 1381: Mann. "Michael and Melba," 16" collectible dolls, sold separately. Porcelain heads, inset brown eyes, glued-on wigs, porcelain arms and legs, cloth bodies. Both of the dolls are all original. Boy has white pants and vest with white and pink striped shirt, girl has matching white and pink striped dress with white pinafore. Marks: #383/MANN HANDMADE/PORCELAIN/MCMLXXXIII, on both dolls.

Plate 1382: Mann. "Lonnie," 14". Late 1980's. Porcelain head, arms and legs, cloth body. Inset dark brown eyes, glued-on synthetic black wig. All original in pink and white striped dress under white pinafore. Doll is unmarked.

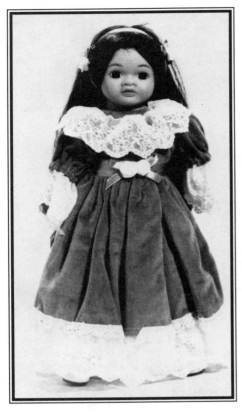

Plate 1383: Mann. "Patty," 14". Porcelain head, stationary brown eyes, long brown crimped styled wig, closed mouth, cloth body. All original in long mauve velvet gown with white lace trim. Marks: #383/MANN/HANDMADE/PORCE-LAIN/MCMLXXXIII, inside maple leaf on head.

Plate 1384: Mann. "Larry," 14". Porcelain head, arms and legs, cloth body; glued-on black wig, inset dark brown glass eyes. All original in blue velvet pants and matching cap with white shirt and bow tie. Marks: 383/MANN/Hand made/Porcelain/MCMLXXXIII, on head.

Plate 1385: Mann. "Edwina," 14". Porcelain head, arms and legs, cloth body with glued-on black curly wig, inset glass eyes. All original in pastel print dress trimmed with lace. Doll is unmarked, clothing marked Mann, 1987.

Left – Plate 1386: Mann. "Carolyn," 14". Collectors doll with the same face as many of the Mann black dolls. Porcelain head, arms and legs, cloth body, inset glass eyes, glued-on wig. All original in ankle-length mauve velvet dress, hooded cape, and matching muff. Marks: #383/MANN/Hand-made/Porcelain/MCMLXXXIII, on head.

Right – Plate 1387: Mann. "Tanya," musical, plays "Hello Dolly." 14". Porcelain head, stationary dark brown eyes, black synthetic wig, porcelain arms and legs, cloth body. All original in mauve velvet dress trimmed in lace. Marks: #383/MANN/HANDMADE/PORCELAIN/MCMLIII, on head.

Plate 1388: Mann. "Tanya." This doll is identical to previous Tanya doll except this one is not musical, is not marked and mauve velvet dress is slightly different.

Plate 1389: Mann. "Chandra," 16". 1990. Porcelain head, arms and legs, cloth body; inset brown glass eyes, glued-on long black synthetic wig, open mouth. All original in mauve dress with net overskirt and ecru trim, ecru pantaloons. Marks: CONNOISSEUR DOLL/COLLECTION/Seymour MANN/(the remainder is covered by cloth body). Limited edition of 2,500 dolls.

Plate 1390: Mann. "Toni," 16". Porcelain head, arms and legs, cloth body, brown stationary eyes, glued-on black wig, open mouth. All original in white organdy lace trimmed dress with matching pantaloons and hat, white stockings and shoes. Numbered limited edition of 2,500 dolls. Marks: SEYMOUR MANN/MCMXC, incised on head; CONNOISSEUR COLLECTION/Seymour/MANN/cSeymour Mann Inc 1990/1,068 (out of) 2,500, stamped on head.

Plate 1391: Mann. "Francine," 16". Porcelain head, arms and legs, cloth body; glued-on long black crimped wig, inset glassine brown eyes. All original in pink dress trimmed in white lace. Marks: inside Mann logo, 383/MANN/Handmade/Porcelain/MCMLXXXVII, on head.

Plate 1392: Mann. "Lisa," 16". Porcelain head, arms and bent legs, cloth body; stationary glass eyes, painted hair. All original in long white eyelet christening gown and cap trimmed in lace. Marks: #383/MANN/HANDMADE/PORCELAIN/MCMLXXXVII, on head.

Plate 1393: Mann. "Rachelle," 11" with porcelain head, arms and legs, cloth body; inset glass eyes, glued-on black curly wig. All original in blue dotted dress with white smock. Marks: 1982/Mann, on head. Original box is marked "Duck House."

Plate 1394: Marian Yu. "Natasha and William," 10" brother and sister dolls. Porcelain heads, arms and legs, cloth bodies. Inset dark brown eyes, glued-on black wigs. Dolls are number 1,547 in a limited edition of 5,000. All original in school clothes with books strapped on belts attached to wrists. Marks: Marian Yu (in cursive writing)/MYD Inc./Marian Yu Design/1547 (slash)5000 (written by hand).

Plate 1396: Maryse Nicole. "Alexa" number 52 from a limited edition of 500 dolls; 19" tall. Fully jointed all-porcelain doll, inset dark brown glass eyes, open mouth, glued-on black synthetic wig, handset human hair eyelashes. All original in beige print dress with burgundy trim and matching pantaloons. Marks: 52 of 500 with signature of Maryse Nicole/1990.

Plate 1395: Marian Yu. "Black Americana." c1988. 11½" tall. Porcelain shoulder head, closed mouth, stationary brown glass eyes, curly black synthetic wig, porcelain arms and legs, cloth body. All original in striped pinafore over mauve print dress. This is doll number 179 from a limited edition of 2,000 dolls. Marks: 179 (slash) 2,000/Marian Yu/MYD Inc. MARIAN YU DESIGNS, on head.

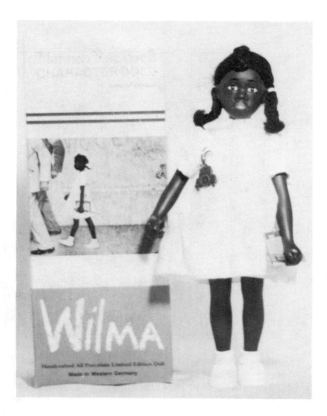

Plate 1397: Mary Moline. "Wilma," Norman Rockwell character doll. 10½". Doll is sculptured by Moline after the famous painting that appeared in the 1964 issue of *Look Magazine* of the first black girl integrating a white school. Doll is all porcelain, fully jointed with painted features, black synthetic wig. All original in white cotton dress, white socks and white tennis shoes like the girl in the painting. c1981 Rumbleseat Press, Inc. Metal Rumbleseat logo charm hangs from belt on dress. The doll is hand painted and numbered on the neck. This doll is 1,470.

Plate 1398: "Tyne Baby," 14" reproduction of an antique doll. Porcelain heads and hands, inset dark brown eyes, painted features, cloth frog body. Marks: 1924 by E.L. Horsman Co. Inc./Mildred Seeley/4/Myla Jan. 1991, doll on left; doll on right is the same except for last line, Clara Jan. 1991. Dolls were made in a porcelain doll making class by author and her sister, Clara Clark. Courtesy of Clara Clark.

Left – Plate 1399: "Grandma." Character doll 16" tall. Porcelain head, arms and legs, stationary brown glass eyes, gray mohair wig, closed mouth, cloth body. Made by Connie Nash in 1990. Marks: ORIGINAL/cL. GARRARD/1979, on head. Courtesy of Clara Phillips Hill.

Right – Plate 1400: "Grandpa," mate to previous doll. 16" tall. Marks are the same. Courtesy of Clara Phillips Hill.

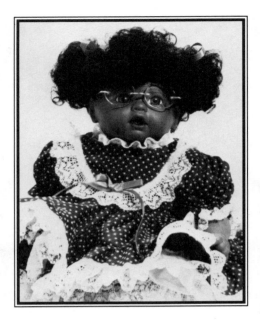

Plate 1401: Reproduction K*R 117. 14" tall. Porcelain socket head, jointed porcelain body, stationary brown glass eyes, closed mouth, dark brown synthetic wig. Made and dressed by Michele Rene Hill-Grier. Marks: K * R/SIMONE & HALBIG/ 117/58, incised in mold; Michelle/1990/ Nash, incised when reproduced. Courtesy of Michele Rene Hill-Grier.

Plate 1402: Price Products. "Naomi," African International doll from the Hello Dolly Signature series. 16½" tall. Porcelain head, arms and legs; stationary brown glass eyes, closed mouth. All original in African styled printed clothing. Numbered limited edition of 2,500 dolls. This is doll #261. Marks: Hello Dolly/ (pink rose logo)/COLLECTIBLE DOLLS/ C1990 A.E.P. Inc./0261/ 2500.

Plate 1403: Mildred Nettles. "Michael," a Millie Billie doll, 14" long. Porcelain head, arms and legs, cloth body; inset glass eyes, glued-on black wig, open/closed mouth. All original in blue dotted swiss dress with lots of lace and wearing "real" eyeglasses. Marks: Milli Nettles #26.

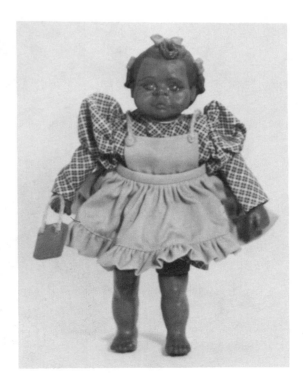

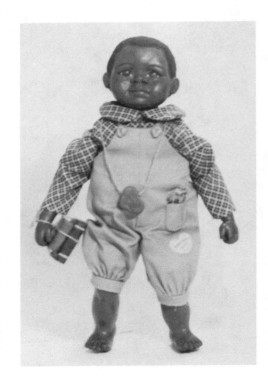

Left – Plate 1404: Sarah's Attic. "Sassafras," School Days, #1680. Limited edition of 2,000 dolls. 12" tall. Wood resin heads, arms and legs, cloth bodies; painted features; molded hair with molded-in ribbons. All original in beige pinafore over long-sleeved blue checkered dress. Doll carries slate in one hand and wears heart-shaped necklace incised "Sarah's Attic." Marks: SAS-SAFRAS/SA c1990.

Right – Plate 1405: Sarah's Attic. "Hickory," School Days, #1766. Limited edition of 2,000 dolls. 12" tall. Wood resin head, arms and legs, cloth body; painted features; molded hair. All original in beige knickers and checkered shirt, matches previous doll Sassafras. Doll carries two schoolbooks tied with string and wears heart necklace incised "Sarah's Attic." Marks: HICKORY/SA c/1990.

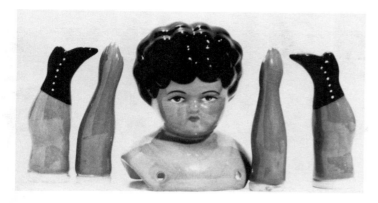

Plate 1406: Standard. "Prissy." Kit to make a china doll nurse of Scarlett's and Melanie's children from Gone With the Wind. Completed doll would be 18" tall. Kit comes with a pattern for body and clothing. Kit was available from Standard Doll Co. from the mid-1970's until the present.

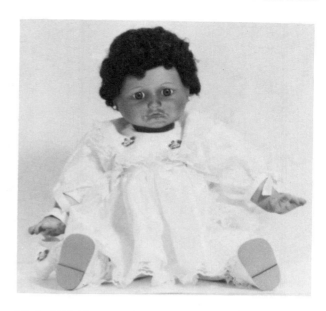

Plate 1407: Treasures in Lace. 15" baby doll with porcelain head, arms, and legs; stationary brown glass eyes; dark brown synthetic wig; closed mouth; cloth body. All original in white dress trimmed with lace and pearls. Marks: D1004, on head. 1991.

Plate 1408: Reproduction Kewpie doll, 7" tall. Porcelain head with brown googlie eyes, painted lashes; jointed porcelain arms and legs. All original in yellow dress trimmed in yellow lace. Courtesy of Karen Ewing.

Plate 1409: Treasures in Lace. 16" tall. Porcelain head, stationary brown glass eyes, black synthetic wig, porcelain arms and legs, cloth body, closed mouth. All original in dark brown and green striped dress with white muslin trim and matching purse and cap. Marks: 2316-2, on head. 1991.

Plate 1410: Victoria Ashlea. 16", numbered limited edition musical doll. Porcelain head with hand-painted features, porcelain hands and feet, cloth body, inset glass eyes. Doll is all original in handmade designer victorian fashioned white print dress with under slip and pantaloons. Doll plays "True Love." Marks: VICTORIA ASHLEA/ORIGINALS/LIMITED EDITION/16/2,000 (hand lettered 16). Doll is No. 16 out of a production of 2,000.

Plate 1411: Victoria Ashlea. "Rita," 12" musical doll plays "Whistle a Happy Tune." Porcelain head, hands, and legs with cloth body; stationary brown glass eyes, black wig. All original in pink cotton dress. Doll #516 in a limited edition of 5,000 dolls. Marks: Victoria Ashlea/Originals/Limited Edition/516-5000, on head.

Plate 1412: Victoria Ashlea. "Patty and Patrick." 5" tall. Porcelain bald shoulder heads, painted eyes, closed mouth, porcelain arms and legs, cloth bodies. Patty is all original in pink outfit with matching pillow. Identical doll Patrick is all original in blue. Marks: Victoria Ashlea Originals/DESIGNED BY Betty Ball/House of Global Art 1986..., tag sewn to body.

Plate 1413: Victoria Impex Corporation. "Jackie," 15" original collectible doll with porcelain head, arms and legs and cloth body. Designed by Cindy. M. McClure, Jackie is doll #51 in a limited edition of 1,000 dolls. Jackie is musical playing "Everything is Beautiful," and was made exclusively for the San Francisco Music Box Co. Doll has inset dark brown eyes and glued-on black curly wig. Marks: Cindy M. McClure/Victoria Impex Corp./1986/51-1000. Doll came carrying a cloth goose.

Plate 1414: Wimbleton. "Samuel," #4014 and "Sabrina," #4015, collectible dolls with porcelain heads, arms and legs, inset eyes, glued-on wigs. All original in blue print for boy and pink print for girl. Dolls are unmarked.

Plate 1415: Marsha Taylor. "Haka." 23" tall. Head and arms are made of "Miracle Clay," black glass eyes with lashes, open/closed mouth, pierced nostrils, cloth body and legs. Marks: Marsha/'91, signed on chest.

GENERAL INDEX

Price Guide

Page 6
Plate #1 ....$700.00

Page 7
Plate #2 ....$700.00
Plate #3 ....$300.00
Plate #4 ....$300.00
Plate #5 ....$400.00

Page 8
Plate #6 ....$300.00
Plate #7.....................................NPA
Plate #8.....................................NPA
Plate #9 ....$200.00
Plate #10 ....$200.00
Plate #11 ....$250.00

Page 9
Plate #12 ....$1,800.00

Page 10
Plate #13 ....$400.00
Plate #14 ....$400.00
Plate #15 ....$400.00
Plate #16.................$35.00 - 150.00

Page 11
Plate #17 ....$1,800.00
Plate #18...................$100.00-275.00
Plate #19...........................ea $100.00

Page 13
Plate #20.....................................NPA

Page 14
Plate #21.....................................NPA
Plate #22.....................................NPA
Plate #23.....................................NPA
Plate #24.....................................NPA

Page 15
Plate #25.....................................NPA
Plate #26.....................................NPA
Plate #27.....................................NPA

Page 16
Plate #28.....................................NPA
Plate #29.....................................NPA
Plate #30.....................................NPA

Page 17
Plate #31.....................................NPA
Plate #32.....................................NPA

Page 18
Plate #33.....................................NPA
Plate #34.....................................NPA
Plate #35.....................................NPA
Plate #36.....................................NPA

Page 26
Plate #39 ....$20.00
Plate #40 ....$20.00

Page 27
Plate #41 ....$900.00
Plate #42 ....$650.00

Page 28
Plate #43 ....$1,200.00
Plate #44 ....$650.00

Page 28
Plate #45 ....$1,200.00
Plate #46 ....$1,200.00
Plate #47 ....$1,200.00

Page 29
Plate #48 ....$1,200.00
Plate #49 ....$1,200.00
Plate #50 ....$1,200.00
Plate #51 ....$1,000.00

Page 30
Plate #52 ....$700.00
Plate #53 ....$550.00
Plate #54 ....$1,100.00
Plate #55............................ea $800.00

Page 31
Plate #56 ....$1,200.00
Plate #57 ....$1,300.00
Plate #58.....................................NPA
Plate #59.....................................NPA
Plate #60 ....$500.00

Page 32
Plate #61.....................................NPA
Plate #62 ....$4,500.00
Plate #63 ....$3,500.00
Plate #64 ....$3,500.00

Page 33
Plate #65.....................................NPA
Plate #66 ....$3,000.00
Plate #67 ....$3,500.00
Plate #68 ....$1,500.00

Page 34
Plate #69 ....$1,600.00
Plate #70 ....$800.00
Plate #71 ....$1,000.00
Plate #72 ....$1,500.00

Page 35
Plate #73 ....$3,000.00
Plate #74 ....$1,600.00
Plate #75 ....$400.00
Plate #76 ....$800.00

Page 36
Plate #77 ....$800.00
Plate #78 ....$800.00
Plate #79 ....$700.00
Plate #80 ....$800.00

Page 37
Plate #81 ....$600.00
Plate #82 ....$800.00
Plate #83 ....$600.00
Plate #84 ....$800.00
Plate #85 ....$500.00

Page 38
Plate #86............................ea $600.00

Page 39 (top)
Plate #87 ....$5,000.00
Plate #88 ....$5,500.00
Plate #89 ....$2,000.00

Page 39
Plate #90 ....$2,000.00
Plate #91 ....$1,000.00
Plate #92 ....$1,800.00
Plate #93 ....$5,000.00

Page 40
Plate #94........................ea $1,200.00
Plate #95 ....$1,000.00
Plate #96........................ea $1,300.00
Plate #97.......................set $500.00
Plate #98 ....$600.00

Page 41
Plate #99 ....$5,000.00
Plate #100.....................set $4,000.00
Plate #101 ....$800.00

Page 42
Plate #102 ....doll only $1,100.00
Plate #103 ....$1,000.00
Plate #104 ....$350.00
Plate #105 ....$1,000.00

Page 43
Plate #106 ....$700.00
Plate #107 ....$2,000.00
Plate #108 ....$2,000.00
Plate #109 ....$2,500.00

Page 44
Plate #110 ....$1,200.00
Plate #111 ....$2,500.00
Plate #112 ....$2,500.00
Plate #113 ....$3,000.00
Plate #114 ....$3,000.00

Page 45
Plate #115 ....$2,500.00
Plate #116 ....$2,000.00
Plate #117 ....$2,000.00
Plate #118 ....$600.00
Plate #119 ....$2,000.00

Page 46
Plate #120 ....$2,000.00
Plate #121 ....$7,000.00
Plate #122 ....$7,500.00
Plate #123.....................................NPA

Page 47
Plate #124 ....$4,500.00
Plate #125 ....$3,000.00
Plate #126 ....$3,000.00
Plate #127 ....$1,500.00

Page 48
Plate #128 ....$1,500.00
Plate #129 ....$2,000.00
Plate #130.....................................NPA
Plate #131 ....$1,500.00
Plate #132 ....$1,800.00

Page 49

Plate #133.................................NPA
Plate #134 ....$350.00
Plate #135 ....$300.00
Plate #136 ....$300.00
Plate #137 ....$1,000.00

Page 50

Plate #138 ....$500.00
Plate #139 ....$250.00
Plate #140 ....$300.00
Plate #141 ....$400.00

Page 51

Plate #142.................................NPA
Plate #143 ....$900.00
Plate #144 ....$400.00
Plate #145 ....$800.00

Page 52

Plate #146 ....$600.00
Plate #147 ....$450.00
Plate #148 ....doll standing $1,500.00
Plate #149 ....$475.00
Plate #150 ....$700.00

Page 53

Plate #151.......................ea $550.00
Plate #152 ....$900.00
Plate #153 ....$550.00
Plate #154 ....$850.00

Page 54

Plate #155 ....$500.00
Plate #156 ....$150.00
Plate #157 ....$50.00
Plate #158 ....$50.00
Plate #159 ....$50.00

Page 55

Plate #160 ....$175.00
Plate #161 ....$175.00
Plate #162 ....$100.00
Plate #163 ....$80.00
Plate #164.................................NPA
Plate #165 ....$100.00

Page 56

Plate #166.....................pair $1,000.00
Plate #167 ....$350.00
Plate #168.................................NPA
Plate #169 ....$70.00

Page 57

Plate #170 ....$65.00

Page 59

Plate #171 ....$450.00
Plate #172 ....$375.00
Plate #173 ....$65.00
Plate #174 ....$55.00

Page 60

Plate #175 ....$175.00
Plate #176 ....$200.00
Plate #177 ....$200.00

Plate #178 ....$225.00

Page 61

Plate #179 ....$200.00
Plate #180 ....$175.00
Plate #181 ....$175.00
Plate #182 ....$150.00
Plate #183 ....$150.00

Page 62

Plate #184.........................set $225.00
Plate #185 ....$90.00
Plate #186 ....$200.00
Plate #187.........................set $185.00
Plate #188 ....$175.00

Page 63

Plate #189 ....$100.00
Plate #190 ....$175.00
Plate #191 ....$165.00
Plate #192 ....$150.00

Page 64

Plate #193 ....$45.00
Plate #194 ....$45.00
Plate #195 ....$1,000.00
Plate #196 ....$165.00
Plate #197 ....$175.00

Page 65

Plate #198.........................ea $45.00

Page 66

Plate #199 ....$65.00
Plate #200 ....$45.00
Plate #201.......................pair $145.00
Plate #202 ....$450.00

Page 67

Plate #203 ....$300.00
Plate #204 ....$20.00

Page 68

Plate #205 ....$400.00
Plate #206 ....$175.00
Plate #207 ....$120.00
Plate #208 ....$350.00
Plate #209 ....$350.00

Page 69

Plate #210 ....$400.00

Page 70

Plate #212 ....$40.00
Plate #213 ....$100.00
Plate #214 ....$50.00
Plate #215 ....$30.00
Plate #216 ....$30.00

Page 71

Plate #217 ....$40.00
Plate #218 ....$40.00
Plate #219 ....$15.00
Plate #220 ....$45.00
Plate #221 ....$25.00

Page 72

Plate #222 ....$15.00
Plate #223 ....$20.00
Plate #224 ....$15.00
Plate #225 ....$25.00
Plate #226 ....$125.00
Plate #227 ....$30.00

Page 73

Plate #228 ....$30.00
Plate #229 ....$15.00
Plate #230 ....$15.00
Plate #231 ....$30.00
Plate #232 ....$40.00

Page 74

Plate #233.........................ea $30.00
Plate #234 ....$25.00
Plate #235 ....$35.00
Plate #236 ....$35.00

Page 75

Plate #237.........................ea $20.00
Plate #238 ....$30.00

Page 77

Plate #239 ....$350.00

Page 79

Plate #240 ....$85.00

Page 81

Plate #241.................................NPA

Page 82

Plate #242.................................NPA

Page 83

Plate #243.................................NPA

Page 84

Plate #244.................................NPA

Page 85

Plate #245.................................NPA

Page 86

Plate #246.................................NPA

Page 87

Plate #247.................................NPA

Page 88

Plate #248.................................NPA

Page 89

Plate #249.................................NPA

Page 90

Plate #250 ....$550.00
Plate #251.......................ea $200.00
Plate #252 ....$2,000.00

Page 91

Plate #253 ....$800.00
Plate #254 ....$550.00
Plate #255 ....$500.00
Plate #256 ....$600.00

Page 92
Plate #257 ....$200.00
Plate #258 ....$850.00
Plate #259 ....$175.00
Plate #260 ....$350.00

Page 93
Plate #261 ....$250.00
Plate #262........................set $250.00
Plate #263 ....$125.00
Plate #264 ....$250.00

Page 94
Plate #265 ....$200.00
Plate #266 ....$125.00
Plate #267 ....$75.00
Plate #268 ....$200.00
Plate #269 ....$65.00

Page 95
Plate #270 ....$75.00
Plate #271...................as is $125.00
Plate #272 ....$1,000.00
Plate #273 ....as is $100.00
Plate #274 ....$175.00

Page 96
Plate #275 ....$125.00
Plate #276 ....$200.00
Plate #277 ....$175.00
Plate #278 ....$500.00
Plate #279 ....$75.00

Page 97
Plate #280 ....$175.00
Plate #281 ....$90.00
Plate #282......................as is $125.00
Plate #283 ....$75.00
Plate #284 ....$125.00

Page 98
Plate #285 ....$125.00
Plate #286 ....$125.00
Plate #287 ....$100.00
Plate #288 ....$75.00
Plate #289 ....$75.00
Plate #290 ....$175.00
Plate #291 ....$500.00

Page 99
Plate #292 ....$125.00
Plate #293 ....$125.00
Plate #294......................as is $75.00
Plate #295.....................................NPA
Plate #296.....................................NPA
Plate #297 ....$275.00

Page 100
Plate #298 ....$225.00
Plate #299 ....$175.00
Plate #300.....................................NPA
Plate #301 ....$150.00
Plate #302 ....$75.00
Plate #303 ....$100.00

Page 101
Plate #304 ....$350.00
Plate #305.....................................NPA
Plate #306 ....$35.00
Plate #307 ....$1,000.00
Plate #308 ....$300.00
Plate #309 ....$200.00

Page 103
Plate #310 ....$65.00

Page 104
Plate #311 ....$50.00
Plate #312 ....$600.00
Plate #313 ....$750.00
Plate #314 ....$300.00
Plate #315 ....$475.00

Page 105
Plate #316 ....$110.00
Plate #317 ....$125.00
Plate #318 ....$475.00
Plate #319 ....$475.00
Plate #320 ....$475.00
Plate #321 ....$475.00

Page 106
Plate #322 ....$475.00
Plate #323 ....$550.00
Plate #324 ....$550.00
Plate #325 ....$450.00
Plate #326 ....$50.00
Plate #327 ....$450.00

Page 107
Plate #328 ....$80.00
Plate #329 ....$75.00
Plate #330 ....$75.00
Plate #331 ....$55.00
Plate #332 ....$75.00
Plate #333 ....$55.00

Page 108
Plate #334 ....$55.00
Plate #335 ....$55.00
Plate #336 ....$55.00
Plate #337 ....$40.00
Plate #338 ....$100.00
Plate #339 ....$75.00

Page 109
Plate #340 ....$65.00
Plate #341 ....$25.00
Plate #342 ....$25.00
Plate #343 ....$25.00
Plate #344 ....$200.00

Page 110
Plate #345 ....$50.00
Plate #346 ....$35.00
Plate #347 ....$25.00
Plate #348 ....$25.00
Plate #349 ....$40.00
Plate #350 ....$175.00

Page 111
Plate #351 ....$10.00
Plate #352 ....$100.00
Plate #353 ....$175.00
Plate #354 ....$15.00
Plate #355 ....$20.00

Page 112
Plate #356 ....$15.00
Plate #357 ....$20.00
Plate #358 ....$15.00
Plate #359 ....$50.00
Plate #360 ....$50.00
Plate #361 ....$50.00

Page 113
Plate #362 ....$50.00
Plate #363 ....$40.00
Plate #364 ....$40.00
Plate #365 ....$150.00
Plate #366 ....$40.00

Page 114
Plate #367 ....$55.00
Plate #368 ....$125.00
Plate #369 ....$95.00
Plate #370 ....$60.00
Plate #371 ....$75.00
Plate #372 ....$125.00

Page 115
Plate #373 ....$125.00
Plate #374 ....$35.00
Plate #375 ....$35.00
Plate #376 ....$45.00
Plate #377 ....$45.00
Plate #378 ....$65.00

Page 116
Plate #379 ....$25.00
Plate #380 ....$15.00
Plate #381 ....$15.00
Plate #382 ....$15.00
Plate #383 ....$15.00

Page 117
Plate #384 ....$10.00
Plate #385 ....$50.00
Plate #386 ....$35.00
Plate #387 ....$60.00
Plate #388 ....$125.00

Page 118
Plate #389 ....$225.00
Plate #390 ....$225.00
Plate #391 ....$225.00
Plate #392 ....$125.00
Plate #393 ....$125.00

Page 119
Plate #394 ....$95.00
Plate #395 ....$25.00
Plate #396 ....$25.00
Plate #397 ....$25.00

Page 120

Plate #398 ....$25.00
Plate #399...........................ea $20.00
Plate #400...........................ea $20.00
Plate #401...........................ea $20.00

Page 121

Plate #402 ....$35.00
Plate #403 ....$250.00
Plate #404 ....$300.00
Plate #405.........................set $35.00
Plate #406 ....$100.00

Page 122

Plate #407 ....$100.00
Plate #408 ....$100.00
Plate #409 ....$30.00
Plate #410 ....$30.00
Plate #411 ....$35.00

Page 123

Plate #412 ....$75.00
Plate #413 ....$65.00
Plate #414 ....$65.00
Plate #415 ....$35.00
Plate #416 ....$30.00
Plate #417 ....$30.00

Page 124

Plate #418 ....$40.00
Plate #419 ....$35.00
Plate #420 ....$40.00
Plate #421 ....$25.00
Plate #422 ....$35.00
Plate #423 ....$85.00

Page 125

Plate #424 ....$75.00
Plate #425 ....$50.00
Plate #426 ....$95.00
Plate #427 ....$75.00
Plate #428 ....$85.00

Page 126

Plate #429 ....$150.00
Plate #430 ....$95.00
Plate #431 ....$95.00
Plate #432 ....$95.00

Page 127

Plate #433 ....$95.00
Plate #434 ....$95.00
Plate #435 ....$60.00
Plate #436 ....$75.00
Plate #437 ....$45.00

Page 128

Plate #438 ....$55.00
Plate #439 ....$55.00
Plate #440 ....$55.00
Plate #441 ....$75.00
Plate #442 ....$45.00

Page 129

Plate #443 ....$100.00
Plate #444 ....$60.00

Plate #445 ....$50.00
Plate #446 ....$65.00
Plate #447 ....$65.00
Plate #448 ....$65.00

Page 130

Plate #449 ....$65.00
Plate #450 ....$80.00
Plate #451 ....$55.00
Plate #452 ....$75.00

Page 131

Plate #453 ....$75.00
Plate #454 ....$80.00
Plate #455 ....$85.00
Plate #456 ....$85.00

Page 132

Plate #457 ....$95.00
Plate #458 ....$95.00
Plate #459 ....$95.00
Plate #460 ....$95.00
Plate #461 ....$95.00
Plate #462 ....$95.00

Page 133

Plate #463 ....$175.00
Plate #464 ....$300.00
Plate #465 ....$75.00
Plate #466 ....$150.00
Plate #467 ....$135.00
Plate #468 ....$85.00

Page 134

Plate #469 ....$75.00
Plate #470 ....$65.00
Plate #471 ....$45.00
Plate #472 ....$20.00
Plate #473 ....$20.00
Plate #474 ....$20.00
Plate #475 ....$25.00

Page 135

Plate #476 ....$20.00
Plate #477 ....$65.00
Plate #478 ....$75.00
Plate #479 ....$35.00
Plate #480 ....$20.00
Plate #481 ....$20.00

Page 136

Plate #482 ....$25.00
Plate #483 ....$30.00
Plate #484 ....$20.00
Plate #485.........................ea $75.00
Plate #486 ....$35.00
Plate #487 ....$40.00

Page 137

Plate #488 ....$30.00
Plate #489 ....$45.00
Plate #490 ....$50.00
Plate #491 ....$75.00
Plate #492 ....$6.00

Page 138

Plate #493 ....$30.00

Plate #494 ....$65.00
Plate #495 ....$65.00
Plate #496 ....$65.00
Plate #497 ....$65.00

Page 139

Plate #498 ....$65.00
Plate #499 ....$15.00
Plate #500 ....$30.00
Plate #501 ....$40.00
Plate #502 ....$200.00
Plate #503 ....$200.00

Page 140

Plate #504 ....$175.00
Plate #505...........................ea $50.00
Plate #506 ....$20.00
Plate #507 ....$30.00
Plate #508 ....$35.00
Plate #509 ....$15.00

Page 141

Plate #510 ....$15.00
Plate #511 ....$20.00
Plate #512 ....$20.00
Plate #513 ....$20.00
Plate #514 ....$20.00
Plate #515 ....$15.00

Page 142

Plate #516 ....$15.00
Plate #517 ....$15.00
Plate #518 ....$15.00
Plate #519 ....$15.00
Plate #520.........................set $20.00
Plate #521 ....$15.00

Page 143

Plate #522 ....$15.00
Plate #523 ....$25.00
Plate #524 ....$25.00
Plate #525 ....$25.00
Plate #526 ....$25.00

Page 144

Plate #527 ....$25.00
Plate #528 ....$6.00
Plate #529 ....$35.00
Plate #530 ....$25.00
Plate #531 ....$25.00

Page 145

Plate #532 ....$75.00
Plate #533 ....$20.00
Plate #534 ....$15.00
Plate #535..........................set $50.00
Plate #536 ....$35.00
Plate #537.........................set $45.00

Page 146

Plate #538.........................set $50.00
Plate #539 ....$45.00

Page 147

Plate #540............................NPA

Page 148
Plate #541 ....$25.00
Plate #542 ....$25.00
Plate #543 ....$25.00
Plate #544 ....$20.00
Plate #545 ....$20.00

Page 149
Plate #546 ....$20.00
Plate #547 ....$20.00
Plate #548 ....$20.00
Plate #549 ....$20.00
Plate #550 ....$250.00

Page 150
Plate #551 ....$390.00
Plate #552 ....$125.00
Plate #553 ....$85.00
Plate #554 ....$50.00
Plate #555 ....$75.00
Plate #556 ....$125.00

Page 151
Plate #557 ....$425.00
Plate #558 ....$125.00
Plate #559 ....$20.00
Plate #560 ....$185.00
Plate #561 ....$185.00

Page 152
Plate #562 ....$195.00
Plate #563 ....$35.00
Plate #564 ....$40.00
Plate #565 ....$55.00
Plate #566 ....$90.00

Page 153
Plate #567 ....$125.00
Plate #568 ....$80.00
Plate #569 ....$40.00
Plate #570 ....$30.00
Plate #571 ....$30.00

Page 154
Plate #572 ....$65.00
Plate #573 ....$65.00
Plate #574 ....$10.00
Plate #575 ....$45.00
Plate #576 ....$45.00

Page 155
Plate #577 ....$45.00
Plate #578 ....$45.00
Plate #579 ....doll only $45.00
Plate #580 ....$45.00
Plate #581 ....$45.00
Plate #582 ....$45.00

Page 156
Plate #583 ....$45.00
Plate #584 ....$30.00
Plate #585 ....$30.00
Plate #586 ....$25.00
Plate #587 ....$30.00
Plate #588 ....$25.00
Plate #589 ....$25.00

Page 157
Plate #590 ....$25.00
Plate #591 ....$30.00
Plate #592 ....$30.00
Plate #593 ....$65.00
Plate #594 ....$10.00
Plate #595 ....$10.00

Page 158
Plate #596 ....$65.00
Plate #597 ....$35.00
Plate #598 ....$35.00
Plate #599 ....$35.00
Plate #600 ....$75.00
Plate #601 ....$25.00
Plate #602 ....$65.00

Page 159
Plate #603 ....$30.00
Plate #604 ....$70.00
Plate #605 ....$40.00
Plate #606 ....$30.00
Plate #607 ....$40.00

Page 160
Plate #608.........................set $40.00
Plate #609 ....$40.00
Plate #610 ....$50.00
Plate #611 ....$75.00
Plate #612 ....$85.00
Plate #613 ....$45.00

Page 161
Plate #614 ....$45.00
Plate #615 ....$35.00
Plate #616 ....$40.00
Plate #617 ....$30.00
Plate #618 ....$35.00
Plate #619 ....$20.00

Page 162
Plate #620........................set $15.00
Plate #621 ....$100.00
Plate #622 ....$85.00
Plate #623 ....$225.00
Plate #624 ....$30.00

Page 163
Plate #625 ....$95.00
Plate #626 ....$95.00
Plate #627 ....$95.00
Plate #628 ....$200.00
Plate #629 ....$65.00

Page 164
Plate #630 ....$65.00
Plate #631 ....$65.00
Plate #632 ....$95.00
Plate #633 ....$95.00
Plate #634 ....$95.00

Page 165
Plate #635 ....$95.00
Plate #636 ....$140.00
Plate #637 ....$125.00
Plate #638 ....$85.00

Plate #639 ....$175.00
Plate #640 ....$70.00

Page 166
Plate #641 ....$40.00
Plate #642 ....$40.00
Plate #643 ....$40.00
Plate #644 ....$30.00
Plate #645 ....$40.00

Page 167
Plate #646 ....$30.00
Plate #647 ....$60.00
Plate #648 ....$60.00
Plate #649 ....$30.00
Plate #650 ....$30.00
Plate #651 ....$75.00

Page 168
Plate #652 ....$75.00
Plate #653 ....$50.00
Plate #654 ....$50.00
Plate #655 ....$30.00
Plate #656 ....$35.00

Page 169
Plate #657 ....$30.00
Plate #658 ....$300.00
Plate #659.........................set $70.00
Plate #660 ....$35.00
Plate #661 ....$40.00
Plate #662 ....$45.00

Page 170
Plate #663 ....$75.00
Plate #664 ....$50.00
Plate #665 ....$35.00
Plate #666 ....$55.00
Plate #667 ....$55.00
Plate #668 ....$45.00

Page 171
Plate #669 ....$45.00
Plate #670 ....$350.00
Plate #671 ....$75.00
Plate #672 ....$25.00
Plate #673 ....$30.00
Plate #674 ....$30.00

Page 172
Plate #675.........................ea $30.00
Plate #676 ....$50.00
Plate #677 ....$50.00
Plate #678.........................ea $40.00
Plate #679.........................ea $30.00

Page 173
Plate #680.........................ea $45.00
Plate #681 ....$35.00
Plate #682 ....$35.00
Plate #683 ....$40.00
Plate #684 ....$150.00
Plate #685 ....$35.00

Page 174
Plate #686 ....$35.00
Plate #687 ....$20.00

Plate #688 ....$20.00
Plate #689 ....$30.00
Plate #690 ....$50.00

Page 175

Plate #691 ....$50.00
Plate #692 ....$50.00
Plate #693 ....$50.00
Plate #694 ....$45.00
Plate #695 ....$45.00

Page 176

Plate #696 ....$175.00
Plate #697 ....$15.00
Plate #698 ....$20.00
Plate #699 ....$35.00
Plate #700 ....$45.00

Page 179

Plate #701 ....$50.00
Plate #702 ....$65.00
Plate #703 ....$60.00
Plate #704 ....$65.00
Plate #705 ....$65.00

Page 180

Plate #706 ....$55.00
Plate #707 ....$55.00
Plate #708 ....$50.00
Plate #709 ....$50.00
Plate #710 ....$120.00

Page 181

Plate #711 ....$55.00
Plate #712 ....$35.00
Plate #713 ....$50.00
Plate #714 ....$120.00
Plate #715 ....$60.00

Page 182

Plate #716...........................ea $45.00
Plate #717 ....$65.00
Plate #718 ....$50.00
Plate #719 ....$65.00
Plate #720 ....$30.00

Page 183

Plate #721 ....$35.00
Plate #722 ....$20.00
Plate #723 ....$45.00
Plate #724 ....$20.00
Plate #725 ....$20.00
Plate #726 ....$20.00

Page 184

Plate #727 ....$20.00
Plate #728 ....$75.00
Plate #729 ....$20.00
Plate #730 ....$20.00
Plate #731 ....$15.00
Plate #732 ....$15.00

Page 185

Plate #733 ....$30.00
Plate #734 ....$50.00
Plate #735 ....$45.00
Plate #736 ....$45.00

Plate #737 ....$20.00
Plate #738 ....$8.00

Page 186

Plate #739 ....$8.00
Plate #740 ....$8.00
Plate #741 ....$25.00
Plate #742 ....$300.00
Plate #743.........................ea $40.00

Page 187

Plate #744 ....$300.00
Plate #745 ....$300.00
Plate #746 ....$35.00
Plate #747 ....$50.00
Plate #748 ....$50.00
Plate #749 ....$50.00

Page 188

Plate #750 ....$50.00
Plate #751 ....$20.00
Plate #752 ....$30.00
Plate #753 ....$35.00
Plate #754 ....$30.00

Page 189

Plate #755 ....$30.00
Plate #756 ....$30.00
Plate #757.........................ea $30.00
Plate #758 ....$20.00
Plate #759 ....set $15.00
Plate #760 ....$70.00

Page 190

Plate #761 ....$70.00
Plate #762 ....$35.00
Plate #763 ....$35.00
Plate #764 ....$50.00
Plate #765 ....doll only $25.00
Plate #766 ....$25.00

Page 191

Plate #767 ....$20.00
Plate #768 ....$15.00
Plate #769 ....$10.00
Plate #770 ....$15.00
Plate #771 ....$12.00

Page 192

Plate #772 ....$12.00
Plate #773.........................ea $20.00
Plate #774.......................set $20.00
Plate #775 ....doll only $50.00
Plate #776 ....$35.00
Plate #777 ....$50.00

Page 193

Plate #778 ....$15.00
Plate #779 ....$20.00
Plate #780 ....$20.00
Plate #781 ....$35.00
Plate #782 ....$460.00

Page 194

Plate #783 ....$500.00
Plate #784 ....$185.00
Plate #785 ....$180.00

Plate #786 ....$140.00
Plate #787 ....$65.00

Page 195

Plate #788 ....$65.00
Plate #789 ....$70.00
Plate #790 ....$20.00
Plate #791 ....$20.00
Plate #792 ....$20.00
Plate #793 ....$75.00

Page 196

Plate #794 ....$75.00
Plate #795 ....$65.00
Plate #796 ....$85.00
Plate #797 ....$65.00
Plate #798 ....$60.00

Page 197

Plate #799 ....$65.00
Plate #800 ....$65.00
Plate #801 ....$35.00
Plate #802.........................ea $30.00
Plate #803.......................set $50.00
Plate #804 ....$70.00
Plate #805 ....$65.00

Page 198

Plate #806 ....$60.00
Plate #807 ....$45.00
Plate #808.......................set $60.00
Plate #809.......................set $60.00
Plate #810 ....$65.00
Plate #811 ....$60.00

Page 199

Plate #812 ....$250.00
Plate #813 ....$45.00
Plate #814 ....$25.00
Plate #815 ....$45.00
Plate #816 ....$40.00

Page 200

Plate #817 ....$45.00
Plate #818 ....$45.00
Plate #819 ....$25.00
Plate #820 ....$85.00
Plate #821 ....$40.00

Page 201

Plate #822 ....$95.00
Plate #823.......................set $20.00
Plate #824 ....$25.00
Plate #825 ....$65.00
Plate #826 ....$35.00

Page 202

Plate #827 ....$65.00
Plate #828 ....$35.00
Plate #829 ....$45.00
Plate #830 ....$45.00
Plate #831 ....$35.00
Plate #832 ....$25.00

Page 203

Plate #833 ....$35.00

Plate #834 ....$15.00
Plate #835 ....$40.00
Plate #836 ....$30.00
Plate #837 ....$20.00

Page 204

Plate #838 ....$20.00
Plate #839 ....$60.00
Plate #840 ....$50.00
Plate #841 ....$15.00
Plate #842 ....$20.00
Plate #843 ....$25.00

Page 205

Plate #844 ....$20.00
Plate #845 ....$60.00
Plate #846 ....$60.00
Plate #847.............................set $45.00
Plate #848.............................set $80.00

Page 206

Plate #849.............................set $50.00
Plate #850.............................set $55.00
Plate #851 ....$60.00
Plate #852 ....$50.00
Plate #853 ....$25.00

Page 207

Plate #854 ....$200.00
Plate #855 ....$125.00
Plate #856 ....$125.00
Plate #857 ....$100.00
Plate #858 ....$80.00
Plate #859 ....$95.00

Page 208

Plate #860 ....$95.00
Plate #861 ....$90.00
Plate #862 ....$75.00
Plate #863 ....$55.00
Plate #864 ....$75.00
Plate #865 ....$55.00

Page 209

Plate #866 ....$90.00
Plate #867 ....$60.00
Plate #868 ....$150.00
Plate #869 ....$50.00
Plate #870 ....$60.00
Plate #871 ....$60.00

Page 210

Plate #872 ....$35.00
Plate #873 ....$60.00
Plate #874 ....$60.00
Plate #875 ....$60.00
Plate #876 ....$60.00
Plate #877 ....$60.00

Page 211

Plate #878 ....$35.00
Plate #879 ....$65.00
Plate #880 ....$35.00
Plate #881 ....$35.00
Plate #882 ....$45.00
Plate #883 ....$35.00
Plate #884 ....$35.00

Page 212

Plate #885 ....$35.00
Plate #886 ....$40.00
Plate #887 ....$40.00
Plate #888 ....$40.00
Plate #889 ....$40.00
Plate #890 ....$40.00

Page 213

Plate #891.............................ea $35.00
Plate #892 ....$35.00
Plate #893 ....$30.00
Plate #894 ....$70.00
Plate #895 ....$30.00
Plate #896 ....$50.00

Page 214

Plate #897 ....$35.00
Plate #898 ....$40.00
Plate #899 ....$30.00
Plate #900 ....$35.00
Plate #901 ....$35.00
Plate #902.............................ea $35.00

Page 215

Plate #903 ....$25.00
Plate #904 ....$25.00
Plate #905 ....$30.00
Plate #906 ....$25.00
Plate #907 ....$25.00

Page 216

Plate #908.............................ea $35.00
Plate #909 ....$30.00
Plate #910 ....$25.00
Plate #911 ....$45.00
Plate #912 ....$40.00
Plate #913 ....$15.00

Page 217

Plate #914 ....$40.00
Plate #915 ....$25.00
Plate #916 ....$40.00
Plate #917 ....$45.00
Plate #918 ....$25.00
Plate #919 ....$25.00

Page 218

Plate #920 ....$40.00
Plate #921 ....$15.00
Plate #922 ....$20.00
Plate #923 ....$40.00
Plate #924 ....$15.00
Plate #925 ....$20.00

Page 219

Plate #926 ....$25.00
Plate #927 ....$25.00
Plate #928 ....$30.00
Plate #929.............................set $75.00
Plate #930 ....$20.00
Plate #931 ....$20.00

Page 220

Plate #932 ....$50.00
Plate #933 ....$20.00

Plate #934 ....$20.00
Plate #935 ....$15.00
Plate #936 ....$10.00
Plate #937 ....$10.00

Page 221

Plate #938 ....$35.00
Plate #939 ....$65.00
Plate #940 ....$25.00
Plate #941 ....$25.00
Plate #942 ....$30.00
Plate #943.............................set $15.00

Page 222

Plate #944 ....$20.00
Plate #945 ....$20.00
Plate #946 ....$20.00
Plate #947 ....$12.00
Plate #948 ....$35.00

Page 223

Plate #949.............................set $35.00
Plate #950.............................set $35.00
Plate #951.............................set $50.00
Plate #952.............................set $30.00
Plate #953.............................set $25.00
Plate #954.............................set $25.00

Page 224

Plate #955.............................set $25.00
Plate #956.............................set $25.00
Plate #957.............................set $30.00
Plate #958.............................set $30.00
Plate #959.............................set $25.00
Plate #960.............................set $25.00

Page 225

Plate #961 ....$70.00
Plate #962 ....$70.00
Plate #963 ....$45.00
Plate #964.............................ea $30.00
Plate #965 ....$75.00

Page 226

Plate #966 ....$50.00
Plate #967 ....$75.00
Plate #968 ....$85.00
Plate #969 ....$50.00
Plate #970.............................ea $45.00
Plate #971 ....$125.00
Plate #972 ....$20.00

Page 227

Plate #973 ....$125.00
Plate #974 ....$175.00
Plate #975 ....$15.00
Plate #976 ....$20.00
Plate #977 ....$12.00
Plate #978 ....$25.00

Page 228

Plate #979 ....$25.00
Plate #980 ....$25.00
Plate #981 ....$30.00
Plate #982 ....$25.00
Plate #983 ....$20.00
Plate #984 ....$15.00

Page 229

Plate #985		$35.00
Plate #986		$20.00
Plate #987		$30.00
Plate #988	ea	$20.00
Plate #989	set	$10.00
Plate #990	set	$10.00
Plate #991	set	$12.00

Page 230

Plate #992	$15.00
Plate #993	$10.00
Plate #994	$35.00
Plate #995	$55.00
Plate #996	$45.00
Plate #997	$65.00

Page 231

Plate #998	$65.00
Plate #999	$275.00
Plate #1000	$20.00
Plate #1001	$20.00
Plate #1002	$60.00
Plate #1003	$60.00

Page 232

Plate #1004		$20.00
Plate #1005		$35.00
Plate #1006	doll only	$150.00
Plate #1007	doll only	$150.00
Plate #1008		$35.00
Plate #1009	ea	$10.00

Page 233

Plate #1010	$20.00
Plate #1011	$30.00
Plate #1012	$30.00
Plate #1013	$10.00
Plate #1014	$35.00
Plate #1015	$35.00
Plate #1016	$20.00

Page 234

Plate #1017	$35.00
Plate #1018	$35.00
Plate #1019	$20.00
Plate #1020	$20.00
Plate #1021	$20.00
Plate #1022	$20.00

Page 235

Plate #1023	$20.00
Plate #1024	$20.00
Plate #1025	$20.00
Plate #1026	$20.00
Plate #1027	$20.00
Plate #1028	$15.00

Page 236

Plate #1029		$15.00
Plate #1030		$15.00
Plate #1031		$15.00
Plate #1032	ea	$15.00
Plate #1033		$20.00
Plate #1034		$10.00
Plate #1035		$25.00

Page 237

Plate #1036		$40.00
Plate #1037	ea	$20.00
Plate #1038		$20.00
Plate #1039	ea	$20.00
Plate #1040	ea	$20.00
Plate #1041	set	$15.00

Page 238

Plate #1042	$40.00
Plate #1043	$25.00
Plate #1044	$15.00
Plate #1045	$15.00
Plate #1046	$20.00
Plate #1047	$30.00

Page 239

Plate #1048	$30.00
Plate #1049	$40.00
Plate #1050	$95.00
Plate #1051	$95.00
Plate #1052	$95.00
Plate #1053	$95.00

Page 242

Plate #1054	set	$95.00
Plate #1055		$95.00
Plate #1056	set	$40.00
Plate #1057	set	$40.00
Plate #1058	set	$45.00
Plate #1059		$125.00

Page 243

Plate #1060	$45.00
Plate #1061	$45.00
Plate #1062	$25.00
Plate #1063	$30.00
Plate #1064	$30.00
Plate #1065	$35.00

Page 244

Plate #1066	$25.00
Plate #1067	$175.00
Plate #1068	$65.00
Plate #1069	$75.00
Plate #1070	$90.00

Page 245

Plate #1071	$25.00
Plate #1072	$300.00
Plate #1073	$300.00
Plate #1074	$200.00
Plate #1075	$800.00

Page 246

Plate #1076	$300.00
Plate #1077	$250.00
Plate #1078	$250.00
Plate #1079	$250.00
Plate #1080	$175.00

Page 259

Plate #1081	$75.00
Plate #1082	$75.00
Plate #1083	$75.00
Plate #1084	$75.00

Page 260

Plate #1085	$30.00

Page 260

Plate #1086	$175.00
Plate #1087	$175.00
Plate #1088	$50.00
Plate #1089	$175.00
Plate #1090	$50.00

Page 261

Plate #1091	$45.00
Plate #1092	$60.00
Plate #1093	$50.00
Plate #1094	$50.00

Page 262

Plate #1095	ea	$50.00
Plate #1096		$50.00
Plate #1097		$50.00
Plate #1098	ea	$50.00

Page 263

Plate #1099		$35.00
Plate #1100		$35.00
Plate #1101		$45.00
Plate #1102	ea	$35.00
Plate #1103		NPA

Page 264

Plate #1104	$35.00
Plate #1105	$35.00
Plate #1106	$35.00
Plate #1107	NPA
Plate #1108	$55.00

Page 265

Plate #1109	NPA
Plate #1110	$60.00
Plate #1111	$135.00
Plate #1112	$135.00

Page 266

Plate #1113	$95.00
Plate #1114	$75.00
Plate #1115	$75.00
Plate #1116	$75.00

Page 267

Plate #1117	ea	$55.00
Plate #1118		$55.00
Plate #1119		$55.00
Plate #1120		$55.00

Page 268

Plate #1121	$55.00
Plate #1122	$55.00
Plate #1123	$15.00
Plate #1124	$60.00
Plate #1125	$60.00

Page 269

Plate #1126	$60.00
Plate #1127	$50.00
Plate #1128	$50.00
Plate #1129	$175.00

Page 270
Plate #1130 ....$175.00
Plate #1131 ....$55.00
Plate #1132 ....$55.00
Plate #1133 ....$75.00

Page 271
Plate #1134 ....$80.00
Plate #1135 ....$80.00
Plate #1136 ....$45.00
Plate #1137...........................ea $55.00

Page 272
Plate #1138 ....$60.00
Plate #1139 ....$55.00
Plate #1140 ....$55.00
Plate #1141 ....$60.00

Page 273
Plate #1142 ....$70.00
Plate #1143 ....$55.00
Plate #1144 ....$55.00
Plate #1145 ....$55.00
Plate #1146 ....$55.00

Page 274
Plate #1147 ....$55.00
Plate #1148 ....$40.00
Plate #1149 ....$40.00
Plate #1150...........................ea $45.00
Plate #1151 ....$75.00

Page 275
Plate #1152 ....$45.00
Plate #1153 ....$45.00
Plate #1154 ....$45.00
Plate #1155...........................ea $45.00
Plate #1156 ....$45.00
Plate #1157 ....$75.00

Page 276
Plate #1158 ....$135.00
Plate #1159 ....$100.00
Plate #1160 ....$40.00
Plate #1161 ....$40.00
Plate #1162 ....$40.00
Plate #1163 ....$60.00

Page 277
Plate #1164 ....$35.00
Plate #1165 ....$55.00
Plate #1166 ....$35.00
Plate #1167 ....$35.00
Plate #1168 ....$35.00
Plate #1169 ....$55.00

Page 278
Plate #1170...........................ea $65.00
Plate #1171 ....$65.00
Plate #1172 ....$20.00
Plate #1173 ....$20.00
Plate #1174 ....$20.00

Page 279
Plate #1175 ....$20.00
Plate #1176 ....$20.00

Plate #1177 ....$20.00
Plate #1178 ....$20.00
Plate #1179...........................set $8.00
Plate #1180 ....$10.00

Page 280
Plate #1181 ....$12.00
Plate #1182 ....$20.00
Plate #1183 ....$15.00
Plate #1184 ....$30.00
Plate #1185 ....$20.00

Page 281
Plate #1186 ....$15.00
Plate #1187 ....$15.00
Plate #1188 ....$15.00
Plate #1189 ....$15.00
Plate #1190 ....$12.00

Page 282
Plate #1191...........................set $20.00
Plate #1192...........................set $20.00
Plate #1193 ....$12.00
Plate #1194 ....$10.00
Plate #1195 ....$10.00

Page 283
Plate #1196 ....$35.00
Plate #1197 ....$50.00
Plate #1198 ....$50.00
Plate #1199 ....$85.00
Plate #1200 ....$85.00
Plate #1201 ....$85.00

Page 284
Plate #1202 ....$20.00
Plate #1203 ....$15.00
Plate #1204 ....$30.00
Plate #1205...........................ea $45.00
Plate #1206 ....$45.00

Page 285
Plate #1207 ....$145.00
Plate #1208 ....$145.00
Plate #1209 ....$25.00
Plate #1210 ....$25.00
Plate #1211 ....$5.00
Plate #1212 ....$15.00

Page 286
Plate #1213 ....$15.00
Plate #1214 ....$25.00
Plate #1215 ....$25.00
Plate #1216 ....$25.00
Plate #1217 ....$20.00

Page 287
Plate #1218 ....$20.00
Plate #1219...........................set $12.00
Plate #1220 ....$15.00
Plate #1221 ....$50.00
Plate #1222 ....$45.00

Page 288
Plate #1223...........................set $15.00
Plate #1224 ....$35.00

Plate #1225...........................set $15.00
Plate #1226 ....$20.00
Plate #1227 ....$25.00

Page 289
Plate #1228 ....$35.00
Plate #1229 ....$70.00
Plate #1230 ....$45.00
Plate #1231 ....$45.00
Plate #1232 ....$70.00

Page 290
Plate #1233 ....$30.00
Plate #1234 ....$125.00
Plate #1235 ....$15.00
Plate #1236 ....$18.00
Plate #1237 ....$25.00

Page 291
Plate #1238 ....$25.00
Plate #1239 ....$85.00
Plate #1240 ....$85.00
Plate #1241 ....$85.00

Page 292
Plate #1242 ....$85.00
Plate #1243 ....$50.00
Plate #1244 ....$50.00
Plate #1245 ....$80.00
Plate #1246 ....$65.00

Page 293
Plate #1247 ....$60.00
Plate #1248 ....$65.00
Plate #1249 ....$50.00
Plate #1250 ....$50.00
Plate #1251 ....$100.00
Plate #1252 ....$125.00

Page 294
Plate #1253 ....$50.00
Plate #1254 ....$50.00
Plate #1255 ....$40.00
Plate #1256 ....$40.00
Plate #1257 ....$35.00
Plate #1258 ....$35.00

Page 295
Plate #1259...........................ea $35.00
Plate #1260 ....$35.00
Plate #1261 ....$20.00
Plate #1262 ....$35.00
Plate #1263 ....$35.00

Page 296
Plate #1264 ....$40.00
Plate #1265 ....$40.00
Plate #1266 ....$40.00
Plate #1267 ....$40.00
Plate #1268 ....$40.00
Plate #1269 ....$40.00
Plate #1270 ....$40.00

Page 297
Plate #1271 ....$30.00
Plate #1272...........................set $140.00

Plate #1273 ....$75.00
Plate #1274 ....$40.00
Plate #1275 ....$40.00

Page 298
Plate #1276 ....$40.00
Plate #1277 ....$75.00
Plate #1278 ....$75.00
Plate #1279 ....$25.00
Plate #1280 ....$30.00

Page 299
Plate #1281...............................NPA

Page 300
Plate #1282...............................NPA
Plate #1283...............................NPA
Plate #1284 ....$60.00
Plate #1285 ....$60.00

Page 301
Plate #1286 ....$60.00
Plate #1287 ....$65.00
Plate #1288 ....$65.00
Plate #1289 ....$65.00
Plate #1290 ....$65.00
Plate #1291 ....$65.00

Page 302
Plate #1292 ....$65.00
Plate #1293 ....$90.00
Plate #1294 ....$65.00
Plate #1295 ....$45.00
Plate #1296 ....$30.00
Plate #1297 ....$20.00

Page 303
Plate #1298 ....$35.00
Plate #1299 ....$40.00
Plate #1300 ....$20.00
Plate #1301 ....$30.00
Plate #1302 ....$35.00
Plate #1303.....................set $20.00
Plate #1304 ....$95.00

Page 304
Plate #1305 ....$150.00
Plate #1306 ....$150.00
Plate #1307 ....$150.00
Plate #1308 ....$10.00
Plate #1309 ....$40.00
Plate #1310 ....$150.00

Page 305
Plate #1311 ....$65.00
Plate #1312 ....$70.00
Plate #1313 ....$70.00
Plate #1314 ....$150.00
Plate #1315 ....$150.00
Plate #1316 ....$175.00

Page 306
Plate #1317 ....$300.00
Plate #1318 ....$85.00
Plate #1319 ....$25.00
Plate #1320 ....$25.00
Plate #1321 ....$35.00
Plate #1322 ....$40.00

Page 307
Plate #1323 ....$650.00

Page 308
Plate #1324 ....$650.00
Plate #1325 ....$650.00
Plate #1326 ....$650.00
Plate #1327 ....$650.00
Plate #1328 ....$650.00

Page 309
Plate #1329 ....$650.00
Plate #1330 ....$650.00
Plate #1331 ....$650.00
Plate #1332 ....$650.00
Plate #1333 ....$650.00
Plate #1334 ....$50.00

Page 310
Plate #1335 ....$400.00
Plate #1336 ....$400.00
Plate #1337 ....$80.00
Plate #1338 ....$400.00
Plate #1339 ....$50.00

Page 311
Plate #1340 ....$250.00
Plate #1341.....................ea $900.00
Plate #1342 ....$900.00
Plate #1343 ....$600.00

Page 312
Plate #1344 ....$600.00
Plate #1345 ....$50.00
Plate #1346 ....$30.00
Plate #1347 ....$80.00
Plate #1348 ....$80.00
Plate #1349 ....$85.00

Page 313
Plate #1350 ....$80.00
Plate #1351 ....$80.00
Plate #1352 ....$100.00
Plate #1353 ....$110.00
Plate #1354 ....$340.00

Page 314
Plate #1355 ....$340.00
Plate #1356 ....$50.00
Plate #1357 ....$50.00
Plate #1358 ....$300.00

Page 315
Plate #1359 ....$250.00
Plate #1360 ....$250.00
Plate #1361 ....$150.00
Plate #1362 ....$100.00
Plate #1363 ....$600.00

Page 316
Plate #1364 ....$200.00
Plate #1365 ....$750.00
Plate #1366 ....$850.00
Plate #1367 ....$400.00

Page 317
Plate #1368 ....$1,100.00

Page 318
Plate #1369 ....$50.00
Plate #1370 ....$150.00
Plate #1371 ....doll only $300.00
Plate #1372 ....$900.00

Page 318
Plate #1373.....................set $60.00
Plate #1374 ....$75.00
Plate #1375 ....$75.00
Plate #1376 ....$75.00
Plate #1377 ....$65.00

Page 319
Plate #1378 ....$65.00
Plate #1379 ....$80.00
Plate #1380 ....$65.00
Plate #1381 ....$80.00
Plate #1382 ....$80.00

Page 320
Plate #1383 ....$80.00
Plate #1384 ....$80.00
Plate #1385 ....$80.00
Plate #1386 ....$80.00
Plate #1387 ....$100.00

Page 321
Plate #1388 ....$80.00
Plate #1389 ....$100.00
Plate #1390 ....$100.00
Plate #1391 ....$50.00
Plate #1392 ....$45.00

Page 322
Plate #1393 ....$35.00
Plate #1394.....................set $90.00
Plate #1395 ....$60.00
Plate #1396 ....$450.00

Page 323
Plate #1397 ....$275.00
Plate #1398 ....$75.00
Plate #1399 ....$200.00
Plate #1400 ....$200.00

Page 324
Plate #1401 ....$125.00
Plate #1402 ....$80.00
Plate #1403 ....$150.00
Plate #1404 ....$175.00
Plate #1405 ....$175.00

Page 325
Plate #1406 ....$30.00
Plate #1407 ....$75.00
Plate #1408 ....$30.00
Plate #1409 ....$45.00
Plate #1410 ....$100.00

Page 326
Plate #1411 ....$65.00
Plate #1412.....................ea $35.00
Plate #1413 ....$150.00
Plate #1414.....................ea $85.00
Plate #1415 ....$190.00

NPA—No Price Available

Schroeder's Antiques Price Guide

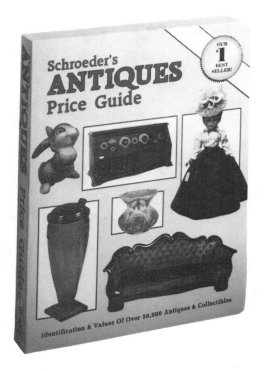

Schroeder's Antiques Price Guide has become THE household name in the antiques & collectibles field. Our team of editors work year-round with more than 200 contributors to bring you our #1 best-selling book on antiques & collectibles.

With more than 50,000 items identified & priced, *Schroeder's* is a must for the collector & dealer alike. If it merits the interest of today's collector, you'll find it in *Schroeder's.* Each subject is represented with histories and background information. In addition, hundreds of sharp original photos are used each year to illustrate not only the rare and unusual, but the everyday "fun-type" collectibles as well -- not postage stamp pictures, but large close-up shots that show important details clearly.

Our editors compile a new book each year. Never do we merely change prices. Accuracy is our primary aim. Prices are gathered over the entire year previous to publication, from ads and personal contacts. Then each category is thoroughly checked to spot inconsistencies, listings that may not be entirely reflective of actual market dealings, and lines too vague to be of merit. Only the best of the lot remains for publication. You'll find *Schroeder's Antiques Price Guide* the one to buy for factual information and quality.

No dealer, collector or investor can afford not to own this book. It is available from your favorite bookseller or antiques dealer at the low price of $12.95. If you are unable to find this price guide in your area, it's available from Collector Books, P.O. Box 3009, Paducah, KY 42002-3009 at $12.95 plus $2.00 for postage and handling.

8½ x 11", 608 Pages   **$12.95**

COLLECTOR BOOKS
A Division of Schroeder Publishing Co., Inc.